Selected Readings

for an Introduction to

HOTEL AND RESTAURANT MANAGEMENT

compiled and edited by

Douglas C. Keister, Ph.D.
and
Ralph D. Wilson, Ph.D.

School of Hotel and Restaurant Management
University of Denver
University Park, Denver, Colorado

McCutchan Publishing Corporation
2526 Grove Street
Berkeley, California 94704

ISBN: 0-8211-1013-6
Library of Congress Catalog Card Number: 78-152403

PREFACE

This selection of readings is intended to give a broad view of some of the current activity and thinking in hotel and restaurant management. The readings do not comprehensively cover all phases of the food service and lodging industry, but represent a cross section of literature currently published in the field.

The wide range of subject matter is appropriate to both introductory and advanced courses in hotel and restaurant management, and can also provide a collection of information for those already working in the industry. The articles are intended to supplement lectures and to provide a basis for discussion and evaluation of changing trends.

We feel that understanding of the industry in general is more possible by presenting disparate points of view and sources than by reading from a few periodicals. In choosing the articles to be included in this book, we examined many articles in various publications. Limited space resulted in the unfortunate omission of many excellent articles. We realize that additional reading is necessary to keep abreast of changing trends.

In discussing the problems that exist now in their areas of interest, most authors also project their visions of the future. They see what is done now is the basis for achieving the desires and expectations of the future. Because of this, readers should gain an overall perspective to solving some of the problems of the hotel and restaurant industry.

CONTENTS

FORECAST FOR THE '70'S

Ralph D. Wilson

The United States in the 1970's will be a dynamic, changing society with built-in opportunities for certain types of food service operations—and with a declining market for others. Social, economic and political changes that will affect American society (and the food service market) in the next decade include the following:

Social trends. (1) Population will increase at a decreasing rate. (2) An increased percentage of the population will be under 25 years of age and over 65. (3) Service occupations will be considered less attractive.

Economic trends. (1) Incomes will continue to increase from the present level (74 percent of families now earn more than $4,000 and six percent earn more than $15,000 annually). (2) More families will have two or more workers contributing to family income. (3) The labor force will increase in size but will be drained by continuing military manpower requirements. (4) A business community that is short of qualified management talent will seek to merge or consolidate in an effort to maintain or improve their sales and market positions.

Political trends. (1) Government spending will increase to meet military and foreign commitments. (2) Government will continue efforts to subsidize the income of marginal workers, to increase social benefits and to increase the job skills of unemployables. (3) Washington will continue support of labor union aims. (4) There will be continuing efforts to increase minimum wages, decrease the work week and to broaden coverage of the minimum wage law.

As a result of all these trends, all segments of the food service industry will grow in the 1970's. However, the growth will be unevenly distributed.

From *Fast Food Magazine*, May 1966, pp. 33-35. Reprinted by permission.

Greatest expansion will probably be experienced by specialty food units featuring informal dining with high-grade decor, limited menu, fast service and convenient locations. These restaurants will meet the needs of the younger, more mobile people with two wage earners, who will most often live in apartments or town-house complexes. The suburban home owner will also be attracted by the lower total check for family dining. Frequently requiring less capital investment and less skilled employees, these restaurants will lend themselves well to franchising and to standardization of design, location, menu preparation and service. They can easily be established in new growth areas.

A second type of restaurant that should increase in importance is the small, personal service establishment with 35 to 50 seats, in which the owner-manager will cater to the ego desires of higher income groups seeking personal recognition, personal service, and who are bored with large impersonal, mass dining. Menus will be limited to a few excellent entrees with a very limited choice of accompanying items. Prices in these establishments will be high; decor will be expensive and in good taste. Such restaurants, which represent a return to the prestige personality dining places of the past, are already achieving notable success in Chicago, New York and San Francisco.

Gigantic Expansion Soon for College Food Service

The number of food service units in colleges and universities will substantially increase, as will the number of students served. The student pressure now being felt primarily on the elementary and high school levels will be felt at the college level by 1975 when enrollments, stimulated by social pressure from parents and the availability of low-cost government loans, will double to nine million students. An increasingly large percentage of the new and expanded college food service units will be served by specialized management companies who, through superior programs of recruiting, training and management development, will be capable of solving management personnel problems that are beyond the scope of most individual schools.

The trend toward building smaller plants near recreational areas, desirable living conditions, labor sources and near markets will result in an increased number of in-plant feeding facilities. However, with increased automation, such plants will be staffed by fewer workers, which indicates that in-plant food service will probably grow at a less rapid rate than other industry sectors.

Persons 65 years of age and older represent a major growth market for the food service industry. Older persons now live longer. They have higher incomes derived from retirement plans and government payments, and are more frequently separated from their children who are now under less obligation to provide homes and support. These factors will result in rapid expansion of housing, food service, recreation and extended health care units. Services provided will ordinarily be above average rather than minimal.

Country Clubs To Get Competition

Traditional country clubs, while they will increase in number, will attract a smaller percentage of the population. Their competitors will be townhouse apartment complexes and planned suburbs with swimming pools that will offer country club-type facilities at lower year-round costs. Recreational clubs—golf clubs, stables, etc.—with relatively low-cost dues structures will be very much in demand.

Hospital food service will expand rapidly as government medical programs, as well as private plans, make better medical care available to all groups in society. Also creating hospital expansion will be programs aimed at care of the entire man, rather than physical illness only.

New Food Developments Predicted

Food processors and suppliers, too, will change methods and products for the 70's. The industry should see the following developments within a decade:

—Fresh vegetables, particularly leafy vegetables that tend to spoil in transit, will acquire new packaging. A possibility: inert gases used as quality-retaining media.

—Less food waste (exterior leaves of lettuce, bone in meat, etc.) will be transported at high handling and storage costs.

—Most pre-preparation and holding of food will be done by the supplier rather than by the food service operation. The pace of this trend will quicken as methods improve and markets for by-products are found.

—Greater efforts will be made to standardize quality, packaging and labeling of foods to meet the standardized requirements of buyers.

Suppliers of food service equipment, too, will move to meet the changing needs of the industry. The following developments can be expected in the years just ahead:

—The kitchen equipped to produce a wide variety of food items will disappear and be replaced by a kitchen with specialized equipment designed to handle pre-processed foods.

—Smaller, electronic units will be designed to produce both heat and cold and will replace traditional equipment. Heat and cold will also be produced from reprocessed circulation of gases and from chemical sources that renew themselves.

—More compact, lightweight specialized equipment adapted from space research will be offered to the food service industry. The new equipment, while expensive, will provide the greater mobility necessary to meet changing operational patterns and changing markets.

Management Gap To Continue

Management shortages will continue during the 1970's, as well as the shortage of training workers and supervisors. Reasons: (1) expansion in the number of units needed to serve the industry's larger market and (2) the time lag between vacancies caused by persons leaving the industry because of retirement, ill health or better opportunities in other fields and the development of new management personnel.

Active recruiting by franchise operations and by others in the food service industry will help close the gap, as will mergers and consolidations that will make possible more efficient use of management talent. Younger managers, able but with less experience, will assume positions of responsibility sooner and will partially meet the shortage.

Not the least among continuing trends that will affect the industry in the 70's is government influence over the operation of businesses. Some predictions:

—The government's social programs will result in more record-keeping and higher tax payments by the food service industry.

—Higher minimum wage laws will be enacted and will be extended to cover all food service employees.

—Government programs to reduce hours of work and to improve working conditions may result in making food service work more attractive to some classes of workers, but *less* attractive to workers who have a choice of jobs because of the need to work on evenings, Sundays, and holidays.

Sales To Zoom in '70's

The food service industry's sales during the 1970's will be up—as will costs. Profits will rise because of the larger volume of sales but will represent a smaller percentage of each sales dollar. Certainly there will be challenge for management in the 1970's, but there will be abundant opportunities for organizations that effectively change their techniques to fit a marketplace that is sure to be different from today.

2

HOTELS IN YEAR 2000

from *Cornell H.R.A. Quarterly*

Yesterday's Soothsayers

To foretell the hotel-motel industry—or commercial lodging—in Year 2000, let's . . . base our trend back one generation, to the 1930's. Hotel occupancy was then 50 percent and the traveling public was finding a new type of lodging—auto camps, auto courts, motels, tourist homes. Leading hotel men, at AHA's 1943 convention, reported an 84 percent wartime occupancy but were anxious about their industry for the years ahead.

Fay M. Thomas, vice president and general manager of Detroit's Book-Cadillac, addressed (*Hotel Bulletin,* November 1943) his fellow AHA members: "The new type of lodging [auto courts and tourist homes] was the result of a majority of the travelers using their personal automobiles and following highways which in increasing numbers were routed around cities rather than through them. All this emphasizes that the post-war problems of hotels are going to be centered around developments in transportation. The training of thousands of American boys as expert fliers and the production of thousands of airplanes indicate that the travel habits of the American public will be changed."

W. Stewart Woodfill, president of the Grand Hotel at Mackinac, Michigan, predicted (*Hotel Monthly,* October 1943): "New resorts are going to spring up all over the world, along the routes of the airlines, just as resorts in other years first sprung up along the routes of coach trails and steamers, and then along the routes of railroads and finally along the routes of highways."

And Seth Ridout, editor of the *Tourist Court Journal* (November 1943), spokesman for a group not accepted in the hotel field, commented with acerbity: "Does the term 'highway hotel' used by some

From the *Cornell H.R.A. Quarterly,* August 1968, pp. 5-8. Reprinted by permission.

hotelmen mean that hotel owners are planning to get into the tourist court business?"

Today, American Hotel & Motel Association members would give these leaders of 25 years ago a Triple-A rating as seers.

Today's Prophets?

What are today's "seers" saying? First, here is an excerpt from an article by Charles A. Horrworth, former executive vice president of AHA, published in the August 1960 issue of ... [the *Cornell H.R.A. Quarterly*] describing the future hotel:

You guide your car through the motorists' entrance and park it exactly where the lighted sign indicates. As you step out, a recorded voice extends a word of welcome and directs you to take out your baggage and remove a numbered metal tag protruding from one of the slots in an adjacent wall panel.

As you take the tag, your car is mysteriously picked up and whisked away to be filed in its own storage cubicle until you return the tag to the numbered slot and reverse the process.

You enter the lobby through a "doorless" door of air and, as you step onto a floor mat you feel its vibrating brushes cleaning your shoes. At the desk, you follow instructions about inserting your credit card into a machine which responds by disgorging a room key and a card bearing an account number.

On the card is information that your account has been established in the local data center and that insertion of the card into the checkout machine will provide you with an up-to-the-minute record of all the charges incurred during your visit.

During the course of your stay, you learn that the various departments in which charges originate use a small dialing device to record your charge in the data center where the record keeping for all of the electronically operated businesses in town is handled.

The trip to your room involves only a few steps to the off-service elevator and a brief horizontal ride on the moving floor of the hallway to your door.

Your room is pleasant and completely equipped with every possible convenience including pneumatic tube delivery of room service orders, adjustable firmness beds, bedside control of lights, shower, TV, door lock, temperature, window drapes and other conveniences.

At mealtime you are, perhaps, a bit disappointed to learn that your dinner is ordered by dialing code numbers. Your meal is delivered in a miniature dumbwaiter appearing in the middle of the table.

You suspect, and rightly so, that your meal was prepared and served without benefit of the human touch. While the food is excellent, you find yourself longing for some small sign that this hotel is staffed by people.

That Mr. Horrworth's Hotel of Year 2000 has solved the worker shortage goes without saying. And that this automated hotel may well be the future prototype is strongly suggested by Prof. Neil H. Cheek's study of workers in four of today's large metropolitan hotels (*Quarterly*, May 1967). He found the median age of city hotel employees to be 46.8 years and that they are drawn from the so-called "marginal" workers in the labor force, workers who couldn't readily find other employment. By Year 2000, these hotel employees will have been retired long ago and the acute worker shortage will be even greater—if . . . [a] bright future world comes true.

Even though animal psychologist Don Smith of Anaheim, California, foresees (*New York Times,* June 18 [1968]) the training of monkeys to perform many unskilled and semiskilled tasks in the years ahead, it seems likely that technology will outstrip animal training. Psychologist Smith claims, though, that "monkeys understand the value of money and will do anything to get out of their cages."

At AH&MA's 1967 convention, Charles B. Alling, Jr. told assembled members they must gear up now for foreseeable changes ahead. If they don't, buses and airplanes may take over the function of providing guest accommodations by further refinements of in-transit feeding, reclining seats, and the like. He pointed out that mobile roomette hotels were already in use and that a German bus operator had successfully used them in the U.S. for tour groups. (Isn't this as clear a warning as that voiced by 1943 doomsayers?)

Alling suggested the concept of dual-purpose buildings in which space used for offices during the day could be changed into guest rooms at night by means of convertible furniture and movable walls. Much more automation in check-in and check-out, increased use of dehydrated foods, infra-red ovens on each hotel floor to replace the coffee shop, and disposable tableware, draperies, and towels were other possibilities mentioned.

"Instant" Hotels

The "instant" hotel is already here—the San Antonio Hilton was constructed practically over night when completely equipped room modules were slipped into a structural frame. More hotels of this type will be prefabricated in factories and assembled in city centers or at remote resort areas.

That hotel operation is becoming highly automated and geared to "instant" service has been published in past issues of this and other industry magazines. The *Quarterly* published the all-inclusive possibilities of computers in November 1967, "instant" reservation systems and Ready Foods in February 1968, "instant" food systems in May 1968, and "instant" roast beef appears in this issue. The School's Research Section, soon to be housed in large new laboratories, will develop experimental guest rooms with adjustable walls, changeable decor, adjust-to-comfort mattresses, self-cleaning room devices, and so on.

"Instant" Hospitality

But of greatest concern to the manager of the automated hotel of Year 2000 may be ways to provide the guest with the "human touch" mentioned by Mr. Horrworth.

What do hotel guests want? Pleasant treatment by management and staff as well as the comforts and standards of their own homes, according to a recent survey made by Market Facts, Inc. for Procter & Gamble and AH&MA. The survey, entitled "The Commercial Lodging Customer—His Attitudes and Preferences," obtained a statistical sample of U.S. hotel guest opinions to learn guest "likes and peeves." Service shortcomings drew the most complaints—26 percent of the frequent guests and 24 percent of the business guests commented on annoyance with a maid or bellman, front desk service, and disinterested personnel. Since the "likes" were such usual ones as cleanliness, comfort, quiet and privacy, as well as good food, they serve to underscore the complaints about service.

(Another complaint found was the lack of sufficient bathroom supplies—not enough towels and wash cloths, and bars of soap too small. While the finding that soap bars were too small may seem mere self-serving on the part of Procter & Gamble, one should consider the nightly laundry ritual of today's drip-dry travelers—it seems reasonable that they really want more soap and might even appreciate special suds and a clothesline over the tub.)

If the future hotel is to be more mechanical and the complaints about disinterested service personnel are to be overcome by more automation (or cheerful trained monkeys) how can the guest be given more of the "human touch"? Should tomorrow's world be as crowded as demographers predict, some guests may deliberately seek isolation. But those on pleasure trips will certainly want to relate to other people in sharing their enjoyment.

Dr. Ernest Dichter, speaking to AH&MA members at their 1967 convention, delved into "the real emotional needs of the stranger in a strange place who may be searching for warmth and hospitality beyond the mere efficient functioning of the mechanical hotel routine." He suggests "instant courtesy" expressed through the registration clerk's concern in meeting the guest's special comfort needs, the placing of "mind-reading" memos in the room to tell the guest how to find and work his mechanical gadgets, and "instant orientation" into the community through a descriptive leaflet informing the guest of the area's features and what to do at 7 p.m., 9 p.m., etc.

Some hotels already provide "instant friends" by placing a community directory of classified club contacts and hobbyists in hotel rooms. Perhaps in Year 2000, guests can dial their needs for human contact into a computer, where their interests will be matched with those of instant-friends in the neighborhood.

Another hopeful trend is that of group travel to conventions, business meetings, or on company incentive award trips and club excursions. Persons nearly everywhere already belong to special interest clubs or can easily join one for a trip—ski groups, ornithology, philatelist, fraternal, professional and other societies. In fact a product of the mid-20th century is "instant groups" who travel at special rates all over the world where they are greeted and entertained by similar organizations who later return the visit.

Lodging of the Future

Max Blouet, general manager of the Geneva Hotel Inter-Continental, writes (*World Travel Tourisme Mondial*) that today's hotels, which will probably be in operation in Year 2000, already include many automated features—electronic elevators, automatic telephones, escalators, guest self-parking garages, individually controlled room climate—and that more automation must be developed, particularly to check in jumbo jet groups of 500 and check them out without chaos. He foresees more hotels and motels being built all over the world—in cities, at the seashore and winter sports centers, at airports—more boatels, officetels, and so on. Even more prescient are his predictions for "a hotel in space not seeing anything but the moon and a hotel deep in the sea!"

Fantastic? Not at all. Where will adventurous people travel in Year 2000 now that African safaris, cruising the Greek Isles and those of the South Pacific, and flying the Polar Route to Japan or to Europe have become commonplace? A generation ago such trips would have seemed fantastic to most people.

That the hotel in space and at the bottom of the sea is feasible has been researched by senior students at Cornell's School of Hotel Administration. Recently, reports have been made available for constructing, maintaining, and operating the Lunar Hilton and a Deep Sea Hotel. (These reports are available at $5 each.)

Tourism's role in upgrading national income and in maintaining a favorable international balance of trade will be stressed even more in the years ahead. Recently, international tourism topped $12 billion and it is growing faster than 10 percent annually. Thus more government incentives for hotel construction can be expected—direct subsidies, low interest rates, tax abatements. Even the United States, which now provides incentives for building hotels in regions of high unemployment, may extend Federal aid to hotels in order to encourage tourism. Presently, U.S. hotel operators are asked to cut their rates to provide more enticing and world-competitive prices for encouraging visits by overseas travelers.

In brief, the hotel industry in Year 2000 will be an extension of trends already discernible to the alert observer.

3

REVEILLE SOUNDS FOR THE HOTELIERS

Roger Beardwood

When corporate chieftains with an appetite for acquisition and an eye for potential look at the hotel and motel industry, they see a rich field that is waiting to be harvested. Last year the industry had revenues from rooms, food, and drinks estimated at $6 billion. By 1978, if current economic trends continue, its revenues should rise about 50 percent, to almost $9 billion. That respectable but unspectacular prospect of growth is not the main attraction for outsiders, however. They are fascinated more by the challenge and the promise of applying sophisticated management, marketing, and financing techniques to one of the last major industries still dominated by small entrepeneurs.

The 10 largest lodging chains control only 15 percent of the 2,500,000 hotel and motel bedrooms in the U.S., though they account for rather more of the revenues. Most establishments are small: the average hotel has about 59 guest rooms, and the average motel only 29. With a few notable exceptions, lodging companies are poorly managed. One result is a generally low standard of comfort, service, and food. Another is the industry's failure to hold its share of the gross national product. In 1939 it accounted for one percent of the G.N.P., but in 1968 for only 0.7 percent.

Because they are labor-intensive, often built on credit, and mainly small, hotels and motels are painfully vulnerable to inflation and to rising wages. But the industry does little research into its problems, relying instead on its customers to solve many of them. To improve labor productivity, for example, a growing number of hostelries force the guest to make his own morning coffee, clean his own shoes, and carry his own baggage. Costs that cannot be passed on in the form of self-service are generally added to the bill—along with a markup for

From *Fortune Magazine,* September 1969. Reprinted by permission of Time, Inc.

the house, of course. Some experts estimate that the *grand luxe* hotels need to raise their prices by 10 percent a year or more just to maintain current profitability. The rise may be smaller in houses offering less prestigious addresses, though it may frighten more of their customers: people who use cheaper hotels and motels are usually more parsimonious than the grand hotels' customers.

Objective: A Total System

Some industries create and control change; others have change thrust upon them. Change in the lodging business is largely generated by relative newcomers from the food, real-estate, construction, communication, and transportation industries. They are ruthlessly casting aside hallowed practices, substituting long-range planning for hasty improvisation, and investing heavily in market research, new construction techniques, and equipment. These are among the ways in which the pacesetters are transforming a somnolent industry.

—Holiday Inns, which has grown in 17 years from a single inn to the world's largest lodging chain, has acquired Continental Trailways. One attraction of the nation's second-biggest intercity bus line is that it can offer package tours to Holiday Inns, thereby building new business for both companies. The acquisition took Holiday Inns further along the profitable road to vertical integration: it owns a furniture manufacturers, a food processor and a distributor, a construction company, a printing plant, and insurance companies.

—I.T.T.'s 1968 merger with Sheraton Corp. of America has borne fruit in an $865-million expansion program—probably the largest ever announced by a hotel company. By 1973 the Sheraton system, including franchised motor inns, will encompass 116,000 guest rooms in 38 countries, compared with the present 45,734 in 14 countries. Some of the capital will come from the Euro-dollar market, which might have been closed to Sheraton as an independent because of its relatively small size.

—Airlines continue to strengthen their hotel interests, infusing a new element of marketing sophistication. Inter-Continental Hotels Corp., founded by Pan American World Airways, and Hilton International Co., owned by Trans World Airlines since 1967, have announced expansion plans. Eastern Air Lines is in the hotel business in the Caribbean and Hawaii. Braniff Airways, with Western International Hotels Co. as one of its partners, plans to become a major force in Latin-American hotels.

—The air-transport-catering-hotel nexus is increasingly emphasized by Marriott Corp., which claims to be the world's largest independent supplier of food to airlines, and by Host International, a bustling, diversified rival. Marriott operates 14 hotels, plans 15 more of its own, and will have more than a hundred inns run by franchisees within five years. Host is co-manager of one airport hotel, and plans a hotel group of its own for the 1970's. Both companies see hotels as profitable new markets for catering skills.

—Car-rental and hotel companies are invading each other's territory. Hilton Hotels Corp., founded 23 years ago and still youthfully nimble, is offering guests a 25 percent discount when they use one of the rental cars in its new fleet, five percent more than Hertz and Avis offer to some business users. RCA's Hertz, on the other hand, operates an airport hotel in Huntsville, Alabama, that may be the vanguard of a new venture. Hertz's main competitor, Avis, is a sister company of Sheraton in the I.T.T. family.

Those and other developments that are enlivening the industry are not haphazard. They are evidence that some of the innovators are moving toward a new concept in which the provision of bed and board is only part of a total system of linked services. With some false starts, and many sideways glances at the Justice Department's Antitrust Division, the pacemakers are putting together polymorphous corporations that provide the hotel and motel guest with many other facilities, including transportation, a rented car, recreation, entertainment, and assured credit. The concept pays off in two ways. It keeps within the corporation revenues and profits that would otherwise go elsewhere; and it puts a big, distinctive umbrella over the traveler. "One of the things we are selling is peace of mind," says Curt R. Strand, president of Hilton International.

At a quickening pace, the old distinction between hotels and motels is giving way to a recognition that they are complementary, serving essentially similar publics. That view is confirmed by *The Commercial Lodging Market,* a minutely detailed study undertaken by Michigan State University's hotel and business schools and the American Hotel & Motel Association. It shows that about half the guests in U.S. hotels and motels are traveling on business. Conventions account for an additional 18 percent of the guests in hotels, and for about five percent of those in motels. The ratios vary greatly in individual establishments, of course; but it is clear that hotels and motels as a whole are not primarily dependent on the leisure market. Only 24 percent of the guests in hotels, and 29 percent in motels, are traveling solely for pleasure. One reason for this rather surprisingly low ratio is, perhaps, the competition the lodging market is meeting from counterattractions: second homes, campsites, yachts, rented summer homes and ski lodges, and hotels and motels overseas.

The more successful of the large lodging corporations are proving that a clear view of the market, better management, and economies of scale pay off in higher profits. While company-by-company comparisons are somewhat misleading because of varying accounting methods and financing techniques, most of the pacesetters are earning higher pretax profits—in some cases far higher—than the average of 11.6 percent achieved last year by the sampling of establishments shown in the chart opposite.

Traffic in the Bathroom

The livelier lodging chains are spending increasing time and money on finding new solutions to the interlocked problems of hotel design, construction, and operating efficiency. "One secret of success in our business is to start with the right structure in the right place at the right price," says Wallace E. Johnson, 67, the massive, rumpled, and folksy president of Holiday Inns. Johnson and Kemmons Wilson, the 56 year old chairman, have been getting the formula right since 1952, when they realized that the growth of the interstate highway system was going to create a need for lodgings of good quality and modest prices, but saw few signs that anybody else was about to provide them.

Figure 1. How the U.S. travel and lodging business grew

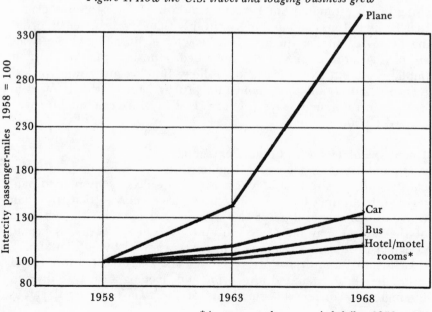

*Average number occupied daily 1958 = 100

Wilson and Johnson, builders and real-estate developers, concentrated from the beginning on building efficiently and well. William W. Bond Jr., a Memphis architect, who is now a vice president and director of the company, has designed about 825 of the 1,150 Holiday Inns that straddle the globe. Bond has standardized many structural elements. He has also reduced wasted space by studying "traffic patterns" of guests and staff in such facilities as bathrooms, kitchens, and laundries. Holiday Inns' market studies have helped Bond to design to an optimum size such public areas as dining rooms and lobbies.

Much of Bond's accumulated knowledge has been stored in a computer that is linked to a Norwegian-made drafting machine. Computerized architecture starts when Bond or one of his staff of 75 chooses the type of bedroom from a catalogue, and makes a rough sketch of a proposed new inn. After being coded, that information is fed into the computer, which records on tape data from its memory store. The tape then activates the drafting machine; in 25 minutes it provides detailed plans and elevations accurate to 0.002 inches.

Speed is important. With interest charges at 8½ percent for prime borrowers (and even higher for those who are less than prime), each month's delay, in effect, raises the cost of a $1-million building site by almost $7,000. Furthermore, the cost of construction is currently rising by an estimated one percent a month. Wallace Johnson claims that Holiday Inns can build more cheaply than any other chain offering rooms of similar quality. In Chicago, for example, where rivals are paying more than $25,000 for a bedroom, including its share of public areas but excluding land, Holiday Inns recently built for less than $12,500—"and our rooms are just as large as theirs, or even larger." In rural areas, says Johnson, Holiday Inns can build for well under $10,000 a room.

The Shape of Things to Come: Pentagonal
Other hotel companies are finding different ways to hold down construction costs. Last May, Sheraton unveiled a copyrighted pentagonal bedroom that not only uses space more efficiently than conventional shapes do, but also will cost less to build—though some of the savings may be swallowed up by the higher cost of specially designed furniture. The room, which was evolved by a "think tank" that included a professor of psychology and an associate professor of visual design, is separated into living and sleeping areas by a divider. By night the divider becomes one of the twin beds; by day it is

folded to become a sofa that also contains a chest of drawers topped by a table. The bathroom juts out from the external wall of the hotel and, as a self-contained unit, can be delivered to the site and hoisted into place by crane.

TraveLodge Corp., a large and aggressive motel chain, is pioneering its own solution to the problem of rising construction costs. The "tri-arc" hotel has a floor plan in the shape of a triangle with concave sides. It uses space economically and, because it has no front or back, can be put on almost any site. TraveLodge is building one tri-arc in Atlanta, and another in San Diego, plans to have ten more operating by early 1970. Each will take between eight and twelve months to build—about two-thirds the normal time needed to construct a 200-room hotel.

Hot Old Properties

Innovation may flatten the curve of rising construction costs, but it cannot do more, short of a technological breakthrough that is not yet in sight. For the customer, the inevitable result will be rising prices. In New York City and other major metropolitan areas, the day of the $50 bedroom is dawning. A generally accepted rule in the industry is that the daily rate for a room should be one-thousandth of the investment it represents. (The investment is defined as the total cost of the hotel divided by the number of bedrooms.) Preston Robert Tisch, president of Loew's Hotels, says that a new *grand luxe* hotel could not be built in midtown Manhattan for less than $50,000 a room—which would indicate a rate of $50. Furthermore, he points out, operators of older hotels are entitled to raise their rates to reflect the increased value of their properties and rising operating costs. Loew's, which built seven new hotels between 1961 and 1963, is now buying existing properties instead. "The cost of construction is just too high," says Tisch. His strategy is to look for well-maintained older hotels in good locations that can be improved by refurbishing, and made more profitable by efficient management and vigorous marketing, such as the Ambassador hotels in Chicago, acquired in 1965.

Such hotels are hard to find. Stephen W. Brener, vice president of the hospitality division of Helmsley-Spear, a New York real-estate brokerage and consulting firm, says: "A hotel built in the late 1950's and early 1960's, in the right location, is the hottest property in the market. A hotel of that age is young enough to be attractive, is efficient to operate, and probably cost about half of what it would today. But I don't think you could build up a chain of them: there just aren't enough to meet the demand at the price people are willing to pay."

With wages and fringes accounting for an average 36.4 percent of operating costs, as shown in the chart above, managements are searching diligently for ways to increase the productivity of labor. One way is to design the structure itself so that staff do not move about it needlessly—an important virtue of TraveLodge's tri-arc concept, which houses all the service areas in a central core. Another is to use materials in construction and decor that need little or no maintenance and cleaning: stainless steel in kitchens, fabrics that do not attract or show dust, and crockery and glassware that can be washed in a machine without breaking, for example. But the industry's favorite solution is still, unfortunately, to make the guest do more of the work. At the *grand luxe* end of the business, customers resist that solution, and rightly: they are paying a premium for pampering. "We can afford to make economies only where guests will accept them," says Roger P. Sonnabend, 43, the bearded, inno-

Figure 2. Where 700 establishments got their revenues in 1968 and how they spent them

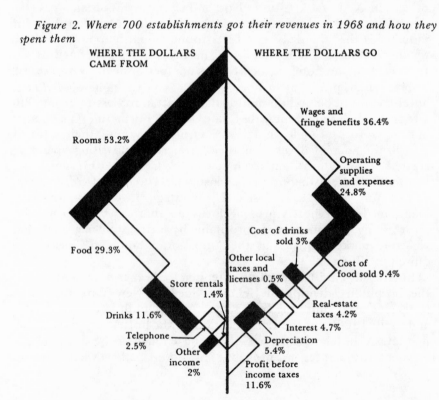

WHERE THE DOLLARS CAME FROM

WHERE THE DOLLARS GO

Wages and fringe benefits 36.4%

Rooms 53.2%

Operating supplies and expenses 24.8%

Cost of drinks sold 3%

Food 29.3%

Other local taxes and licenses 0.5%

Cost of food sold 9.4%

Store rentals 1.4%

Real-estate taxes 4.2%

Drinks 11.6%

Interest 4.7%

Telephone 2.5%

Depreciation 5.4%

Other income 2%

Profit before income taxes 11.6%

vative president of Hotel Corp. of America. "At the Plaza in New York, for instance, we still employ elevator operators and starters because guests expect them there. We would lose more than we would gain by installing automatic equipment in passenger elevators."

An old joke in the industry is that somebody will one day invent a machine to make beds. Henry O. Barbour, the newly appointed vice president for manpower development and director of research at Inter-Continental Hotels, is trying to turn the joke into fact. The device will be operated by a chambermaid. but it will change the linen or smooth a rumpled bed faster than she could do the job unaided. "There's absolutely no reason why such a machine shouldn't work," says Barbour, an adjunct professor of hotel administration at Michigan State University. "It's just a matter of thinking from first principles, and designing the bed, the machine, and the linen as parts of the same system." He hopes to build and test a prototype within the next year.

Holiday Inns is tackling the housekeeping problem from a different angle. It is experimenting with disposable paper sheets, pillowcases, towels, and staff uniforms. If they went into general use, Holiday Inns could make large savings in linen inventories and storage space. At present, each room requires three sets of linen, one on the bed, one in reserve, and one in the laundry (some inns keep a fourth set in reserve). And, of course, disposable linen needs no laundering. But Holiday Inns still needs to be convinced that its customers will accept without protest such a radical innovation.

The more enlightened corporations are coming to believe, however, that the best way to improve the productivity of labor is to attract better employees. Western International Hotels offers its staff health- and life-insurance plans, a stock purchase program, and complimentary rooms in its hotels during vacations. Furthermore, Western has a sophisticated training program that enables it to promote from within: each of its top corporate officers has worked his way up through the ranks. "Our philosophy is that if we treat our employees right, they will treat others right," says Gordon Bass, the executive vice president for operations. Holiday Inns offers comparable benefits, with the addition of a profit-sharing scheme and, for lower-paid employees, a credit union as well.

Western, Holiday Inns, and a handful of others are exceptional, and farsighted. Most hotels and motels offer low pay and few fringe benefits, and get left either with people who cannot find jobs elsewhere, or with those who mean to move on to something better as soon as they can.

Thieves in the Kitchen

Dishonesty is another reason for the industry's poor record. Some establishments build into their prices an assumption that dishonest members of the staff will pilfer a sizable but unknown percentage of the food and drink. "They have a thousand ways of getting the stuff out," says a hotel purchasing director who prefers not be identified. "Kitchen workers walk out with steak strapped round their waists. Some supplies are not even delivered: somebody in the hotel is on a kickback." The same executive adds: "I can't really blame all the pilferers. Some are treated like dirt. Pay a man the minimum and you will get a minimum man."

In the kitchen three solutions are being tried, sometimes in combination. The first is to supervise more closely—which is both expensive and less than thief-proof, because even supervisors can be corrupted. The second is to employ men of high caliber, in the hope they will remain honest. The third is to have food delivered in portions of specified size and quality (which doesn't always stop pilferage, but does make it measurable). Instead of buying a side of beef, for example, the hotel will buy a specific number of individually cut steaks. These become part of the inventory, and are checked out of cold storage against written orders for meals.

A popular new gadget that keeps barmen honest is the AutoBar, manufactured by Inter-American AutoBar Systems of Miami. It eliminates the ease of "kicking back" the profits on undelivered bottles, and the possibility of serving short measures. Each bottle is locked, upside down, into a dispenser; to get a measure, the barman presses a glass against two prongs, and a metered drink is poured automatically. At the end of each shift, the barman has to account for the day's stock in metered drinks instead of in bottles.

Recipe for Failure

Hoteliers are also attacking the problem of guests who refuse to eat in hotels. *The Commercial Lodging Market* reports that only 60 percent of the people questioned ate all their breakfasts in the hostelries they slept in; only 13 percent ate all their lunches; and only 20 percent ate all their dinners there. The study doesn't show where they took their other meals; but many of them must have voted with their feet against hotel food by going to restaurants that offered better cuisine, service, and atmosphere.

Too many hotels regard food as a service to be offered grudgingly instead of seeing it as a potential moneymaker—or in the jargon of these times, a profit center. Hotel dining rooms tend to be cavernous and dull, motel dining rooms small and dull. Both try to be all things to all people. If the restaurant industry did business the same way, it would long ago have gone broke. John D. Lesure, a partner in the hotel accounting firm of Laventhol, Krekstein, Horwarth & Horwarth, which also offers consulting services, says: "The lodging industry needs to develop more specialty restaurants, appealing to a particular group, and it needs to compete with nonhotel restaurants."

Some of the trailblazers are proving that good food can be a palatable part of the income statement. Western International Hotels and Hilton offer notable examples of in hotel restaurants that are varied, excellent, and busy. At a lower price level, Holiday Inns is adding to many of its establishments specialty restaurants that feature ingenious decor: they are tricked out to give fox hunting, nautical, and other salable flavors. Some outsiders view the hotel business as a huge new market for catering skills developed elsewhere. Marriott Motor Hotels, owned by Marriott Corp., makes an average 25 percent departmental profit on restaurant sales, about double the industry average. Marriott relies increasingly on pre-prepared and convenience foods, puts its staff through intensive training courses, and keeps its restaurants busy with local customers as well as hotel guests. "I'd say our success isn't based on just one factor, but on making everything work together well," says J. Willard Marriott Jr., president and son of the founder. "In this business, you have to shave points off a lot of percentages, and when you add up all those little points you have a nice edge on the competition."

The industry could greatly improve its financial showing by keeping its bedrooms busier. The breakeven point ranges widely in different establishments—from an occupancy rate of 40 percent, to 60 percent or more. But once that point has been passed, the ration of profit on room rentals rises dramatically. A study by the hotel accounting firm of Harris, Kerr, Forster & Co. shows that the industry is treading water. In 1968 the 300 transient hotels studied had an occupancy rate of 66.4 percent, down from 67.4 percent in 1967. The 300 motels studied did somewhat better, achieving an occupancy rate of 74.4 percent in 1967 and 74.3 percent in 1968.

The Stay-at-Homes

So far, the lodging industry has sold its services mainly to people who are better educated and more affluent than average. *The Commercial Lodging Market* reports that in 1966 more than 75 percent of the respondents in its study had family incomes over $10,000—

i.e., they were from the most affluent third of the U.S. population at that time. Thus hotels and motels are competing for the custom of a very small segment of the population. The big challenge before the industry is to change the spending, social, and vacation habits of the majority of Americans. An American Automobile Association study made in 1966 showed that half the civilian population had never spent a single night in a hotel or motel, and that 52 percent had never traveled more than 200 miles from home. What keeps half the population in its own beds is not primarily the cost of travel, however. According to a Louis Harris & Associates poll, cost is less of a deterrent than "uncertainty." The industry has done more to perpetuate than to cure inhibitions about travel schedules, tipping, and dress.

Until recently, few hotel chains, and even fewer independent hotels and motels, either understood or used sophisticated marketing methods. Furthermore, they failed to offer the salaries and status needed to attract the marketing experts who could develop those methods. Frank W. Berkman, executive director of the Hotel Sales Management Association, says that even today some sales and marketing executives earn as little as $7,000; the maximum is around $60,000.

Marketing strategy starts with the decision to build a hotel or a motel in a particular place. The decision should be based on research of the market potential, and of the probable effect of future travel patterns. Hilton Hotels uses such preresearch, and the results demonstrate its value. Hilton's establishments have an over-all occupancy rate of 68.3 percent, and its net income from operations last year was $12,200,000, about 25 percent more than in 1967. Most hoteliers, says Berkman, rely on hunch: "I'm afraid our industry is still full of people who believe they have an intuitive 'feel' for a situation, and refuse to invest in original research."

Hotels in city centers have a more formidable marketing problem than the motels and motor hotels near airports and in suburbia. Many city hotels have lost trade for a complex of reasons that require them to devise a new marketing philosophy—and a new aggressiveness. The increasing speed of air travel has made it possible for businessmen to make day trips to a city instead of staying overnight. Traffic congestion has forced travelers by car to seek motels in suburbia; with the rise of the "grand motel," a hybrid that offers full service at relatively modest prices, the conventional hotel has lost the advantage of greater comfort. And urban violence has discouraged tourists and business groups from visiting some cities. Hotel Corp. of

America lost $666,000 on the Hotel America in Washington last year largely because of the summer riots. "It was cancellations, cancellations, all the way," says Roger Sonnabend of H.C.A. The hotel is doing better now, but still has problems.

H.C.A.'s misfortunes in Washington reinforce the view that a lodging chain needs to straddle a number of markets. In New York, for example, H.C.A.'s Plaza had a record year, with sales of $22,260,000, and profits of $2,131,000 before income taxes. The venerable Plaza's buoyancy is demonstrated by the rise of occupancy rates and of the average charge for a room. In 1961 the occupancy rate was 59.9 percent, and the average room rate was $19.25. In 1968 the occupancy rate was 85.1 percent, and the average room rate was $28.07. Both rates are still rising.

The Plaza is proof that vigorous salesmanship can give an old hotel new life. Hyatt Corp., a California based chain of hotels, motels, and coffee shops, is proving that good marketing allied with striking architecture and decor can turn a new hotel into an institution almost overnight. When Hyatt Corp. bought what is now the Regency Hyatt House, Atlanta, in 1966, it was a half-finished shell. Today it is the flagship of the Hyatt fleet, an airy structure that soars 21 stories above Atlanta's Peachtree Street. The hotel is built round a covered courtyard that contains an "outdoor" continental restaurant and a cocktail lounge perched on a pedestal and overhung by a 13 ton, Tiffany-style parasol.

It is always hard to get a room at the Regency, and at times it is impossible: the hotel has $40 million in bookings from clubs and conventions that stretch ten years into the future. Hyatt Corp.'s performance is almost as impressive as the Regency's. Its sales rose from $17 million in 1964 to $36,500,00 in 1968, and its net income from $407,000 to $1,700,000. In 1969, predicts President Donald N. Pritzker, 36, sales will be some $105 million and net income $5,500,000.

Keeping Them on the Circuit

The electronic reservation network is one of the most useful of the new marketing tools. It enables a customer to get a confirmed reservation within seconds at any hotel or motel on the network. It enables the chain to know precisely how business is shaping up that day—and in the days ahead. And it keeps travelers on the circuit: the guest leaving a hotel in one place is encouraged to make a reservation for his next destination. The cost of such a system is formidable. Holiday Inn's Holidex system, which consists of twin I.B.M. 360

computers interconnected with regional offices and inns by 50,000 miles of leased wires and by communication satellite, represents an investment of $12 million. But the daily volume of business, some 120,000 reservations on average, has brought huge economies. Each reservation costs about 17 cents, compared with $1.50 to $4 on the older, slower, and now vanishing manual systems used by smaller lodging chains. Every major hotel chain now has switched to an electronic system; for the airlines, the possibility of using their seat-booking systems for room reservations is an added attraction of the lodging industry. Inter-Continental Hotels, for example, is hooked into the Panamac reservation network owned by its parent, Pan American—which uses its airline sales staff to sell I.H.C. bedrooms as well as aircraft seats.

Independent hotels and motels are looking with increasing interest at cooperative reservations systems; only by banding together will they be able to afford the high capital cost and obtain the volume to justify it.

The pacesetters are busily and successfully tapping the new sources of finance they need to expand and to re-equip. Indeed, since such corporations as Hilton, Hyatt, Holiday Inns, and Western International showed that good management could bring high profits, hotel stocks have become high risers on Wall Street.

Public ownership gives the industry access to additional sources of capital that are badly needed. Traditionally, the industry has been built on a shaky pyramid of first, second, and even third mortgages, many of them at short term. The big financial institutions, which were hurt badly by overbuilding of hotels in the late 1920's, have until recently looked on the industry as poorly managed and risky.

One factor that favored the tremendous growth of motels at the expense of hotels in the 1950's and early 1960's was the willingness of local investors to put money into investments on which they could keep watchful eyes. Holiday Inns, and other chains that offer franchises, expanded mightily by putting their seal of approval on such relatively small local projects. The franchised chains not only offer hardheaded appraisals of a project's future, but also supervise franchises, and help their business by making it part of a coast-to-coast "brand name."

The financial institutions are going back into the lodging business. And some major manufacturing corporations, seeing real estate as a hedge against inflation, are putting their money into hotels. One of them is Alcoa, which has two joint projects with Western International. The first is the huge and successful Century Plaza in Los

Angeles. Alcoa financed the construction, aided by a mortgage from the Equitable Life Assurance Society. Western operates the hotel, and holds the lease jointly with Alcoa. The second Western-Alcoa project is the 700-room Washington Plaza in Seattle, a spectacular amalgamation of an existing hotel with a new one.

The Bankers' Bet on Las Vegas

Investors looking for proof that professional management is at work appear also to have found it recently in Las Vegas—long thought to be a city of casinos that provided bedrooms as an after-thought. As it now turns out, that view is obsolete. When Howard Hughes started buying Vegas hotels and casinos in 1966—he has paid some $85 million for six—he gave the city respectability. Since then, rival hoteliers have issued a flurry of corporate prospectuses and given the Vegas hotel business visibility. The hotels, it becomes clear, are successful in their own right: on average, they make about half their profits from gambling, and half from selling rooms, food, and beverages.

"To put the business in its true perspective," says Robert Maheu, chief executive of Hughes's Nevada operations, "we operate hotels that provide a number of recreational facilities: one of them is gambling, which makes money. Another is entertainment, which loses money. But both attractions have this in common: they are necessary because we have to give people reasons for coming to this particular spot in the desert. And people will not come here in suffi-cient numbers unless we continually devise new attractions, such as golf tournaments and rodeos. Gambling is not enough by itself."

Hughes was only the vanguard of a less publicized invasion of new money and new ideas. International Leisure Corp., controlled by aviation entrepreneur Kirk Kerkorian, has gone public on the strength of owning the Flamingo, and of building the $60-million Inter-national, billed as the world's largest resort hotel; Levin-Townsend Computer Corp. has bought the Bonanza from Kerkorian for $10 million; Parvin/Dohrmann, which sells a wide range of services and equipment to hotels, restaurants, and other institutions, has acquired the Aladdin, the Fremont, and the Stardust; and Continental Con-nector Corp., a diversified company with interests in electronics, trucking, retailing, and real estate, has acquired the Dunes. It is also buying the Golden Nugget.

"The pioneers are moving out," says E. Parry Thomas, who is chairman of both the Bank of Las Vegas and Continental Connector. "As the business got bigger, it required greater financial and management depth. Only the professionally managed corporation can obtain the institutional and public backing that Las Vegas needs."

Although Las Vegas draws about 70 percent of its business from the West Coast, it is looking toward the East, the Pacific, and Europe for much of its future growth. Sig S. Front, vice president for sales at the Hotel Sahara, which is owned by the publicly held Del E. Webb Corp., was an organizer of an airline-hotel seminar last year that considered the implications of the 747 jumbo jet, and of supersonic jets. "If we start early enough," says Front, "we can make Vegas into a 'must' for tourists from overseas. We have to do our planning *now,* though—and we have above all to start thinking globally."

Globalists Old and New

All the major U.S. chains, and some minor ones, are trying to become global. There are some encouraging precedents for them to follow. The pioneers of the U.S. hotel abroad are T.W.A.'s Hilton International and Pan American's Inter-Continental. Between them they operated and franchised 91 hotels in early 1969; since then they have announced plans for 39 more. Despite their apparent similarities, the two chains operate quite differently.

Hilton International's hotels are usually owned by local investors, who contract with Hilton for management services. The contract normally gives the owners two-thirds of the gross profits, and requires Hilton to make only a minimal investment: "We like the investors to supply even the egg cups," says President Curt Strand. That technique has been highly profitable. In 1968 the 41 hotels, with a total of 13,930 bedrooms, produced a net income for Hilton International of $6,200,000. In contrast, Inter-Continental had a net income of only $1,600,000 from 42 hotels with a total of 12,264 bedrooms. (Five hotels were franchised.)

The contrasting histories of the two chains help to account for that difference. Hilton International's hotels are in places chosen purely because they are buoyant markets. T.W.A. is not about to change that formula; Hilton's profits are more important than its role as a provider of bedrooms for T.W.A. passengers. Inter-Continental, on the other hand, has in the past built some hotels that fitted Pan American's needs better than its own. Some were built because a developing country would grant Pan Am landing rights only if it provided a prestigious hotel. Others were built because Pan Am thought a first-class hotel would help it to increase traffic on a new route. That strategy is changing. In the future, Inter-Continental will build hotels only if they can be profitable in their own right. Today's feasibility studies of projects are detailed and hardheaded—models for the industry, in fact.

Inter-Continental's history has bequeathed benefits, too. Some of its older hotels, built when costs were lower, are now highly profitable. And because of Pan American's extraordinary sensitivity to local political problems Inter-Continental has typically favored partnership with local investors. Usually, it has bought the land, and developed the hotel jointly with its partners. Thus its hotels are appreciating assets. Hilton's are waning ones: it owns management contracts instead of land and buildings. The two groups run their hotels differently, too. Hilton hotels are standardized American oases; Inter-Continental's are more varied, reflecting the country in which they are situated. One at least, the Mandarin, Hong Kong, has a place on any list of the world's best (see "The Great Hotels," *Fortune*, November 1967).

The U.S. invasion of foreign markets is becoming a stampede. Loew's, for example, is building its first foreign hotel in London, following there such trailblazers as Hotel Corp. of America, Hilton International, and Knott Hotels Corp. Inter-Continental Hotels is involved in two London projects—both of them in partnership with British Overseas Airways Corp. The ubiquitous Holiday Inns is planning or building 124 inns in more than 30 countries. As it does in the U.S., Howard Johnson is sticking close to Holiday Inns' heels; it, too, is building in Canada and the Netherlands. (Howard Johnson will be forced to lessen the shock of its hideous orange gables in places where local sensibilities are backed by strong planning regulations.)

Rivalry From the Old Masters

In Europe, particularly, the U.S. chains face heavy competition from local rivals. At the *grand luxe* end of the business, the competition is fierce. "The Europeans have a long and formidable tradition of providing first-class food and service," says Henry W. Beardsley, senior vice president for marketing at Inter-Continental. "What we add, I think, are modern management methods, modern design, and the advantages of being a member of a worldwide group." Unlike smaller local rivals, for example, Inter-Continental has easy access to world markets for food, where it buys in bulk, usually flying consignments via Pan American to hotels that order them. (Inter-Continental also has the muscle and knowledge to help local suppliers improve their efficiency and even to make new products.)

Following their U.S. counterparts, the big European chains are also starting to cross frontiers. Forte's, the British airline catering and restaurant company, which already owns 19 hotels in Britain, recently acquired three first-class Paris hotels, including the George V. Trust Houses, another big British chain, is operating in Spain, the Caribbean, and elsewhere, and is a member of a foreign consortium that has bought 27 percent of U.S. TraveLodge. A third British group, Grand Metropolitan Hotels, has proved its global ambitions by buying the Hotel Manhattan in New York City. Meanwhile, foreign airlines are following T.W.A. and Pan Am into the hotel business.

The U.S. lodging industry is thus being cross-fertilized with ideas, with techniques, and with competition from a multiplicity of sources. For small, independent operators, the next decade will be crucial. If they cannot improve both their efficiency and their standards they will be swamped—and there are few signs at present that most of them have either the ability or the access to capital that will enable them to survive. For the customer, on the other hand, the ferment in the industry will be almost wholly beneficial. Standards have been so low for so long that they have nowhere to go except up.

4

TRAINING HANDBOOK

Frederick H. Antil

"Training doesn't work in our business." I've been hearing this cry for years from managers and corporate officials who think they've given employee training a chance. Most managers haven't really tried it. Their excuse is: "I know I should do something about training, and as soon as things slow down, I will."

We all know that time is money, particularly in our business. But is there a conscientious manager anywhere who can honestly say he doesn't have to:

—reduce employee turnover and absenteeism?
—reduce costs?
—improve service?
—maintain high sanitation and good quality standards?
—improve "atmosphere" by changing employees' attitudes?
—increase sales?

Surely we all can find time to increase profits and productivity. Training isn't magic, but it can achieve dramatic results if it is carefully planned *and* if management is committed to the plan. Training isn't mysterious. It merely means making a change in an individual. It means adding to, or changing, what he knows—what he can do—or the way he feels about his job. It's that simple. In brief:

Frederick H. Antil is Vice President of Education Systems for Aims Education, Inc, Lake Success, New York, a firm that develops and markets a multimedia systems approach to employee training. He was also Director of Training and Management Development for the Marriott Corporation and Playboy Clubs International.

From *Volume Feeding Management*, September 1970, pp. 19-26. Reprinted by permission of the author.

Knowledge is the *what* of any job.
Skill is the *how* of any job.
Attitude is the *why* of any job.

What I want to do here is explain: What training is, to increase your knowledge of it; How training can work, to increase your skill as a manager; Why training is necessary, to change your attitude about it.

Whatever your position—owner, manager, supervisor—you are a manager. As such, you will be involved in two types of training. The first is "Formal Training." This includes any regular classes held for individuals or groups of employees. The second is "Informal Training." This includes daily on-the-job training that goes on constantly in your operation. The coaching and counseling you provide your individual employees can also be called informal training.

The basic principles that lie behind successful training are merely common-sense rules for dealing with people. Something of your attitude toward customers should carry over in your treatment of employees. The most expensive training program will flop unless you and your employees are prepared for training, and the atmosphere is right.

Create Interest

Adults will learn only what interests them. Their first (usually unspoken) question is: "What's in it for me?" You have to assure them that training can mean a new job opportunity, more money, greater safety—in short, training has to mean something to them personally.

I remember working with a new large dishroom crew at an opening. The men were sullen and indifferent. It wasn't until they found out that the equipment and supplies they were responsible for cost more than a new luxury car that I was able to convince them of the importance of their job to the whole operation. Every job is important. You know that, but it's up to you to convince your employees. Each operation has its own peculiarities; with a bit of imagination, you can get your employees interested in learning. For instance:

—A bulletin board set up to display both complaining and complimentary letters will provide incentive.
—Make kitchen employees responsible for sanitation inspections. By rotating the inspectors every week, you can assure impartial inspections, and the competitive aspect will improve sanitation conditions enormously.

—Establish a scale of promotion, so that busboys, for example, know your criteria for a waiter's position.

—Initiate waiter-waitress training by demonstrations of good preparation.

—Encourage fountain help, sandwich or salad men, to create new menu items (perhaps for a holiday or new season). Then encourage training to prepare them to make and serve their own suggestions.

—Hold group employee meetings to discuss problems that can be solved by training.

—If practical, have kitchen or service employees come back after work as guests, so they can see their jobs from another point of view.

Communicate Clearly

In our business, as in any other, we use hundreds of terms and expressions which are meaningless to new employees. Even if your trainee nods his head when you give directions, don't let it go at that. Make sure he knows what you want him to do. Ask him to repeat them in his own words. And, no matter how busy you are, check on him occasionally.

A classic case of misunderstanding occurred a few years ago when a young assistant manager trainee reported to a restaurant for his practical, on-the-job training. Because he reported late in the morning, the manager was too busy to say more than: "I want you to watch the door through lunch. I'll see you after that to work out your schedule."

About 1:30, a steaming manager called company headquarters to complain about the "idiot" they'd sent him. The trainee, it turned out, was doing what he was told, without really understanding the order. He sat in the front lobby and "watched the door" during lunch.

The manager, of course, wanted him to stand in front of the dining room, greet the guests, pass them on to the floor hostesses, and issue menus. But all he said was "watch the door." The manager had blamed the young man when the problem really was his own poor communication.

Another case involved a young lady training to become a kitchen supervisor for a tollway operation. After she had observed for a few days, the manager told her to wear her uniform the next day because he wanted her to "work stations." Out of inexperience and nervousness, she imagined herself pumping gas at the adjacent service station. She almost quit. The next day, of course, she found out about the various "stations" in the kitchen. The manager knew what he meant, the employee thought she understood—but they failed to communicate.

Repeat Yourself
Consider these truths about learning:

—a trainee learns more, the more often an instruction is repeated;
—no one learns from one experience, he needs several;
—the brighter and more interested trainee will learn more quickly;
—training is a never-ending process; repetition must be built-in.

How do you turn nagging into repetitive training? Let me repeat again: Use your imagination.

—Repeat yourself by displaying pictures of beautifully prepared foods in strategic places in the kitchen.

—Repeat by posting printed reminders or check lists in the dining room (where customers can't see them, of course).

—Repeat by initiating menu drills before each service period for your dining room employees. (Providing a taste of special dishes takes the "drill" out of practice here.)

—Post a cleaning schedule, based on employee suggestions, if possible, and institute a regular "inspection" to see that it's followed.

—Establish a personal sanitation routine for everyone, with posters or notices in entryways, locker or clothing storage areas, employee restrooms, etc.

Keep Current
Another important fact about learning is this: the more recently a person learns something, the more likely he is to remember it.

When one company with a very thorough new-waitress training program decided to give the program's final examination to the girls who had been on the job for some time, it was shocked. Invariably, the older waitresses had forgotten much of what they learned initially. The company then had to retrain them.

—Ask your more experienced employees a few informal questions, to check their knowledge, skills, attitude.

—If you find that they are "slipping," get some repetition and reminder routines going.

—Older employees, far removed from the so-called training period, may exhibit habits that will confuse the new people working with them. You might find that newcomers, if well trained, keep the others on their toes.

Insure Satisfaction

Unless your people get some personal satisfaction out of learning, they won't learn.

Training people by ridiculing them, by replacing them even temporarily, or by pointing out their faults without mentioning the good qualities of their work can be worse than no training at all. A damaged ego will not be receptive to anything you have to say. Here's where you need *your* sensitivity again.

Create an "un-threatening" atmosphere. Remember that some of your employees have not been in school for many years, and may not have liked it back then. Formal schoolroom training can make them resentful.

One operation solved the problem of busboy turnover by taking a "personal" interest in the problem. When formal training was set up, a head busboy was selected and involved in the training. The busboys and the trainees were encouraged to participate by choosing their own uniforms. They even changed the title of their job (they preferred Service Attendant). Turnover was dramatically reduced.

Make a Survey of Your Training Needs

You know where your operation sticks, stumbles, or halts. Get those rough spots down on paper; decide who needs training, who should do it, and how it should be done. If your organization has a training department, use it for advice and implementation. But don't expect the training department to make your major decisions or do all the work.

Any operation, regardless of size, will require certain minimum training:

1. Orientation for all employees.
2. Periodic refresher training for everyone in:
   —courtesy and customer relations,
   —sanitation,
   —fire prevention,
   —safety.
3. Supervisory and management development for the supervisory staff.

Using your own experience, plus that of your staff, investigate your operation for training possibilities. Ask yourself these questions to spotlight those areas where formal training might pay off.

—What is your largest group of employees?

—In what group does the greatest turnover occur?
—Where are your major service problems?
—Which job is the most complex?
—Where is quality control hardest to maintain?

In certain jobs you'll find little turnover and professional, experienced employees. Yet, even these jobs require clear-cut standards and supervisory follow-up. I am reminded here of a case where lack of planning seriously hindered a well-intentioned training effort. It started when corporate officials took a quick look at service in their various field units—probably through the eyes of unit managers and assistant managers.

Management decided to hire a professional training person to "solve the service problem." Unfortunately, management neglected to tell the trainer that they wanted him to work personally with individual waitresses on the job. All they said to him was "solve the problem."

The trainer spent months developing materials to be shipped to all the units, because he felt that individual managers lacked the materials to train their people. Management meantime saw "no progress," by their definition of progress, and fired the trainer. Had management done a careful study of the problem beforehand, they'd have avoided a wasteful mistake.

As a manager, you should snoop around, watch what's going on, and talk the operation over with your supervisors. Once you decide which areas need help, you can go on to tackle the specific training problems of personnel, schedules, and materials.

As a general rule, I think that most of your employee training should be as self-instructional as possible, and highly visual. Written materials are nice, but too often just don't get read. Movies are effective but expensive to make. Film strips or slide programs are more reasonable. Gimmicks don't work, if you treat them merely as gimmicks, and expect them to do all the training for you.

One large operation achieved a great deal of notoriety in the trade by installing individual teaching machines to train employees. There was tremendous excitement about this program, but a follow-up revealed that the "miraculous" machines were gathering dust. Management expected the machines to take over its responsibility for training, and these were not made an integral part of a total training program. Because the machines were expected to do everything, they accomplished very little.

Once you have established which areas need training, you should take the next step. Analyze each job that needs training, break it down into its components or steps, and spell out the knowledge of skills, and attitudes that are required. From this breakdown, you can develop training "objectives." These are a list of what the trainee should know, what he should be able to do, and what his attitude toward the job should be once he's been trained.

Training should not be a shotgun blast you hope will touch on something the trainee needs to know. It should be rifled at his specific needs.

The manager who runs a union operation may feel his hands are tied in regard to training. He does have less flexibility in moving his employees from one area to another and he must compensate them for any meeting or training session they attend.

As a consequence, many managers of union shops give up any thought of training at all. And yet, training in a union house can pay many dividends, as in a non-union one. Actually *any* training time should be compensated whether you have to or not. The trainee should not be penalized for being trained.

Training can, and should be, used to qualify employees for the next higher level. By training them yourself, you can develop employees who have not yet learned all the bad habits that new outside "fully-trained" employees sometimes bring.

The Four-Step Method of Training

During World War II, we turned ordinary young men into pilots, riflemen, communications experts, and military leaders. We turned housewives, secretaries, and coeds into defense workers. In doing this we found out, through necessity, how best to train people. What we developed then, and have since refined, we call the Four-Step Plan. We have learned we can teach any subject with this method. The four steps are:

First, *explain* the whole job in detail—the what, the how, and the why. Use an experienced employee, a film or other visual aid, reading material, or all three.

Second, have an expert *demonstrate* what the job is and how to do it, explaining why each of the steps is necessary. Encourage questions. Then ask the employee questions to be sure that he understands what he is supposed to do and why.

Third, let the trainee *try out* the job, under supervision, correcting him, answering his questions. It is important here that he be asked some direct questions to make sure he knows why he is doing the various steps of the job.

Fourth, arrange periodic *follow-up* observations to be sure the employee is not making mistakes or taking shortcuts. Your interest should encourage him to perform the job right.

These four steps are simple. But don't be fooled by this simplicity. I think you'll find that if you neglect the explanation, or the demonstration, or the try-out, or the follow-up—you'll be in trouble.

Implementing Training

The kind of training that is most common is "on-the-job training." This is where one employee performs his job under the guidance of a more experienced employee. The danger in on-the-job training is that the new employee may not learn how to do the job properly. Older employees are often proud of short-cuts they've invented. So beware of:

—the bartender who free-pours instead of measuring;
—the cook who holds the meat in his hand on the automatic slicer instead of using the hand guard;
—the cook who doesn't measure or follow approved recipes;
—the carver who uses a knife with a great deal of "style," but only nearly misses taking his fingers off, and
—the assistant manager who hastily accepts deliveries without measuring or weighing.

These examples also point out the importance of explaining *why* to a trainee. If a trainee knows why he is doing a certain thing, as well as *how* to do it correctly, he will be much more likely to perform the job correctly when the supervisor is not around. Don't wait for an accident or a mistake that fouls up your procedures to stop and explain things. Think *prevention*. This is only one of the benefits of training, and the one most often overlooked.

Know who are your good trainers. Good trainers are experts at their jobs, and articulate enough to explain what they do. They are also patient with newcomers, and can understand a trainee's problems. But, no matter how suitable your trainers, you can handicap them by failing to provide them with materials and equipment.

Finally, reward your trainers. Make training worth their while by rewarding them with bonuses or status or some recognition.

Each job and each training program should have its own materials. You can use a series of pictures showing the steps in preparing or serving a certain product, or another kind of visual program (film-strips, movies or slides). You can use audio tapes that explain certain information. To be sure that all training materials are available when you need them, you should designate one person responsible for developing, securing, maintaining, and issuing training materials.

Ideally, you will have a complete library of manuals and visual programs available for new employees. Many establishments use small, rear-screen projection units with cartridge-loaded film or film-strips; all the trainee needs is a few minutes by himself with the projector.

An increasing amount of commercial training material is being developed for food service management. You can choose among film-strips, movies and slide programs, posters, booklets, textbooks, audio tapes, records, and programmed instruction courses. Subjects range from waitress training, to operating a dishroom, to understanding wines, to becoming a better manager.

You will find that few, if any, off-the-shelf programs meet your needs exactly. But you can be discriminating and build this material into your program. Do not build your program around the material.

For example, there are a number of poster programs available. These are designed to hang on the employees' bulletin board, or in a locker room. By themselves, these posters accomplish almost noth-ing, but, if you can incorporate them into your own well-planned training program, you can achieve good results.

Beware of fads. No salesman is going to solve all of your problems with a "fantastic course." Training is a slow process and a continuing one. There are a few short cuts, and no instant remedies.

Training Really Begins Before You Hire

For some time now the reputation of the food service industry as a place to work has ranged from mediocre to unsatisfactory. Man-agers have had to work long hours under heavy pressure. Employees often have lacked any sense of pride in what they were doing.

Take the situation of the waitress who won a local restaurant association award as the Outstanding Waitress of the Year. She wouldn't allow her picture to appear in the local paper because she didn't want her neighbors to know she was a waitress. This situation is sadly indicative of the problem we face.

One of the most important steps you can take is to see that your employees begin on the best possible basis. If they feel enthusiasm about their jobs, and pride in working for your organization, you'll have eliminated, or at least diminished, many potential problems.

Actually, an employee's training begins even before formal job orientation. A prospective applicant will remember vividly how he is first treated, and that memory will influence his later behavior.

I remember a manager who opened a nonunion hotel in a highly industrialized and unionized area. From the beginning stages, he involved his employees and supervisors in the venture. He created tremendous enthusiasm among his people, so that word-of-mouth had it that this was going to be an exciting place in which to work.

As further incentive and evidence of his interest in his people, the manager waived certain restrictions on corporate benefits, stock purchases, and so on. He set up employee committees to handle safety, training, sanitation, and service. These committees became a genuine decision-making body, instrumental in selection of uniforms and other basic policies. He invited employees' families as his guests at the hotel's opening. Not coincidentally, the hotel was soon very profitable, and within two years doubled the number of rooms available!

If you have pride in your business and enjoy running it, then the atmosphere of your operation will reflect it. Too many managers confuse perspiration with good management. Foodservice is a tough business, but not as tough as many managers make it. The manager must build his staff if he is going to keep his health and sanity. This can be done through training, but the image you create sets the stage for any training you do. The climate you create will determine how well your training pays off.

One company that was opening new units at a rapid rate developed an "opening task force." A number of experienced employees would go to each opening to train new employees and to help for the first week or two of operation. When it came time for his unit to open, the manager of one of the new operations questioned the make-up of the task force. He had worked for this company for many years. He had even worked with some of these "task force" employees. He questioned why they were included in the task force, saying "they're not so hot."

At the opening, he was amazed to see the outstanding job performed by each of the members of the task force. He finally realized that each member of the group was convinced that this was an elite group of the best employees in the company. And so they worked doubly hard to justify this belief.

I have mentioned several times that training must be constant if it is going to be successful. Another way of saying this is that the manager must be totally and truly committed to training. It can't be a fad or a phase that comes and goes.

Management and Supervisory Training

Management development, your professional growth, and the growth of your management staff should be a continuing process. Can you imagine an engineer, doctor, or lawyer not continually studying and learning, to stay abreast of what is happening in his field? Yet how many managers feel that because they have worked for 10 years they know all they need to know?

A cynic once said that experience is a great teacher because it enables you to recognize your mistakes the next time you make them. Joe Powell, a management lecturer, counters with: "Does the manager with 10 years experience really have 10 years experience, or does he have one year's experience repeated ten times?"

A word about your own development, as distinct from that of your staff. Here, the impetus has to come from you alone. If you, or any member of management, expect to become managers, it has to be because you want to, and very badly.

Managers have to be proficient in three areas:

1. *Technical Subjects.* You have to know the business you're in: Food purchasing, preparation, service, and controls; Beverage purchasing, service, and controls; Accounting and bookkeeping methods and an understanding of equipment and its use and maintenance.

2. *Supervision Skills.* You must understand your responsibilities as a supervisor in working with and through your subordinates. A keen understanding of human nature—skill in human relations—is absolutely necessary. More young supervisors fail because they lack this skill than because they lack technical competence.

3. *Basic Management Practices.* The higher you go in management, the more you need skills in: Planning your operation; Organizing your staff capabilities; Motivating and directing your staff to accomplish your plan, and Controlling your operation to guarantee you meet your plans.

As in training at the employee level, the manager sets the pace in Management Development. I remember one eager young assistant manager who wanted to complete his college work, even though he was working over 60 hours a week in a very busy restaurant. He went to school at night and managed to perform very satisfactorily at the restaurant during the day.

The manager, who did not have a college degree, began to harass the young man about this "moonlighting." "You don't need a college degree in this business," and like comments, began to demoralize the young man and he eventually quit—the restaurant, not college.

This is a sad example of the type of manager who frustrates a sincere desire for Management Development.

Let's look at each area of management needs and investigate how a manager might train himself and his subordinates in these areas.

Training in the first area—technical subjects—is fairly easy to find. There are various schools with both short and long courses; local and national restaurant associations conduct various seminars, and the American Motel Association correspondence courses teach certain technical subjects.

In addition, the manager can call weekly staff meetings where problems can be discussed and solutions found by the staff. Portions of this meeting should be devoted to reviewing certain aspects of the business to teach newer members, and re-train older ones.

It is much harder, however, to teach human relations and management principles. Various graduate schools of business devote years to mastering the intricacies of these subjects. There are a number of excellent books available, but the greatest impact will be the example of the manager himself. Unfortunately, your people are more apt to imitate your weak or bad management practices than they will your good ones.

Don't neglect trade periodicals and journals as sources of information. These publications can be an effective way of sharing common experiences and problems. This material can be used in your weekly staff meetings.

One of the most difficult things to teach management is the ability to "see," that is to notice what is going on around you. Working in a busy operation, you easily lose your ability to critically observe.

You can't change something unless you know about it, and the only way you are going to know about it is to see it. You have to train yourself and the staff to see.

One manager who understood this principle was faced with a problem. His night manager, well qualified in other respects, seemed to show no interest in the quality of the food itself. This was a particularly high volume restaurant. The manager was concerned about the night man's apparent compromise on quality. He suggested that for a three-week period the night man guarantee that one particularly fast-selling item be prepared and served correctly. The manager, of course, wanted everything to be served correctly, but he knew that you must change behavior gradually. Because the night man concentrated on only one item at a time, he became more conscious of looking. In several months, the manager was very pleased with the food standards of the night manager.

Another technique that I have used successfully is inviting staff members, perhaps with their families, to visit the operation as guests. Seeing the operation from the customer's vantage point can open up the eyes of even the most complacent employee. Follow-up discussions of what each saw, and ideas to improve problems, can involve everyone in upgrading the operation.

Summary

I hope that I have shown that training isn't complex. It is merely the application of sound management principles along with a lot of common sense, and a sincere interest in people. I also hope that I have convinced you of the absolute need for total management commitment; not just when it's slow, not even when it's just convenient —but all the time. Training does not exist in a vacuum. It succeeds because a number of other things are being done well at the same time. Training has to be put into perspective. Understand what it can do, and what it can't do.

I think here, particularly, of a large company that was having trouble with one of its oldest divisions. Sales in this one area were falling off; while other divisions were growing rapidly. Management's first reaction was to stiffen up training programs, to get the failing operations back on their feet.

Before plunging into a full training push, though, management took time to do a thorough study. They discovered a number of reasons for falling sales: changes in the customer population, locations, pricing, style of service. Many of these problems were unrelated to training. As a result of the study, many units were closed down or shifted, and others were modified. The thorough analysis is the key here.

Training need not cost a great deal. Your biggest expense will be the salary of the person doing the training, and the people being trained. But, no matter how expensive this is, it is still cheaper than the turnover, waste, inefficiency, and customer dissatisfaction caused by an untrained staff.

Training can be inconvenient but it also can be a blessing to a manager in a number of very tangible ways. Having more than one person trained for each job allows you to more easily schedule days off and vacations. By making people flexible, you add interest to their job and broaden their perspective of the total operation.

No discussion of training would be complete without recognizing the importance of recruitment. Admittedly, for certain job categories and certain geographical areas, recruitment is a most difficult task.

But, understanding your employees and your operation pays dividends here, too. I recall an operation with the usual high turnover of dishwashers and pot washers. Busboys, however, made excellent tips, so there were a number of applicants waiting for this desirable job.

The manager made a rule that the busboy job could only be filled from the dishwasher ranks. Turnover of dishwashers nearly stopped. The men waited their turns for the busboy job, even though they weren't enthusiastic about dishwashing. The manager benefitted, too, because he could replace absent dishwashers with the newer busboys; their background qualified them for both jobs.

I hope that I have convinced you that training makes good sense. Training is good management, and good management pays off.

5

MANAGE YOUR CLUB FOR A CHANGE!

John F. Duncan

Every club manager thinks he works too hard. The truth is, he works too long.

When every self-respecting business executive is expected to get his job done in 40 hours (while plumbers and electricians get it done in 32), the country club manager frequently works a 70-hour week in the summer.

It's not impossible to cut down the hours at the club.

Like going on a diet, or maybe like joining Alcoholics Anonymous, a club manager first has to determine there's something wrong with the way things are now. After that, he has to really want to do something about it.

The two stipulations eliminate a lot of managers—just as they eliminate a lot of fat people and drunks—because not all 70-hour managers really want to do something about it.

Although a manager who works 70 hours neglects his wife, kids, home and social life, he usually rationalizes that his work week is not unreasonably long "because" . . .

A friend, knowing how strongly I feel about waste hours at the club, asked me some time ago, "How do you get away with it? My members expect me to meet them every time they come to the club, whether it's 8 a.m. or midnight."

Good old Bill no longer is in the club business. The 70-hour weeks he put in "because his members expected it" became too much for him.

Another of my 70-hour friends recently put it another way: "I owe it to my members to be available to them anytime they're in the club."

John F. Duncan is the Manager of the Point Grey Golf & Country Club, 3350 J.W. Marine Drive, Vancouver, British Columbia.

From *Club Management*, November 1969, pp. 26-28. Reprinted by permission of the publisher and the author.

This is drivel.

The maitre d' has to be on hand when the dining room is open. The bartender must be at work when the club is pouring martinis. The accountant should be on the job when the books need keeping.

Mark this carefully: The manager who says he works long hours because he owes it to the club, or because his members expect it, is testifying to his inadequacy as a manager.

What he really is saying is that he isn't sure he is doing a good job of managing. In fact, he is so insecure that he probably is spending a lot of time around the club proving to his members how hard he is working. His rationalization is, "They certainly can't criticize me for the number of hours I put in around here!"

There's another category of managers we can't help: People so dedicated to their work that the club becomes hobby as well as work. For some, the club is also home and family.

Pity these men, who will go to their graves under-paid and unappreciated in spite of their dedication. These managers get up in the morning, read the paper and go to the club. They come home at night, sip a brandy and go to bed. And they like it that way.

There is a third category: Managers who can be saved! These are the people who work 70 hours because they haven't learned the difference between operating the club and managing it.

I believe that in every club in the country the manager, if he is truly hired to manage, can get the job done in 40 hours. All he has to do is manage more and operate less. Without exception, both he and the club will benefit.

To do this takes a little soul-searching; and if a manager has been at his club several years it also takes considerable courage.

The first thing to decide is whether he wants to work a nine-to-five day like other human beings in business—with Saturdays and Sundays off. Why not? Business is like that when it has the word "company" at the end of its name instead of the word "club." Ours is a business, and we as managers have supervisory people just as they do downtown. We call them maitre d', bartender and accountant. They are supposed to do our operating while we manage.

Although it is necessary that a manager have some specialized knowledge, he need not be the "compleat" authority on everything. He has supervisors or department heads for that.

The manager's primary function should be to look into the future, not into tonight's party.

Some time ago I was in the office of a fellow club manager when the chef burst in, breathless from a dash down the corridor, to exclaim, "Boss, the freezer's out! We've got those 300 New Yorks for tomorrow's party and I figure with the other meats we could lose about a thousand dollars!"

My manager friend, reacting instantly to the emergency, leaped out of his chair and dashed to the kitchen, where he inspected the freezer and the refrigeration unit. Once he determined the scope of the problem he set about solving it.

Oh, he was a "man of action." He called a refrigeration man, arranged to borrow some freezer space, supervised an inventory of meat, helped transfer some meat to a cooler and watched the kitchen employees as they moved the rest of the meat to the borrowed freezer in a neighboring building. He then called his meat man and held up the order for the next day and, finally, told his chef how to get dinner out without using the freezer.

My friend is an operator more than a manager; it's no wonder he works 70 hours a week. My chef doesn't burst in on me with a problem like that. He knows my reaction would be to ask, "What have you done about it?"

My chef would come to me after the crisis and say, "Mr. Duncan, the freezer went out this morning, but the refrigeration people said they'll be over to fix it. Meantime, I sent most of the meat we had in the freezer over to Dunnigans—they gave us a little space."

The difference between an operator and a manager is illustrated very clearly.

Some managers, reading these words, are saying to themselves, "That makes sense, all right. But it'll never work in my club. The chef just couldn't take care of an emergency like that."

Are you sure? Have you ever given the chef any responsibility? Has he ever had to make decisions? Or are you really the executive chef as well as the manager? And if you're the executive chef, because you don't rely on the man in the kitchen to take care of that kitchen, perhaps you're also the head bartender, head accountant, purchasing agent and chief of the locker room.

We're approaching a subject on which hundreds of books have been written. They usually call it "delegation of authority," and I guess that's what we're really talking about.

My own description of the technique for getting somebody else to do your work is "using people." I "use" my people. I manipulate staff, committees, directors, the membership in general *and myself*— to the highest and best use for the good of the club and all its members.

True enough, some club managers cannot "use" their employees properly because they don't have the proper employees. In some clubs, the freezers wouldn't be fixed and the thousands of dollars worth of meat would be spoiled if the manager didn't get the job done. But this may be the manager's fault.

Because it is necessary that responsible people take over all operating chores if a manager is to have a shorter work week, he has but two choices: (1) Develop every supervisor's responsibility and extend his authority, or, (2) get new supervisors who can do those things.

Authority and responsibility are in themselves motivators, and with proper motivation we can get our staff people to do our work for us—to do all the supervisory work we managers assign to them. We're not going to discuss training here, but motivation is even more important than the kind of training in which a chef is told where to buy his meats and how he should compute his food cost.

Committees

Committees also are made up of people who can shorten the manager's work week. *Operating managers usually over-burden their staffs with things done by committees in well-managed clubs.* Such managers say, "Well, this committee isn't going to get the job done, so we'll have to do it." Or the manager reasons that a committee might go over the budget . . . or do the job inadequately . . . or maybe, heaven forbid, do it so well the manager doesn't get the credit for it.

A good manager not only lets his committees do the work, but seeks to involve more members in committee work. Then he restricts his time and effort, during the committee's tenure, to playing the old political game of selling, persuading and cajoling in hopes that the project is completed properly.

That kind of effort is not only fun and a challenge, but it saves hours of a manager's time.

Members in General

A manager also can save hours in dealing with his members. The operator spends a lot of time being lovable. He smiles at his members at every meal and regularly strolls through the bar and sometimes as far as the first tee, greeting, smiling, playing the "utter host." He strives to be well-known and hopes to be popular.

Unfortunately, that kind of manager not only gets the complaints, but he encourages them. He's the kind of manager who says, "Thank you, Mr. Gideon, for what you have told me. If we didn't have members like you to point out what's wrong in the club, we wouldn't know that it should be corrected."

Bah!

Complaints should be meted out to the people who provoked them: The bar manager, chef, maitre d' or greenskeeper. The good manager doesn't get such complaints because he really isn't that well known. Some of our best managers are virtual nonentities to their members.

They're better managers because they don't have to waste time dealing with the problem of why Mrs. Smythe's steak was over-cooked. (In a well-managed club, the maitre d' or chef has to answer that one.)

In an attempt to be of service to the members, as a group, let's not make the mistake of personally hunting for the wallet Mr. Sheffield thinks he left in the locker room, personally carrying the cold cup of soup back into the kitchen when Mrs. Bergh complains, personally checking the bar to see if the henpecked Mr. Linville has left for home yet. Let the operators do those things.

Board

Relations between the manager and board of directors is different in each club; and, more than that, different each year in every club: Your board must know you're a manager, not an operator.

Many a good manager has ruined his image and betrayed his status by being seen changing a faucet washer. While none of us should be above changing a faucet washer in an emergency, it must be obvious that a businessman downtown who is paid $15,000 doesn't replace faucet washers; and directors who see the $15,000 club manager with a wrench in hand quickly will consider him more menial than manager.

Managerial skills are difficult to define. Suppose we start with awareness, or perception, and add intuition, extrasensory perception or clairvoyance. A manager must exude confidence and trust, offer cheerfulness and hope, bring in an element of salesmanship and show humility.

Putting intuitive skills in proper perspective with the learned skills of the operator is usually a quandary for a manager. The size of the club will dictate the amount of time and energy a manager should put to managing and operating.

My own rule of thumb is that in any club which does a gross of at least $500,000 (including dues, initiation fees, everything) the manager should spend 100 percent of his time managing. At $250,000 he should spend half his time managing and half operating.

At $125,000 it would be 75 percent operating and 25 percent managing.

My own rule of thumb is that in any club which does a gross of at least $500,000 (including dues, initiation fees, everything) the manager should spend 100 percent of his time managing. At $250,000 he should spend half his time managing and half operating. At $125,000 it would be 75 percent operating and 25 percent managing.

When you manage instead of operate, what do you do? One way to describe it is to say that *as a manager you're looking into the future, and as an operator you're concerned with the buffet tonight.*

Projecting the club operation into the future is your responsibility as manager. How many members will you have in two, five and 10 years? What will be their needs? How should these be measured in dollars and cents? From these elementary questions, a manager proceeds by surveys, questionnaires, investigation, etc., to arrive at answers needed for decision making by the board and long-range planning committee.

He is a manager!

6

MERCHANDISING FOR THAT EXTRA SALE

Hans Prager

How do we get the people to spend more than they really thought they were going to; and how do we get them to eat the hot appetizers and salad and dessert and wine, and have the after-dinner drink?

It is all within the realm of possibility. We know that they came in just knowing that they were going to have an entree. As long as they came into the dining room, chances are 99.9 per cent of the people will order an entree. We have to sell more.

The first prerequisite is that instead of having an order taker, you have a salesman or sales lady take an order. Anyone can walk up to a table with a pad and pencil in his hand and say, "Good evening, what will you have for dinner?"

"I will have the roast beef."

"And you?"

"The duck."

But that is not the way it should be done. Your people should be sales people, just like the people who sell stoves, light fixtures or carpeting.

First, when you take a guest to the table, don't take a menu with you. Leave the menus somewhere at the desk or scattered about the dining room. You seat the people and the hostess will say, "Have a nice evening, enjoy your dinner. Miss So-and-So will be right with you," or whatnot.

The waitress comes to the table. "Good evening, I am Miss Sapain. I will have the pleasure of serving you this evening. May I bring you a cocktail from the bar?"

Hans Prager is Assistant General Manager of the Lawry restaurant organization in Los Angeles as well as a lecturer in restaurant management at the University of California at Los Angeles.

From *Club Management,* April 1967, pp. 62ff. Reprinted by permission.

Chances are in our area people will have a drink, and she will get the drink, serve it—still no menu. Now the people have something to do; they have something in their hands. They are talking and the waitress takes five to 10 minutes, until she sees the drink is halfway down or three-quarters of the way down. Now she brings the menu because now she has the opportunity to say, "Would you care for another cocktail?"

Had the menu been with the people the second time she came back, she would have had to take the food order.

Okay. Now they have the menu, they are studying it. Now the waitress comes up to the table and starts suggesting some things.

"We have a special salad in this restaurant. Have you ever tried our Granada salad? The specialty tonight is so-and-so." And she describes it.

Know the Product

But unless she knows what it is and how it is prepared—knows her subject—she can't really sell it. And how many serving personnel really know their product?

I know it happens to me every once in a while. "What kind of soup do you have today?"

The waitress will say, "Just a moment, I will go check in the kitchen."

It's happened to you, too. Knowing what you are selling is half the sales job.

Now, for all the girls, even in the other restaurants that have more than one item on the menu—and none of our restaurants have more than 12—each entree is broken down phonetically: How it is pronounced, what is in it, and how it is prepared.

The new waitress gets a session with the chef. She knows the menu frontways, sideways and backwards. I think if the cooks didn't show up, we could probably take some of these girls and put them in the kitchen and they'd know how to prepare the food, too.

The problem, of course, that you have that we don't is that your repeat clientele is far heavier than ours. We may see a customer once a month, once every six weeks. You may see a guy every single day for golf and lunch.

I think then you come to a happy medium where you have different menus for five weeks in a row and then you repeat them.

We have given our sales people, as I would like to call them, the means with which to sell—sales gimmicks—and we have them all over the place. I'd like to mention some of them.

At one of our restaurants, the Mediterrania, we have a wine cart. It is not just a little cart with a little barrel on it; it is a huge thing. It has features on it, it is a take-off on a Syrian donkey cart. Built in underneath is a hurdy-gurdy, a music box. When you turn the handle, it tinkles. It is supposed to be some operatic tune, but you could never make it out.

It has two barrels on it, one Burgundy and one Chablis. Why? Because people don't have to be afraid of mispronouncing a French name in front of their guest or choosing the wrong type of wine to go with the right entree. It is either red or it is white.

And it is dispensed in a glass liter or a glass half-liter; and it is reasonable: $2.50 for the full liter, $1.25 for the half liter. The full liter is enough for four, and the half liter is enough for two.

It's gotten so that just to have the cart come by the table and hear the tinkling, people order the wine—because it is a little bit of show business.

Lawry's serves truly but one entree, prime rib of beef. The average dinner count is about 700 people at night. Now, the roast beef is no better than it is next door at another restaurant. In fact, I think there are restaurants that serve prime rib maybe a little bit better than ours.

Yet we are more successful than any other restaurant in town, and I think we know why. Being that we only serve this one entree, we merchandise it to the hilt.

First, all the prime rib is cooked in rock salt. It is buried in salt and again it doesn't make it any better, it really adds nothing. It prevents the rib from roasting. It stews it to a point. But it gives us something to tell people.

We felt we had to do something to add romance to the words "prime rib"—by telling the story as to how we prepare it, then bringing it right up to the customer's table. We have the huge silver-domed carts rolling around the dining room. There is a man dressed as a chef, though he is not, carving your slice of beef to your specifications.

We feel that if we brought the prime rib out of the kitchen, we'd close in six months.

People who come into restaurants don't just do so to eat; they come to be entertained a little bit and to find something other than just the food on the plate. I don't believe that the only function your club dining room serves is to satisfy an appetite.

Sure, the primary reason for having come into the establishment was to eat. But if you are able, after an hour and a half of his being there, to give your guest or member a little more than what he ordered off the menu, I think the repetition of the times he will come into your dining room will be greatly increased.

We have some specialty items. We have an item called cappuccino, and I know most of you know what that is. In Italy, instead of hamburger specials they have espresso bars. And out of these beautiful, gleaming espresso machines they make some awful coffee and a drink called cappuccino.

That is a mixture of coffee, chocolate and milk, and it is steamed up and served in America in a restaurant we visited, where it tasted like hot Bosco with booze in it. But it was selling; it was really selling.

We put in a cappuccino machine, changed the name to cappuccinero and are now selling 2,000 a month. It costs 24 cents each to make; we sell it for $1.25.

Success with Desserts

We instruct our girls, "If you are going to ask the customer, 'Would you care for dessert?' chances are he is going to say 'No.' But if you just bring the dessert cart right up to the table and say, 'What may I serve you?' like he wants something, you are telling him that he should have it."

And you know something? The worst thing we can do in our business is say, "I hate to throw these eclairs away. They don't look 100 per cent right, but I think we can go with them one more day."

Wouldn't you rather have a 43 percent food cost on $80,000 a month than a 38 per cent food cost on $40,000 a month?

We don't worry about desserts being 50 per cent cost. If they are not 100 per cent fresh, out they go, because chances are people are really much smarter than you think they are. And they can tell when an eclair is not fresh or when a strawberry torte looks just a little dilapidated.

They won't buy them.

So food costs are going to come into line all by their little selves, as long as you do that gross volume. Gross volume pays for the lights and your salary and the chef's salary and the overhead. That is constant, that is a fixed cost. And the only cure for that is growth, dollar volume.

Lawry's also serves a salad. When I say a salad—just one!

We in Southern California think that we have mastered or pioneered the salad business. California offers a fine supply of lettuce and romaine, and Lawry's feels that 28 years ago when it went into the salad dressing business it was able to merchandise this better than anybody else.

We bring the salad to the table in a bowl with crushed ice—a plastic bowl has crushed ice in it; the salad greens are in a stainless steel bowl that sets in the ice.

The waitress has learned to spin the stainless steel bowl in the ice; and as it's spinning she uncorks a bottle of dressing she has shaken and lets the dressing flow in while the salad is spinning.

It creates a little bit of appeal. It is different from the ordinary restaurant where they set down the salad with dressing already plunked on top of the greens. It makes the salad just a little bit different, and it didn't cost any more.

None of the things that set the good apart from the bad really cost more. It is just the manner in which they are done. Merchandising for that extra sale does not always come in what you sell, but in what you give.

We feel we can charge more for some items because of what we give around the plate, not on the plate. Anything you give on the plate will cost money. Anything you give in decor or service or in little niceties that you do here and there, those are the things that cost you nothing.

It is not what we do but how we do it. It is not what you do in your club but how you go about getting to the same place everybody else wants to reach. You just want to take a different route instead of going the straight and easy way. You don't mind being the type of manager who goes out of his way in order to come up with a new gimmick, with a new idea.

Bar Merchandising

The bar is something that interests me very much, and some people have done a great job on bar merchandising.

Consider what one place has done with orange juice and pineapple juice and some rum in a beautiful-looking glass—$1.75. The drink is in a tall glass with a chopstick in it and a clay parrot sticking on it; it is beautifully colored.

You still pay $1.75, only you get to keep the parrot. You can take that home.

Just to illustrate how these things work, I took my sister to San Francisco to lunch, and she saw a waiter walk by with three of those and she said, "I want one."

I said, "You don't even know what it is."

She said, "I don't care."

That is really the truth.

In what manner do you serve your drinks in your club? Do you use the same glass everybody else does?

There are many ways to merchandise bars. A bartender with personality, for instance.

I haven't visited too many clubs, but most have the austere-looking dining room, which is fine, and then they bring you a printed menu that was typewritten that morning in the office. It has about as much appeal as a piece of scrap paper.

They don't use any words to describe the item, so there is no romance that goes around the menu. Our menus don't cost more than 18 or 19 cents apiece. We are happy to have people take them with them; and we throw them away when they are dirty.

We dress the waitresses according to the overall theme of the place. I guess in clubs it could be accomplished just as well, instead of that same old red jacket and black pants, or black skirt and white blouse.

Of course, it costs a little bit of money to maintain these uniforms, and initially they may cost a little more to order. But the results you are going to get from them are fantastic.

We have a restaurant that is not doing quite as well as it should be, and we have tried this and we have tried that and it hasn't helped. You may ask, "Well, where is the Lawry image that you have talked about?"

For some reason, there is this one intangible that we can't put our fingers on. I think personally from my experience, having worked in the place before while it was busy, it is because of the people we used to have that we don't have any more.

What has happened to that restaurant? It had a manager who was killed on the freeway, who was a very vibrant type of personality. It was really a swinging place and he made it so.

Hopefully, soon we will come up with the one little merchandising gimmick that will solve that restaurant's problems.

We have a steak over there right now that we are advertising. It is called a culotte. It is from the end—that is what culotte means, a piece of the end.

We have advertised that in such a manner that we now are slowly having people come in and ask for culotte. Our ad reads, "Reserve a steak tonight because the number that we have is limited."

And people actually are calling up and reserving a steak. We may only have 30 or 40 a night because we can't get rid of the rest of the top sirloin (from which the culotte comes).

7

THE GREAT AMERICAN GET-TOGETHER

from *Forbes*

Here they come: Accountants and chiropodists. Biscuit bakers and broadcasters. Chemists and coin-laundry operators, dentists and dry cleaners. Systems analysts. Salesmen. Stenographers and steel workers. Just about everybody, from tailors to taxidermists to top executives.

Here come the conventioneers—flocking to some 300,000 meetings, 40 million strong last year and growing in number all the time. "Back in the Fifties," says Philip Harrison, publisher of *Sales Meetings* magazine, "there were about 20,000 association conventions a year." The number was up 75 percent to 35,130 last year, attended by some 12 million people, conducted by everyone from the American Medical Association to the National Crushed Stone Association.

Of these, 6,330 were international or national conventions, while nearly five times as many, 28,800, were state or regional association conventions. While the number of association-sponsored conventions has been growing, the number of *corporation* meetings has been growing at an even greater rate. Business meetings have become a great industry. In the Fifties there were about 60,000 to 70,000 of them a year. The number has since quadrupled to over 280,000 with an estimated attendance of about 28 million in 1968.

Altogether, this makes conventioneering a very big if unsung business. According to Harrison, at least $6 billion was spent on conventions and business meetings last year—$2.2 billion for all association conventions and $3.9 billion for corporate meetings and participation in trade shows and exhibitions.

That includes only what is spent to put on conventions or to attend them. In addition, delegates spent upwards of $1 billion for transportation to and from association and corporate meetings. Add it all up and you have at least a $7-billion business.

From *Forbes*, February 15, 1969, pp. 28ff. Reprinted by permission of the publisher.

The dollars spent for conventions and business meetings have enormous economic significance for cities, hotels, airlines and the whole fast-growing tourist and travel business and its related services.

For example, the average delegate to a national convention spends about $35 a day for hotels, food, car rental and entertainment, according to Joseph S. Turner, executive manager of The International Association of Convention Bureaus. This means that a city playing host to a four-day, 10,000-delegate meeting will take in close to $1.4 million that wouldn't have been spent there otherwise.

Some conventions attract really big spenders. The 41,000 delegates who attended the 25th annual convention of the National Association of Home Builders in Houston last month, says the association's director of conventions and meetings, Don S. Vaughn, spent close to $10 million in the five days they were there. That was an average of about $50 a day each.

A place like Atlantic City, of course, could not live without conventions. (With only 60,000 residents, it pulls up to 500,000 conventioneers a year.) But conventions are economically important even to New York City (population: 8 million). "Last year we had 12,733,350 delegates to 812 conventions, and they spent $267 million in the city," says Charles Gillett, executive vice president of the New York Convention & Visitors Bureau. "They also returned home to promote further travel by others to the city." To New York, the last is vital because tourists bring an estimated $1.5 billion into the city every year.

While conventions are important to a city's total economy, they are crucial to hotels. For almost half of what an association convention delegate spends goes to the hotel that houses him, either for his room or his meals. The rest is spent for food and drinks elsewhere in town, purchases in retail stores, local transportation, sightseeing and the like.

"The hotels of the future that are going to be successful are those that are all-purpose, accommodating conventions as well as pleasure travel," according to James C. Collins, sales vice president of the Hilton chain.

Today most big hotels in most major cities already are dead if they do not do a sizable convention and corporate meeting business. "Depending on the size, type and location of the hotel," says Frank W. Berkman, executive vice president of the Hotel Sales Management Association, "conventions and corporate meetings could range anywhere from 25 percent to 65 percent of their total business."

"We get about 40 percent of our business in our chain from conventions and corporate meetings," says Preston Robert Tisch, president of the 14-unit Loew's Hotels. "We built the Americana in New York specifically as a convention hotel with its 2,000 rooms, five restaurants, 10 ballrooms and 41 public rooms."

Hotelmen like Tisch love conventions for a lot of reasons. For one thing, they help fill up "the property" (as hotelmen call a hotel or motel) in the off season and in the Sunday-through-Thursday "dead time" when room occupancy is normally quite low. For another, "a convention or meeting delegate is not like an average guest who may eat one meal in a hotel and do the town in the rest of the time he and his wife are here," says Tisch. "If he's booked with us, more often than not it's for breakfast, lunch and dinner for the three or four days he's with us. Or pretty close to that. It depends on the kind of meeting it is, of course."

So lucrative are conventions that convention hotels will go almost to any lengths to drum up business. For the past few years, for example, Del Webb's Sahara Hotel in Las Vegas has run an annual World Airlines Christmas party, attended by a total of about 10,000 airline personnel who come in and out over a two-week period. Being airlines employees, most of them can get to Las Vegas for practically nothing. "We give them special rates for rooms when they get here," says Sales Vice President Sig Front. Whatever it costs, the hotel is worth it. Front can be assured that there is an employee in every major airline in the country who is prepared to extol the virtues of the Sahara as a convention or tourist site.

Spreading the word does not hurt the airlines a bit, either. For the airlines also are becoming more and more dependent on convention and business-meeting business. A little over a decade ago, according to the International Association of Convention Bureaus, probably only a little more than a third of delegates to national association conventions got to them by plane. By 1966 another IACB survey showed that more than half of the delegates got to national association meetings by air.

W. Scott Supernaw, acting manager of convention sales for TWA, estimates that something like 15 percent of his airline's total business comes from convention travel. He expects "our convention travel in 1969 to approach $100 million." The airlines not only profit from the boom in conventions; in a way they are responsible for the boom. They have made it easy to get to a convention anywhere in the U.S. "People think in terms of the time it takes to travel, not the distance," says Desmond Kelly, manager of the Las Vegas Convention Bureau. Las Vegas is 2,249 miles from New York, but only 4 hours and 25 minutes by nonstop jet. "Moreover, excursion and group rates make travel less expensive," Kelly adds.

The American Way

But jets are only one of perhaps a dozen or so interrelated reasons why the convention boom is what it is. "Without our wonderful tax structure, we would hardly be in business," says one association convention manager. He refers to the fact that most convention costs can be taken as business expenses, and are thus a deduction from taxable income. But, again, this is only part of the story. At the heart of it all, perhaps, is that getting together for a convention is a basic part of the American character. Jet travel and tax deductions for business purposes only make it easier for Americans to express that character.

"The Americans of all ages, all conditions and all dispositions constantly form associations," Alexis de Tocqueville, the French statesman, wrote after visiting this country in 1831. Today, Charles Gillett says, "Nobody in the world is really like us when it comes to conventions. People in other countries, particularly businessmen, simply do not get together the way we do to share information. They are much more secretive."

Learning what's happening in their business or profession is the No. One reason why most people attend conventions, according to a recent survey conducted by Opinion Research Corporation for the U.S. Chamber of Commerce. But it's not the only reason. Almost as important is the opportunity to meet with colleagues or friends who are in the same business or profession. "Some guys come and go to only a few meetings," says Gillett. "They sit around in their room with a bottle of whiskey and talk, talk, talk. To them, that's as good as anything—maybe better." Some go for the social life (12 percent, according to the ORC study).

"Why, I've been to sales incentive meetings where several dealers who are close socially and close businesswise, spent their entire week sitting at the same table every morning, going on the same things, sitting together for lunch and dinner," says a leading Philadelphia appliance dealer.

Looking for a new job is another reason for attending a convention. At the Modern Language Association annual meeting of 15,000 or more people, says Gillett, "We set up hiring booths where people who want jobs or want to change them can be interviewed. It's part of our deal with the convention manager. We even supply the girls to help with the clerical work involved."

All in all, for whatever reason they go, most people seem to think most conventions worthwhile. For example, 92 percent of those interviewed in the ORC study for the Chamber of Commerce, said attending conventions was worth whatever it cost. More than half of them said they attend three or more a year; 39 percent of the professional men said they attend six or more.

Over the years the character of conventions has changed. Time was when they were very much stag affairs, replete with electric canes and water bag bombs dropped from the top floor of a hotel. No more. What with group air fares, today's convention is more often than not a family affair. Wives accompany over 50 percent of convention-bound husbands to New York, while about 75 percent of the convention goers to Florida bring their wives. A recent survey of 1,326 associations by the American Society of Association Executives shows that 80 percent of their members invite wives to attend conventions and trade shows. "You get the guy's wife wound up about getting away from home and you get the guy to come," says James P. Low, executive vice president of the ASAE.

Today almost all major conventions feature everything from bridge shows to fashion shows. "The department stores just love big conventions," says Candis O. Ray, one of a handful of consultants who have come into being in recent years to help convention managers set up programs for wives. A case in point: At last month's meeting of the National Association of Home Builders, in Houston, Neiman-Marcus put on a fashion show for more than 900 wives of conventioneers at the Shamrock Hilton Hotel. Following the show chartered buses were made available to transport intrigued customers to Neiman's downtown store in Houston.

Recently, there has been a trend on the part of both companies and associations to involve the wives in convention meetings themselves. The theory is that the more they understand their husband's industry and job, the more emotional support they can give them, according to Dr. Joel E. Ross, marketing specialist at Florida Atlantic University.

As a result, it is not unusual to see convention programs featuring a psychologist or a psychiatrist or two discoursing on such subjects as "Are You Helping or Hindering Your Husband?," "The Husband-Wife Team—Working Together," or other specialists discussing "What to Feed an Executive" or "How to Handle a Possible Heart Attack."

The California Trucking Association even trains wives in public relations for the industry. "This year," says Thomas Schumacher, assistant managing director of the CTA, "we're having one program to show wives how to explain trucking activities to local groups like the PTA. They'll really go for it."

Companies make a point of inviting wives to their sales meetings. Since 1965, for example, Jerry P. Solomon, convention manager of Ford Motor Co.'s Philco-Ford Corp., has been running what he calls "the Philco airlift." Each year the company has chartered thirty 707 jets to ferry 5,000 appliance and electronic dealers and their wives to such places as Puerto Rico, Hawaii, Las Vegas and Paradise Island in the Bahamas. "We bring them in—all expenses paid—in six successive waves for five days and four nights," explains Solomon. The average annual cost to Philco: $2.5 million.

The payoff? Solomon says Philco signed up $26 million worth of orders from dealers the first year, 1965; $56 million the following year; some $70 million in 1967 and around $100 million last year.

One of the big features of the Philco dealer convention last year (as every year) was a four-hour musical show introducing the new line. "It was a $300,000 production with 20 scenes, 32 stage hands, 10 in the cast and a 12-piece orchestra, all flown into Paradise Island beforehand," says Solomon.

Spectacular as the Philco show might seem, the fact is the convention business wouldn't be the convention business without show business, whether it's a magician or contortionist hired to demonstrate new building materials or a full-scale musical sent on a nationwide tour at a cost of $1 million or more to herald the latest auto models. Ford Motor gets top songwriters like Jule Styne ("Gypsy," "Funny Girl") and Cy Coleman ("Sweet Charity") to turn out complete scores for its extravaganzas. "We have made a full-cast recording—just like Broadway—and send it out to the dealers beforehand as a come-on," says Bill Winn, vice chairman of Wilding Inc., which regularly puts on the Ford shows.

Along with show biz have come trade shows. In fact, the rise of trade shows and exhibits by industry suppliers at conventions has practically made salesmanship the name of the game at most of the big business or professional meetings.

Since the Fifties the annual number of trade shows and exhibitions held in North America alone has risen 40 percent, totalling 4,500 last year at all levels. Moreover, in the past five years the bigger industrial or trade exhibitor has practically doubled his participation, going into ten convention shows a year, with an annual budget up to

$500,000 and even more. Some, like General Electric, participate in about 400 trade shows a year.

In fact, the business has gotten so big that by last year 200 participating companies had banded together in their own trade group, the National Trade Show Exhibitors Association. They, too, held a convention last August in Philadelphia.

Why a trade association for trade show exhibitors? "One of our reasons for getting together was to find a common ground for dealing with labor problems in setting up exhibits at conventions," says President Raymond R. Remaley, exhibit manager for the American Can Co. "You know, you can't just move your stuff in and set up. In New York, you can't put up your own sign, even if it just says, 'Enter Here.' A union carpenter has to do it. Unpack a case and you use another union where you have to pay a fork-lift truck operator and *his* two helpers under the union contract with the convention hall. At the New York Coliseum we had to have an electronic oven completely rewired to meet New York City electrical code specifications. When we went into another convention, the damn thing wouldn't work."

Inexpensive Marketing

Despite these problems, there's hardly a cheaper way to set up a sale than at a convention trade show. "On the average it costs a company at least $40 to send a salesman out to call on a potential customer," says *Sales Meetings'* Phil Harrison. "The average price of a single sales contract at a trade show can be as low as $7 with all those people circulating around. Also, a salesman can't lug something like farm machinery around to every place he goes. But it will be right on display at a convention."

The *quid pro quo* in all this is the income an association gets from selling convention exhibit space which it has rented from a convention hall or hotel at a much lower price. In fact, a business, professional or trade association can get 10 percent of its operating income from conventions and expositions, according to figures put out by the American Society of Association Executives. That, however, is an average. There are plenty of associations that get almost all of their operating income that way. And it can add up to help pay for the association's operation.

A prime example is the kind of money brought in at the trade show sponsored by the National Association of Home Builders in Houston last month. About 470 exhibitors were featured in the 16-acre Astrohall exhibit center just opposite the Astrodome.

"We rented the space for 35 cents a square foot from the Astro-hall," says director of conventions and meetings Dan Vaughn. "And we charged exhibitors eight dollars a square foot for it. Nine dollars for prime corner locations. I figure, with everything, we made any-where from $750,000 to a million dollars on this part of the conven-tion alone, the best in the association's history."

All this, in turn, has made the availability of good exhibit space one of the greatest bargaining weapons a city or hotel can use to attract a major convention. In fact, some convention men say it is *the* deciding factor when it comes to selecting a site.

"You take a place like Atlantic City that has a municipally owned convention hall," says a rival convention bureau manager. "I know they'll rent that to an association for just a lousy dollar to get all those people into town and into the hotels. And there are other places in the country that also give away exhibit space to get them in. How can an association stay out when it can make all that money selling the free space to exhibitors?"

In hotels, the pattern is the same, with meeting rooms as the bait, according to Frank Berkman of the Hotel Sales Management Associa-tion: "It works on a sliding scale, depending on the number of sleep-ing rooms an association can fill and how badly a hotel wants a particular convention that may lead to other business. Say an associa-tion can fill X sleeping rooms with delegates, we'll give it meeting rooms without charge and it can rent them to companies."

The Rush to Build

Such economics, in turn, go a long way toward explaining the big rush on the part of cities and hotels in the past decade to build convention halls and meeting rooms. For example, according to the International Association of Auditorium Managers, the annual expen-diture for construction of multipurpose civic halls—for everything from concerts to conventions—is now about eight times what it was ten years ago. In 1963 about $125 million went for such municipal caverns. By 1966 it was up to $800 million. And Charles R. Byrnes, executive director of the auditorium manager's group, expects up to $8 billion more to go into such facilities in the next decade. In recent years halls have been going up almost everywhere, from new conven-tion towns like Anaheim, Calif., with Disneyland as a big attraction, and Duluth, Minn. to expanded facilities in old ones like Atlantic City. "You can't get or keep the big conventions," says hotelman Bob Tisch, "unless you've got the hall. I know we've lost out many times because the New York Coliseum is not big enough."

The trouble is, it is not enough just to have a convention hall. "You're dead if you don't have hotel space," says the ASAE's Jim Low. That, for example, is one of the criticisms of a place like Detroit, with its great big, beautiful Cobo Hall, opened in 1960. "Sure, it's one of the nicest around," says one association convention manager. "But where the hell are the hotel rooms? I can't book my convention in Detroit because I have no place for my delegates to stay." What is more, the more convention halls that go up, the more murderous has become the competition among cities for big conventions. Three years ago New York City's Charles Gillett had two salesman working full time on the American Medical Association alone. The AMA had just about decided to skip New York in 1969 after failing to get its traditional June annual meeting date in the city because of exhibition problems at the Coliseum.

"We had to go all the way up to the AMA's House of Delegates, its most powerful body, to get them to switch the meeting date to July," says Gillett. "You don't know what that meant. That meant changing tradition. That meant keeping out Miami, which was making all kinds of offers to give them this and that."

Gillett's most successful ploy was to appeal to the pride of the large and influential Medical Society of the State of New York. "We got them on our side and we had them arguing for us. They helped us counteract all those arguments about not being able to get eminent speakers in July. They really helped us sell it. We expect the young doctors will want to bring their families to New York in the summer after school is out."

Established convention centers in New York and Chicago are facing increasing competition from places like Las Vegas, which has gone all out to sell itself as a convention city. Until the late Fifties, Vegas meant gambling, girls and gangsters; but the high rollers and the high livers weren't enough to keep the hotel rooms filled or the crap tables jammed year round. So, in 1959 the city opened a $10 million convention center on a 67-acre site, one of the most modern in the country. At the same time it set up a convention bureau financed by a tax on hotel rooms, which is why the Las Vegas promoters are now considered among the sharpest and most aggressive in the country. Des Kelly, who ran the Miami convention bureau for 13 years before coming to Las Vegas, is the only bureau manager with convention salesmen permanently stationed in Washington and Chicago which (along with New York) are the main headquarters for most of the national associations in the country.

The result is that Las Vegas now books almost 250 conventions a year worth close to $50 million. It gets everybody from the National Education Association to the National Council of Catholic Women and the National Automobile Dealers Association. "We also get them back," says Kelly. "The American Dental Association will make its second trip here in 1970."

What is more, today almost every major hotel along the city's famous Strip has added convention halls and meeting rooms. And more are being added all the time—for example, Kirk Kerkorian's new 1,500-room International Hotel, now building adjacent to the city's Convention Center (*Forbes,* January 15, 1969).

The more, the merrier, says the Sahara's Sig Front. "The more people who come to this town the better off we all are. We know they aren't going to stay in one hotel all the time, the way they do some place else. This is really the entertainment capital of the world, and a guy and his wife are going to go all over the place before they leave. They'll come in here, too, and watch our show. And they'll gamble in our casino."

One of the most important recent developments in the convention business is the trend to booking meetings further and further in advance. "You have to do it if you want to get into the best hotels in the best cities and you have a lot of delegates," says Al Winstead, manager of national meetings for the American Chemical Society. Winstead knows. Each year, he runs two annual conventions averaging 12,000 delegates each. "I've already got all my cities lined up to 1976. Now I'm working on 1976 through 1980."

Almost all convention men are looking to the jumbo jet to take their delegates to even more exotic places. "You just can't keep going to the same old cycle of cities these days," says Frank Berkman. "You have to keep looking around. The 747s could be a bonanza." For example, Hawaii could become a major contender, as could Europe.

One convention man who is counting on delegates' ennui with the "same old cycle" is John T. McDonnell, a lively Irishman who runs, of all things, the Japan Convention Bureau in New York City. A nation of go-getters, Japan so far is the only overseas country with a convention bureau in the U.S. It opened three years ago, and Japan has been putting up convention facilities like mad at home, including the Kyoto International Conference Hall.

"Sure, I don't try to kid anybody. It costs a hell of a lot to go to Japan," says McDonnell. "But how exotic can you get? We've got the world travel convention, sponsored by the American Society of

Travel Agents, booked for this year. And also the Lions International Convention."

Mexico also is moving up in a big way. Six years ago there were something like 300 annual international conventions held there. Now the country has newly created an international convention bureau, jointly supported by the Mexican government and businessmen and expects 814 international meetings this year. One reason is the big push given hotel building by the Olympics in Mexico City last year.

If the U.S. balance-of-payments situation ever eases, there will almost certainly be an upsurge of conventioneering in foreign lands.

A crazy business? Perhaps, but it plays a big role in our economy and conforms well to the gregarious American character.

8

MASTER PLAN

Robert E. Burns

Planning is the essence of a successful convention. You can have the most money, the best theme, and the greatest idea, but without proper planning, the convention will have little chance for success. Plan it properly and the convention will be a satisfying experience for both you and the delegates.

The successful convention is one that satisfies a need. One company's need may be to bring people together for social, business, or educational reasons—another company wants to provide motivation or public exposure. What kind of convention will be most productive: educational, social, business, or a combination of all three? Establish the need and you have the goal. The attainment of that goal now depends upon the single most important factor—planning.

In order to begin, let's make a few educated guesses. How large the convention will be, what type of audience will attend and how much time and budget is involved need not have definite answers at this point. Educated guesses will do. Many people run into trouble when they believe that a plan has to be final in every detail and not subject to change. We start with a good, basic premise and constantly examine, implement, and re-examine. The original plan is only a starting point.

There are several ways to finance a convention. One is through exhibitors, another through registration, still another through a combination of funding methods. We finance our convention exclusively through registration. Let us say that the cost is twenty thousand dollars. We would build the registration fee upon the anticipated number of people expected to attend. For example, 225 members at $55 each, plus 175 spouses at $45, would give us a working budget

Robert Burns is Secretary of the California Land Title Association.

From *Meetings & Conventions*, December 1969, pp. 72ff. Reprinted by permission.

of $20,250. Before we determine the actual expenses, which is done four to five months prior to convention, let us discuss a decision that needs to be made some two to five years before convention year. That is, site selection. When the site location is decided, part of the expense tabulation is told.

My preference in choosing a site is a property which will accommodate five hundred people under one roof, provide two-hundred and fifty sleeping rooms, dining and meeting facilities for five hundred, and two other separate dining enclosures large enough for two to three hundred people. All this, plus aesthetic value for the audience. This is when the hotel representative can enter the planning picture.

Is it necessary to use a hotel representative? Can he help? I believe the answer to both of these questions is "yes," primarily because the representative's responsibility is a dual one. He not only represents a number of hotels, he represents you. He tends to be more objective than hotel sales personnel and can appreciate both the advantageous and detrimental aspects of a potential site. The representative can gather all of the information required for your decision, obtain commitments on dates and times, and even provide you with floor plans. I use their services extensively, and find they will search out new locations, come up with interesting ideas, and handle negotiations with difficult hotel properties. The first step that I take, in selecting possible convention sites, is to go to various hotel representatives and provide them with my basic requirements. Whether or not the properties will be available for my convention schedule, or on alternate dates, can be established at this time.

When discussing the convention date, include both the pre-convention and post-convention activities. In this way, the possibility of the hotel property limiting itself to booking for the convention period only, will be eliminated. In the past, when the pre-arrival pattern was not established, we had the added responsibility of providing accommodations at locations other than the convention hotel, because they could not accommodate us before the convention. This situation will not occur when proper planning is followed. I establish the pre-arrival pattern by having the hotel convention sites provide me with their record of our past convention. Most hotels will be very helpful. They appreciate the fact that the assembled information, in return, will be furnished to them at some future date.

A hotel is able to give the best service when you approach as early as possible and are totally honest with your needs. In the past we booked our convention two years in advance. Now, it is four to five years ahead and in some areas, on a national basis, bookings are made ten years prior to actual convention date. Providing the hotel representative with last year's attendance, type of functions, activity arrangements, along with the dates and arrival pattern, will enable him to expedite all required activities. You will be told which hotels are able to meet requirements, their policies, and what the "complimentary" accommodations are to be.

It is customary for hotels to provide, in conjunction with a convention, a certain number of complimentary rooms. Since individual policies vary, it is wise to establish what the policy will be at the time of the convention. Selecting the convention site five years in advance sometimes brings a breakdown in communication, so it is essential that both you and the hotel understand each other's obligations.

With the help of the hotel representative, we are in the process of creating a file on five locations for the 1974 convention. I will organize this file and then turn it over to a site selection committee that has been appointed by the President of the Association. The committee members select the site from a pre-qualified site location list. In some cases, where they are not familiar with the locality, arrangements are made to inspect the property before passing judgement. This is done only when necessary, or when the choice is down to one of two hotels. For these visits most hotels are both generous and cooperative, since they hope to be selected as the convention site. We caution our committee to be prudent in taking advantage of their generosity.

All of this planning has been four or five years prior to the convention date. Finally, the convention year arrives. In our particular case, the Association's year runs from convention to convention. At each May assembly a new president is elected and he, in turn, appoints a site selection committee for the convention four or five years from that date. Also, he appoints a general chairman for the convention after his term.

Theme Lends Coordination

Around one year prior to convention date, and after the site location has been decided, a central theme should be developed. You want to lend a spirit, a special identification to the upcoming convention, so the delegates do not superimpose their past experiences on what is yet to happen. A strong, new central theme will have them looking forward to the event. Sometimes the convention site itself will lend the theme idea. Is the geographical location near water? This could suggest a nautical motif. Historical monuments nearby?

Go into the past for your central theme. Keep in mind that the idea should lend itself to dramatization and an eye-catching design for a Convention Logo. The theme can be present in everything from speakers' topics to hotel shop windows. Often, because of cost, a theme is not utilized.

By planning and coordination, the cost can be brought within any company's convention budget. In the art and printing department much of the true need can be accomplished by duplication and variance of size and color. Use the Convention Logo throughout the programs, on tickets, badges, signs, registration kit, and if possible, on letterheads. Inform your program speakers of the theme, as this will enable them to incorporate the subject into their presentation. Instruct all committee chairmen to use the Convention Logo whenever and wherever possible. Making your convention theme come alive, will attract potential delegates and create anticipation.

Approximately nine months before convention date, I accompany the president and general chairman to the chosen site for initial planning and inspection. This enables us to meet the personnel, obtain a visual concept of the facilities, and appraise the suggestions given for the type of convention we are going to have. At this time I give the preliminary function schedule to the hotel. This schedule is a plan through which the days are translated into functions. The hotel will superimpose the location and conditions onto the schedule, thus establishing the basis for final planning. We discuss with the hotel, room reservations, rates, cost of beverages, complimentary sleeping units, public rooms, required facilities for planned functions, photographer, audio-communications, display cases, prizes and awards, and the message center. The meeting is followed up by a written letter stating my understanding of the conversation. Between now and convention date, this letter can become a very useful reference.

The inspection trip also familiarizes the general chairman and the president with the facility. This is of benefit to the president as, emotionally, it is his convention. Any way that you can provide him with security, in the form of familiarity, function schedule, programming, and progress to date, will help relieve the details of planning and enable him to thoroughly enjoy the convention. Present him with enough information, so that he feels confident.

Selecting Committee Heads
Seven months before convention date, the general chairman selects his committee chairmen and informs them of their convention assignments. If you provide the general chairman with a program, general

ARRANGEMENTS COMMITTEE CHAIRMAN

Prior to Convention:

Six Months—Appoint 2 members to work with you on Committee and submit the names to the General Chairman.

General Convention Planning Work Shop.

Become familiar with hotel facilities and appropriate personnel. Arrange for necessary meeting rooms and other facilities and/or services that will be required. Have a firm agreement on costs such as rates, food, drinks, tipping, use of special equipment or special services.

Establish liaison with other committees to coordinate activities, particularly Business Program, General Entertainment, Golf, Hospitality, Ladies Entertainment, Nominating and Reception Committees. Determine their needs in regards to hotel facilities and services along with any special jobs required.

Four Months—Prepare a budget covering expenses to be incurred with the convention hotel, such as costs of meeting rooms, use of equipment or facilities, etc., and submit to the General Chairman.

During Convention:

Keep a running check-off list, as the Convention shapes up, to be sure that all arrangement with hotel necessary to the various committees has been met.

Have someone available prior to each meeting or group activity for check-out on requested hotel equipment or last minute changes in requirements.

CONVENTION VICE-CHAIRMAN

Assist General Chairman in every way possible.

Prior to Convention:

Nine Months—Initial Planning Session and Convention Site Inspection.

Six Months—Make arrangements for first meeting with committee chairmen to discuss duties of each in detail.

Five Months—Initial Business Program Meeting.

Four Months—Final Business Program Meeting.

The chairman of each committee should be requested to submit their portion of the budget to the General Chairman.

Three Months—Submit consolidated budget of costs and Business Program to staff.

Two Weeks—Final pre-Convention Planning Meeting.

BASIC SCHEDULE FOR GENERAL CHAIRMAN

It is the responsibility of the General Chairman to direct the activities of the Convention Committees. He should delegate as much responsiblity and authority as possible and keep in touch constantly with his General Vice Chairman and the chairmen of the various committees.

Prior to Convention:

Nine Months—Initial Planning Session and Convention Site Inspection.

Eight Months—Select Chairmen for the various committees and submit for approval.

Six Months—Make arrangements for first meeting with committee chairmen to discuss duties of each in detail.

Five Months—Initial Business Program Meeting

Four Months—Final Business Program Meeting

The chairman of each committee should be requested to submit their portion of the budget to the General Chairman.

Three Months—Submit consolidated budget of costs and Business Program to staff.

Two Weeks—Final pre-Convention Planning Meeting

GENERAL ENTERTAINMENT COMMITTEE CHAIRMAN

Prior to Convention:

Seven Months—Select 2 individuals to work with you on the committee.

Six Months—General Convention Planning Workshop

Four Months—Submit budget to General Chairman.

With the Arrangements Committee, check out the hotel facilities to plan where each of the programs for which you are responsible may best be held. In each case, have a firm understanding as to costs to be charged for room, food, drinks and extras.

Be sure that date and time of rooms desired for the various activities are reserved.

Responsible for:

Arrange for annual Dinner Dance. Reserve the Ballroom for the desired night. Make arrangements for an orchestra for dancing determining: hours to be played, charges by the orchestra, charges of playing overtime, traveling charges (if any), charges of rehearsal time is necessary with other entertainers. Check the contract for accuracy.

Arrange for Floor Show (if one is included in program). Usually this can be bought in a package, complete with M.C. and three or four acts. Where you can't audition acts of M.C., a phone call to the Entertainment Editor of the local paper will help your decision. A standard contract with a booking agent is normal here.

Sightseeing or side trips: decide on routes to be taken, etc.

Complete all arrangements for entertainment functions on a signed contract basis. Make final check up on entertainment arrangements to make sure that every detail has been covered.

HOSPITALITY COMMITTEE CHAIRMAN

Prior to Convention:

Seven Months—Appoint approximately 5 members to work with you on Committee.

Six Months—General Convention Planning Work Shop.

Coordinate with Arrangements Committee to set time and dates of hospitality hours.

(There are generally three hospitality hours: One prior to dinner of each Convention day.)

Make arrangements to reserve a room for the hours specified, for complete bar service, waiters necessary, etc., snacks or hor d'oeuvres, arrangements for tips.

Have a firm understanding as to cost per drink to be charged and method of counting drinks served (by bottle count or chit).

Before each Hospitality Hour is scheduled, check to make sure all arrangements are complete. Plan to have someone there during each event and to settle the drink account at their completion.

Four Months—Submit budget to General Chairman.

LADIES ENTERTAINMENT COMMITTEE CHAIRMAN

Prior to Convention:

Six Months—Appoint 7 or 8 wives to work with you.

General Convention Planning Work Shop.

Four Months—Submit estimated budget to General Chairman along with your program.

Three Months—Selection of Bingo Prizes.

Suggestions:

Combination Fashion and Cosmetic show, Individual Hair Styling and Luncheon.

Bingo Luncheon (almost a must).

Local Luncheon and Tour.

RECEPTION COMMITTEE CHAIRMAN

Prior to Convention:

Seven Months—Select 3 or 4 individuals to assist you.

Six Months—General Convention Planning Work Shop.

Obtain list of Guests from staff.

a. Meet all guests, show around and introduce at the registration desk.

b. Each morning, list guests that have arrived for introduction at Business Meeting.

c. Make arrangement for one or more of the company's representatives to have lunch with guests.

Four Months—Submit estimated budget, if any, to General Chairman.

BUSINESS PROGRAM
COMMITTEE CHAIRMAN

Six Months—Appoint 9-10 members to work with you.

General Convention Planning Work Shop.

Five Months—Initial Business Program meeting to discuss plans, decide on speakers, arrange a tentative program and assign duties.

Four Months—Prepare a budget covering probable expenses (transportation, accommodations, etc., for speakers) and submit to General Chairman for approval.

Appoint liaison to work with other committees (particularly Arrangements Committee) so Business Program will work in smoothly with the whole Convention.

Contact prospective speakers for availability and notify them of subject matter and time allocated. This must be done as early as possible. At this time, please notify them that a copy of their speech and a photograph will be required.

Three Months—Confirm speakers and firm up program so that it may be included in plenty of time for the printing of the program.

Check overall arrangements at the Convention site for an accurate idea of the physical set-up and any recommendations you may have to be made to Arrangements Committee such as:

a. State location

b. Rostrum—Speakers' Table

c. Microphones—Sound Equipment

d. Lighting—ventilation

e. Decorations

Make arrangements with Hospitality Committee to meet speakers at train or airport and see to their accommodations at hotel.

GOLF COMMITTEE
CHAIRMAN

Prior to Convention:

Seven Months—Appoint three vice-chairmen for Handicapping, Starting, and Prizes Committee.

Six Months—General Convention Planning Work Shop

Make arrangements with Golf Course, setting time and date for exclusive use, caddies and equipment desired.

Five Months—Determine budget for prizes, entertainment, any fees, etc., and submit to General Chairman.

Contact all members announcing the Golf Tournament, giving place, date, starting time, events.

Work with Arrangements Committee to coordinate Golf Tournament with meetings and other activities, being sure to set up time for dinner and awards.

Four Months—Submit Golf Registration copy to be included in pre-Registration packet to staff.

Vice-Chairmen Duties:

Handicapping: Determine method of Handicapping and assignment of one to those without an established handicap.

Set up alphabetical "form chart" for quick reference and in determining winners.

Starting: From list of entrants, assign starting times with attention to those who have declared a preference as to partners.

Determine awards to be made and select prizes. Have prizes in plenty of time to put on display.

Contact Arrangements Committee Chairman for setting up of display case in prominent position making sure case can be adequately locked.

timetable, individual committee budget guides, and a material/ manpower timetable, he will be able to do a very successful job, because he can superimpose his personality and ideas onto the basic plan. After the assignments are received the committee chairmen, general chairman, and myself meet for a convention planning workshop. We discuss what happened last year and relate it to what we should do this year. This effort helps the individual committee chairmen to understand the entire convention picture and enables them to coordinate their efforts. Around the first of the year, we announce to the delegates the date and place of the convention. This alerts them to set aside certain dates five or six months hence so there will be no conflict. Also, at this time, we give them some idea of the general format plan.

Using Workshops

In determining the program, one should always be aware of the human element—the social, fellowship, and educational needs of the delegates. We are now in the process of identifying the major delegate strata by writing to members and asking each to identify his role in his particular company. If we find that the multiplicity of delegate strata is too great for one meeting and one type of speaker to satisfy, we will move toward individual workshops. The workshops would culminate in unified general discussion. It is important that each year audience "needs" be identified.

One of the most critical aspects of a convention is the program itself. Too often we allow a program speaker to select his own subject without considering audience interests. For an interesting program, you have to communicate with the speaker so he can identify with his audience. I schedule the selection of a speaker seven to eight months in advance because high caliber speakers tend to book themselves early. If you are considering industry speakers, rather than those of general interest, your timetable can be shortened.

While on the subject of time I'd like to emphasize that the arrangements committee coordinates all conventions. This group will back up the staff when a job needs to be done, plus provide any time extension necessary. All committee members, with the exception of the business program chairman, should be chosen from those members who live near the convention site area. It is to your benefit to have local people on the scene to cover assignments.

An assignment that is significant is the one given to the Ladies Entertainment Committee. One year we had a limited ladies program, and it almost ruined the convention. For ladies, the convention is a social outing. They are there because their husbands are, and as a consequence, they expect to be entertained. If there is going to be a ball or cocktail party, give plenty of time for female preparation. And make sure that the husbands will be available for the event. Most men, when they get together, tend to lose track of time. Events that are well coordinated and identified in advance will remind delegates and their wives of approaching functions. Contented wives help guarantee a successful convention.

Guaranteed Schedule

There is one other form of guarantee that can save you time and money. This is the guarantee spelled out on the function schedule. Because of guaranteed control planning on all convention functions, we saved ten percent on our over all budget. Preliminary planning of the function schedule begins nine to twelve months prior to the convention. As arrangements finalize, the plan becomes much more definitive and this is where you save money. On the function schedule, for instance, instead of a meeting from "two to five p.m.," there is now a designated meeting, in a specified room, with final numbers for the setting and guarantee, and the type of service or food specified. During a convention the hotel personnel will not itemize tables as they would in a restaurant. They figure out how many dinners are needed, then serve as fast as possible. In order to save their time (which in essence is money) they will accept the figure that you give them. For instance, we did not know how many tickets were sold for our grand ballroom dance. We guaranteed 375 and asked them to set for 425. Later, because of high registration, I increased the guaranteed figure to 410 and asked for a set of 460. It is possible that more than 410 attended, but the billed price was still based on the guaranteed figure. Only in the absence of knowing does the hotel implement their figures. If you furnish educated figures and guaranteed attendence, you will keep financial control over the convention.

Post-Registration Tally

Not until after registration do we really know how many delegates will attend. From the day you make the first reading until the date of the convention, many things change. It's wise to sit down and recap everything in it's final form. I tend to handle all negotiations with the hotel, since I want to be aware of any changes. A letter is sent, just prior to the convention, stating the understanding that I have of final arrangements. In effect, it is the contract under which I intend to operate. If there is a disagreement, it will be settled before the convention, not during or after.

I believe that the planning, attention to detail and exacting work that make up a good convention are well worth the effort. A convention is an ideal time to give a person a new outlook on life. Removed from his regular environment, he is in a position to be receptive to new ideas. If you try to interject these same ideas into his usual environment he will not be as receptive because they are competing with his normal routine. I feel there is tremendous value in giving him this new exposure—and a good convention is the most stimulating way to do it.

9

CUSTOMER DROPOFF:
ONLY GIANTS RIDE OUT COST CRUNCH

Michael Whitman

Listen carefully. You can almost hear the current crunch of extinction as thousands of restaurant men struggle under tremendous economic pressures.

Latest government figures provide fresh evidence that, at midyear, customer traffic was plummeting in the nation's restaurants—and that only large companies wielding impressive market power can stay securely in the growth groove.

For most food men, sales "gains" this year are wholly dependent on menu price increases that have neatly disguised what's really been happening. Things shape up this way:

1. The entire away-from-home food and beverage industry showed a six-month "gain" of just 1.1 percent in sales, dangerously close to the zero point.

2. Chains of 11 units or more, on the other hand, chalked up a stunning 17.9 percent increase over the first six months of 1968.

3. Extract those chains' contribution from gross industry data and you shove the figures downward into the negative column.

4. Even more to the point, subtract from that 1.1 percent overall sales "gain" the component accounted for by menu price hikes, and you find that the industry as a whole is serving far fewer customers—and moving significantly less tonnage—than it did last year. About 4.4 percent less. Valued in 1968 prices, that is about $551 million less merchandise.

5. Meanwhile, big chain gains, even when adjusted for higher menu prices, indicate an increase in tonnage movement of at least 12.5 percent over last year. And that figure would no doubt be

From *Nation's Restaurant News*, September 1, 1969. Reprinted by permission.

higher if it included new multi-unit operators presently entering the market with fresh concepts.

More Hikes Coming

The gap between chains and independents is certain to widen in coming months and would include yet another bout of menu price hikes. That is because there is a three-to-six month lag between a rise in food costs and any menu changes, so there is undoubtedly a drastic upshift in menu prices on the way—stimulated by those painful May-June runups in meat, fish and poultry. But another lifting of menu tabs could spell disaster at most eateries. For if the figures say nothing else, they prove that customers today aren't going along with increased costs of eating out—never mind what operators claim. If it were otherwise, sales would be up more than prices. But prices in reality are up 5.5 percent and sales are up only 1.1 percent. Since food service prices generally ratchet upward while supermarket prices are flexible, there's little likelihood of restaurants reducing prices as meat costs begin to fall.

Which means that customers, cash-short because of governmental measures to curb inflation, are going to be increasingly aware of the cost differential between eating out and eating at home. Supermarket sales are already far ahead of supermarket price increases, indicating at least a short-term flow of customers from restaurants back to their kitchens.

The combination of all these factors leads to the conclusion that the current crunch has triggered an irreversible trend that will alter the structure of food service. After all, chains are still pulling them in, the figures show.

To fully comprehend the dimensions of this shift requires close inspection of a boom-within-stagnation: chain growth in the face of an industry-wide standstill. It's all been said before in one form or another, but it's still worth repeating:

1. You can't make it in today's market unless you possess the ability to finance a strong impact on consumers. That means heavy advertising and promotion—and chains can spread costs over many units, while independents cannot. Chains are convincing customers that eating out is worthwhile, even at higher prices.

2. You must have the ability to finance costly locations to get where the traffic is. And with money tight and expensive you're automatically behind unless you swing corporate borrowing influence.

3. You must be able to effectively utilize the market power of advertising, promotion and package design to suck enough customers into your units to justify costly locations. That means paying for top professional talent.

4. You must be willing to experiment, and you must have the funds to diddle with, because it's what's new that will be luring customers from the competition. To stand pat in an era of innovation is to die.

New Growth Phase

Why is "new" so vital today? Because it appears likely that the initial phase of postwar food service growth—pulling people out of their kitchens is now at an end. The old theory of market segmentation—that you could tap a hamburger market from among people who were still eating home; and then a roast beef market among people who stayed home because burgers weren't attractive; and then a fried chicken market among eat-homers who were tempted by neither burgers nor roast beef; and then a pizza market among stay-at-home folk who didn't think much of any of the above—that theory is dead.

New restaurants coming on-stream today are pulling their customers primarily from other restaurants, not from the kitchen. It's doubtful, for example, that all those new fish 'n chips restaurants are *expanding* the eat-out market so much as they're *reducing* the customer flow at more traditional eateries. This is not just a fast food franchising phenomenon, either.

Each new food service concept that mushrooms into a string of eateries—oriental restaurants, Mexican foods, units tied to TV personalities, who-knows-what-next?—will affect the industry in two ways:

1. It will accelerate the draw of people away from conventional feeders: and,

2. It will provide a pool of customers who pretty soon will trade up to a new class of big-tab service restaurants that take their cues from fast food operators—short on menu and long on concept and promotion.

The crucial factor here is that the customer base is now firmly established. It can be enlarged in the short run, to be sure, by massive increases in disposable income (something not about to occur), and in the long run by normal population growth. But most people now in the market are experienced eat-outers, and as such they're typical consumers searching for the new.

The emerging battle for these existing customers in food service is not likely to differ significantly from the struggle for space in a supermarket's detergent display, or in its dry cereal department.

The market for detergent is pretty well defined, and the only way to keep your share-of-market is to continue bringing new products to market, replacing those older products whose sales have started to lag. That's the way things are developing in food service. The big chains recognize that a restaurant, no less than a box of Sudzy Wudzy, is a product with a measurable life cycle and that it is patronized by increasingly fickle customers.

Hence, astute feeders are continually filling the pipelines with "new products"—new eateries that will capture customers looking for "something else." You can see it happening at International Industries, probably the first company to fully comprehend the perishability of a restaurant. What began as International House of Pancakes now includes Wil Wright's ice cream parlors, Copper Penny family coffee shops, Orange Julius snack stands, and House of Pies.

On a smaller scale, Jerry's Restaurants in Lexington, Ky., began as a coffee shop chain and has now expanded first into hot meat sandwiches (Lott's) and into fish 'n chips (Long John Silver).

You could string all the above-named restaurants along a highway and they probably wouldn't hurt each other one bit, because they'd still be able to pull customers from off-the-road mom-and-pops units that are rapidly being killed off. . . .

But once the balance of power has finally shifted to the chains, as it is now happening, the struggle for share-of-market should be something fierce to behold.

10

MANAGEMENT MAKES THE DIFFERENCE

from *Hotel & Motel Management*

The Arizona Biltmore is part of a 1,164-acre complex in Phoenix known as Arizona Biltmore Estates, Inc. The Estates includes the hotel, two dozen privately-owned homes around the golf course, La Colina Solana—formerly a winter home of the Phillip K. Wrigley family—and the 30-acre Biltmore Fashion Park shopping center.

The Arizona Biltmore is one of the best known U.S. resorts because of its unusual architecture, spacious grounds, continental cuisine and gracious service. There are 243 guest rooms in the hotel section, including 15 de luxe cottages, and most rooms provide a view of nearby Camelback and Squaw Peak mountains.

The hotel's distinctive architecture (Frank Lloyd Wright was consultant) was planned as a style which would not become outmoded. The mass of ramparts represents the first large-scale U.S. use of convex-faced concrete block. No major additions have been built to threaten the hotel's architectural integrity.

Last September 27 [1968] the Arizona Biltmore opened its doors for its 40th consecutive season. This season, ending May 20, will be the longest in the hotel's history.

The season's increased length is only one reflection of the success of a sales-oriented management team which took over operation of the Biltmore in the late summer of 1966.

Indicators of Success

The Biltmore's season once lasted only three or four months. By 1964-65 there were 185 operating days, last year there were 228 days and this season 239 operating days.

Total guest count (vacation and convention guests) has risen from 5,236 in 1964-65 to 10,142 in 1967-68, and will exceed that figure

---

Reprinted with the permission of *Hotel & Motel Management,* Clissold Publishing Co.

this year. There has been a 71 percent increase in vacation guests, and vacation guests returning year after year are increasing—705 coming back for the 1965-66 season, 944 last year.

Simultaneously, first-time vacation guests increased 68 percent last year. And the Biltmore's February occupancy this year was near capacity as compared with a 56 percent occupancy last year.

Business produced by travel agents has doubled in the past three years. Group business, too, has far exceeded goals set by management. The number of convention guests went from 3,568 in 1964-65 to 7,133 in 1967-68. In 1965-66 the hotel booked 12,000 convention room nights; this year it will show an increase of more than 75 percent with 22,000 convention room nights booked already.

During the past 40 years, the property has been maintained impeccably and the changes which have taken place in the past three years have been primarily operational rather than physical. These changes reflect the shifting pattern in traditional resort business and travel.

Three years ago, principal stockholder Philip K. Wrigley determined that a new way of operating was called for and business that in the past had not been important must be sought out. His first step was the selection of Lawrence J. Boyle as president of Arizona Biltmore Estates in June 1966 to supervise the complex and to build an organization which could hold its own in the resort field.

People are Important

As Boyle puts it, "The Arizona Biltmore is one of the best-known American Plan resorts in the country, of just the right size to do a quality job of guest service. We wanted to make it contemporary in its marketing policies and its approach to business." Wrigley gave Boyle overall responsibility, asked him to create and to be the "motivator" of an experienced team which could carry out the objective.

In August 1966, John F. Clifford was named GM of the Arizona Biltmore. The rest of the marketing-oriented management team developed that fall included John Sienold as general SM, O. Karl Giesen as controller, and Henry Warren as food and beverage director.

Their mix of background encompassed Boyle's city hotel, resort, chain and property management experience; Clifford's city hotel and resort experience; Sienold's city hotel and convention sales work; Giesen's hotel chain and advertising background, and Warren's international experience. Though varied, these backgrounds have meshed to produce an effective marketing, sales and service force which has nearly doubled the sales volume of the Biltmore in less than three years.

The Plant

The Arizona Biltmore occupies 67 acres, includes trails, citrus groves and landscaped areas. There are 130 rooms in the main building, 30 in a garden wing, 70 in 15 de luxe "casitas" and 13 in La Colina Solana. Guests have their choice of European or American Plan; most choose the latter. The AP double rate range is $54-$60, except for the February/March social season when it is $66-$72. EP is $12 less a person.

The hotel is like most major resorts in its wide variety of recreational activities. Golf is offered on its own adjacent 18-hole championship course. The greens fee is $6 for guests, and support facilities include a practice range, golf shop and putting green. The Biltmore has 45 Cushman "Golfster" carts available at $9 a round.

The Arizona Biltmore Equestrian Center has 80 stalls, provides guest riding ($3 an hour) as well as horse boarding facilities for Phoenix horsemen. There are 26 miles of desert and mountain trails for riding on the property. The center also gives the hotel such merchandisable, built-in attractions as rodeos and horse shows.

Four tennis courts can be illuminated for night playing. A lawn bowls court has been installed.

A heated pool and 50 cabanas around it ($12 a day) are supplemented with a massage parlor, steam bath and exercise equipment.

Meeting Facilities

A theatre-auditorium seats up to 400, and there are six additional rooms which accommodate from 15 to 200 persons.

Space, while it appears to be limited, has two flexible characteristics. First, the balmy Phoenix weather makes outdoor functions practical. Poolside space, patios and terraces are almost always usable. In addition, the acreage has room for picnic and cook-out areas.

Interior space also has been made convertible. For example, a remodeled cocktail lounge is equipped with moveable walls; the Gold Room (main dining room) also is used for food functions for up to 500-plus persons; daily teas are held in a nook of the spacious lobby.

In addition, La Colina Solana gives the Biltmore management a top facility for small, special groups. Four large bedrooms, dining room, breakfast room, living room and library are suitable for top-echelon seminars. The east wing of the house has 10 smaller bedrooms and preparation and service kitchens. Food functions and receptions for up to 60 persons may be held here.

Last summer the Biltmore carried out several improvement projects—made possible because of added income from new business and made necessary because of the needs of business to be developed.

A new cocktail lounge provides additional seating and a more inviting atmosphere. A portion can be converted, with folding walls, into a room seating 150 for meetings. A sunken bar area and a new dance floor were included.

The lobby was refurnished and recarpeted as was the Gold Room. Guest rooms, too, have had refurbishing and installation of TV.

A new front entrance provides easier access at 24th Street, the bordering thoroughfare, which itself has been widened and extended.

In summer 1967 a parking area for 139 cars was created near the hotel's main building, and, several years ago, all buildings were air-conditioned.

The Program

Under Clifford's direction, the new management group analyzed departmental operations and staff needs and began to develop programs. Consensus was that the resort's fine reputation and steady business did not indicate the full possible potential.

A management program was initiated, with authority precisely distributed among team members. Improved communication on all levels—with ownership on objectives and policy, with guests by management, as well as with department heads and employees—was instituted.

Employees were offered stability so that a well-trained, knowledgeable staff could be maintained.

"We try to give our staff a sense of security," says Clifford. Weekly meetings for department heads help create *esprit,* and every group booked is reviewed at a briefing for all staff members involved.

Local Sales Development

The Arizona Biltmore is unlike many classic resorts in two important aspects. First, it is immediately accessible to the city of Phoenix and its airport. Secondly, it has successfully attracted group business.

Traditional resorts were built to attract visitors, not local residents. A major policy of the new management was to turn the Biltmore's business around and to make Phoenix an important part of the activity.

When the Biltmore first opened in 1929, it was eight miles from the nearest boundary of Phoenix. Today it is within the city limits and, in effect, surrounded by the city's 500,000-plus residents.

A conscious attempt was begun to get closer to the local market, rather than remain separate and detached. Community leaders in business and social circles, as well as the local press, were invited to meet the new management executives.

A more direct line of communication was established with the local community. Local advertising and public relations programs were effected, and management took an active part in community affairs. Clifford, for example, serves on the tourism committee of the mayor's task force, as a past president of the Phoenix Valley Inn-keepers, is secretary of the Arizona Hotel & Motel Association and a director of the Valley of the Sun convention bureau.

A credit privilege mailing was made to 16,000 Phoenix residents. There was an enthusiastic response of 38 percent, and 2,100 conversions to actual city ledger accounts.

The Biltmore's public rooms are advertised in local papers, offering dining, lounge entertainment and dancing.

Weddings, balls, dinners and other prestigious social events have been attracted to the Biltmore, as have local blue-chip business groups.

Another facility of Arizona Biltmore Estates which brings the city and the hotel more closely together is the Biltmore Fashion Park shopping center located at a corner of the property, about a mile from the hotel. It has 25 "name" retail and service outlets, such as Elizabeth Arden, Saks Fifth Avenue and I. Magnin, and a full-line department store. The hotel provides complimentary transport for guests to the well-landscaped center.

The National Effort

On the national level, the Biltmore's advertising and promotion budget was increased 120 percent and an over-all marketing and advertising program was developed by Gardner, Stein and Frank, Inc., Chicago.

The sales representation firm, Robert F. Warner, Inc., was retained to represent the hotel in key areas and to research specific markets.

With the help of these firms, the Biltmore team precisely defined each market and developed programs to reach each one.

Contact with major airlines led to the establishment of cooperative promotion ventures. In addition, travel agent mailings, agent familiarization tours and packages of interest to agents were created.

The Warner offices in New York, Washington, D.C., and Chicago, and Leonard Hicks, Inc., offices in Los Angeles and San Francisco, sell the hotel. Careful recordkeeping indicates which types of sales

Figure 1. Data extracted from Comparative Guest Survey. Record is kept for seven years to show trends. Helping to arrest length-of-stay decline has been 5 percent discount on rooms offered on stays longer than two months.

ARIZONA BILTMORE—GUEST MIX

	Individuals	Groups
Ratio to Total Demand	35%	65%

	February/ March	Other
Average EP Rate Per Occupied Room	$47.71	$28.50

ARIZONA BILTMORE—COMPARATIVE GUEST SURVEY (Excluding groups)

	1967-68	1966-67	1965-66	1964-65
Number of Guests	3,009	2,517	1,898	1,758
Average Stay	6	5	9	9
Number of Guests— length of stay more than 3 days	1,833	1,649	1,316	1,143
Number of Guests— length of stay 10 days or more	699	--	--	--
New Guests— first time arrivals	2,065	1,661	1,193	1,047
Past Guest Return	944	856	705	711
Percentage to Total— first time arrivals	68.6	66.0	62.8	59.6
* * *				
Convention Guests	7,133	6,860	5,071	3,568
Regular Guests	3,009	2,517	1,898	1,758
Total Registrations	10,142	9,377	6,969	5,326
Total Operating Days	228	216	194	185

Figure 2. Portion of Biltmore's Guest Survey showing source of individual guest business. Careful records kept for seven years indicate shifts in generators of demand, permit more effective advertising.

ARIZONA BILTMORE—GUEST SURVEY
1967-1968 SEASON

	NO. OF GUESTS	%
CALIFORNIA		
Los Angeles & Terr.	260	8.6
San Francisco	57	1.9
Other California	283	9.4
	600	19.9
SOUTHWEST		
Arizona	72	2.4
Nevada	6	.2
New Mexico	5	.2
Utah	23	.7
	106	3.5
PACIFIC NORTHWEST		
Idaho	2	.1
Oregon	26	.8
Washington	11	.4
	39	1.3
WEST NORTH CENTRAL		
Denver	97	3.2
Other Colorado	36	1.2
Kansas	22	.7
Montana	9	.0
Nebraska	19	.7
North Dakota	0	.0
South Dakota	0	.0
Wyoming	0	.0
	174	5.8
SOUTH CENTRAL		
Arkansas	9	.3
Louisiana	5	.2
Oklahoma	18	.6
Dallas	32	1.0
Other Texas	56	1.9
	120	4.0
EAST NORTH CENTRAL		
Chicago	335	11.1
Other Illinois	107	3.5
Indiana	21	.7
Iowa	4	.2
Kentucky	3	.1

Detroit	21	.7
Other Michigan	29	1.0
Minnesota	30	1.0
Missouri	41	1.4
Cleveland	14	.5
Other Ohio	48	1.5
Wisconsin	35	1.2
	688	22.9
SOUTHEAST		
Florida	13	.4
Alabama	15	.4
Georgia	5	.2
Mississippi	4	.2
North Carolina	8	.3
South Carolina	0	.0
Tennessee	7	.2
Virginia	11	.4
West Virginia	0	.0
	63	2.1
MIDDLE ATLANTIC		
Delaware	6	.2
District of Columbia	54	1.8
Maryland	28	.9
New Jersey	100	3.3
New York City	356	11.8
Other New York	291	9.7
Pittsburgh	11	.4
Philadelphia	28	1.0
Other Pennsylvania	68	2.2
	942	31.1
NEW ENGLAND		
Connecticut	76	2.5
Maine	6	.2
Massachusetts	69	2.2
New Hampshire	4	.2
Rhode Island	8	.3
Vermont	4	.1
	167	5.5
HAWAII	5	.2
ALASKA	2	.1
CANADA	46	1.5
OTHER FOREIGN	57	1.9
TOTAL	3,009	100.0

effort are producing and which cities are most lucrative for the hotel.

Travel-agent business, on the increase, now accounts for about 15 percent of total room nights. Here, again, careful records are kept indicating the most productive agents and cities and even the number of cancellations and no-shows.

A direct mail program was refined, using automatic equipment, producing letters to inform past guests of the hotel's progress, to invite the local community to use personalized credit services and to establish a continuous mail effort reaching past guests and prospects.

Control of Markets

One of the Biltmore's two primary markets is individual business —older, affluent persons on vacations. This is mixed with some family business during the Thanksgiving, Christmas and Easter periods. During the peak of the social or "high" season (this year, February 1 through March 15—43 days), no group business is accepted.

The other major demand consists of groups. Obviously, the size of the group which can be accommodated is limited. Goals were set by establishing allocations of rooms available on each day of the season for vacation guests and for groups.

The Individual Market

One of Clifford's basic tools is a sell-and-report chart used by the Warner and Hicks organizations with "open," "crowded" and "sold out" dates clearly marked for weeks ahead and updated regularly.

Another sales tool is an elaborate guest history card system. Each card has detailed preferences—even friendships and habits—of many regulars.

"This kind of sales control lets us begin personal service before the guest arrives," says Clifford. The records enable management to make personal contact with the regular guest at about the time he should be making his reservations.

Or, when the guest calls to inquire about reservations, Clifford's secretary is able to put into his hands almost immediately a "dossier" on the guest's likes and dislikes.

A day-by-day flow sheet with specific house counts of rooms and guests permits effective scheduling of payroll and supplies and is used by housekeeping as well as food and beverage departments.

Arrival sheets for the day ahead are detailed with special requests, orders for complimentary flowers, etc.

At the beginning of the Biltmore season, personal letters are sent to all past guests inviting them to return. And thank-you letters are sent out upon departure of long-stay guests with an invitation to come back the next season.

"We also make ourselves a visible part of the operation," says Clifford. During the social season, Clifford hosts a weekly cocktail reception. Teas, cotillions, parties, fashion shows, tours and champagne hours are regular activities with management invariably on the scene.

The result of all these efforts has been a 92 percent increase in gross sales with 35 percent of total demand derived from the vacation guest.

Special Promotions Help Fill Gaps

Thanksgiving, Christmas and Easter periods also are carefully controlled and merchandised in preselected, accessible markets.

The Thanksgiving package, for example, draws family business from Denver, San Francisco, San Diego and Los Angeles and has grown in the last two years. Five days, four nights, with four breakfasts and three dinners and complimentary riding, is $89 a person, double occupancy.

The Christmas package calls for a minimum 10-day stay, with a daily double rate running $52 to $58, AP. The Biltmore's Christmas guest list survey for 1967 shows that top generating areas for the hotel were New York, Chicago, Los Angeles, Canada, Pennsylvania, Denver and Maryland.

"Christmas promotion has had a good history," says Clifford, "but cancellations are a problem." In a recent season 400 reservations were sold, but only 180 were taken.

"Christmas-season vacationers finally pick the warmest spot they can find," Clifford says. He has countered the cancellation problem with a deposit policy asking for $150 for each room reserved, and this has been successful in reducing cancellations to 20 percent. (During the rest of the year, low deposit is required since guest arrivals are more dependable).

The Easter holiday, whose date changes, also attracts family business. However, school holidays, which also change, must be determined if families from particular cities or states are to be sold.

This year the Easter package (April 1-6) offered six days, five nights, for $119 a person, double occupancy, with special rates for children. Breakfast on five days, riding at any time and four special dinners—western cook-out, Hawaiian luau, Charleston party and champagne dinner dance—as well as ping-pong and other tournaments for the children, were included.

Figure 3. *Arizona Biltmore's Flow Chart shows convention group rooms booked, identifies low periods, permits the acceptance or rescheduling of groups to attain full potential occupancy.*

ARIZONA BILTMORE HOTEL—CONVENTION ROOM SALES
(as of 2/10/69)

	Sept	Oct	Nov	Dec	Jan	Feb	Mar	Apr	May
1		50	70	150		66		30	170
2		30	50	185	65	35			170
3		6		200	75				40
4		55		200	100				
5		37	45	162	200				200
6		85	165	200	200			Easter	200
7		155	210	60	200			150	200
8		165	210	60	200		Social	150	215
9		173	152	200	135			150	50
10		155	203	200	135			215	50
11		180	203	200	135			105	100
12		180	215	50	165			205	230
13		220	160	10	165			215	230
14		220	220	18	165			215	230
15		220	220	18	70		70	215	20
16		60	220	18	70		66	210	220
17		150	220	18	70		70	180	220
18		175	30		20		10	190	220
19		200	170		60	Social Business Only	25	20	220
20		180	185		60		130	40	
21		180	185		20		130	210	
22		180	15		120		125	210	
23		227	15	Christmas	120		125	210	
24		190			135		132	200	
25		220			135		95	35	Closed
26		118			135		100	35	
27	25	200			135		97	160	
28	55	200	Thksgng		135		145	160	
29	50	200			140		190	155	
30	50	200			96		190	130	
31		180			190		190		
Total	180	4,791	3,163	1,949	3,651	101	1,890	3,795	2,985

Room Nights Total { 1968/69   22,505   1967/68   17,245   1966/67   15,165

Figure 4. Travel agent survey shows who generated business, with careful recording of package guests. In combination with a geographical breakdown, the summary will show exactly how much business is being derived from each source. Last year some 4,800 guest nights were generated by travel agents, golf packages, air line promotions, etc.

ARIZONA BILTMORE—TRAVEL AGENT SURVEY

	NAME	ROOM NIGHTS	GUEST NIGHTS	ROOM VALUE	COMMISSION	WARNER	HICKS	GOLF	AIRLINES
California									
Los Angeles									
Meadows Travel	Mr.&Mrs. B. J. Barnes	2	8	$88	$8.80		$1.10		
Bryan Travel	Mr.&Mrs. L. Sharman	10	20	610	61.00				
Wilson Travel	Mr.&Mrs. S. Kahn	4	8	120	18.40		4.60	x	
		4	28	315	31.00				

The shorter holiday is promoted successfully in southern California and Texas cities as well as in the Denver area.

Biltmore golf packages have been merchandised by the property and, recently, have become part of American Airlines' Astrojet Holiday plan, widely advertised in northern cities. The plan offers a choice of the Arizona Biltmore or any of four other Phoenix-area resorts. American reports they will sell about 500 this year—150 percent more than last.

The golf package gives guests seven days, six nights, EP, with greens fees included, at $126 a person, double (except $176 February/March). This year it should gross more than $50,000 for the Biltmore.

A running count is kept of golf package as well as holiday package guests as a guide for determining the effectiveness of advertising efforts. Ad coupon respondents are even checked against eventual registration lists so that ad effectiveness can be precisely measured.

Another variation from classical resort philosophy has been the Arizona Biltmore's successful solicitation and scheduling of group business. A primary cause of the longer seasons is the hotel's increasing popularity as a relaxing meeting site for business and professional groups.

In 1965-66, 49 groups came to the Biltmore; last year there were 75 groups, most staying three to four days. Convention groups are all AP and, by definition, are those requiring 10 or more rooms. Currently they account for 65 percent of the hotel's total demand.

Close control, from the placement of sales emphasis to the recording of guest stays is, here again, the keynote of the Biltmore's management team.

Says John Sienold, who knows both, "Resorts are a different product, more complex than the city hotel. Careful coordination of social and meeting facilities is required."

Sienold says that in city hotels the emphasis is on room sales; in resorts, it's the over-all sale which counts. In addition to the room, food, entertainment, golf, swimming, tennis, etc., are all potential added-income sources.

And groups, generally, spend more per capita than do individual guests—especially on an American Plan basis, despite a lower average room rate.

The selectivity of group sales is stressed. Obviously, the size of the group which can be accommodated is one factor.

"We also prefer mixed groups," says Sienold. "We want groups which will use our facilities." These tend to be prestigious groups—

insurance organizations, professional associations, manufacturing institutes, etc., whose members will bring wives along, use the resort's facilities and make all areas productive.

"Resort guests are a 'captive audience' and have to be catered to accordingly," Sienold says. "Most city hotels find that their rooms are used for sleeping while the guest spends the rest of the day and evening away from the hotel. In resorts, guests are drawn to the total environment and reputation which must be enhanced at all times.

"When it comes to double occupancy, resorts generally have the advantage over city hotels. Single reservations are the exception, and become a problem only with group bookings. These are carefully screened at the Biltmore, and preference naturally is given to an account which can fill 200 rooms with 400 guests rather than with 200 guests," Sienold says.

Scheduling is important as the sales department probes for Sunday-Wednesday and Wednesday-Saturday group stays. This sales approach is based on knowing the number of rooms available in order to develop a steady flow of business. Painstaking control is kept of rooms available in the form of a "flow chart" which is updated regularly to show group rooms booked.

Jack Clifford believes, "The flow chart is one of the most important tools we use. It shows room bookings for months and years ahead. It's the simplest but most sensitive barometer by which the entire operation is guided. When carefully maintained, it forecasts trouble spots well in advance and in time to correct the situation."

Resorts, more than city hotels, must be assured of a steady room demand since the possibility of short-stay group bookings, unexpected walk-ins or referrals from neighboring properties cannot be relied upon for fill-ins. "Therefore, the client booking a group must be made aware of his responsibility to fill his commitment to the same extent as he expects the hotel to fulfill its promises," says John Sienold.

A master of telephone selling, Sienold uses the phone for personal touch and quick action. He begins calling prospects in the East, two hours ahead of Phoenix time, "working his way" westward, following the time changes across the country to Chicago, to Denver, to Los Angeles, as the day goes on. Sienold has two phones—one a private line, free of incoming calls, specifically for phone solicitation.

A crucial fact gleaned in these phone conversations is the date on which the group's meeting site selection is to be made so that a timely follow-up can be established. Each call is followed with an information kit and letter tailored to the group's needs, size, dates

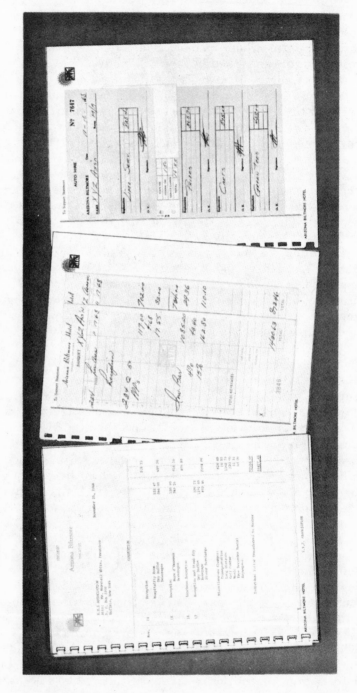

Figure 5. Plastic bound, 8½" x 11" folder itemizes charges, contains copies of group's bills. Format ties in with prestige image of hotel, leads to prompt payment.

and interests. If nothing else, the eventual follow-up call at the right time permits Sienold to free the dates for sale to another group.

Information gained in these phone calls also is fed into the automatic equipment for continuous direct mail effort. It's coded as to status (past client, prospect), size of group, geographical location, number of rooms required, dates, etc. Letters are produced automatically with proper information based on this code.

A geographical file also is arranged to provide ready reference on prospects in any city, or even any portion of a major city.

Personal Contact

The new management team established a travel budget for field trips to supplement other efforts and to bring the personal touch into group sales. During the summer, for example, Sienold makes a six-week sales trip through northern cities. He calls on companies, associations and airlines in serving cities, carrying files organized for efficient use of time. Other sales trips are scheduled at times that will not deprive conventions-in-residence of his personal attention.

A newsletter is mailed several times a year to convention prospects with timely information about meeting equipment, new ideas for meeting planners and subtle Biltmore sales messages.

"There are lessons to be learned by city hotels from resort selling," says Sienold. "The resort SM is geared to the entire complex. And the resort concept of 'carrying the group'—creating an event for a group's free night to keep them in the property, for example—is applicable to selling other types of hotels."

Once a group has contracted to meet in the Arizona Biltmore, its over-all program is established, including meeting schedule, social and recreational activities, early arrivals and overstays. This enables the sales department to book additional small groups without inconveniencing any and helps to maximize occupancy.

The Biltmore's convention coordinator takes care of day-to-day details during the group's stay, but the entire management team is in direct contact with the group at all times. "Repeat business from convention accounts is a necessity and takes constant servicing and anticipation of needs, 24 hours a day," says Sienold.

Such personal interest has often resulted in the re-booking of the account for the future, often before it has departed.

Food and Beverages

Henry Warren supervises and arranges food and beverage functions ranging from French silver service in the main dining room to western cook-outs.

"We had three goals," says Warren, "—to increase local functions and fill gaps such as Saturdays, to build up conventions and cater to them, and to provide superb food and service to all—conventions, social guests and locals."

"To sell local functions, we zeroed in on the top 20 prospects, knowing we were able to accommodate up to 500 persons in one room," says Warren. "We invited the organizations' chairmen for dinner, stressed our fine service."

For group functions, Warren developed new ideas—Western hoe-downs, luaus at poolside, Mexican fiestas, Chinese and Oriental buffets—all with menu specialties, music, costumed servers and appropriate decorations. "We know we must be creative to get repeaters," Warren says. "We even produced a wine tasting for a group which increased our dining room sales of wines."

Local residents also were promoted for the Biltmore's food and beverage rooms. "Our per person dinner check averages $10.32, and our no-cover, no-minimum dancing hours in the lounge also bring local support," says Warren.

Food service becomes more efficient with guests on American Plan service. "The more guests on AP, the better for planning," says Warren. "We can budget our staff and our buying. Good food and service keep guests on AP, which 68 to 72 percent now select. Our target is 75 percent."

AP is $12 additional per day per person, with children under 12, $8 a day. For guests on EP, meal prices are Breakfast $3, Luncheon $3.50 and Dinner $8.50, or a total of $15.

However, AP service means that quality must be maintained. "You can't say 'No' to an AP guest," says Executive Chef Franz Nikodemus. Guests enjoy asking for and getting special items such as Nova Scotia salmon, caviar, special veal chops, or some other personal culinary delight, for which they are willing to pay a surcharge. "They're hypercritical of food and service," he says, "but it's our job to please them."

Breakfast business runs heavily to room service—with 35 to 40 percent of breakfast orders in that style. Luncheon is served regularly at poolside, and dinners are rather formal, with most guests preferring black-tie attire on Wednesday and Saturday evenings.

Controlling It All

Controller Karl Giesen brought a basic philosophy to the team which implies that new systems which improve the operation must not only increase efficiency and conserve profits but also must enhance sales and take all phases of good public relations into consideration.

The Arizona Biltmore's increased volume of business made it necessary to re-evaluate methods of operation and uses of equipment. Giesen prepared the documentation which led to capital improvements. In the past three years, some $700,000 has been spent on new equipment and contruction. Included was the recreated cocktail lounge at a cost of $80,000, parking spaces, TV, meeting room equipment, riding stalls, etc.

As the new management team set its goals, it was Giesen's job to prepare forecasts and put into effect the changes necessary to handle the increased business. Working three to five years in advance, the management group forecast rate structures as well as costs in order to set goals and maintain profits.

Short-term investments are used to create profit dollars which help the cash flow of the operation. Thus any temporary excess of funds is put to work. Giesen has arbitrarily set as his goal the earning of a certain portion of his department's cost through investment. The interest income naturally flows to the greater profit of the total operation.

Giesen has been described as "sales-minded," is aware of the importance of guest contact. For example, the billing format devised for groups takes the form of a handsome bound folder of itemized charges. It leads to prompt payment in full of these large amounts, reducing any confusion. "It's our last contact with the group," says Giesen, "and we're still selling. As a result, customers have even thanked us for the bill."

Other techniques installed in Giesen's department include the use of electronic data processing for payroll and the microfilming of data to eliminate storage problems.

All equipment, from mowers to office machinery, was evaluated. As a result of Giesen's equipment study, the 45 golf carts, which had previously been rented, were purchased. They'll pay out in a year and a half, turning a rental expense into a profit figure.

Income also comes from a profitable sundry shop operated by the hotel, geared to guest demand with many regional products; the stables; apparel and gift shop rentals; bicycle and cart rentals; and some citrus "ranching."

The Biltmore's large payroll requires careful scheduling, with 305 regular workers (200 are housed). Also included in the operation are valet, print and furniture repair and upholstery shops. Landscaping service is contracted.

Careful control records are kept on each new service. Following the creation of the lounge, for example, data indicating the dollar volume between certain hours were recorded to measure the pay-out of the new facility.

The Future?

"Extension of the season to a year 'round base is a long-range target," says Clifford. Currently the four-month summer off-season provides an opportunity for sales calls as well as major maintenance. Except for the golf course, the hotel's facilities are closed during the summer. Clifford and a 50- to 60-person office and maintenance staff remain at the hotel, while other members leave to work in northern summer resorts, returning in the fall.

"Our problem in staying open year 'round is the lack of Phoenix-area promotion," says Larry Boyle. "We know we must compete with other cities. The Arizona Biltmore's own $200,000 promotion effort exceeds the tourism allocation for the entire state of Arizona."

The future of the Estates may see more commercial development. A 23-acre parcel recently was sold to American Express Co. for a regional credit card computer center with a $10,000,000 payroll and 2,000 new jobs.

Residential development of the country-club type is also a possibility, as is a second golf course.

In the meantime, every member of the Biltmore team will be endeavoring to maximize volume and profits through progressive marketing, sales and service techniques.

11

HOW WORD-OF-MOUTH ADVERTISING WORKS

Ernest Dichter

Each year members of our organization talk to over 10,000 consumers in various parts of the world. "What made you buy this brand or particular product?" is one question which usually is part of our motivational study. No matter how our depth interviews approach the question, the answer invariably reveals that there he is again—the mysterious friend, expert, or relative who "told me about it." At times, the figures show this influence of "recommenders" to run as high as 80 percent. Why in a time of increasing advertising volume does Word-of-Mouth recommendation loom so high?

Apparently, there are several ways of influencing people that coexist with, or go beyond, radio, TV, magazines, and newspapers as media for recommending goods and services. These unconventional forms of "advertising," or influence, include *Consumer Reports* and similar publications; refrigerator, freezer, and pantry shelves ("Every time I look at my shelves, I am sold or unsold on products which I bought"); seals of approval; and, most important of all, the advice of a friend.

We decided, therefore, in order to develop a better understanding of the mechanism involved in these informal channels of communication, to initiate a research study of our own .... Then, as we proceeded, listening to consumers recalling their experiences, a number of key research questions emerged. The most significant of these included:

—What are the reasons for the growing importance of Word-of-Mouth recommendation? In what psychological needs is it rooted?
—What motivates people to talk about their experiences?

—What motivates them to listen to recommendations? To act or not to act on them?

—How does Word-of-Mouth recommendation affect advertising, and how does advertising affect Word-of-Mouth?

—How does this whole process influence the purchasing behavior of the contemporary American consumer?

Answers to these questions have now enabled us to develop recommendations as to how the processes involved in Word-of-Mouth can be successfully adapted and used by advertising and public relations practitioners.

Effective Advertising

We all have the desire to re-create the situation where the shoemaker, the tailor, or the grocer gave information and friendly advice based on personal knowledge of the consumer, his or her family, and their needs and means. Such intimate relationships created a feeling of trust and security and reduced the confusions of cold "commercialism."

When the consumer believes that an advertisement is more of a sales tool than information and guidance, he feels threatened. He rejects the advertising claim. He turns for a solution of his buying problem to Word-of-Mouth. When the consumer feels that the advertiser speaks to him as a friend or as an unbiased authority, creating the atmosphere of Word-of-Mouth, the consumer will relax and tend to accept the recommendation.

There are two kinds of Word-of-Mouth: pre-decision and post-decision. They do not have the same object, and they probably do not take place in the same way. The most effective Word-of-Mouth for the advertiser is the post-decision speaker who is bent on eliminating all dissonance in his post-decision situation. He is the man to sell to because he will be an active propagandist. For this same reason, advertising should perhaps be oriented much more toward present than potential customers and use them to spread the good word.

Effective advertising and effective Word-of-Mouth are *not* worlds apart. On the contrary, it is the sense of our findings that *the most effective advertising is that which follows the same psychological channels of communication and satisfies the same motivations on which the whole importance and success of Word-of-Mouth rest.*

This article is organized into two parts. Part I—the psychological findings about Word-of-Mouth—deals with the discovery and charting of the channels of communication. Then, in Part II, the findings obtained are applied to the practical problems of advertising.*

Part I. Psychological Findings

I shall first focus attention on the two specific problems of the psychology of Word-of-Mouth recommendation:

1. What motivates a person to *talk* about a product or service?
2. What motivates a person to *listen* to a recommendation and to act on it?

Speaker Motivation

The power and the significance of everyday Word-of-Mouth lie mainly in the *speaker's* lack of *material* interest. This does not imply, however, that he has no investment in the process of recommendation. Our investigation confirms that—generally—nobody will speak about products or services unless the talking itself, or the expected action of the *listener*, promises *satisfaction* of some kind—popularly speaking, unless he "gets something out of it."

We found further that the speaker is likely to choose such products, such listeners, and such "words" as are most apt to serve his underlying needs and ends (of which he is only rarely or partially aware).

---

*This article is based on research findings of the Institute for Motivational Research, Inc.

Depth interviews were conducted with 255 consumers in 24 localities in the United States, with emphasis on the New York metropolitan area. Respondents were encouraged to recall freely (and in full detail) conversations in which products, services, and advertising had been discussed, including recommendations made as well as received.

Conditions and circumstances under which recommendations were accepted or rejected were carefully probed. Altogether, 352 individual instances of what we call "active Word-of-Mouth" recommendations and 488 instances of recommendations received and acted on (purchases) were reported. (There were some instances of negative Word-of-Mouth, which are beyond the scope of this article.)

Verbal tests regarding the most "talked about" advertising were conducted with 103 adult persons in the New York metropolitan area—to get some indications about the nature and structure of sales messages which, in themselves, invited Word-of-Mouth.

Also included is research material developed by the Ziff-Davis Publishing Company, under the direction of its marketing vice president, Stanley R. Greenfield, which the company has kindly put at our disposal.

Involvement Categories

Motivations to talk about products or services were found to fall into four main categories, frequently overlapping or combined. I shall identify these categories briefly, and then discuss each in turn:

1. *Product-involvement.* Experience with the product (or service) produces a tension which is not eased by the use of the product alone, but must be channeled by way of talk, recommendation, and enthusiasm to restore the balance (provide relief).

2. *Self-involvement.* In other cases the accent is more on the self of the person than on the product, with the latter serving as a means through which the speaker can gratify certain emotional needs. As we shall see, there exists potentially a whole host of them, but they can all be subsumed under the overall category of "self-confirmation."

3. *Other-involvement.* Here the product chiefly fills the need to "give" something to the other person, to "share" one's pleasure with him or her, or to express care, love, or friendship. In these instances the recommendation takes the place of a "gift," just as a thoughtful gift often expresses a tacit "recommendation." ("Because I have had pleasure in this, I want you, too, to have it and here it is.")

4. *Message-involvement.* This refers to talk which is mainly stimulated by the way the product is presented through advertisements, commercials, or public relations, but is not necessarily based on the speaker's experience with the product proper.

Naturally, products and services will vary, according to their potential role in the consumer's life, in their capacity for producing excitement, expressing care or love, and so on. And, certainly, the kind and degree of emotional involvement aroused by a car and a detergent, a dish and a dress, or a cigarette lighter and a perfume will differ a great deal. (This study presents the average reactions in a number of incidents covering a wide variety of products. It could be refined by future investigations aimed at product categories.)

Product-Involvement

Of the 352 talking episodes reported by our respondents, 33 percent belong in this category.

Distinctly pleasurable (but also certain unpleasurable) experiences have a tendency to call for mental repetition in the form of speech whenever a fitting occasion offers itself. This category includes incidents of strongly felt, gratifying experiences with a product or a service which make the speaker "flow over." Talk in this case may also serve to relive the pleasure the speaker had obtained, such as on a boat trip to Europe, or from a dish served in a restaurant, the pickup and power of a car, and so forth; it also helps to dispose of the excitement aroused by the use of the product, or by the fact of having obtained it. In many instances it is talk about the product which confirms for the speaker his ownership and joy in the product, or his discovery of it. For example:

"She asked if I'd ever used Guardsman. She said, 'You ought to get some—it's terrific!' Well, I said I'd try it, and I did. I mentioned to this friend later that I had used it, and she seemed pleased that I had bought it and anxious to know if I'd liked it. I told her it seemed to be pretty good, but she was hardly satisfied with that comment, and began to rave about it all over again. I don't rave much as a rule anyway. She seemed convinced she'd done me a huge favor by recommending it, and if I wouldn't get all excited after using it, she had to get excited for me. You'd think there was something in it for me."

The question, "What's in it for me?" is brought up by another respondent, a New York housewife. But one can easily see from her response that her "reward" is in the "verbal consumption" of those precious cookies:

"You'd think there was something in it for me the way I talk it up for Sandies. I think they're the best cookies ever, and that's why I like to have other people try them. That's the way I got to know about them. I was spending a weekend with an old girl friend of mine at her house on Long Island. She served these cookies in a dish, and they tasted so delicious and had such a real home-made flavor and look that I congratulated her on making such wonderful cookies. I really thought they were homemade. They don't look all even and perfectly rounded like the usual package cookies. And besides there was something about their taste that I can't describe but that usually seems to go with homemade cakes and cookies. I was amazed when she told me what they were. I had never heard of them."

Self-Involvement
The depth interviews revealed, in 24 percent of all talking instances, that self-confirmation plays the major part in motivating talk.

Here the experience with the product is immediately put to use in the service of self-confirmation of the speaker and of his need to reassure himself in front of others. The product is employed in many, often clever, ways as a vehicle to carry him safely, even victoriously, through his self-doubts and insecurity. Most of us use such techniques occasionally and involuntarily, without being aware of it.

The most frequent goals of self-confirmation through talk about products and services are:

Gaining attention. The products and services which, in their totality, represent what could be called the "machinery of living" take the place of topics centered around people or ideas. (Introducing a product into a conversation can be a way of "having something to say.")

Showing connoisseurship. Talking about certain products can serve as proof of being "in the know," or having refined judgment, and so on.

Feeling like a pioneer. Newness and "difference" of products provide the speaker with an opportunity to identify with them and their makers.

Having inside information. Some products or services permit the speaker to feel clever—that is, to know "more" about them and their production than the listener is expected to know.

Suggesting status. Talking about products with "social status" provides an "elevator" for the talker by which he can reach the level of the product and its users.

Spreading the gospel. "Converting" the listener to using a product can provide the speaker with occasion to enlist the listener in a "good cause"—that is, to "preach the gospel."

Seeking confirmation of own judgment. The more people there are who follow the speaker's advice, the more justified will he feel in his own judgment; he needs followers to feel reassured about his own decisions.

Asserting superiority. Recommendation of products can be used as a tool for assuming leadership and exercising power over the listener, and may even serve as a sort of test to determine whether the listener really respects the speaker ("Will he or won't he heed my advice?").

Here is but one example from many reported in which self-involvement is channeled through product recommendation:

"I recommended it to my sister-in-law Ruby and to Rosie Gibson, my friend up on the hill, and I don't know how many more. And I feel rather good that something I recommended was so well liked because it makes me feel that my judgment is good, and I know that people respect my judgment. Yes, there's been many a time when one friend or another would ask me how I felt about a certain thing, and I'd tell them. Many times that was all they needed and went along on my advice. I'd say that if you establish a feeling of confidence about yourself, and there's a feeling of dependability about you, people sort of take your word because they know that you have had some experience with the thing they are talking about, and that you will tell all you know about it and if you don't, you won't."

Usually, the follower is reassured by the power and strength of his leader. However, in Word-of-Mouth we often found the reverse to be true: followers are sought by the leader (speaker) so that he feels less lonely and more secure in his own product choice. Knowing that others will conform to his choice makes him feel good. Consider:

"I want to feel there are others. . . . I use this as a test. . . . If he comments favorably, he's your kind of guy. . . . You know you share not only the product but your approach to the world."

The "bandwagon effect" is reversed in cases in which consumers are proud to use what they consider an "underdog" product. They feel gratified in defying the majority by publicly using an unpopular brand; but the real self-confirmation lies in converting others to their own "peculiar" choice:

"People think I'm an odd duck for smoking Raleighs. Although Raleigh is one of the popular brands, in the sense that one sees them everywhere, they're hardly popular from the standpoint of the number of people who smoke them that I see. It's as if buying them makes you stand out like a jerk or poverty-struck, a guy who can only afford to smoke Raleighs if additional merchandise is added. So I say, 'Look at me!' by recommending them. . . . Also smoking an unpopular brand makes me feel I'm bucking the headwind. I'm handicapping myself in advance, saying to people, 'You're going to like me in spite of my peculiarities, maybe even because of them.' If I can get them to smoke Raleighs, that really clinches it. Maybe that's why I recommend them."

The degree to which the need for self-confirmation motivates Word-of-Mouth recommendation is reflected in the speaker's reaction to a rejection of his advice. In cases of nonacceptance, the self-involved speaker feels hurt, rejected, or abandoned as a person:

"I think when people reject a suggestion violently, they are aware that in a sense they are rejecting the person. And, on the other side of the coin, I do feel rejected when somebody won't take a suggestion I've made. I feel real bad when they refuse out of hand to consider the idea. I'm likely to sing its praises even louder—and that's not really because I think I've not been convincing, but because either my ideas are worthwhile and acceptable, or in some small sense I'm not."

Rejection is particularly resented when another person's advice has prevailed:

"Well, I don't mind telling you I felt pretty angry about it, but I didn't say much. I felt like I had been kicked in the face. Here I tell her about something I think tastes good; then someone else tells her it's no good, and she takes this other person's opinion just like that—just as if I didn't know the difference between a good taste and a bad taste. It's really not anything to get excited about, but sometimes things like that get under a person's skin."

Frequently, the hurt and resentment about nonacceptance turn into hostility against the unwilling follower. In a rapid process of depreciation, the erstwhile friend or neighbor, or relative, is now accused of "double-crossing" the speaker; he is called stubborn, set in his ways, lazy, foolish; and the aggrieved speaker's sentiments range from false pity to malice:

"Now he is having mechanical difficulties with it [the car purchased against the speaker's recommendation]. He made his bed, and now he has to lie in it. He has to live with his decision. That's all there is to it."

Generally, the self-involved speaker feels that the listener has a moral duty not only to try the recommended product, but also to share his—the speaker's—feelings about it, to report back to him, to be grateful, and thus to confirm the speaker's judgment. It is one of the characteristics of the next category that these symptoms of intolerance on the part of the speaker are missing.

Other-Involvement
This motivation appeared to prevail in 20 percent of all talking events.
Here the prevailing attitude is the need and intent to help, to share with the other person enthusiasm in, and benefits of, things enjoyed. Products serve mainly as instruments which help to express sentiments of neighborliness, care, friendship, and love.
This case example was chosen to illustrate the way in which an "other-involved" person accepts and respects the reasons for the rejection of her recommendation, however strongly she may feel about the product as such:

"I was telling my mother about Ivory Liquid and how much I liked it. She said she would try it, but just couldn't because she has an allergy condition with her hands and finds it impossible to use any kind of detergent. I felt that it was so good I wanted her to know about it—especially for her dishes. I was at my mother's house and just happened to mention it in the course of conversation ... about the sample and how I had tried it and all that. I was pretty enthusiastic about it, and wanted to share that enthusiasm with her—especially because it was my mother. I did try hard to convince her—even advised her to use rubber gloves in order that she could use it and see how wonderful it was—but Mother said she can't do a thing with gloves on, and we dropped the whole subject. Well, there just wasn't anything I could do about it. Knowing the condition of her hands and knowing that it is important, I didn't renew my efforts for her to try the detergent any more."

Message-Involvement

That the current "age of advertising consciousness" leads to a particularly strong position of Word-of-Mouth has been previously mentioned. However, this very orientation of sophisticated skepticism toward modern sales messages is accompanied by three other consumer attitudes which, strangely enough, give Word-of-Mouth a good chance to operate by using them as the topics of talk and thus, in many instances, making them "sell" in an indirect way. The three phenomena that ushered in the age of advertising consciousness— similarity of claims, conspicuousness of the advertising profession, and intrusion of advertising into most aspects of living—have also produced several widespread audience attitudes:

"The Show Is the Thing." Since it is difficult for consumers to avoid exposure to advertising, many people have turned to accepting it for its independent attraction and entertainment value and originality of ads have become topics of talk.

Shop Talk. Knowing that hundreds of highly paid brains are competing for their favor, readers and listeners have become judges and experts of advertising effectiveness. They assume the critical attitude of an advertising manager and tell each other about "clever" ads.

Verbal Play. Whether or not the product is desired or the content of the sales message is of interest, readers and listeners like to quote playfully and apply verbally ad lines and slogans. Even where the original mood is one of mockery or irony at the ad, the advertiser, or the product, it is usually superseded by the pleasure gained in the act of the perhaps often-repeated and varied application. A certain gratefulness is the price one pays for the opportunity offered by the ad to "play" with it.

Listener Motivation

Whereas in the preceding discussion I explored the motivations of the speaker (the one who recommends), in this section I shall explore the motivations of the listener in those instances in which he or she *acted* as a result of the recommendation—that is, purchased the product in question.

What—on the basis of our investigation—are the factors that decide whether a recommendation is to be rejected, or accepted and acted on? The answer is that to make a recommendation "carry," the three points of the triangle—speaker, listener, and product—have to "fit" each other in certain ways. (To some degree the quality of the message also is involved.) We found to be of particular importance the *speaker-listener* relationship, as seen by the listener, and the *speaker-product* relationship, again as the listener perceives it.

Naturally, we do not intend to minimize the importance of the listener's "need" for the product. The degree of need-urgency, the propinquity of points of sale, and all other factors which make up the "logistics" of the situation contribute considerably to every buying decision. However, we have accepted the fact that need is not necessarily a "given" entity; it can within certain limits be produced or stimulated. Where this is not the case, it has to be added to those variables which cannot be controlled anyway and therefore do not belong within the scope of this study.

Key Conditions

In analyzing the 488 instances of purchases ensuing from Word-of-Mouth, we found that in weighing the value and validity of a recommendation, the listener is primarily concerned about two conditions: (a) that the person who recommends is interested in him and his well-being, and (b) that the speaker's experience with and knowledge about the product are convincing. More or less consciously, the listener asks himself a number of tacit questions:

"Is it the speaker's intention to sell me the product for any material reasons, or to help me with his true experience? What is his relation to me? May I fully trust him as a friend? What is the speaker's relation to the product? How authentic is it? How much does he know about the product, apart from his experience with it? Does he know more about it than I do?"

"Influential" Groups

The factors that make a recommendation "click" are not always clear-cut and definite. In many instances several determinants combine in bringing about the decision. But it was our goal to trace through careful probing the main motivational emphasis in each case to the most decisive single condition. Therefore, it became important to define as closely as possible the main sources of potentially successful recommendations and the respective psychological forces behind their effectiveness.

Analysis of our sample yielded seven divisions among the recommending groups:

1. *Commercial Authorities.* Under this heading are listed those persons who, on the basis of their training and/or work, appear to be

closer to the product and more knowing about it than the average consumer.

Recommending groups within this commercial authority division include *professional experts* and *sales persons*. To the former group belong, for example, mechanics (in the case of car recommendations), pharmacists, beauticians, and so on. Recommendation by experts was responsible for the buying decision in 3 percent of the cases. On the other hand, advice from sales personnel was instrumental in 6½ percent of all the buying events we analyzed. (I shall later discuss incidents of salesmen's influence in which factors other than the mere "authority" of the salesmen were involved.)

2. *Celebrities.* Included are movie, theater, TV, and radio personalities whose "authority" is attributed to prominence in show business, also persons prominent in any other fields not directly connected with the product. Although these speakers are in the strict sense part of advertising, we include them here because they have actually entered our living rooms and represent industry's closest approach to a synthetic Word-of-Mouth production. In 7½ percent of our incidents, a celebrity's recommendation was directly responsible for the purchase.

3. *Connoisseurs.* Into this group fall those cases in which the listener was chiefly influenced by the speaker's close and authentic, but nonprofessional, contact with the product. The connoisseur may know as much or more about the product and its background than the expert, but he does not make his living in connection with it; he merely enjoys it and his know-how about it. But he is still a consumer, and as such is perceived by the listener as someone like himself but with more special product knowledge. This kind of product relation provided the main motivating force in 10 percent of the purchasing events.

Such a group of connoisseurs are, for example, the readers of *Car & Driver* magazine. Research on members of this group demonstrated conclusively that they do play a major role in influencing the automotive brand decision making of millions of Americans. One study indicated that 50 percent of *Car & Driver's* subscribers were asked for their opinions or advice on cars more than 50 times in one year, and another 20 percent reported that they were asked at least 12 to 18 times a year. In other words, since the magazine has over 300,000 subscribers, this 70 percent gave advice or opinions to literally millions in the consumer audience. Or to put it in another way, several million decisions on automobile purchases were to one degree or another influenced by this group of opinion leaders.

It is also of extreme importance to note that opinion leaders rap as well as boost. In fact, the tabulation of brands mentioned as having been discussed in the last interaction reported in the study showed that there were 80 percent as many raps by brand as there were boosts by brand.

4. *Sharers of Interests.* The influence of speakers in this group rests on the fact (or impression) that they have something special in common with the listener, be it a definite life situation (they are both young mothers, or they are junior executives living under similar circumstances) or a similarity of interest or taste. This sort of influence prevailed in 18 percent of all buying decisions.

5. *Intimates.* What is meant here is the influence of mother, father, big brother or sister, husband, wife, boyfriend or girlfriend which expresses itself not necessarily by means of verbal communication, but by the speaker's action. Thus, for example, keeping in the house a certain brand of soap, cigarette, toothpaste, and so on, may replace verbal advice or recommendation. Life in a family, marriage, or in any close relationship includes to some degree the taking-over of prevailing patterns of product-use and buying, "empathic" adaptation to the leader's habits and taste. The kind of "authority" which operates in these cases is, of course, one based on personal closeness and not, as in the commercial group, on relation to the product. (The effect on the listener may, in accordance with the emotional trend of the relationship, not always be acceptance of, but sometimes rebellion against the speaker's choice of product or brand). Our depth interviews revealed that 14 percent of the buying instances analyzed fall into this category.

6. *People of Goodwill.* In these instances, the listener sees the speaker as a person who is genuinely interested in his well-being. The speaker is trusted as a genuine friend, or as a friendly neighbor, and shows the sincerity of his intention and interest in the listener frequently through his knowledge and understanding of the listener's special and individual needs. Such feeling on the part of the listener was responsible for 24½ percent of the buying decisions.

7. *Bearers of Tangible Evidence.* Where the speaker has at his disposal perceivable proof of a product's efficacy, this fact may override all other factors of personal and product relations and easily tip the scales. Demonstrable effects ("before" and "after") of cosmetics and home remedies, observable or somehow memorable performances of household machines, cars, and gadgets, belong in this group. Combinations of this motivation with categories of personal relationship are frequent. However, we have tried to isolate in this

group only those instances where tangible evidence prevailed (16½ percent of the purchase decisions).

Role of "Intention"

An analysis of the foregoing frequencies reveals the predominant position of "intention" in the listener's motivational system. The "hierarchy" of factors which were instrumental in bringing about the buying decisions is:

People of goodwill	24½%	"Disinterested"	
Intimates	14	friendliness	38½%
Sharers of interests	18	Community of	
Connoisseurs	10	consumership	28%
Salesmen	6½	Commercial	
Celebrities	7½	authority	17%
Professional experts	3		
Bearers of tangible evidence	16½		
	100%		

As the tabulation shows, closer knowledge of the psychological forces at play leads to the reduction of the seven influential groups into three main categories of motivating factors. (The "bearers of tangible evidence" may belong to any of the three categories.) Let us examine them:

"Disinterested" friendliness. The first two groups, i.e., "people of goodwill" and "intimates," were formed into a unit because their main motivating power rests on the listener's feeling that the speaker (or, in the case of "silent" Word-of-Mouth, the "model") is motivated to contribute to the listener's well-being or, at least, that his intention is divorced from material interests.

Community of consumership. The next two groups which were combined are "sharers of interests" and "connoisseurs," since in both of these the common interest in the product is the bond that united the speaker and the listener.

Commercial authority. The Word-of-Mouth influences by sales personnel, professional experts, and celebrities were combined because in these instances a certain "authority" is assigned to the speaker on the basis of his *position,* without his necessarily having the backing of a strong inner conviction about the product or a personal relationship to the listener.

"Aha" Experience

Our research at the Institute has shown that only a dialogue—that is, a two-way communication—is truly effective. This applies to formal communication in mass media, but even more to the informal influence of Word-of-Mouth interaction.

Many advertising copy tests are based on the erroneous assumption that the recipient of a message "gets the word" passively. Thus Ad A, if it makes a deeper groove in his brain, is assumed to be more effective than Ad B.

In reality we are dealing with what we call a motivated reaction. It is a dialogue between the sender and the receiver of a message. Three different people, a hunter, a forester, and an artist, going into the same forest see three different forests. Their interests differ, and a varied communication dialogue takes place.

The same thing applies to commercial communication. When the reader or viewer can say, "Yes, that's true," or nod in agreement, we talk about an "aha" experience. But it is this "aha" experience which mass media often fail to produce.

Appraisal of advertising effectiveness often does not match what actually happens between a commercial message and a consumer. Criteria such as attention, recognition, and recall were not the key factors which differentiated successful commercial campaigns from unsuccessful campaigns.

The reason for this is that most advertising effectiveness testing, as it has been practiced up to now, seems to have proceeded on the premise that commercial messages represent a stimulus; the consumer is exposed to this stimulus, and something registers in his mind. This registration has been researched in terms of the attention aroused, the recognition created, and the recall brought about. At first glance, these approaches sound reasonable.

However, our practical experience and modern psychological understanding challenge the whole basis on which these research approaches have been built; they violate everything we know about how perceptive processes really take place.

The "recommender" is often much more capable of establishing this "aha" experience, this dialogue of conviction. In doing so, four factors help him a great deal:

"Expressive Movements." Psychologists have established the fact that "truth" in terms of a person's inner experience is expressed by the conveyance of emotions in the form of "expressive movements" which can be perceived by the other person. Indeed, it is considered

one of the functions of emotions to inform the other person about the speaker's inner experience. Thus the real meaning of a product and of its effect to the user is revealed not only through the choice of the speaker's words, but also through the discharge of emotions in inflection, face and body expressions, and gestures.

A Philadelphia housewife, for example, expresses her desire to be swayed by the speaker's enthusiasm for the recommended product:

> "I'm not really an explorer; I'm a creature of habit. I don't try new things. Someone has to try them and rant and rave, ooh and ah . . . and then I'll try them."

Understanding of Needs. That the speaker is genuinely concerned with the listener's well-being or has his advantage at heart becomes eminently believable in cases in which the recommendation is geared to, and takes into account, the individual needs or special circumstances of the listener. This serves, as it were, as a "passport" for the message to the listener's heart. Consider this listener's response:

> "Well, I have very fine hair and not everyone knows how to set that type of hair. If done wrong, it's a great waste of money and time for everyone concerned —the beauty operator and the one getting her hair done. But, you see, in the first place, the person who recommended the beauty shop knew about my soft hair and didn't send me to just anyone. She was thoughtful enough to know just what I wanted in a beauty operator. Oh, she was a new neighbor—a very lovely person."

Tangible Evidence. In our tabulation we have treated "tangible evidence" as a separate group. However, it frequently serves to strengthen the impact of an ad or of a recommendation in cases in which personal intention are not sufficiently convincing in themselves.

In instances of home appliances, food, or garden equipment, the results are often at the listener's disposal right in the speaker's home, yard, or garden. In the case which follows, the combined strength of an attractive product name, advertising, and the "commercial" authority of a salesgirl did not suffice to motivate the purchase; it was the "tangible" proof of the speaker's beautiful skin that clinched the sale:

> "I think an ad that stands out in my mind was a product put out by Revlon called Moondrops. It is a skin lotion, and I saw the ad on TV and in the magazines and newspapers. The ad stressed it was good for the skin and made one look younger. The name also attracted me—it sounded so cool and pretty. Some girl who worked in a cosmetic department in a department store here also

told me about it. I was not very friendly with the girl, but she had such beautiful skin. It may not have anything to do with the lotion, but after seeing the lotion so nicely advertised and then the recommendation from her and her lovely skin—well, I just thought I would invest in it."

Secrecy or Hesitation. Expressed in the form of a paradox, the best proof of the speaker's disinterestedness is his reluctance to divulge the source or brand name of a product which is wanted by a "listener." This refers to the well-known psychological phenomenon that the harder it is to get a desired object, the more desirable it becomes.

In Summary

In talking to other people about products and services, "speakers" expect and/or receive certain gratifications; they will not recommend things "for nothing." However, in typical Word-of-Mouth incidents, these rewards are always purely psychological, and never material. This very assumption—that no material interest is involved in the recommendation—is the most basic motivation for the "listener" in accepting and acting on the recommendation. He desires to learn the "truth" about the product and expects to obtain it most safely under two conditions: (a) that the one who recommends is interested in him and his well-being, and (b) that this recommender's experience with and knowledge about the product are convincing.

If we transfer these conditions to the relationship between advertiser and reader and consider the former the "speaker" and the latter the "listener," it becomes obvious that the advertiser faces a fundamental difficulty in filling this psychological role. Is it not the avowed purpose of advertising to sell and to make money? And is not the product to him a means to this end rather than an object of personal experience and interest? And yet the ad-conscious attitude of modern audiences compels the advertiser to attack the problem of closing this gap and to try to absolve himself of his "original sin."

Part II. The Applications

In the preceding section it was reported how, in the light of our investigation, everyday Word-of-Mouth processes come about in the area of product and service recommendations. However, in order to utilize some of the selling power of Word-of-Mouth in advertising, it will be necessary to apply our findings to the practical realities of advertising. Specifically, the two main problems are:

1. How to *simulate* Word-of-Mouth.
2. How to *stimulate* Word-of-Mouth.

Simulation Requirements

If we see in the advertiser the recommending "speaker," he has to be as effective as possible in making his "listener" accept his word and act on it. No commercial ad can help having the ultimate intention of selling for monetary profit. On the other hand, the foremost source of selling power in Word-of-Mouth lies in the belief that this very intention is missing. In order to escape this contradiction, the advertiser has to attempt to approximate, at least, the position of the disinterested and noncommercial speaker, and to absolve himself to some degree of his original sin.

According to the study findings, there are two approaches which can lead the advertiser closer to the position of the reader's friend and fellow consumer: (1) proving his "intention," (2) improving his authentic relationship to the product. Practical applications of these findings open up a number of ways to which other-than-profit motives can be expressed.

Proof of "Friendship"

Most consumers have a strong secret desire to be "loved" by their suppliers for their own sake. Thus every time an advertiser "speaks," he has to *separate himself,* as it were, from the commercial camp and become an intermediary between the producer and the consumer— but one who can be believed to be a "friend" of the consumer. He must give proof through understanding, attitude, and action that he is one of them, or at least that he has their well-being at heart. This may, according to the size and scope of operations, extend to community, country, or even to mankind.

There are a number of methods by which you, as the advertiser, can prove your intention and ally yourself with your readers (listeners):

Anticipate Consumer's Attitude. Meet the consumer's ad-consciousness by showing that you are ad-conscious yourself! Once you anticipate the increasingly ad-conscious attitude of your audiences, your ads will avoid a sense of grim urgency and gain a more pleasurable attitude toward themselves and their audience. Invite readers and listeners to join you in the fun of advertising, even to some extent at your expense!

By taking the audience into your confidence and placing it on your own level, you will prove your friendship for it and absolve yourself, within limits, of the original sin.

"Gift Package" Sales Message. Go beyond the selling purpose of your ad by giving it some independent value which the reader-listener can enjoy. In expressing your sales message by means of something genuinely beautiful, exciting, entertaining, insightful, or humorous, you reveal your care for your listener, who is free to benefit from your thoughtful efforts—whether he follows your recommendation or not.

Understating the actual sales message may in such ads even enhance the selling effect. For example: "We must be doing something right"—the Rheingold ad.

Establish Audience Kinship. Match yourself and your product's appeals with the customer you are aiming at. Prove to him that you and he understand each other, that you have something in common with him, and that in some way you and he are kindred souls. (This, remember, is the feeling which in everyday Word-of-Mouth makes a listener so much more susceptible to a speaker's message.)Refer to some of his most probable group or individual characteristics, leanings, tastes, and needs; make him feel that the man behind the ad is his kind of person.

Make the style of your ad your password to your consumer. The choice of medium and style of artwork and copy is in itself an important step in the establishment of a community of taste and interest between advertiser and audience. The style reassures the consumer: "See, you and I have a similar taste, style of life, and so on; this is why I feel that this product which I am recommending is just right for *you.*"

Initiate "Exclusive" Group. Join your prospective customers, through your ad, in an act of initiation: suggest that the product is not meant for everybody, and only those who belong to the circle of the initiated (which includes the advertiser) may know about and take advantage of it. Again, some proof should be in the ad that the advertiser understands the prospective members of the "exclusive" group and shares with them that of which they are proud.

Be a Friend of Man. There is nothing new about institutional advertising and the use of public relations for the creation of good-will in the interest of large companies. Ford Motor Company, Humble Oil & Refining Company, Container Corporation of America, and many others, have—through their foundations, donations, general research, and rewards—demonstrated that they are interested in the community at large. But one does not have to represent a giant corporation in order to prove that the company has nonprofit interests and is a friend of man. The yearly pleasure trip on which a Florida businessman takes his 47 employees every Christmas may make a more personal and moving impression than the millions spent by those whom everbody knows have millions to spend. Small but thoughtful and original acts of friendship may do a lot to prove a company's intention.

Convey Personal Experience. We have seen that the Word-of-Mouth recommendation draws a great deal of its power from the fact that the speaker is in a position to convey his personal experience with the product, and to express it in the authentic language of his experience or enthusiasm. The advertiser, however, has not always really "experienced" his product, and often does not know enough of its effects on others to talk about it in an authentic, spontaneous way.

Ads that express and reveal genuine interest in and love for the advertised product, and understanding of its role in the consumer's life, will go far in proving the advertiser's intention above and beyond his monetary motivation.

Relation to Product

The second role to be played by the advertiser is his authentic relation to the product. The following suggestions can serve as guideposts toward the application of this principle:

Become a Consumer. From our findings, we remember that the greatest chance for the salesman to sell is in leaving his role as a salesman and momentarily slipping into the role of a consumer who has had (or witnessed) a genuine experience with the product in question. Accordingly, give yourself a chance to "live with your own product" as a consumer. Thus you can step out of the (suspect) role of advertiser and tell your audience of your real experience.

Personalize the Producer. Demonstrate an immediate relationship between producer and product which should show some of the love and care the old craftsman used to feel for the things he made. If this is not feasible, personalize the people who are closer to the product: the brewmaster, the engine designer, and the like.

Trace "Company Myth." Find out about the circumstances under which the company was organized, and how its product or products were created or adopted. In many cases someone will be found who was once creatively involved in, or "obsessed" with, the product. On other occasions, interesting material about the product may come to light. Such material can help the advertiser to show his or the company's product involvement, and thus help to "absolve" him.

Instances of this sort which have proved effective in advertising and public relations are: the cooperative founding of Nationwide Insurance by 26 farmers who needed inexpensive insurance for themselves; Sell's Liver Paté, which owes its existence to a gourmet-turned-producer; Mrs. Pepperidge's bread which, we are told, she first baked herself for her sick son, and later for the many thousands of "sons" and "daughters" who became her customers; and Mrs. Gerber, as the developer of baby food for her children.

Describe Organization Climate. Find an aspect of the product or its production which calls for special care or is unique or exciting. Fit this into the company climate and describe it as one of general care, appreciation, respect, and love for the product.

Reflect an Adventure. Whenever possible avoid the polished anonymity of the conventional copywriter and turn your ad into a personal statement about some kind of adventure with the product. Try to embed the product into your private life—that is, let your friends and family make contact with it, and turn your ad into a "documentary."

Consumer Testimonials

In cases in which the advertiser's own voice is not convincing enough, he may call in a third person as an intermediary between him and the listener (testimonial). What happens in testimonials comes particularly close to the Word-of-Mouth process; here a "user" or alleged user of the product is called on by the advertiser to convey to the nonuser or prospective user his experience with, or opinion about, the product. Consequently, everything that applies to everyday Word-of-Mouth can be applied to testimonials, and gains particular significance in this advertising technique. The principle of "fittingness" among the three factors—speaker, listener, product—prevails.

The success of the message, therefore, will rest to a large degree on the reader's (listener's) belief that the auxiliary consumer (speaker) is talking to him spontaneously and disinterestedly, that he has *not* been called in as a "hired hand," and that he has no monetary interest whatsoever in the matter. Being a paid agent is the endorser's "original sin." But the reader's belief in the endorser's message will also depend on the believability of the latter's relationship to the product and the authenticity of his language.

For example, sometimes it is better to state, "I really don't drink Lipton tea, but I have been told it is very good."

Stimulation Appeals

Another of the advertiser's tasks is to provoke, stimulate, and produce Word-of-Mouth about his product, company, or message. He must supply his messages with motivations and ammunition to this end, and turn them into topics of talk.

We have seen from everyday Word-of-Mouth incidents that "a person does not talk for nothing"; if one wishes to motivate him to talk, the message has to offer him a promise of emotional gain or some sort of mental gratification. This, as we have seen, may be the chance to channel the excitement aroused by an experience with a product, to obtain some kind of self-confirmation and enhance his ego, or to get the satisfaction that he has shown interest in or care for others. Finally, the emotional gain may consist of those gratifications which derive from an involvement in the message rather than in the product, leading to talking about or quoting from an ad or commercial.

Topics of Talk

Numerous applications for the advertiser suggest themselves to stimulate Word-of-Mouth:

Use the "shock of difference"—but with an orientation. Try to stop reader-listeners in their tracks by presenting your cause from an unusual angle, showing a not-so-obvious facet of your product, setting it off sharply from or against what others are doing in the same area. But don't be "different" at all costs and without an orientation. Successful applications of this technique are the Schweppes bearded Commander, who lends his product the desired touch of upper class distinction; Hathaway's black eyepatch, which endows its shirts with an atmosphere of adventurous and romantic virility; Maidenform's dream-walk in the seminude, which associates the bra with "wishful dreams" of passion; the glamorous hand from nowhere, which offers an attractive promise to the simple man; and so on.

Accordingly, let the incongruency, extremity, or unusualness of your ad express the "climate" in which you expect your product to thrive or the direction in which you want it to "move" psychologically. The shock of difference is likely to produce in the reader-listener a "tension" which in turn may use talk as an outlet. People also like to show their alertness in spotting the "difference."

Employ the effect of "heightened reality" (stagecraft). All talked-about ads, commercials, and so forth have one thing in common: they use the artistic effects of heightened reality; they "stage," as it were, their content by transforming the features of reality into a selective, condensed, symbolic, and stylized presentation—whether visual, audible, or both. If you want your advertising itself to stimulate talk, don't be satisfied with presenting "reality as is." Do make use of the expressive power of the art forms—the suspense of drama, the lifts and moods of poetry, the relief of comedy, the irony of anecdote, the bluff of paradox, and the startling truth of a documentary close-up.

Invite "listeners" to join you in poking fun at yourself. We have previously discussed this friendship-promoting aspect of self-mockery in advertising. The same feature that makes the consumer feel the advertiser takes him into his confidence also loosens his tongue. Where you intend to use humor or comedy, include humorous and consciousness in your advertising performance; it will encourage and stimulate the reader-listener to join you in this vein and to prolong and vary the fun through his own Word-of-Mouth.

Equip your message with "wings." Verbal play is not a child's prerogative; people will quote widely, and often with compulsive repetitiveness, what is made easy and pleasurable for them to quote. See to it that your message contains some good *coinage*—a sequence of words (and sounds) which provokes verbal play through its rhythm, alliteration, and pointedness. It should be applicable to a wide variety of life situations and should offer a plug for symbolic, figurative, ironic, aggressive, or suggestive use.

Leave room for your reader's wit or ingenuity. In coining your slogans or jingles, give your reader-listener a chance to fill in left-out words or to exploit ambiguous meanings for his own purposes! In this way you provoke him to make your message really his own.

(Whether such verbal play will tend to preserve the original sales message, or will bypass and eventually obliterate the product-association, is another problem which cannot be elaborated on in this study.)

Do not leave your customer alone with your product. Advertising in order to win customers is not enough. If you wish them to become your product's advertisers, if you want to stimulate them to talk about your product, you cannot afford to leave them alone with it! You must try and meet their experience with your product along the lines which you expect will make them talk.

For instance, if you advertise a cleanser, ask your customers whether they notice that in using this product they no longer have to bend down in order to get the dirt rings out of the bath tub. Ask them for a report about their experience, and they surely will be talking about it. If you advertise a car, tell those who own it how to turn the key, open rear doors in station wagons, and make them aware of pleasurable driving experiences peculiar to your make. (Ford is doing an excellent job with its approach: "Ford has a better idea.")

Most products have an aspect which answers some specific need or emotional desire on the part of the public. Often that desire is not quite obvious and the customer is only vaguely aware of it. The advertiser should have his ear to the ground to find out about this desire and to make his customers aware that his product does answer it.

Link your products with needs and trends of the time. Certain topics are "in the air" in certain periods of time. It is the job of the advertiser to hit on that aspect of his product which can be most readily and productively linked with these topics and trends, and thus to secure the product a place in the "talk of the time."

Satisfy the urge for "newness." Present your product from time to time from a new angle. The best product is usually taken for granted and ceases to be discussed once it has become part of the accepted pattern of use and of living. From time to time it has to be revived, rejuvenated, and brought in line with changes which have already occurred. Moreover, it has to be presented in ways which *anticipate* such changes and, through new facets of the product, make the public aware of them. The reward will be not only sales, but also talk, and thus more sales.

Give your reader a chance to gain attention. Supply him with "unusual" and interesting material which might be anything from impressive or sensational to anecdotic. See to it that the product or company forms an indispensable background for the "story" or is meaningfully linked with it. Give him cultural, scientific, or technical ammunition, but always make it pointed and highlighted so as to be "ready for use." Again, don't allow the product or company to get lost in the process. In a general way, *The New York Times* began appeal to this desire with its slogan: "It's more interesting—and you will be, too!"

Provide him with "inside information." Take the reader behind the scenes of your product or company and give him the feeling of being in-the-know. The information may refer to the making of the product, to company personalities, or to product history. The interest-value of the piece of knowledge will promote and facilitate talk about the product.

Give him the feeling of secrecy or exclusivity. Analysis earlier pointed to the fact that, in all probability, the spreading of a message will be facilitated when a certain degree of secrecy or exclusivity is connected with it. What motivates the one who "gives it away" is the desire to show that he himself is initiated, and that he is gracious enough to initiate the listener into a chance that is restricted or rare.

Supply users of your product with material to show them that in using the product they have, as it were, joined a "club" of people who really "know"—have more taste, understanding, or connoisseurship than most others—and you will have propelled them psychologically in the direction of "talk."

If your product shows some new angle, or represents an attempt at a new solution, do not try only to sell or to convince your reader, but "hire" him in the role of a pioneer. Your ad should leave him with the feeling that in understanding and accepting the novelty and "differentness" of the product, he can share some of the credit that will go to it, and that it is his job to pave the way for it in talking to others. Let your ad mobilize his ambitions and supply him with the "weapons" for assuming his leadership and exerting his power in the interest of the product.

Make your reader feel that recommendation is a gift. We pointed out earlier how close the recommendation of a cherished product comes to being a gift, and that, conversely, a thoughtful gift always represents a recommendation. Make your readers aware of what your product can do for those for whom they "care," and that a recommendation can take the place of a gift: without the reader acting as an intermediary between the product and the cared-for person, a wish may remain frustrated and a gratification missed. Thus talking about the product can do a lot for the reader in his relation to those he cares for; it will give him a chance to do a favor, earn praise, make friends, or simply express his attention, care, or love.

Offer a bridge of friendship. Make it easy for consumers who like or cherish your product to send a free, gift-packed sample of it to their relatives or friends. It can be accompanied by a brief, personal-looking note which explains that "this is one of the things that has made life more enjoyable (or easier) for me, and I don't want you to miss it." All the giver has to do is to send you his personal signature and the names of his friends. Keep the company in the background; make the "gift" serve as an invisible bridge.

Conclusion

I consider the establishment of a close link between successful, everyday Word-of-Mouth recommendations and effective advertising to be one of the implicit findings of the present study. It emphasizes the new role of the advertiser as that of a friend who recommends a tried and trusted product, as against that of a salesman who tries to get rid of merchandise.

Tracing the reasons for effective advertising in step-by-step fashion back to its person-to-person roots will, we hope, help the advertiser in reviewing his mass media approaches and in carrying through his new role. It is evident that in addition there are other avenues that *complement* mass media advertising. There is a symbiotic relationship between the impersonal and the personal, or the formal and the informal, avenues of communication.

I have tried to demonstrate in this presentation that mass media advertising does indeed make people aware of a product and may stimulate sufficient interest in the product to make it desirable. Mass media advertising may even be sufficient to sell the product. But for the latter statement to be true, generally speaking, the risk factor has to be extremely low. Consider the difference, for example, in the choice between detergents and in the choice between two automobiles. In the first case there is little economic or psychic risk; in the second case the economic risk is great, and important psychological and sociological considerations are involved.

I have also tried to demonstrate, particularly with products whose risk value is high, that Word-of-Mouth recommendation is a strong, if not the strongest, ally a product can have. Recent anthropological, sociological, and psychological studies have shown that mass media can raise questions or define issues; they can be informative and entertaining, and, to some degree, they can influence public opinion, but in the final analysis they cannot shape or mold it. People mold opinion. The glossy, brightly colored magazine page or the 21-inch TV screen can never replace the influence and the value of a personal recommendation. Were that the case the consumer would have to be very passive—simply sitting back and receiving information, and enough of it to permit proper evaluation.

However, our recent studies have shown quite the opposite: the consumer public is in fact active. Consequently, in a buying situation a dynamic interpersonal relationship—where ideas are discussed, opinions are exchanged, questions are asked, and answers are given— will frequently exist. Moreover, such an exchange will almost always outweigh the passivity of a one-sided and purely formal advertiser- audience relationship. Advertising cannot sell against personal influ- ence.

We have further endeavored to point out that there is a ready- made market of "influencer," "experts," and "aficionados," who can be reached and, in turn, influenced by advertising in existing special- ized publications or by the appropriate creative approach.

The advertiser with a good product to sell will do his best to stimulate information seeking by prospective buyers, and he will make every effort to have as much favorable information as possible in the hands and heads of these various influentials. The "afici- onado" is the person who can take the buyer into his confidence and make him a "member of the club." The bond created by this rela- tionship of people dedicated to the same hobbies can often replace, and often produce, real friendships. To the extent that the advertiser joins this club, he too offers friendship, trust, and confidence.

12

DIVERSIFIED FOOD MANAGEMENT

Frank J. Haberl, Jr.

Martin Marietta Corporation's Denver Division is located some 25 miles southwest of Denver in the secluded canyons of the Rockies. Here more than 7,500 people are intently and vigorously involved in the business of space ships, ballistics missiles and the attendant arts and sciences.

The nearest community is 20 minutes away—by car, not space ship. There are no nearby restaurants, hotels, or lunch counters. Hence, to serve these thousands of workers, Martin has established the largest, and one of the finest, food facilities in the inter-mountain West.

The business of Martin is as complex as it is vital. Parts of the Denver facility are located over hundreds of acres, in deep canyons, and high on strategic hills. Thousands of engineers, scientists, and their associates work in these areas. Thousands more are in the laboratories, offices, factories, and test facilities. There are many departments, many shifts, and constantly changing conditions. These complexities dictate the food service facilities required to adequately support a great and important effort. So, we have of necessity become:

A Variety of Food Services in One

It goes without saying that most food facilities, especially in industrial service, have obligations other than that of providing good food and reasonable service. Martin management has always been particularly aware of these other important services and of benefits that

---

Frank J. Haberl, Jr. is Manager of Food Services for the Martin Company's Denver Division. He is a member of the National and Colorado Restaurant Associations, the National Industrial Cafeteria Managers Association, is a trustee of the Winter Park Ski Area, and is a lecturer at Denver University.

From the *Cornell H.R.A. Quarterly*, May 1962, pp. 35-43. Reprinted by permission.

food and food facilities can supply. It is policy that they be perpetually considered and aggressively pursued. These services and benefits are motivated by such factors and influences as:

—Being twenty minutes away from the nearest community, hotel, restaurant, or lunch counter, our food clientele is definitely "captive";

—The very dynamics of Martin's business creates a problem of intensity that must have alleviation and change;

—Costs are a two-edged sword: they must give the employee a maximum of food and satisfaction for his dollar without incurring costs that might accrue to Martin and, subsequently, to the Air Force and the taxpayer;

—There is a responsibility to combat the highly accentuated problem of monotony;

—Where the commercial restaurant creates an atmosphere of hospitality and sophistication, we must develop a rapport of fraternity, happiness, informality, relaxation, etc, and supply the necessary break from routine.

—We must have foods and service on a constant and "immediately available" basis. The time element can be crucial. Variety, per se, is not a problem; selecting a generally acceptable variety of foods is a problem.

—The anticipations and realities of meal time enjoyments must at least be relative in all areas where meals or snacks are served.

So, the multiplicity of types of service tax ingenuity and experience. To accomplish our objectives, some very interesting approaches have been tried.

Food Service Facilities

Because of needs created by the very complexity of both the type of business and the plant and facility deployment, the food services at Martin-Denver are also relatively complex. There are three basic cafeterias, two service dining rooms, two mobile food service vans, snack bars throughout the Denver complex and a box lunch department.

Food is prepared and served on an almost around-the-clock basis. Breakfasts, lunches and dinners are served for two or three shifts. Many employees use the food services several times a day. Transactions usually number more than 10,000 per day; gross yearly volume is about 1¼ million dollars.

Martin-Denver Cafeterias

The three cafeterias seat a total of 1,000 people at one time. Two of the cafeterias are in one major building; the third is in another building, about 300 yards away. Normal service now is about 75 people per minute. This rate must be met because approximately 700 people are scheduled into the food facilities every ten minutes during the luncheon period from 10:15 until 12:45.

Basic cafeteria layout . . . provides two serving lines for full meals, a separate snack bar, and separate dishwash rooms.

Menu boards offer both a la carte foods as well as combination lunches. The combination lunches are reduced in price about 10 percent to encourage employee-customers to eat a complete, well-balanced meal. The increased check average results in a lower payroll cost per customer and thus allows more and better foods to be served without increasing prices.

Self-service is developed to the maximum. Customers help themselves to coffee, hot and iced tea, milk, bread, rolls, butter, salads, dressings, desserts, ice cream, and even milk shakes. After their meal, customers carry their trays to the dishwash windows where flatware and paper are removed and each placed in a separate chute. The dirty dishes are placed on stainless steel shelves.

Self-service facilitates speed, helps hold labor costs in line, and has a definite psychological value in allowing maximum choice and individual initiative. (As yet, we haven't let the customer ring up his sale and deposit his money in the cash register, but we'd like to.)

Service Dining Rooms

Like all other food facilities at Martin, the service dining rooms have a specific purpose, present their individual problems, and are integrated into the complete food operation in somewhat unique ways.

Until 12:30 each day these rooms are reserved for executive luncheons, during which classified information is being discussed. Service requirements for such groups include security-cleared people who are fast, efficient, and quiet.

During the other hours of the luncheon period, hospitality and cheer may be both needed and expected. But during these special "classified luncheons" a particular type of service has been developed. We call it "unobtrusive service." The waitress is supposed to be omnipresent and neither seen nor heard.

To do this we have developed a system where the guest orders his foods by designating his wishes directly on his copy of the menu.

This has several advantages: it allows conversations to continue uninterrupted; gives a detailed order at one time; induces the guest to give a complete order while he is hungry (thereby increasing check average because almost everyone specifies a dessert); and creates a meal charge slip that is used in charging the guest for his meal. Charges are collected through salary deductions.

Menus in these dining rooms are the same as those of the cafeterias, with a few specialty items added. The pictures of the menus indicated that items and prices are the same for both types of service.

Obvious advantages include those of single-purpose preparation. All basic items are prepared in the main kitchens, making it possible to have only service and dishwashing equipment in the kitchens of the service room areas. Noise and activity can be held to a minimum. Leftover foods are the same as for the other types of service and can be combined and reworked without extra processing.

With uniformity of food and price, management is constantly aware of the types, quality, and quantities of food being served. There is, of course an obvious psychological benefit when management and workers have exactly the same menus.

While daily fare is planned to be just good, plain, generally accepted, and well-prepared food, opportunity is frequently presented to roll out the red carpet. Several of our supervisors and cooks have had fancy food experience in hotels and clubs and enjoy the challenge of *haute cuisine*. The tent card illustrates the type of fine menu we occasionally present to serve management's purpose in internal or public relations activities.

Mobile Cafeteria Service

We have our own "Cape Canaveral" right here in Denver—the giant test stands on which the Titan missiles are test fired without leaving the ground. These test stands are located in canyons, isolating the stands from each other and also from the main plant buildings. Test-site personnel work under most exacting schedules, and often in adverse weather. To provide maximum support to these important operations, Martin Company policy requires that these people be provided with the best mobile food service possible.

These mobile cafeterias provide, at twelve separate locations, the same foods available in the service dining rooms and cafeterias. To meet the dish and utensil problems, we adopted disposable ware, similar to tha used for TV dinners, and a heavy grade of plastic knives, forks, and spoons. These mobile units carry quite a good selection: soup, chili, entree (two on days of specific religious requirements), vegetable, potato, salads, pie, cake, ice cream, coffee, iced tea, Coca Cola, and selections of candies and tobaccos. These mobile cafeterias serve at scheduled stops for 10 to 25 minutes, depending on the number of employees at the stop. The driver opens the folding covers, and plugs into local electrcial outlets to provide power for lights, heating, and refrigeration. Patrons walk around the truck, gathering their food on a disposable tray. The single driver-attendant acts as a cashier at each stop, replenishing food and supplies before proceeding to the next stop. During peak programs, 1000 to 1200 people are served at a given location from two trucks, frequently on a three-shift basis.

An interesting and sometimes difficult problem is the selection and "just-right" preparation of foods so they will look and taste good when finally served at the sites. Doing this for the third-shift personnel requires considerable ingenuity.

In keeping with Martin policy of providing more than food and service, these mobile units were given a personality by decorating them with art work and naming them "Ridge Runner." This little touch has proved very effective. It gives the unit a positive personality by creating a "conversation piece" of pleasant connotations.

Snack Bars

Several snack bars are operated within the Denver complex. These provide adequate but slightly limited food service to sizable groups of employees temporarily located away from the main food service facilities.

There are times when we need to divert excess business away from the cafeterias. The snack bars serve this purpose well. On occasion, vending machines are used at the snack bars, but generally Martin Company purposes are best served by regular snack bar foods. Here again the responsibilities of variety and acceptable menus dictate the type of service.

Since several of the snack bars are located in areas not too distant from the main plant and offices, many employees desiring only a snack for lunch or dinner will patronize the snack bars. They seem to enjoy the break of getting away for a few minutes and usually obtain a completely adequate selection of foods. With these snack bars we are able to keep excessive snack business away from the cafeterias, and at the same time provide a "variety" of places to eat.

We will soon operate cigarette vending machines, placed throughout the factory, warehouse, and office buildings. The purpose is to make it convenient for employees to buy cigarettes in their areas.

The vending machines will be operated by food services personnel. Revenues will be used to help offset continuously rising food and labor costs. There are no plans to expand into other vending lines.

Preparation Facilities and Production Procedures

The kitchens at Martin-Denver are large and particularly well equipped. We are able to produce foods in large quantities and still maintain the desired taste and quality controls.

From the beginning of the Denver operation, equipment and lay-out were planned to allow us to produce good Western, family-type food and avoid the onus of so-called "mass feeding." We do a considerable number of those little extras that make the difference. For example, we grind our stale bread for breading cutlets, rather than buy commercial breading compounds. Pastry dough is mixed by hand to avoid the toughening often caused by machine mixing. All stew or soup ingredients are diced to uniform size. The stock kettle is going all the time, supplying rich, naturally flavored stock for soups, gravies, and such.

For our purposes we use women cooks only. We find they are particularly amenable to following recipes, eliminating waste and reworking leftovers. They expend the extra care and energy necessary to produce the types and quality of foods we need.

Kitchen preparation is generally one half to one day ahead of service needs, short order items excepted. On Tuesday morning, for example, the grinding, peeling, chopping, weighing, and so forth would be for Wednesday lunch. Foods are purchased from one-half day to five days in advance—sometimes even longer when suppliers need extra time to fill such large orders. Green peppers for stuffing, corn on the cob, smoked pork chop, ham hocks, and knockwurst, are all items that require extra lead time in ordering, as local suppliers do not carry 2000 to 2500 orders on hand.

A daily production log is kept of food quantities produced, sold, and left over. Entrees are usually scheduled in pairs so that the relative amount of each to prepare is easily computed. Corrections are made to production estimates when necessitated by such factors as changes in plant manpower, changes in the weather, the day of the week relative to pay day, heavy vacation schedules, and the usual slumps following Christmas, income tax deadlines, etc. We are usually within 3 or 4 percent of actual needs.

Menus and Special Events

Monotony with a capital "M" is not an unusual problem in industrial feeding. At Martin it is accentuated by the absence of other immediately available restaurants or coffee shops. It is, therefore, expedient that we combat this morale killer with judgment and applied imagination.

We use every trick of the trade but have found the most gratifying results by careful menu planning, and in presenting special events and different types of service.

A cyclic menu has been developed that has proved particularly successful for our employee clientele, within our price range, and suitable to this part of the country. It coordinates soup, two hot entrees, vegetables, potatoes, a hot sandwich feature, and cold plates for variety. Such a menu does not overload specific pieces of kitchen equipment or any one section of the service counters.

Entrees are seldom repeated more often than every seven or eight weeks, some only every fourteen or fifteen weeks. Our menu file of special entrees includes almost a hundred tried and tested items. The menu is altered for market bargains, or for seasonal dishes like sauerbraten and lasagne in the winter, or cold buffet service in the summertime. If one item is a poor seller, it is either changed for a new recipe that may sell better or scheduled less frequently.

Daily menus feature homemade chili (this is the West, Suh), soups, two hot entrees, one cold plate or salad bowl (two in summer), and a hot sandwich feature. Additional variety is offered in a selection of freshly made cold sandwiches, a la carte salads, or vegetables. Metrecal is on our menu. (And therein lies a good example of customer humor. We posted a sign offering Metrecal at 35c. Some waggish customer added his bit—"with whipped cream—50c.") We serve a 59c and 69c lunch each day (exclusive of dessert). A huge meal consisting of soup, entree, potatoes, vegetable, salad, bread and butter, beverage, and dessert a la mode, need not exceed $1.10.

Special meals at special prices are designed for holidays. The greatest change of pace is the Buffet Day. This was first tried with fear and trembling, not knowing whether unlimited food for a set price would mean 4 ounces of meats, or a pound. The first time it was tried, customers consumed an average of 8½ ounces of meat. In successive times since then the average is 4½ ounces of meat per customer.

The appeal, we believe, is in the customer being able to help himself to everything. Steam tables are left cold, glass fronts are removed, and the regular serving areas are covered with tablecloths. Setting the cold buffet up this way it is both attractive and convenient. Traffic flow is about normal. The average plate comes out just about right for 75c, excluding dessert. The huge serving pictured in the illustration is usually balanced by small servings, as some take very little. All in all, the change is appreciated and enjoyed, and our regular service has new vitality and charm because of another break in routine.

Buffet Day is our most frequently used device for changing pace but we take advantage of holidays, changing seasons, and special events. Menus are designed and dining rooms are decorated according to the event. Sometimes the furniture is moved about, just so the patron can look out a different window. One particularly successful special event was our Fifth Anniversary party.

Purchasing and Inventory Control

Since we use a cyclic-menu system, our purchasing is generally for specific need. The production order specifies how much to cook. The recipe card tells how much of the various ingredients to buy, staples excepted. This system keeps inventory down and helps turn it five to six times per month.

Purchasing through semiannual or annual commitments, and incurring warehousing handling costs, is seldom appropriate for this operation. However, the yearly need of turkeys is purchased at the end of the growing season. The turkeys are frozen and stored in a downtown warehouse. Savings usually amount to 15 or 20 percent, after paying storage costs.

Frozen and canned foods are purchased by brand name, which is determined by testing samples. All are so called "Grade A." We do not buy fancy sizes or cuts.

Meats are bought by competitive bid from vendors of known quality and dependability. Meats purchased are U.S. grades "Good" or "Choice" only. A slight premium is paid for selected and guaranteed fruits and vegetables. This way, any significant defect or spoilage is replaced without charge and the labor of trimming and reworking such perishables is saved.

The thorough security guard system within the company precludes the necessity of maintaining a perpetual inventory, or requisitioning foods out of a storeroom. Occasional spot checks prove that loss is virtually nothing—certainly far less than it would cost to control it.

Repetitive daily ordering is phoned by office personnel, according to par stock requirements. Meats, canned and frozen foods are ordered for specific use by the production supervisor, with all orders documented in writing. All deliveries are checked for quantity, price, and quality.

Accounting and Controls

The major accounting functions such as accounts payable, payroll, and general ledger are performed by the Finance Division. Food service office functions are primarily those of cash handling, person-nel records, and purchase order processing.

Here is our condensed operating statement for the eleven months ending November 30, 1961.

	Dollar Volume	Percentage
Sales	$1,010,737	100.0
Cost of Merchandising	590,749	58.4
Payroll	358,644	35.5
Expendable Equipment and Supplies	62,682	6.2
Profit or Loss	$ 1,338	0.1

This statement portrays the real status of our food operations—an employee cooperative benefit.

Martin Company wishes to return the maximum value to the em-ployee so there are no charges to the food facilities for utilities, administration, space or depreciation—just the direct costs of food, labor, supplies, etc.

A measure that can be applied to labor efficiency is a comparison of annual sales per employee. In the food facilities at Martin-Denver the sales are $9,547, as compared to the national average of the restaurant industry, $6,500. If adjusted to comparable commercial prices, our annual sales per employee approximate $11,080.

Twelve cashiers collect up to $5,000 per day, with a high percent-age of the sales under a dollar. Register tapes are totaled and audited by office personnel. Cashiers are not told how much to turn in, or if they are over or short.

Personnel and Systems Control

Food services manpower totals 104 people, 9 in management, 2 in the office, 70 women employees, and 23 men.

For female employees turnover is usually below 2 percent; for men it is about 3¼ percent. Female absenteeism is very low. Women are clean, they will follow instructions, and their relationship with customers is excellent.

Older women are preferred: 40 to 50, and in exceptional cases 60 to 65 years old. The ones with the greatest need for work are usually selected.

Of the 18 employees that were here at the opening of these facili-ties five and one-half years ago, 13 are still here. Of the five gone, none left for another job in this area.

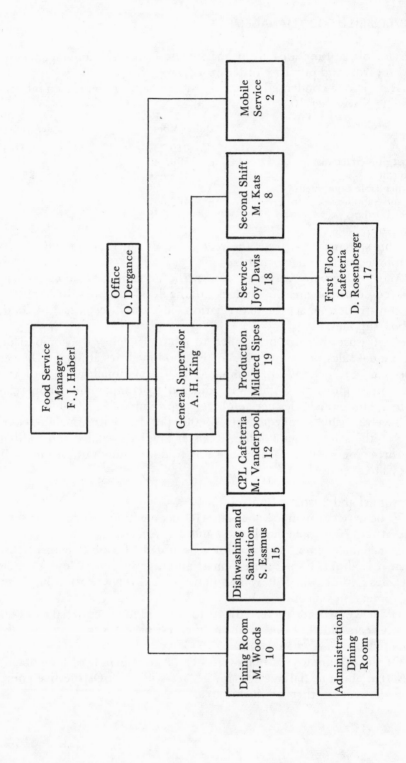

Over a year ago we undertook a program that looks like a solution to some of the problems with dishmen. In conjunction with the Colorado Department of Rehabilitation, four mentally retarded young men were employed. We failed with one of them, but the other three are doing very well. In fact, they are above average in attendance, job performance, and amiability. They require more thorough training and patience, but to date, the results far outweigh the effort.

The organization chart shows the supervisors, their functions, and the number of personnel under the control of each. What is not shown, and really can't be, is the interconnecting responsibilities between these areas. For instance, the production supervisor is primarily responsible for food preparation in four kitchens, standardization of menus, recipes, quality, and costs. The sanitation supervisor is responsible for the dishwashing operation in five dishrooms.

All daily operational problems are discussed, and resolved in a supervisors' meeting each afternoon. The menu, portions, and personnel changes for the next day are reviewed by Harold King, the General Supervisor (operations manager), and individual supervisors discuss their operating problems with their counterparts.

With the exception of management and office personnel, all food service employees are members of the UAW-CIO Aircraft Worker's Union. Martin Company policies on job security, seniority, work classifications, representation and grievances, and the rights of employees are clearly defined and acknowledged.

Management's prerogatives, too, are equally upheld. Activities are not hampered by slowdowns, featherbedding, make-work provisions, restrictive classifications, or jurisdictional disputes.

13

CENTRAL KITCHEN CONCEPT

from *Food Management*

Quite suddenly, the food service industry is becoming aware of the depth of commitment being made to a "new" concept—the central kitchen. Not only has this concept become a reality in a stunningly short time, it is rising toward levels which, until 36 months ago, would have seemed impossible.

Yet, even as the concept gains a strong control over today's operational thinking, there are old-timers around who shake their heads in amusement. "Central kitchens new?" they laugh. "Why look at Horn & Hardardt, or how about Cease's Commissary up in Dunkirk, New York. He's been using the idea since 1919!"

The old-timers are right; there is nothing new about a central kitchen. The newness is in the minds of the food service operator of today who must plan for tomorrow. And therein lie the reasons for the rebirth of the central kitchen. In the days of the flapper and the Model-T, labor was plentiful and cheap. There was still enough of an "old-country" aura surrounding food service to attract good talent for both the front and the back of the house.

No imagination is required to contrast that era with the realities of today.

The answer for today is the central kitchen. And the answer is in direct reply to the simple fact that the food service industry has reached the breaking point in cost control. Deficit operations can no longer be condoned. Within the framework of what the patron can pay and what the operator can charge lies the central kitchen concept.

While there are some self-styled critics who enjoy taking pot-shots at what they consider to be industry weak points, these same critics are notably silent in the face of the explosive growth of the central kitchen phenomena.

From *Food Management*, March 1966.

Common sense has prevailed, and while growth of the concept has been rapid, clear thinking and sound planning have heralded its approach. Even the antagonists who see little advantage to the concept are cautious in their pessimism.

For 45 years the central kitchen concept has been a sleeping giant. Lack of managerial talent, scarce and high-cost labor, an affluent society, and inflation have poked the giant into wakefulness. How the concept fares, just how useful it will be, and whether or not it is *the* solution to the food service industry's problems is a matter for history to record.

Putting the past behind us and letting the future take care of itself, what is today's thinking about the central kitchen concept? What do its apostles have to say for it? Conversely, what do its antagonists proclaim? Herewith are both views.

"One of the greatest concerns of the food service industry has long been the management of food, labor, and equipment costs. Today we must add two more major concerns: intelligent planning to meet future demands, and trained personnel to serve tomorrow's food service industry."—Helen Jenkins, Director of Food Services, Emory University.

With these concerns uppermost in planning, food service management would be wise to consider the concept of the central commissary. The food service industry is massive, yet is often likely to operate many small, repetitious businesses within one organization.

On the college and university campus it is not uncommon to have five or six kitchens doing the same jobs each day. Hospitals and nursing homes are likely to have, under a single roof, one kitchen for patients, another for employees and staff cafeteria, and often a snack bar or vending area under the direction of another firm or organization. Many times one management in these areas is responsible for all food service operations, but makes no effort to centralize or combine functions and procedures.

In many instances centralization is a step toward solving problems, but is not recommended for all organizations. Here, then, is how one could consider the advantages and disadvantages of the central kitchen concept.

Because of centralization there will be a reduction in the number of personnel—a need for fewer high-salaried, skilled employees.

Reducing the number of personnel is accomplished by cutting out entire departments. The vegetable preparation area, for instance, can be centralized or completely eliminated by the use of convenience foods. Centralizing a bakery is another common practice.

Butcher shops, too, are easy to centralize, again resulting in a reduced labor force.

To centralize certain functions of preparation and cut out entire areas, there definitely will be less need for major equipment installations. If equipment is already in existence it can be used in other installations or disposed of as trade-in on new equipment.

A fleet of trucks and transportation equipment is needed. These items are nominal in comparison to costly kitchen equipment. Maintenance and upkeep of trucks can not be overlooked, but here again the costs are slight in comparison to that of maintaining several kitchens.

In buildings today the kitchen area is one of the most costly. The square-foot cost often doubles or triples that of other areas. To eliminate the need to build and equip large preparation and cooking areas certainly reduces the initial cost of construction.

Satellite areas call for planning of dining rooms, serving pantries, and dishwashing areas. Because the preparation area can be eliminated, more square footage can be utilized for other purposes.

Through one central office the work in various food units, regardless of the distance, can be coordinated to standardize all working procedures. Recipes, menus, portions, and prices can be standardized and, through centralization, can be better controlled. Definite cooperation among the top supervisors of each food operation working through a central office can offer a check against each other and an opportunity to establish correct costs.

Centralization of food service will, at the outset, definitely eliminate some jobs, and initially may cause some personnel problems. If displaced employees are transferred to other jobs this first change will not present unsurmountable problems, however.

Without centralization the end food product is only as good as the top manager of each operation. In some locations (within actual sight of each other) the entire food picture can be different because the management differs. Through a central commissary, all food will be uniform in quality, and appearance if controlled and supervised.

A central commissary definitely calls for one administration with a desire to centralize. But unless there is a willingness by "the boss" to stand up for centralization, it will not work.

"By utilizing the central kitchen concept we have achieved certain savings, and gained benefits which would not have been possible under a program of self-contained cafeteria preparation and serving areas."—David R. Page, Director, Division of Food Services, Board of Education, City of St. Louis, Missouri.

In our elementary schools we have in recent years embarked on a program of complete centralization of preparation. All foods in the schools will eventually be prepared in a central kitchen (we refer to these as area kitchens).

We have six area kitchens scattered around the city, preparing foods for 36 receiving schools. These kitchens are located in schools, and in addition to serving as centers, also serve the school in which they are housed. Thus we have 43 schools under centralized operation.

In our area kitchens the ratio of man-hours to meals served is far better than in the self-contained elementary units. Our weighted salary cost per hour (total amount of salaries paid per hour, divided by number of man-hours) is far better than in self-contained units. This saving is achieved even though we are paying a higher daily wage for the persons assuming top responsibilities. This we have been able to do by making the area kitchens high production areas—by installing labor-saving equipment that economically we could not have installed in each unit.

In our view there are other possibilities with regard to centralization. There is the idea of centralization of preparation of bakery items, certain meat and entree items—a whole host of possibilities.

Another saving achieved locally is in the cost of original installation. Through the use of area kitchens we have been able to plan our new elementary school kitchens as rather simple serving areas. The installations were made with a minimum of equipment. No preparation equipment is installed.

This concept of centralized preparation with the use of receiver satellites provides a very flexible arrangement in a situation where demands for food service could change from year to year. The program can be started, changed or transferred from school to school at a minimum of expense and effort.

The other side of this issue also needs some consideration. The idea of doing all food service from centers is completely unrealistic in my opinion. In areas where there is a large volume in one operation, I believe a self-contained kitchen and dining area is well justified. In our St. Louis system we have large high school cafeterias serving schools with enrollments of from 1,500 to 3,000. In these schools the volume is such that a large production job may be installed and operated efficiently and economically.

In substance, I am saying that there is no simple, single answer to this matter of centralization. Each individual situation needs to be studied on its own, but when school officials and others are planning for the future the concept of centralized preparation needs to be considered.

"Many seem to think that the central kitchen concept is the answer to all food service problems. Nothing could be further from the truth."—Christine Pensinger, President, Food & Equipment Counseling, Inc.

Before management considers a central food preparation area, a careful study and survey should be made by a competent consultant. Such a study will show whether the central facility is practical and will provide an estimate on the cost, savings, and method most suitable for operation. This study will first carefully review the existing menu, method of preparation, and execution.

The factors which should be considered when making a study of the menu, and which will influence its planning are:

1. The food budget and raw food costs (do they relate directly to the economic level of the persons being served?)
2. Labor costs and how they relate to food costs.
3. Is the menu, variety, and quality of the foods served acceptable to the clientele?
4. Are seasonal foods purchased, and are available convenience foods used to advantage in order to keep labor costs to a minimum?
5. Is the available cooking equipment adequate and being used properly?

The menu pattern defines the scope of food service activities, and must be used as the basis for the design of all food service facilities. An efficient operation, however, will depend on management. Too often the failure of food service is blamed on layout rather than efficient management.

The main reasons for considering a central food preparation operation are:

1. To improve efficiency of the operation.
2. Combat high labor costs.
3. Take advantage of purchasing food in volume.
4. Proper utilization of space and equipment.
5. Provide more efficient management supervision, and better utilization of employees' time.

Certainly the central facility will make it possible to reach all of these goals, providing the various units to be served are operating under the same policy, have the same basic dietary standards, operate on the same economic food level, and are within a reasonable distance from the central facility.

Transportation costs, which include motor transportation or shipping, salary of driver, and the additional equipment needed for holding food at proper temperature during transportation, may be the deciding factor in determining the practicability of the central food service facility.

The central food production kitchen or commissary is usually advisable for a large hospital complex, which might include a general hospital, nursing home, geriatric unit, T. B. unit, employee cafeteria, staff dining room, and a public coffee shop. These areas might be in the same compound, within walking distance of each other, or one or more of them might be far enough away from the main kitchen to necessitate the transport of food by truck.

When preliminary planning is done on a central food service facility, the question usually comes up as to whether it is best to build a new structure or remodel an existing kitchen. Due to new methods of operation and the size of food preparation equipment, it is often possible to remodel an older kitchen and triple its capacity.

It is not wise to have extensive bakery operations in most institutional kitchens, but in a central commissary it is practical. With the automated equipment available today, a bakery can operate with limited manpower, and the savings can be noticeable.

At the present time, several hospital and nursing home chains are considering the feasibility of a central commissary. These chains, if their volume is large enough, and providing there is an adequate food budget, could certainly support a central commissary—at least for many of their food items.

Feeding elementary and secondary school children is big business today. When this lunch program was first started, it was thought necessary to place a kitchen in each school.

This is a very costly operation. The space in the building is valuable, and the equipment expensive just for the preparation of one meal a day. Also, labor is high-priced and often not too efficient. With this system of operation, many school lunch programs must be subsidized. During the last few years, many school districts have been preparing food for several schools from one kitchen. Large cities have set up commissaries for certain items, if not for the total service.

The school lunch program is an ideal spot for the central commissary, but due to management and personnel problems, such a changeover will take many years to effect in most of the districts.

*"In the university field it is generally agreed that a student popula-
tion of 3,500 is minimum for commissary feasibility; the break-even
point at about 4,000 resident students."*—Forrest Howards, Carl Han-
son, Fred Schmid Associates.

In the commercial field it is generally agreed that eight to 10
operations are necessary to justify the expense of a complete commissary. Retail products, either for "take-out" or food stores, greatly
enhance such an operation.

However, with the continued pressures of major packers and can-
ners to procure more of the available market, it becomes increasingly
difficult to justify the expense of building, maintaining, and operating a commissary.

A continuing trend is evident by commercial interests for expanding the available variety of processed and prepared foods.

Best reason for commissary considerations is quality control—by
professional talent—and the advantage of seasonal purchases.

One of the greatest problems of the commissary is adequate flexibility to accommodate growth of the facilities it serves. Once the
operational scope and physical boundaries of the commissary are
established, further growth is difficult.

Many commissaries operate on a partial or limited basis, and may
include vending operations, baking (no bread), storage (dry, refrigerated, freezer, and flash freezer), preparation of foods (some butcher-
ing, no cooking).

The complete commissary will include cooked foods which are
usually frozen for distribution, a test kitchen, controlled thaw facility for frozen meats and poultry, and the production of salad
dressings and preserves.

*"The biggest problem to the highly centralized commissary con-
cept lies in the lack of resources—time, qualified personnel, and
money—to finance the detailed research necessary to place such an
operation into effect."*—J. P. Tice, Director, Food Services, Western
Michigan University.

The food service operation on most college campuses is a con-
tinuum of productivity peaks and valleys. We begin operations in
September and stop for a few days for the Thanksgiving holiday.
Activity then picks up until the Christmas holidays, when most
campuses are closed for two to three weeks. After Christmas, and
until early in June, activity is on a level keel, except for a break for
spring vacations. Summers tend to be "down" periods.

The direct result of this cyclic business is clear. The labor force is compelled to be transient. It is expensive to retain key people on a 12-month pay status, but impossible to recruit good people unless we do so. Consequently, the labor force is frequently made up of house-wives and other local personnel who are agreeable to sporadic income and employment. Training of these people is expensive, and I'm afraid the resulting work force is frequently less than what should be described as a "professional food service organization."

Further, where food production is completely decentralized, not only is there costly duplication of production equipment, but this equipment stands idle for much of the calendar year.

Ideally, all students, irrespective of residence hall and food service assignment, should receive a uniformly excellent product, and food and labor costs should be similar, without regard to point of production.

It seems to me that the *concept* of centralization is not at question so much as the *degree* of centralization. If centralization of these functions can be successful, then why not centralize the complete production function of a food service operation?

I believe the answer to greater centralization of food production lies in manufacturing in bulk quantities, in accordance with tested formulae that are designed for finalization at point of service in a given piece of equipment, and then frozen or refrigerated and stored for future menu requirements.

In my opinion, the biggest problem to the highly centralized commissary concept lies in the lack of time, qualified personnel, and money to finance the detailed research necessary to place such an operation in effect. This research, it seems to me, must be done by each institution contemplating such a system, since it must be designed to accommodate the peculiarities of that institution.

"The size of a school is not necessarily a factor in the decision to have a central food service commissary."—Dorothy O. Bell, Director of Food Services, Stanford University.

The Central Commissary can be justified by determining the economic benefits to a school, as well as the services necessary to aid the food service director in achieving her responsibilities.

It is my belief that a central commissary, wisely planned and based on need, has a real economic value to the school and the food-consuming units. Better controls are possible in one unit than in 15 or 20 individual units. Direct volume buying and one-spot delivery will give better quality and price control, as well as reduced delivery costs. Requirements can be anticipated and inventories controlled.

The central bake shop and pre-preparation of fruits and vegetables will eliminate duplication of equipment and cut down labor costs. It is my belief that there will be some sacrifice of quality, however, especially in baked goods. For example, a hot breakfast roll going direct from the oven to the student is bound to be of higher quality than one which is several hours old when reheated before serving. The same thing is true of lunch and dinner rolls, pies, cakes, and cookies. In these times of high labor costs, can one afford the luxury of an individual bake shop in each unit? I think not.

The test kitchen would be a real asset to such an operation. It need not be elaborate but should be well equipped.

A central commissary is not the answer to all food service problems. Its main function is to stretch the dollars that students pay for food. Once the central facility is justified, however, benefits can be derived by the food-consuming units.

"In the not too distant future, food preparation as it is being done today by hospitals, institutions and industrial plants will disappear from the picture. This means more will be done, by fewer specialists, in a commissary-type operation supervised by trained personnel with up-to-date equipment and quality controls."—C. J. Parmor, H. Oliveri, R. E. Davidson, A. N. Wladis and J. H. Riehl, Cease Food Management Services, Inc.

The strength that can be generated by the unification of a multiple food service operation and an efficient commissary operation is unlimited. A properly guided program and a combined team effort at the top management level of both will produce excellent service, quality, and variety to customers at reasonable cost.

The disadvantages and limitations of a commissary operation based on the above premise will be almost negligible. A basic understanding as to what is expected of it with the addition of a good system of communications can eliminate most problems. Commissary production and service must be tailored to meet the requirements of each.

What are the advantages of a good commissary operation? Among several, it:

1. Allows food service managers to check inventories and order all items at one time.

2. Requires a smaller inventory because of split case and more frequent deliveries.

3. Lets food service managers devote more time to final food preparation and service.

4. Provides greater menu variety.

5. Reduces number of on-site personnel needed.

6. Requires fewer items of equipment on site.

7. Allows greater use of seasonal items, and specials that are available periodically because of alert purchasing and commissary support.

8. Affords on-site food cost control which reflects in lower food costs.

9. Assures quality control by consistent purchasing and production procedures.

10. Permits closer control of accounting procedures.

15

CONVENIENCE FOODS: THIRD ANNUAL REPORT

from *Volume Feeding Management*

Convenience foods is today's "in" term. Almost everybody talks about it. Everyone wants to know more about it. In some quarters it's the panacea for everything that hampers good, efficient and profitable food service.

If such an elixir exists, then many would find reasons to doubt its effectiveness. But a wide assortment of convenience foods do exist. And more and more operators are willing to listen to how these foods can be used in their operations. Many are using these products on a system basis, others on a trial basis. Some are satisfied with the results. Others complain about quality, consistency, product variability, methods of re-heating, sameness, etc.

Last year VFM did its second analysis of a large group of operators who use convenience foods. The statistics showed that the number keeps increasing. We know that from visits in the field. We see it happening. And many of the times—most of the times—the results are favorable.

But few operators are willing to go on record that using a convenience foods system is effective, efficient, commendable. It is too bad. The stories they tell are frequently very good. The methods they use to add "their touch" to these products show ingenuity, care and creativeness. But it is limited.

There still remains a dread when you ask for the story. "Don't tell our story. Our customers are not aware of our new practice. Our competitors will have enough ammunition to destroy us." It's a plaintive plea. It's frightening. The fear of insecurity hangs like an albatross around their necks. It shows. *But* their fortitude to try new ideas is great. We commend them for it. Some day they will rise above this fear. And, that, too, shall come to pass.

From *Volume Feeding Management*, September 1969. Reprinted by permission of the publisher.

In this issue we have gone into another area on the same subject. This year we decided to interview and poll the distributors of convenience foods. We wanted to learn from them: (1) To whom do they sell product; (2) In what operations are they most successful in sales; (3) What segments of the market are responding most actively to their sales solicitations; (4) What percentage of the distributor sales dollar is being spent for what items; (5) What is the relationship between canned, frozen-prepared and freeze-dried foods; (6) What segments of the market are most lax in responding to the convenience foods concept.

To get this information we decided to survey the outstanding distributors of frozen, freeze-dried and canned convenience foods. They totalled 364. They were located in every part of the United States where such foods are sold.

We asked them a variety of questions. Forty specific items among appetizers, soups, entrees, vegetables, fruits, bread, rolls and mixes, specialties, desserts and freeze-dried products. We asked them for package sizes and portion sizes. Then, we further asked them to give us percentage of sales to restaurants, hotels, hospitals, clubs, schools, colleges, military and other.

The information we were seeking required a mammoth effort. It presupposed that many of these companies were computerized (oddly enough they aren't) and hence such data would be easy to cull from the records. We learned that this was not so. In the responses from 67 wholesale distributors, that's an 18 percent sample, we discovered that the information was not easy to dig out. Furthermore, many did not want to reveal the types of organizations they sold to.

However, those who did respond indicated that 100 percent of those who filled out the questionnaire sell their products to restaurants. Frozen appetizers are a popular item and are being used more and more. By the same token, canned appetizers are popular in fish, seafood, liver and pates and fruit juices.

In the area of soups, the bulk of sales were in the canned product category to restaurants. On the rarest occasion did one say that they sold frozen soups. Since frozen soups come in cans, we assume that most of the respondents considered a canned soup—whether condensed or frozen—just a canned soup.

Among the entrees, frozen products play a major sales role. Restaurants everywhere are either using or experimenting with convenience frozen entrees made with beef, poultry, lamb, pork, fish and seafood. No respondent indicated either a canned or frozen pasta. Did the word pasta stump them? After all, spaghetti and ravioli and pasta products see an extensive use in a variety of high volume operations. But what gives the clue is the fact that in the schools and colleges categories pasta was left blank. From our experience in past research of these institutions, we know that canned spaghetti and ravioli as well as other pasta products (pizza, for instance) receives favorable reaction every time it is offered.

Restaurants have for long periods of time used canned and frozen vegetables and fruits. It is apparent from the answers that almost every respondent indicated that these product lines are "in."

They dittoed it for bread, rolls and mixes. The chart for Specialties is cross hatched rather oddly. The only canned products considered of a convenience nature are pickles, relishes, sandwich fillings and whipped toppings. Frozen products include eggs, sausage, waffles, pickles and relishes, cheese, butter and toppings. Is "frozen" and "refrigerated" used interchangeably here?

Restaurants are using more and more frozen-prepared desserts in all categories shown although some canned items make the grade here, too. The lack of acknowledgment of freeze-dried products is puzzling. In the previous surveys a number of operators indicated that they are using some of these products. Is it possible that the method of sale and distribution is via other channels?

The food service operations in hotels and motels indicates a lack of adequate sales pattern in both canned and frozen convenience products. By their own admission, the distributors indicate a woeful weakness in sales here.

Soups show the greatest strength in both canned and frozen products. Vegetables and fruits are also bought in both categories. Then, there is a smattering of sales activity in the desserts category. The cross hatch between canned and frozen in cakes, puddings, pies, custards and cookies spells out a haphazard use of these products.

Of the respondents, 64 percent said that they sold some products to the hospital field. However, in their responses it became obvious that although they consider this area part of their total market, the amount of product moved is very limited.

Hospitals, a rapidly growing area in the volume feeding industry, are also prime targets for distributor sales efforts. Of the respondents, 65 percent said they sell to this market—or make calls and try to convince them of the use for these products. Still, on careful examination of the responses, it is odd that distributors indicate an almost identical pattern for hospitals and hotels. The pattern is so closely related that one wonders how it is possible.

In our survey of the field, it seemed to indicate that hospitals were gravitating more rapidly to test and experiment with a wide variety

| Restaurant | | PRODUCT |
Canned	Frozen	
		APPETIZERS
✓	✓	Fish
✓	✓	Seafood
✓	✓	Liver & Pates
	✓	Egg Rolls
	✓	Hors d'Oeuvres
✓	✓	Fruit Juices
		SOUPS
✓		Vegetable
✓		Beef
✓		Chicken
✓		Fish
✓		Seafood
		ENTREES
✓	✓	Beef
✓	✓	Poultry
	✓	Lamb
✓	✓	Pork
✓	✓	Fish
✓	✓	Seafood
		Pasta
		VEGETABLES
✓	✓	All kinds
		FRUITS
✓	✓	All kinds
✓	✓	**BREAD, ROLLS, MIXES**
		SPECIALTIES
		Eggs
		Pancakes
	✓	Sausage
	✓	Waffles
✓		Sauces
✓	✓	Pickles
✓	✓	Relishes
✓		Sandwich fillings
	✓	Cheese
	✓	Butter
✓	✓	Whipped toppings
		DESSERTS
	✓	Cakes
✓	✓	Puddings
✓	✓	Pies
	✓	Custards
✓	✓	Ice Cream
✓	✓	Cookies
		FREEZE DRIED FOODS

of frozen and freeze-dried products (the latter seemed most apparent in nursing and convalescent homes). But oddly enough, one of the most taciturn of the group were hospital dietitians. They did not want to talk about these ideas. They, it seemed, were not ready to accept them. Where they did, they felt their patients would resent it, if they knew.

We talked to quite a few distributors whose kitchens had shifted to complete convenience foods. But they did not want to go on record evaluating their experience or commenting on the product. They were long on complaints about quality, stability, variety. Some implied that it was a course that management decided. And there the conversation stopped.

Clubs are one of the smaller segments of this market and make up 33 percent of the customers of the distributors who answered. There are vast vacant areas in usage. According to the answers from these convenience food distributors, much in the nature of fresh product is bought here. Still, a large percentage of this group buys frozen beef, pork, fish and seafood entrees. Vegetables and fruits are accepted in the canned and frozen state. But beyond this, the interest is sparse.

The schools and colleges reflect an almost identical mirror image in the products they use in the various product categories. The picture here may be partly lopsided. There are many colleges and private schools that are catered by specialized catering organizations. Their sources for product both canned and frozen may come from sources that are different than the standard buying patterns. The responses here must be viewed with caution.

The sales to the military, in so many cases, are direct sales. As a result it seems from the sales pattern here that few convenience foods reach this market. Many frozen, canned and freeze-dried products show up here but they are purchased through other channels.

Few question the broad interest in the convenience foods market. Operators, when their anonymity is protected, admit much more freely to the use of these products.

The movement, as our other annual surveys showed, is slowly gaining momentum. It's a hard row to hoe. The labor picture and the people profile are forcing the hands of some operators. But it's far from a landslide. To bring more operators to accept the philosophy will require stronger, more pointed information dissemination. It will mean greater emphasis on systems change in the menu concept of the various restaurants, hotels, hospitals, clubs, schools, colleges, etc. It also means that this is not the answer for everyone but it could, in some part, help many people solve problems that they are facing with greater frequency.

14

THE CONVENIENCE FOOD EXPERIENCE AT LUTHER COLLEGE

L. E. Price

Part 1

It would be hard to find a situation in another industry where innovation has created so much confusion as now obscures attempts to evaluate the practicality of the convenience foods. Available information too often reflects a commercial bias. But convenience products available on the market now are often so much superior to the conventionally produced item that it would be tragic if honest and factual appraisal did not bring out all necessary facts.

Against this background, we projected a convenience food test program at Luther College designed to produce validated records of performance achieving ten objectives. The cost figures were to be authenticated by certified public accountants, and the student-customers evaluated the quality by questionnaires.

We arranged with George A. Hormel Co. of Austin, Minn., to prepare the food, which we paid for at the going distributor's price.

During the last three months of 1967 and January of 1968, we tested samples of frozen prepared entrees with our Student Food Service Management Council, composed of sixteen representative students of our group, to identify those entrees they felt would appeal to the entire student group. The Management Council then prepared a six-weeks cyclical menu of convenience foods which was used exclusively in the program, beginning February 5, 1968, and continuing through the end of the school year: 96 days.

Standards of performance were set up in ten separate areas of activity to enable comparisons with conventional methods of operation. The minimum performance set by these objectives was either equal to, or superior to, those which had been acceptable in the conventional method of operation. Six of these objectives contained

From *Institutions Magazine*, January and March 1969 issues. Reprinted by permission of the publisher.

minimum performance standards in excess of anything before achieved by conventional method of operation. Five objectives could not be obtained by conventional operation at all.

Objective Number One was the adaptation of the convenience concept to the convenience kitchen. The food facility on this campus is located in the student center building. The dining room seats 780 guests. Two thousand students are in attendance. About 1,800 students participate in the prepaid boarding plan. The snack bar is located one floor below the dining and kitchen area. Another dining area, accommodating catered events, is above the kitchen.

One walk-in freezer, with a capacity of 528 cubic feet is located in this kitchen. There is also a reach-in freezer, with a capacity of 70 cubic feet. There are 15 square feet of griddle area, four 40-pound fry kettles, and two types of ovens. The stack ovens have a capacity of 20 standard 18-in. by 26-in. bun pans. Two small rotating ovens have a combined capacity of 20 standard 18-in. by 26-in. bun pans. There are also two steam-jacketed kettles with a total capacity of 120 gallons. Four walk-in coolers with a combined capacity of 2,112 cubic feet.

Objective Number Two was that no additional equipment was to be acquired to accommodate the convenience foods operation.

Objective Number Three was to reduce the space requirement in the food service preparation facility. Since we had listed as our first objective no alterations of the existing physical plant, we did not reduce our space requirement. However, with less need for storage of inventory we were able to release space which has been assigned to other departments.

Objective Number Four was reduced inventory of food. In September, 1967, we had a $36,000 food inventory. In one year, we reduced this inventory to $2,000 by using the convenience concept. Today, we carry a working inventory of $2,000 to $3,000 which has proved entirely adequate.

Objective Number Five was the simplification of the purchasing function. A college of 2,000 student enrollment will, in the course of one year, buy about half a million dollars worth of merchandise. Something near $450,000 of this will go for raw foods. Anywhere from 10 to 25 purveyors usually participate in supplying these raw foods. Many colleges maintain three sources of supply for each major item used. Generally, a minimum of two suppliers is maintained.

By concentrating this purchasing power among fewer purveyors, better results can be obtained. If each purveyor is given a copy of the menu, particularly a four or six weeks menu, this will give the lead time needed in order to service the account properly. No purveyor is going to look lightly upon any account providing a substantial volume of business. This purveyor will provide the purchasing supervisor with certain market information he is not likely to acquire from any other source. In the interests of economy, the college is not likely to find a better friend than an interested purveyor. Obviously, the best way to secure this interest is to extend to the reputable purveyor a substantial amount of the dollar volume of purchases.

In the convenience food concept of operation, we are simply transferring food preparation out of the institutional kitchen over into the purveyor's kitchens.

We need to examine only a few of the entrees in common use today to determine the extent to which the purchase of these frozen prepared items greatly minimizes the number of purchases which would have to have been made if these items had been prepared in our kitchen.

Item	Ingredients
Macaroni & Cheese	12
Sliced Beef & Gravy	12
Tuna Chow Mein	13
Tuna & Noodles	13
Chicken Chow Mein	14
Beef Stew/Vegetables	14
Chicken a la King	15
Spaghetti & Meatballs	16
Beef Goulash	17
Sloppy Joes	17
Meat Loaf w Tomato Sauce	18

Obviously, in the preparation of many of these dishes, we use many of the same ingredients. However, in the preparation of those listed above, actually 64 different items must be used. This simply means that we would have purchased 64 different items.

The sheer mechanics of the convenience food concept, particularly the prepared frozen entrees, gives tremendous promise of relieving the college food facility of the need to maintain elaborate purchasing paraphernalia it has had to use.

Objective Number Six was easy adaptability to a cost accounting system that provides management with a daily food and labor cost analysis. By incorporating a convenience food system, we are now able to make a daily accounting of labor and raw foods as well as processed foods used.

Objective Number Seven was an increased total of student jobs beyond the number presently available in the conventional operation. By eliminating the need for skilled workers and substituting simpler skills, we can now incorporate a greater number of students in the labor force.

Part 2

Tremendous costs savings and a positive student response resulted when we switched to a 100 percent convenience food operation at Luther College.

Costs savings came about for three reasons:

(1) Convenience foods in themselves are labor savers because of their built-in labor factor.

(2) By weeding out the incompetent food service employees, we were able to achieve greater productivity from the fewer but better paid workers that we retained.

(3) By patronizing a single supply source, we saved time and expense on paper work. Food costs were reduced too, because of the lesser cost of one big delivery compared with many small ones.

Student Reactions

Samples of frozen prepared entrees were served to 16 members of the college's Student Food Service Management Council during a three-month test period. The purpose was to identify those entrees the council felt would appeal to the entire student group. The council then prepared a six-week cyclical menu of convenience foods which were used exclusively in the program, beginning Feb. 5, 1968, and continuing throughout the semester.

A six-week menu, with no changes permitted, gives the purveyor the assurance that he isn't going to be stuck with an inventory of unrequested items. The menu range, incidentally, was very similar to that offered by some 250 other colleges. This makes mass purchasing more reasonable for the supplier.

The seniors were polled just prior to their graduation in June as to the quality of the food. They were asked to answer a list of ten questions. Their evaluations were expressed in terms of degrees of satisfaction or dissatisfaction from +5 to -5.

Question No. 1 asked whether the students' complaints and suggestions about food service prompted more effective action this year than in previous years. Over 71 percent answered affirmatively.

Question No. 2 asked for a general evaluation of the food served this year as compared to that offered in previous years. The answer was 76 percent better.

Questions Nos. 3-8 covering specific categories of food offered averaged to 45 percent better.

Question No. 9 asked specifically for the students' reaction to frozen prepared entrees. In reply, 25 out of 207 saw no difference in quality over the same items prepared in the college's kitchen. And 67 said they were inferior while 115 said they were better. The net position was 23 percent better.

Question No. 10 asked, "How would you compare the food served this last year with that you have been served in an average restaurant?" The response was typical of the attitude of the student consumer in the quantity food situation on the American college campus. The answer was 50 percent negative.

This accurately reflects the disenchantment of the student customer and the less-than-acceptable performance of the college food facility to meet the demands of its student consumers. This attitude is not going to be rationalized with such assertions as "students cannot be satisfied."

Cost-wise, the convenience food operation at Luther College was an outstanding financial success. For the fiscal year ended June 30, 1968, income from the 2,000 students for their food was $909,665, or about 50 percent of the income dollar. Labor costs were $184,065 or 20 percent. All other expenses amounted to $38,685 or 4 percent. The gross profit was $229,804 or 25 percent of income.

That brings the average price per meal to about 63¢, of which 49.4¢ is the actual cost of the meal and 13.6¢ is the profit. The figuring: 2,000 students times 3 meals a day, times 7 days a week, times 34 weeks in the school year, equals $1,428,000. $909,665 divided by $1,428,000 equals 63¢.

I doubt if any other college food service in America, charged with the responsibility of providing food for 2,000 students, has ever equaled this financial record. Perhaps some people might contend that we subjected our students to near starvation to achieve this record. This, of course, isn't true. We have a policy of unlimited seconds.

A study in depth made by the National Assn. of College and University Food Services in 1965 revealed that the cost of raw foods, expressed as a percent of the income dollar, varied between 45 percent-50 percent among the 36 schools examined. Our food costs of

50.2 percent would put us at the top of the range. Labor costs in these 36 schools varied between 30 percent to 34 percent.

A food cost of 50 percent is livable, but such a high labor cost is not. Our labor costs at Luther last year were 20 percent, which I think is still too high. I'm sure I can shave it down to 18 percent.

A year ago, before the new program went into effect at Luther, there were 65 full-time people employed in the food service. This was a ratio of one full-time employee to each 30 students served. This isn't considered low by today's standards. The average among host-operated food services in educational institutions is nearly 25 to 1.

This "before" staff was hopelessly inefficient and badly paid. Not one of them could qualify as a second cook.

Today at Luther there are 30 full-time employees in the food service operation. This is a ratio of one full-time employee to 68 students served. Both last year and the year before, the part-time student payroll was constant at $30,000 a year.

Our reduction in labor costs is only partly due to the obvious labor-saving nature of convenience foods. Some of the savings came from improved quality of labor. Before, my staff was so large that I could not afford to pay a competitive salary for a truly competent kitchen professional. Today there are two young, capable chefs in the kitchen. One year ago there were no first line supervisors. Today there are nine.

In instituting the convenience program at Luther College, we spent not one cent on additional kitchen equipment. We had, and still have, just 625 cu. ft. of freezer capacity—less than one third of a cubic foot per student served. We have one stack oven of three compartments and two small, rotating ovens. We have three grills and four fry kettles. Two steam pressure cookers complete the preparation equipment in our kitchen.

Before I tried out the program at Luther, everyone told me that I would have to increase the freezer space. Nothing could be more wrong. I actually need less capacity than I do with conventional foods. Many incoming shipments don't even go directly into the cooler for defrosting. We do the defrosting two days in advance of their use.

Our present purveyor (Hormel) is situated 80 miles from the Luther campus. You might think that this would be a highly adverse situation. It would be if we were buying from them in small quantities, but we aren't. We have embraced the one-source purveyor concept.

A year ago there were 23 purveyors calling regularly on us, supplying food items. Nine more called on us irregularly, from whom we purchased such items as paper goods, detergents, ceramic ware, silverware, etc. Today there are two suppliers from whom we purchase everything—Hormel and Hoxie Institutional Wholesale Foods. We will eventually purchase all Hormel products, including fresh meats, through Hoxie.

A year ago the flow of incoming shipments into our kitchen was almost ceaseless. Today we get five shipments a week—two from Hormel and three from Hoxie.

Certainly the many outstanding results of the convenience food program has assured its continued use at Luther College.

It has long since become a truism in American management that small business cannot give the kind of service that it must in order to compete in today's highly-competitive system. It would therefore seem to be a logical consequence that food preparation be assigned into the purveyor's kitchens where superior capability is feasible without an economic burden.

16

CONVENIENCE FOODS: A DISSENTING VOICE

Fred G. Young

Letter to the Editor

I would like to voice my objections to the feature stories now being circulated in trade magazines about convenience foods and the savings they can produce.

I am the food director for a large boarding and day school in College Park, Ga., just south of Atlanta. We have an enrollment of over 1,000 plus faculty and other employees. The school is Woodward Academy, formerly Georgia Military Academy. I have been food director here for nine years. I read Institutions magazine regularly and enjoy it very much. My total experience with food is 23 years.

I will get right to the point. In the March, 1969 issue of your magazine, Mr. L. E. Price concludes his article on convenience or prepared foods. He seems to be quite sure he is both saving money and satisfying his students. I hope to point out here that I doubt that he is doing either.

1. The $.63 average per meal food cost is not a good average meal cost. The truth is, there is not a precooked frozen entree on the market that any qualified food man can't prepare in his own kitchen at almost half the cost of frozen entrees. My average per meal cost is $.31. I have helped one of the largest food service companies in the world experiment with frozen and/or canned foods, and after two years of tests we can safely say that frozen entrees will increase your food cost around 30 percent, possibly more.

2. I would have to agree with Mr. Price when he says you are merely transfering the preparation from your kitchen to the purveyors when you switch to convenience foods. But I would hasten to add this: In my opinion you are either admitting that you cannot

---

From *Institutions Magazine*, June 1969. Reprinted by permission of the publisher.

organize your own employees or you would rather pay some other company to supervise preparation for you because you are not sure yourself of what you really want and don't know how it should be prepared in the first place.

3. Along this same line, Mr. Price says that before his convenience program was put into effect he had 65 inefficient employees on his staff. Why were they inefficient? Were they untrainable? If so, why did he keep them on his staff? Here again I ask, is Mr. Price really a food director with food experience or is he just an administrator? There is quite a difference.

Another statement he made causes me to have grave doubts: A year ago his staff was so large he couldn't pay a competitive salary, but now he has two young chefs. Something is fishy, organizationally or otherwise. As for the term two young chefs, I wonder if the term chef is not misused. I have worked with some of the best in the country and, as food men will tell you, no self-respecting chef would be caught dead opening a package of precooked sliced meat and gravy.

4. This all smells like a well-planned advertising campaign for convenience food companies, using Institutions Magazine as the bait and students and ignorant food service managers as the scape goats. If you need proof that most of his story (Mr. Price's) is misleading, here is one specific test conducted here in our kitchen:

Beef stew with vegetables prepared here: Total cost is $.19 for an 8-oz. serving (4 oz. meat and 4 oz. vegetables and gravy). This includes food and labor. Customer reactions were excellent.

Beef stew with vegetables frozen precooked, (2 oz. meat and 6 oz. vegetables and gravy). Cost is $.33. This must be opened, heated and served. The meat is usually tough and the potatoes are gray in appearance, the gravy is slimy. Customer reactions were complaints from a great majority of the students.

Difference in cost: Convenience entree costs $.13 more per serving for a very inferior quality. In the interest of honesty, the product tested was not manufactured by the same people Mr. Price used. However, it was a well-known brand and I find very little difference in the leading producers of frozen precooked foods. There are several claims they all make in common. Their claims sound exactly like Mr. Price's.

In closing I would like to make this challenge to Mr. Price and to the magazine itself: He can buy any entree he chooses to name, or any number of entrees, plus vegetables. My staff and I will prepare and serve the same thing at a lower cost with better quality. We will be glad to prove our own conventional type food is not only far ahead of precooked foods in quality but also far more economical. Our cost is $.31 per meal ... served, compared to Mr. Price's $.63 per meal. We also serve unlimited seconds on all items except solid meat, and we always serve seconds on all meats after everyone has gone through the serving line.

The thing most pathetic about misleading stories such as this is that many young and inexperienced managers in our profession are so naive and gullible they fall for this and in many cases they are ruined before they get started.

This is my main concern: the food profession. It has been exploited long enough. I am speaking for myself and other individuals of our profession. Let the food folks hear both sides of the story, please.

Fred G. Young
Food Director,
Woodward Academy
College Park, Ga.

Mr. Young has forcefully raised a number of critical questions about costs, administrative skills, quality, and professionalism that certainly rate airing. They are vital to the business, and Institutions is always happy to provide a forum for discussing them (e.g. February 1968 Institutions). The proper response to Mr. Young's point, of course, must come from operators—and there are many—who have undertaken convenience foods programs and are satisfied with them.

Institutions is prepared to give voice to any expression of opinion having a bearing on these questions.

We'd like to know what other readers thought of the article "The Convenience Food Experience at Luther College."

Ed.

17

PERSPECTIVE ON CHALLENGES IN AIRLINE FOOD SERVICE

Philip J. Parrott

The common approach is to refer to the problems of airline feeding. But those elements which affect the quality of our inflight food product are all pretty well defined; and, as such, I prefer to think of them—not as problems—but as challenges.

Ours is a very fluid, ever-changing operation. I suspect it may well be the most stimulating, the most entertaining, and the most enjoyable segment of both the food service and the airline industries.

My purpose here will be to define some of the elements, to relate them to the present state of the art, and to point out the directions from which, with the food technologist's help, we feel the ultimate solutions must come.

Problem: Kitchen Manpower

The operation of an airport kitchen is always a problem. Commuting and parking are difficult. Skilled, proud food-handlers probably would rather work closer to the end product, where they can see that the buyer appreciates their efforts. In a Flight Kitchen, the Chef wouldn't even know what plane his masterpiece would go on, who would eat it, who would serve it, or even whether it would be served at all.

And (airline) unions, insisting that seniority and qualification are synonymous, have forced the cooking job onto inept persons without sufficient pride in their trade to recognize their limitations.

Solution: More Convenience Foods

The solution has been to purchase factory-produced, pre-cooked, frozen foods of high quality and to turn our kitchens into assembly

Philip J. Parrott is Director of Food Service of Continental Airlines at Los Angeles International Airport.

From *Food Technology*, Vol. 23, December 1969, pp. 41ff. Reprinted by permission of the publisher.

points charged with the task of cleaning, storing, and assembling equipment together with prepared foods—on-site preparation being restricted to salads, appetizers, etc.

Today, nearly every major airline has taken, or is considering, this course. With our next generation of wide-bodied jumbo jets, all will do so.

Unfortunately, acceptance of the convenience food system by those who want to use it, and obviously the conversion of those who are fighting it, has been slowed by the lack of quality and consistency of product available.

Those of us who tout the system, piously praise its obvious virtues: quality, consistency, variety, and control. And, too often the product delivered fails to live up to the sample that generated the order.

In the airline then, instead of a small batch of badly prepared food, we can end up with thousands of portions at a number of locations, and with no available kitchen capacity or kitchen skills to provide a substitute.

In the last several years, more and better sources of product have been entering the field. But the demand is growing equally fast— perhaps even faster—as hotels, hospitals, and franchise units discover the potential of the system which just a few years ago a handful of us in the airlines had to ourselves. Where, in the past, we could create only sufficient demand to inspire a few specialty houses to enter the field, we are now a small part of the total market *competing for the services of the new producers.* And our standards of quality and variety are such that many sources would prefer to meet the less critical and less demanding requirements of hospitals, schools, etc.

With acceptance accelerating as it is, it is *not really a buyer's market,* and I don't see it becoming one in the near future. But I do believe that there will be new equipment, new technology, and new participation by reliable suppliers which should provide a gradual but constant product improvement. And the new conglomerates entering the field have the resources, both capital and technical, to provide the essential R&D.

Problem: Extreme Peak Requirements

Today, at any major catering point, it is common to have ten or more meal kitchen-departures within an hour. This means that every appetizer, every salad, every entree, every dinner roll, every piece of cheese, every dessert, every dish, every glass, and all of their containers must be ready at one time.

The personnel and space required to accomplish this within the limits of heat, cold, and sanitation standards defies the imagination of the food man from other sectors of our business.

Because most of our food people have come from outside, because our kitchen design consultants are primarily experienced in hotel and restaurant needs, and because of our phenomenal growth, nearly every existing flight kitchen is poorly planned and grossly inadequate.

Solutions: Several Are Possible

The solution here comes from several directions. The first is the elimination of large cooking staffs and large hot preparation areas by using frozen food.

The second is in re-design. Multi-unit caterers and airlines who have their own kitchens are developing their own design specialists, fully cognizant of our growth potential and special space and flow requirements, and conditioned to the planning requirements of convenience foods. Our kitchens are getting bigger and better.

The last is to use disposable equipment wherever the state of the art permits its use without seriously affecting quality. This should be the area where we will see the most advance in the next few years.

Problem: Equipment Distribution

One of the big differences between airline food service and other kinds is that every day, and sometimes several times a day, we ship our dinnerware from one city to another, usually to be handled at the other end by an unrelated organization. Even a small airline like Continental serves 13,000 meals per day, and every single meal on equipment that came in dirty from some other location.

Our problem here is the caliber of personnel handling our equipment, the capability of the caterer to accept it and wash it in time for his next need, and the tendency of his staff to board only enough to cater to the particular passenger load of the next flight.

Because of these problems, even though *every* flight is supposed to carry a full set of equipment, most do not. The result is a constant imbalance of equipment, with excesses where they're not needed and shortages where they are needed.

Solutions: Redistribution or Full Control

We at Continental try to cope with this problem by requiring weekly inventories from which we can issue redistribution instructions. The weakness of this method is that the same people who caused the problem are the ones who are taking the inventories and handling the redistribution. And they don't do any one job better than the others.

The final solution is not obvious. Some airlines, Continental as an example, minimize the problem by building their own facilities wherever they can justify them. Other airlines try to have the same caterer at all locations. This can help, but is possible only in a few geographical areas. And another approach is maximizing the use of disposables.

Quite often the cure is as bad as the disease. This is probably true because we fail properly to plan beyond the cure to handle its side effects. Certainly, this is true to some degree in our use of disposable equipment and frozen foods.

Problems: Warehousing and Freezer Space

With disposable equipment, we were so impressed with the elimination of dishwashing, labor, and replacement costs that we underestimated the logistical and warehousing problems that disposables create. Nor were we prepared for the geometric increase in trash facility and trash removal cost.

With frozen foods, too, logistics are complex. We hailed the cost saving virtues of eliminating cooking areas and cooks, without adequate planning for the freezer warehouses that the system requires.

Solution: Off-Airport Warehouses

The cure on the airports is not easy. Land is either costly or non-existent. And the employee problems of transportation, traffic, parking, etc., grow increasingly worse.

I believe the answer is in developing off-airport warehousing services designed to the specific needs of the airlines and offering frequent small quantity deliveries to the various kitchen assembly points.

Problems: Capabilities of Hostesses and of Heating Devices

Creating our end-product are our in-flight cooks. Some airlines call them stewardesses. No domestic airline fully faces up to the fact that they must be knowledgable enough to provide the T.L.C. that delicate foods and sauces require. Few of these girls, despite their many (mostly obvious) talents, come to us with any knowledge of the chemistry of food or the basic physics involved in transforming it from a chilled or frozen mass to the appetizing, attractive, and properly conditioned quality entree the passenger deserves—and expects.

We take these attractive young ladies and spend six weeks teaching them important elements of human behavior such as charm, poise, makeup, as well as other essentials that a flying crew must know. Then we turn them loose with an instrument of food torture called— depending on the airline—a convection oven, a quartz radiant oven, or even (on a very limited basis) a microwave oven. And to help them, we give them a great device called a variable thermostat.

I have yet to find a non-technical woman who understands the principles involved. Many a married man lives with a woman who thinks of the furnace thermostat as she would of an automobile gas pedal. In the cool mornings, she wants the house at 72° quickly, so she sets the thermostat at 90° to get the house warmer *faster*, and then proceeds to forget it until everyone is stifling.

And this is just what our girls do in flight. If we tell them 350°, they'll go to 500° settings to get hot "faster"; and then when everything is hot, they turn off the heat so the food will be properly hot when they need it. They've never heard of, nor do they comprehend, the residual heat that is there—and cooks and cooks and cooks. After all, they turned it off, didn't they?!

And the fact that your steak was steamed, your gravy dried out, your peas shriveled, and your noodles hard, was obviously the fault of the flight kitchen or caterer.

We cannot blame these young hostesses for all of these defects. We must blame the industry which has not kept pace with the ever-increasing requirements generated by competition.

For example, we use conventional, mechanical thermostats that easily lose calibration and, at best, are not accurate throughout the entire range. Even girls with aptitude and experience don't ever find the same conditions twice. This brings us to aircraft ovens and related equipment.

With the increasing need to eliminate flight kitchen labor, the trend—as I mentioned earlier—is to pre-cooked, frozen food. However, a factor which limits the airlines from using this to its fullest cost saving and quality enhancing potential is the inadequacy of existing aircraft ovens.

The first airline to use this convenience food system was Pan Am. The year was 1945. Convection ovens were used. Today, they are still the best available outside of the R&D labs, and they are not greatly improved over those that Pan Am used 24 years ago.

Solution: Better Heating Equipment

We cannot hope to change our girls, and why should we? Their primary role is not that of a technician. The only solution is to develop ovens that are idiot-proof, reliable, and capable of conditioning *all* types of food without damaging *any*.

Within the past year, several new approaches reached the developmental stage and promise to improve our capabilities either as replacement for, or as part of, a system in conjunction with convection.

1. A conduction heating system developed by the 3-M Company (St. Paul, Minn.) which utilizes a conductive coating on the casserole, making the casserole itself the oven. In this system, the box which we would call an oven serves only the purposes of container and as a means of supplying electric current to each casserole. By using dry ice, mechanical refrigeration, or cryogenics, this box could easily serve as a storage freezer up to the point of heating, with no effect on cooking time. 3-M has successfully demonstrated the heating of typical airline meals from zero to 190 degrees in 15 minutes.

2. A conduction oven developed by Dale Engineering (Sun Valley, Calif.) which promises performance comparable to 3-M, but which uses heated racks which conduct heat to the casserole. The obvious advantage here is that existing ceramic or other high-heat conducting casseroles can be used.

3. A radiant oven by Foster Refrigeration (Hudson, N.Y.), an adaptation to aircraft needs of the Foster Recon.

4. A microwave oven by Litton Industries' Atherton Division (Minneapolis, Minn.). After a disappointing prototype several years ago, Litton has now developed a system which promises to provide the reliability under difficult flight conditions which makes it practical. In all probability, this oven will be used by some airlines for special applications, and as a supplement to other units which will be needed to heat volume items.

5. A thermal container-tray developed by Aladdin Industries (Nashville, Tenn.) to help improve food quality and variety on the very short routes where any oven heating in flight is not possible. The problem here is that it reverses the trend and makes us heat the food on the ground, but it does allow us to provide convenience food even on short flights.

So—what's in the future?

As to type of heat—radiation, convection, conduction, or any combination of the three—I don't know. Regardless of the type of oven we use, some of the improvements we must have—and I believe we will have—are:

—Improved design to deliver heat evenly. Hot spots are still one of our greatest problems.

—Transistorized, push-button, pre-set temperature controls that will control temperatures to ±2°F in place of the ±50°F we now have.

—Computerized tailored time/temperature sequencing where our cook/hostess will just place a program into a slot.

—Effective elimination of residual heat so that cooked food can be held at ideal temperature but will not continue to cook.

—Modular construction for ease of quick component replacement at transit points, and a foolproof warning system that tells the crew when operation is abnormal and repair is required.

Food Technologists Help Meet the Challenge

The challenges created by the scope of our operation, the high cost of airline labor, and the shortage of basic kitchen skills has forced the airlines to pioneer in the use of convenience foods.

We are in large measure responsible for the sources of high quality now in existence. We are responsible, too, for much of the innovation in packaging. We have constantly raised our standards so that today our economy services are superior to what our deluxe services were twenty years ago.

And with your help in the future, we will develop the reliability of source, the control of quality, the desire for quality, the reliability of equipment, and the accuracy and simplicity of operation that will guarantee continuing improvement.

18

A NEW HOTEL MANAGEMENT SYSTEM

C. I. Sayles and H. A. MacLennan

Why a New Hotel Management System is Necessary

This new hotel management system, summarized from a more complete report which is available on request, is designed for a group of independent hotels using data processing in a computer center. It is a management system, not a data processing system. Before hotel operators can reap the real benefits of data processing, they need to plan for and approve of a new management system.

Data processing machines have a tremendous capacity to do repetitive jobs. They are also accurate when the "input" is accurate. Several methods to check for accuracy of input and to make instant corrections have been built into this new management system. They are set forth under Accuracy Control.

The work data processing machines are meant to do must be carefully designed into the management system, down to the smallest details. The reason is that once the system has been established, it is both expensive and time consuming to make modifications. Fortunately, hotel operators are accustomed to following standard systems of hotel accounting. Most of them already have well-established procedures for dealing with departmental details.

Now for the first time through data processing, it is possible to design a system of operation which meets the needs of management. A group of independent hotels can adopt this system and be serviced from a common computer system.

Accuracy Control

The management system has worked into it all possible checks for accuracy and the means for instant correction. In some cases it is

C. I. Sayles is Research Director and H. A. MacLennan is Senior Research Associate at the School of Hotel Administration, Cornell University, Ithaca, New York.
From the *Cornell H.R.A. Quarterly*, August 1966, pp. 34-48. Reprinted by permission.

possible to have the computer check for accuracy. This is fine. An example is a charge to the guest ledger. In the computer, the room number is the key, plus three significant letters from the guest's name. If the room number on the charge cannot be correctly located, the computer immediately rejects the charge and the cashier can check and correct the room number while the guest is still available.

A second method of checking for accuracy is to obtain a print-out from the computer as it accepts the data. If the print-out is read by a person other than the one who made the input, there is a good chance that any error will be detected. In the confirmation of a reservation, the computer prints out reservation details which are sent to the prospective guest. If the input is in error, the confirmation will also be in error and he will be requested to let the hotel know if such a mistake has been made.

A third check is to have the input operator examine the print-out. This is not as effective as the other methods, but fortunately there are not many cases where the system is dependent upon this check.

The efficiency created by these checks is reflected in payroll savings. Using present manual methods, first the error must be found, sometimes by trial balance; then the error must be corrected. Correction frequently entails changes in many figures and correspondence with guests. This in turn results in delayed reports, which are less effective than ones sent out on time.

This new management system provides many advantages and much better operating results, as noted below:

1. The area for misunderstandings with guests is greatly reduced because

—Reservation confirmations are produced by the computer. If the reservation is posted in error the confirmation is in error.

—Names, rates, addresses, etc., are all confirmed to the guest by the computer in writing at registration.

—Charges cannot be posted to wrong accounts and problems of correct room numbers, etc., can be solved while the guest is still available.

—Restaurant checks are fully printed (item as well as price), priced, totaled and tax computed and added by the computer.

—Banquet charges are recorded as they occur and a statement can be presented at the time of the banquet.

2. All manual bookkeeping including night audit is eliminated after the original input. This refers to revenue, accounts payable, accounts receivable, expenses including payroll and all balance sheet accounts.

3. The input for telephone revenue and expense is automated.

4. Credit controls are automatic.

5. Circuit clerks are eliminated.

6. Inventoried items can be controlled from purchase to sales.

7. Purchasing agents have valuable data for use in buying.

8. Sales records are sufficiently complete to be able to fully rate room clerks, waiters and other sales personnel.

9. Banquet and convention data is complete for use by sales department and the time for solicitation comes up automatically.

10. Data concerning reservations and walk-in sales is available to ensure full sale of rooms without overbooking.

11. Expense control data is automatic, complete and effective for food, beverages, payroll, fuel, electric consumption and various supplies.

12. All reports are timely, accurate and complete. Unsatisfactory conditions are highlighted for easy recognition.

13. All information is highly private.

14. All reservation replies, all bank checks (accounts payable and payroll), all statements of accounts receivable are produced, signed and mailed automatically.

15. Instead of department cashiers turning their daily receipts over to a general cashier they prepare them, in the amount given by the computer, as bank deposits and put them in a night deposit for the hotel's bank account.

16. Much filing of records and documents and all room and information racks are either automated or eliminated.

Reservations

Reservation data is keyed into the computer by means of a serial number. This number might indicate the month and day of arrival and a serial number for that day. Or, since the reservation input is by date of arrival, the serial number for the day may be sufficient. Each part of the reservation data would be keyed under that serial number, as is now done in the American Airlines system.* The serial number would give the total number of reservations that have been accepted or tentatively accepted for that day without reference to

---

*The organization of the data pertaining to the reservation is entered in a planned order or address. The city from which the guest comes is always located so that it is possible to ask the computer to list all reservations from that city. If one piece of reservation data has to be corrected or auded at a later time, it is possible to call up that one piece and correct or direct the addition to its proper field without destroying, changing or re-entering the whole reservation.

later cancellations. It does not represent the number of rooms committed.

There is some flexibility in the necessary timing of the input of data for reservations by letter or telegram and, as will be noted later, this is important. However, since it is essential to have an accurate report on commitments at least once a day, this flexibility is limited.

Reservation Requests

1. Requests Received by Letter. A reservation clerk would read the letter, note the essential data and put it into the computer. The reservation request would require one of several answers:

—Accepted without change.
—Modified and regarded as a confirmed reservation.
—Modified and subject to confirmation.
—Given a tentative acceptance subject to later ratification.
—Rejected.

There would be a form letter for each of these answers and the proper one would be produced by the computer. The reservation details as confirmed by the hotel would be printed by the computer in the reply. This reply would request the patron to inform the hotel if there should be any inaccuracy.

A tentative reservation acceptance may be given, subject to ratification later on. It is possible to key this information into the program so that on a later date it will come up automatically for re-consideration and possibly final disposition. This procedure would give prospective guests a valuable service, one presently neglected by most hotel front offices.

Reservation data is always automatically available when a serial number is used. The original request can be readily located, amended and re-confirmed. The confirmation letter is typed by the computer so that the patron sees what is actually in the reservation file. Data from a second letter requesting a change in the reservation can be flagged so that the original is located before the computer accepts the amended data. There is little chance for human error or for duplication of the reservation.

2. Requests Received by Telegram. The method of processing reservation requests received by telegram is essentially the same as that for letters, except that the confirmation can be produced in the Western Union office by the computer.

3. Requests Received from Captive Reservation Offices and Special Travel Agents. Many hotels now have leased wires to out-of-town reservation offices and even to high-producing travel agency offices. These leased wires can feed requests directly into the hotel's computer. And immediately the computer will return the confirmation, including its serial number, to the office requesting the reservation. Clerks in these offices will be trained in the same manner as reservation clerks in the hotel.

4. Requests Received from Other Travel Agents. All conditions of payments to travel agents can be automated. Advance payment with commission deducted or with instruction that the guest will pay, etc., will be entered into the computer as part of the reservation data. This represents an advantage over present procedures. When the guest checks out, the programed commission will be calculated by the computer and posted to expense; payment to the agent will be posted to accounts payable and to the agent's account. The agent's account will have a pre-assigned payment date so that the commission on this reservation and all other reservations by the same agent are automatically paid on the scheduled date. The amount will also be posted to "cash required" for that date.

Agents can be rated as to volume of business, quality of business, number of "no shows" or cancellations. They can be further rated in terms of the volume of business sent in slow periods as compared to capacity periods. New agents can be encouraged and old ones who are not sending expected volume of business can be solicited. The data for all such reports is automated and the report printed in the desired form.

5. Reservations Received by Telephone or Sold Over the Desk. At the time he is taking the reservation, the operator or clerk can also enter the relevant data into the system. Here it would be desirable to have a delayed input until all terms of the reservation are complete and confirmed. Since changes are frequently made during the call, the clerk endeavors to obtain full registration data from the patron and have it confirmed as correct before the computer is requested to accept the reservation. After accepting it, the computer produces a print-out which the clerk will read back to the person who is still on the phone. If time permits, a confirmation from the computer can be mailed. Human error is kept to a minimum.

(Note: All changes in reservation are so keyed that the computer will not accept the change until it has located the original and canceled it. This can be overridden if necessary.)

Reservation Service

This proposed reservation system makes it possible to flag reservations with minor requests, such as for a special room location or type of furnishing. On the morning of the day for arrival, these special requests can be automatically sorted out and printed. As rooms meeting each request become available they can be assigned. It is not advisable to tie up too many rooms in this way, for perhaps as many as 20 percent of these reservations may end up as "no shows."

Reservations Volume Control

While no exact mathematical control of reservations in terms of rooms which will finally be sold is ever possible, the number of rooms required for reservation commitments can be counted. It is also possible to figure the number of rooms that will be available by ascertaining when guests now in the hotel will check out. However, people are unpredictable. Some leave early, others overstay, and there are varying numbers of "no shows." Since "no shows" cannot be identified in advance, the limit on the number of reservations to be accepted can only be an estimate.

The volume of reservations to be accepted can be controlled up to a certain period (generally the day of arrival) by the number of reservations in the file, which are counted by serial numbers for that day. Where this control is not good enough, a finer control can be applied, as will be described later. In any event, the number of reservations to be accepted on a given day can be established in the computer, and this number can be varied as desired for individual days. When the serial number of a reservation exceeds the set number, the computer does not accept the data and gives a signal. The reservation manager can override the stop, either by raising the control number or by introducing the finer control described below.

Reservation cancellations, "no shows," walk-in business and all other factors affecting rooms volume follow reasonably fixed patterns. In the past, certain rough formulas have been used to control overbooking, so that all reservations are honored without there being vacant rooms on nights when business has been refused. These formulas can now be more complete and thus more effective. On the day of arrival—when the demand for rooms is greater than the hotel's capacity—status reports of vacant rooms, reservations still to be picked up, expected check outs, etc., can be had instantaneously and as frequently as needed. The office manager can thus control the acceptance of walk-in business to assure a full house and still honor all reservations.

Comments

1. Note that all confirmations come from the computer. This prevents errors. The prospective guest is given the data that is in the reservation file, not something that a clerk thinks he put in the file.

2. All confirmations are machine produced (probably in the computer center if so desired), thus eliminating typing and clerical staff for this function.

3. Many reservations are handled without any staff action being required in the hotel.

4. Agency accounts and the record of their activity on behalf of the hotel are accurate and timely. Payments to them are automated requiring no staff in the hotel.

5. During sell out periods the hotel's obligations for space can be checked every hour if necessary and the information is accurate.

6. Danger signals related to overbooking can be automatic.

7. The danger of vacant rooms on sold-out nights is greatly reduced.

8. Past experience can be analyzed automatically for future guidance.

9. Repeated "no shows" can be identified. If so desired, letters can be addressed to them.

Registrations

Walk-ins may register even when there is a full house. People whose reservations are tentatively accepted are alerted to conditions but are not denied an opportunity to register and talk to the room clerk. If no vacant rooms become available, the hotel has the opportunity to send the prospective guest a "regret" letter and invite him to send in his next request for reservation. The input operator puts the data from the registration form into the computer so that the walk-in is essentially the same as an unconfirmed reservation. All persons desiring rooms have complete registration data in the computer by the time they get to the room clerk as follows:

Patrons with reservations, including "walk-ins," are served as follows. If there is no line up, the room clerk can carry out the entire procedure. This will upgrade the room clerk, as it gives him access to an input device and the ability to enter alpha as well as numeric data into the computer. During busy periods, the room clerk uses only numeric data, as a reservation expediter does the rest.

When many guests are waiting to be assigned rooms, all guests form a single line. One or more expediters will serve this line in the

manner of airlines at busy terminals. The expediter has the means
and the ability to put data into the computer. First, she (a smartly
uniformed young lady) finds if the guest has made a reservation. If
so, the expediter requests a print-out. Reservation data is obtained
by using the serial number on the guest's confirmation. If the
number is not available, the reservation data can be located by using
the guest's name. Once the data is obtained, the serial number is
available for all further processing.

The computer print-out is a sheet divided by perforation. The top
of the sheet is a registration form with all available registration data,
including the serial number. The bottom is a memorandum of the
additional data required for the assignment of a room, and lists the
guest's name and the serial number of the reservation. The expediter
asks the guest to sign the registration form, make any corrections and
fill in any missing data. When this is done, she separates the stub
from the registration form and asks the guest to hand the stub to the
room clerk. Any additional registration data or any corrections are
put into the computer. Handwriting of any additional data on the
stub is good enough.

The guest goes to the first room clerk who is free (there is no need
to be held up behind a guest with reservation problems) and gives the
memorandum stub to the clerk, who then negotiates for the room. If
the expediter is not on duty, one clerk can serve as both expediter
and room clerk.

Every room in the hotel has a tab card, comparable to the room
sale cards now used in most hotels, with all necessary room data both
punched into it and interpreted on it. This includes rates—single,
double, triple; special rates for clergy; and other categories as well as
complimentary. There is a means of overriding these rates and establishing others.

When arrangements are complete, the clerk inserts the room-sale
tab card into a reader, enters the reservation serial number, and
activates the input. This act transfers data from the reservations file
—closing it out—and opens an account with full essential data in the
guest ledger. If there is a special rate or the room is complimentary,
the clerk puts this information into the computer before activating
the input. The computer establishes the proper rate, number of
guests in the room, and the computer's address (key code) to the
account, which is based on the room number and significant letters
of the registrant's name.

An immediate print-out is handed to the guest, who checks all
data, rate, spelling of the name, address, credit card, company affilia-

tion, check-out date, etc., before he leaves the desk. Mistakes and misunderstandings can be immediately corrected. A carbon copy of the name and room number only is given to the bell boy for rooming. The registration form is attached to the room-sale card (they are both the same size) by a paper clip or other suitable means.

The guest's name and other data are correct, are in all information files, and an account is opened before the guest leaves the desk. Advance payments or charges are immediately and automatically posted to the account.

There are no room or information racks. All information is obtained directly from the computer. It can be searched for alternative spelling and confirming data for identification. Telephone operators get their own information, thus eliminating circuit operators (and also eliminating much human error).

The status of room availability and reservation commitments is always up to date. Information can be made available as to people with reservations but not yet registered and also as to those who have checked out.

If for any reason there is no room assignment after a person has registered, the reason is noted in the computer and the reservation is closed out. In all cases the room clerk is identified with the sale or the non-sale, which can prove useful in sales analysis.

Room Revenue

The computer calculates and records the difference, if any, between the actual rate and the regular rate.

At a proper time at night the computer posts the room revenue, and the desired reports are made. It is not necessary to list rooms with regular rates. For these rooms, the computer merely counts the people and the revenue and prints the totals. Next follows a listing of all other occupied rooms with the details of special rates: the number of people, the revenue, the reasons for and the amount of the discount and the identity of the room clerk who handled the registration. At the end of this room revenue report is a summary which includes each classification of special rates, plus the total discount by that classification and also the total of discounts given by each room clerk. The computer then totals all vacant rooms at the single rate. No night audit of room revenue is required. It will be possible to compare actual revenue against the potential revenue.

Details will be given later concerning a possible automatic credit control on all accounts. Here it is sufficient to mention that the amounts of the outstanding accounts, the type of charges, and the timing (all of which is excellent information for credit control) can be automatically supervised for all accounts. Thus, the credit department can be kept alert to accounts needing close supervision.

Most hotels have a policy that, under certain conditions, when a guest wants a room at a certain rate and none is available, he is given one with a higher rate at the rate he requested. Clerks frequently follow this procedure, making little effort to sell the guest on the value of the higher rate room. Salesmanship is missing. This new management system makes available a frequent measure of the extent of salesmanship practiced by room clerks.

The control and sales data which can be automatically obtained from the computer system will not be fully described at this point. Besides the usual room averages, the following data can be obtained automatically and accurately, on regular schedule or by special arrangement with the computer center:

1. A list of people who wanted to stay at the hotel and did not get in.
2. An accurate evaluation of a room clerk can be based on
    (a) his accomplishments in obtaining high average room rates;
    (b) the sale of problem rooms;
    (c) the number and amount of special rates by category;
    (d) the number of failures to make a sale and reasons;
    (e) the number of registrations handled.
3. An analysis of the acceptability of rooms of various types by reference to the number sold in relation to the number available, thus permitting intelligent
    (a) adjustment of rates to keep the hotel in balance,
    (b) changes or improvements in facilities of each type of room.
Note: There is a tremendous variation in the opinion of management as to the acceptability of studio rooms.
4. Guest history.
5. Geographical analysis.
6. Analysis of special rates for possible adjustments.
7. Analysis of travel agents as to
    (a) the volume of business they generate;
    (b) the average rate of rooms sold by them;
    (c) the number of rooms they sell
        (1) in dull periods,
        (2) under sold out conditions.

Food Sales and Settlements

It appears possible, by slight modifications in present procedures, to design an operating system for food sales, service and settlement

that will fit all restaurants in the hotel except small island operations
—such as a coffee counter—and banquets. These two will be dealt
with separately. Other modifications will be based upon individual
management decisions as to the need for certain controls.

Restaurants, Including Coffee Shops

The system of operation can best be outlined by following, step-
by-step, the service to a dining room guest:

1. When a guest is seated at a table, the waiter takes the order
(fully or up to the entree, as is desired) on a memo pad.
2. The waiter then requests a restaurant check from the system.
To get this check he inserts his badge identification. The check (a tab
card) is then issued and charged to the waiter. A serial number is
punched in it. The meal period will be on record as will the dining
room identification.
3. The waiter puts the check into an input device and indicates to
the computer the items he has on his memo card. These are all identified by menu item numbers. When he activates the input all items,
or those which may be selected by management, are printed on a
stub which the waiter gives to the kitchen station in return for the
food.
4. At the same time, the names and prices of all items are printed
on the restaurant check and the data is filed in the computer as a
charge against the waiter. These procedures are followed until the
meal is fully served.
5. As soon as the meal is completely served (the waiter will not
await a summons from the guest), the waiter will return the check to
the computer which totals it, calculates and enters the tax and
again totals. If, after a check has been finally totaled, the guest
wishes more service, a new check is used.
6. The guest may add a tip to the check. The waiter will return
the check to the computer and punch the tip key and amount. The
system will print the tip on the check, will add it in and give a new
total, and will throw off a stub for the waiter. It will total his tips for
the meal, and settlement with him can be as desired by management.
Checks will either be spot checked or fully checked to see that the
waiters enter the tip amounts authorized by the guests.
7. After the check has been finally totaled it may be
    (a) paid in cash,
    (b) charged to a room,
    (c) charged to city ledger.

The waiter will make sure that the instruction is clear, since up to this point the amount of the check is charged to him. Unfortunately most hotels do not require the guest to have identification or a serial number for city ledger accounts.

8. The waiter, with priority over all other functions, will take the check to the settlement station where

(a) Cash is taken by the cashier and the payment is recorded in the computer. The amount of the payment is taken from the computer. Since the amount on this check is now charged against the cashier, it is his responsibility to see that the waiter pays him the correct amount. As the cashier records the payment, the computer issues a receipt for the waiter.

(b) If it is a guest ledger charge, the cashier enters the check and and addresses it to the proper account. If there is no account or if the room number given by the guest is wrong, the computer rejects the check while the guest is still available for further consultation. If the guest ledger address is correct, the amount of the charge is taken from the computer, not from the check. The computer produces a receipt for the waiter and the responsibility for the amount passes from him to the guest ledger.

(c) The procedure for a city ledger charge is the same, except that the responsibility for the amount passes from the waiter to the city ledger.

9. These transactions are given high priority so that the amount can be properly settled before the guest gets too far away from the dining room. In case of rejection for lack of proper account address, the guest is still available to make corrections. If the guest is not on hand, a supervisor will authorize a charge to a suspense account. The burden of proper address being placed on him, the waiter will take care to see that the guest has given proper identification. It is to be noted that the computer can give periodical reports on which waiters are lax in this operation. Since in the present set-up guest identification may cause trouble with as many as one charge in seven or eight, this new system warrants adoption even though there may still be some remaining problems.

10. Now and then waiters make errors while entering items on checks. Also guests may return unsatisfactory items or request changes. In such cases the original item is cancelled and the new is entered. The cancelled item is not lost sight of, however—it is recorded as such and the waiter's identity is retained. An analysis of these "correction" items can be very useful in control of the waiter and of the acceptability of food items to the guests, etc.

11. At the end of his watch the cashier asks the computer how much he owes, and he counts out of his bank this amount and makes a bank deposit as described next. If he has made a mistake, it is reflected in the amount of money left in his bank. It is not likely that the mistake, for which he is held responsible, will be in his favor.

12. This system makes it possible to greatly simplify the functions of the general cashier. All obligations of all cashiers, whether from front office, restaurants, bars, newsstands, etc., are recorded in the computer; and at the end of each watch the cashier counts out of the bank the amount the computer tells him he owes, and makes a bank deposit of this as mentioned above. The general cashier does exactly the same thing but his amount may be a negative one, i.e. he may have paid out more money than he took in. All cashiers handle their deposits in the same manner as night deposits in a commercial bank. The hotel's bank has established the necessary facilities *in the hotel*. The following morning an employee of the bank, on behalf of the bank for the hotel account, cleans out this night deposit. All cashiers with a minus deposit are reimbursed.

To Summarize

The waiter cannot get major food items without giving the kitchen a stub, which provides one side of the food-cost control described later. Once the amount is on the check there is documented responsibility throughout. Missing checks are the responsibility of the waiter, who must either have the check or the receipt. The receipt can only come from the computer and then only if the amount is charged to a cashier or to an identified account. If the check is missing, full details of items on that check are available from the system.

Tips are printed on a waiter's receipt so that he has an accurate record of what is coming to him. Tip amounts also are detailed in the computer by the waiter and at the end of the watch the machine can produce the total when the waiter's badge identification is used. When the cashier pays out tips, he gets an automatic machine-produced receipt. The waiter's badge identification is the only means of getting this amount during the meal period. This procedure keeps accounts for these gratuities and relieves the hotel from certain reports to the Internal Revenue Service.

Banquets

When a banquet or a convention is booked, an account is opened in the computer. All charges are entered against the account as soon as they occur. To illustrate, assume the hotel has bought flowers for

$100 and will charge the association $150. The following procedures will take place. The invoice for the flowers is approved by the banquet department which makes out a sales slip for $150. This is sent to the central input station which records the $150 sale to revenue and processes the invoice ($100) to expense, accounts payable (posting to the proper florist), cash required, etc. These postings will be held in suspense accounts until the date of the banquet.

On the day of the banquet, these and all other postings for the function are processed to operating accounts before the representative of the function leaves the hotel. Substitute invoices can be used where necessary. Food, beverage and payroll costs are all processed by the regular operating procedures. Guests should be given a printed statement of their accounts in full before they leave the hotel and duplicate statements can be mailed the next day. All revenue and all expense is posted on the day of the event. If it is a convention, daily postings can be made and full current statements can be given daily to the convention officers. Data processing and proper efforts by the banquet and convention departments can produce immediate billing and thus avoid misunderstanding and delay in collecting accounts receivable.

Small Island Operations (Coffee Counter, etc.)

These small operations would function much as they presently do on a cash register basis with accurate records of issues and payroll. The totals would be entered daily into the over-all computer system. The detail in the expenses would depend upon the operation's volume.

Beverage Sales

In restaurants on restaurant checks. Orders for drinks would be handled by the waiter in the same manner as the food items on the check. When the waiter put the drink on the check, the computer would produce a stub which the waiter gives the service bar in return for the drink. The bartender now has credit for the drink, which permits proper control in the service bar. The waiter has the drink charged against him and he effects settlement in the same manner as for the food items.

In cocktail lounges. This is a lounge where waiters take orders, have them filled by a bartender, serve them and collect from the guest. The creation of the check and the print-out for the bartender are the same as in a dining room. Settlement follows the same procedure, except that since cash settlements are generally more numerous than charges, the waiter may prefer to hold his cash settlement to a more convenient time as long as charges are processed immediately. The need for immediate processing of charges is probably greater than in the food operation.

If the bartender also sells drinks over the bar, he can be given input and print-out devices so that he can operate in the same way as the waiter. Alternatively this operation can be controlled on a revenue basis, as described next under bars.

Bars. Probably the best control of sales in a bar is to issue all liquor to the bar at retail prices. Because drinks are mixed, a bartender should return from 108 percent to 110 percent of the theoretical revenue.

Banquets. Where banquet waiters are circulating through a banquet room taking orders, the control is the same as for a cocktail lounge.

Comment. Some hotels may prefer a more elaborate control, with the amount of each kind of liquor issued related to the number of drinks sold in which that liquor is an ingredient. This detail is readily available, but being more elaborate it will also be more costly.

Telephone

The telephone company will have direct input to the computer.

Local calls. These are posted immediately as they occur. The 20¢ service charge is posted to accounts receivable in the guest ledger and to revenue. The 5¢ which the hotel has to pay the telephone company is posted to accounts payable, to expense and to cash required. If it is of any advantage, all postings except accounts receivable can be tallied by the computer and posted automatically at the end of the day.

Long distance calls. We assume that the telephone company pays the hotel 15 percent commission and that the hotel makes a service charge varying from 15¢ on any call below 50¢, 20¢ on any call between 50¢ and a dollar, and so on with a maximum charge of $1. We assume also that there are taxes to be paid by the telephone company but charged to the hotel. These are included in the amount reported to the hotel as the cost of the call. It may be that the service charge is permitted only on calls within the state. This can be provided for in the computer.

The telephone company identifies the guest's name and room number, the number called (also probably the name if it is person to person) and a serial number for the charge. The computer adds the service charge to this, prints out all of this information and makes the following postings:

(a) to revenue—the full amount including service charge;

(b) to accounts receivable—the guest ledger account, same amount;

(c) to expense—the amount of the call as given by the telephone company, less 15 percent;

(d) to accounts payable—the amount posted to expense;

(e) to cash requirements—the amount posted to expense.

If more convenient, the computer can separately total the amounts in (a), (c), (d) and (e) and post them automatically at the end of the day. The posting to accounts receivable will include the serial number.

Hotel charges. All hotels have local calls and long distance calls for their own account. These can be handled similarly to the guests' calls; however, when posted to the hotel account all service fees, mark up, etc., are eliminated. These calls are automatically charged to the proper department in the hotel.

City Ledger and Credit Controls

The computer would have a black list and a gray list. As guests register, they would be checked by the computer against these questionable credit lists before the computer would open their accounts in the guest ledger. Those on the black list would be requested to see the credit manager before being given a room. Those on the gray list would be roomed but the credit department would be immediately and automatically notified.

Certain safety factors would be programed so that all accounts would be machine supervised. There are many ways to detect bad risks. A guest is suspect when he charges everything including tips, newspapers, cigarettes. If a guest indulges in and charges all of the most expensive services, foods and particularly beverages, he may also be a poor credit risk. These and other trends indicating possible credit problems generally begin as soon as the guest reaches his room. Some can be detected by data processing and the credit department, automatically alerted to the situation, can take necessary steps. This machine supervision of accounts should greatly reduce exposure to losses.

The city ledger can be highly automated for the scheduling of billings. Certain collection procedures such as inserts, special letters, etc., can also be automated. Successful accounts receivable data processing systems in operation in other businesses can form a basis for the system best suited to the cooperating hotels.

It is interesting to note that other equipment can be used in connection with the computer, so that statements of accounts can come directly from the computer and be automatically processed ready for mailing, including the application of postage.

Check Outs

Guests can go to any window to check out. They can get a statement at one window and pay or settle the account at another. Supporting vouchers are required only for challenges and for this reason need not be kept at the cashier's station. Therefore, the check-out procedure will be greatly speeded. If there is no question as to the items on the account, settlement will be very rapid whether it is cash, city ledger or credit card.

The guest will ask for his statement, which is produced by identification of room number and letters of his name, obtained from his registration card. If the account is agreed to by the guest, settlement is recorded on a stub by the computer and given to him. The stub is not available until the cashier has actually processed the settlement. If it is cash, accounts receivable is credited with the payment (the amount coming from the computer, not the amount of money received from the guest), and the cash is charged against the cashier. The cashier must then be sure that he has collected the amount the computer told him was owing.

When the charge is to city ledger, the proper city ledger account must be located and the charge posted to it before the stub receipt for the guest is printed by the computer. Again the amount is taken from the computer. It may be advisable to transfer the account in detail rather than just the total.

If settlement is made by credit card, the cashier will process the form of the credit card company, recording on it the identification of the account as obtained from the computer. The cashier will then transfer the account with the same identification to the account of the credit card company. The detail and the total is transferred from one account in the computer to another in the computer and not by a manual input, thus eliminating transfer errors.

As previously noted, charges in the hotel bearing guests' signatures are probably on tab cards. These are serially numbered and can be filed in a convenient place after being machine-sorted by number. Other charges can be filed according to the source (laundry, valet, C.O.D., etc.) by the guest's serial number. All serial numbers appear on the guest folio.

As mentioned, these charge cards all can be filed in one convenient place under the supervision of an assistant manager or of another person qualified to answer questions as to guest accounts and to make adjustments. These charge cards should be located in an office near the cashier where the guest can sit comfortably and discuss the basis for the challenge. The original document can be quickly located and in most cases the guest can be shown his signature on it. The number of challenges should be only a fraction of those now made because the guest is given a copy of his room rate at registration and all other charges are identified by his room-name code, eliminating wrong postings.

Purchases, Inventory Control and Issues

Food Purchases for Direct Issue

Perishable foods are generally purchased for direct issue to the kitchen and are charged directly against food cost. (Further operation will be detailed under food cost control.)

The chef or steward prepares a market list of required items. This would be processed through the computer so that each item is as fully described as possible, concerning where it was previously purchased and at what price. The purchasing agent uses this market list to place orders. The purchase data consisting of identification of the purveyor, quantities, and prices from the purchase orders should be entered into the computer at the central input station.

When the supplies are delivered, the receiving clerk checks quantities (this is best when done without reference to invoices) and records them on a delivery record. The data from this record is entered into the computer again at the central input station. If it differs from the corresponding data of the purchase order, the computer reports the difference. These differences may be significant or of little importance. Depending upon the policy of the hotel, the differences are adjusted.

The computer, using the prices from the purchase order and the quantities from the receiving record, computes the extensions and totals and posts them to the purveyor's account as described elsewhere. A print-out should be made of this information and a copy sent to the purveyor as a receipt for the food and a verification of the price. Note that the invoice is not required—the purveyor should understand that this record is the one upon which payment to him will be made. Company policy may require reconciliation with the purveyor's invoice.

Since these items are direct charges to food cost, the quantities are direct issues for food control and are posted as such for the controlled items.

Food Purchasing for Inventory and Subsequent Issue

Each bin in the food stores has a pocket for tab cards. There is a tab card for each item in the inventory. Each can of peas has a tab card in the pocket. At a proper place in the tab card file is a re-purchase tab card with a record of recent prices obtained and the details of the last two purchases. It also has specifications for acceptable quality.

When requisitions are filled, a tab card is removed for each item taken from inventory. The tab cards are collected, run through a reader, the food cost posted to proper accounts and the quantities posted to the proper control accounts.

As supplies are issued, the tab cards are removed as noted above and in a predetermined order a repurchase tab card is exposed. These repurchase cards are run through the computer and from them a market list of inventoried items is prepared. This market list has full information as to the purveyor of the last order and the quantity and price. It gives other information as to normal quantity for purchase, the specifications, and the last competitive prices.

The purchasing agent provides the central input station with the data pertaining to orders placed and this is entered into the computer which prints out the purchase orders. Following the same procedure as defined for direct issue items, a receiving record is made. Again the quantities from the receiving record and the prices from the purchase orders make the final record of purchase. All purchase data is posted to accounts payable, the purveyor's account and the inventory accounts. Here again reference to invoices is unnecessary, and a copy of this purchase record should be sent to the purveyor.

Taking Physical Inventory

All tab cards but one are removed from the bin. The repurchase card is removed. These bin cards are then run through the computer, which makes allowance for the tab card left in the bin and then calculates the inventory as represented by these tab cards. This inventory is checked against the book inventory, of which details are in the computer.

Those taking the physical inventory count the number of items in the bin and note the number on the tab card which was left in the bin for this purpose. The number of items in the inventory is punched into this card, and all these cards are run through the computer. The total represents the physical inventory.

For beverages, the retail price must also be on the bin card so that, when issues are made, the cost is posted to expense and the retail price is posted to the control accounts.

Thus we have three inventory records: the computer inventory, the inventory as represented by the bin cards, and the physical inventory. Adjustments are made and new computer inventories established. Differences or losses are charged to proper expense accounts. By using the computer, physical inventory histories can be analyzed to find recurring losses by items and controls can be established accordingly.

There is nothing new in this system and it has been used in other industries. This same procedure can be used for all inventoried items including china, glass, silver, linen, kitchen utensils, supplies and beverages.

Food Cost Control

Dollar Control. There is nothing new in this. Generally the cost is related to revenue in terms of a percentage and this is the control figure. Sometimes, under manual operation, this is augmented by a cost figure by classification. The cost of items in each classification—such as meat, poultry, fish, vegetables, etc.—is totaled and the amount calculated in percentage to the total cost. This control by classification has always been of doubtful value and with the volume control related herein it is useless.

Volume Control. Items covering about 80 percent of the food cost can be controlled to a greater or lesser degree by volume as per example, so many pounds of rib beef are issued to the kitchen and so recorded in the food control account.

As previously described, the computer has the number of portions of roast beef sold. However, the portions were not all the same size, as a portion of roast beef in the coffee shop is smaller than one in the à la carte dining room. The largest size sold (à la carte) is considered a "standard portion"; the coffee shop portion is a fraction of a standard portion. The computer converts all portions to standard portions.

After a period of experience, during which an item has been subjected to careful supervision, a par is determined such as one pound of rib beef issued per standard portion sold or 1.5 pounds, whatever is agreed upon. This par is then established in the computer. All discrepancies are then readily available to management and corrective steps can be taken.

As will be described later, reports will be complete. Unsatisfactory conditions will be flagged for ready recognition.

It is to be noted that volume controls are based upon the relationship of food purchased (inventoried items would be volume issued) to portions sold. The cost side of this equation is reconciled exactly with purchases and the revenue side is reconciled exactly with sales. This is important. These controls have been attempted many times under manual operation and sooner or later rejected because of errors. With the computer the records should be accurate.

Since many foods are charged out to the kitchen and are not consumed for several days, there is a kitchen inventory. This inventory may fluctuate greatly from day to day but will average out to a reasonable constant. To have both the dollar and volume control reasonably reliable there will be a seven-day roll up. This means that in addition to the results of the single day there will be totals for seven days. As the new day results are added, the results of the oldest day are dropped. The average for seven days will neutralize the effect of fluctuations in the day to day kitchen inventories. Taking actual kitchen inventories is expensive, inaccurate and unnecessary.

Purchases and Accounts Payable

Supplies and services. The methods of handling invoices for foods and beverages have been outlined above. All other invoices are approved for payment and proper expense or inventory accounts are indicated on them. Where applicable proper control accounts should also be indicated. These are then sent to a central input station for entry.

Each purveyor has an account number in an account payable ledger. An account is opened where one is not already established. Payment of accounts is distributed throughout the month in a manner convenient to the hotel with reference to anticipated cash receipts and other payments such as taxes, interest, etc. Some companies such as the telephone company require more than one payment per month. Other accounts are subject to discounts if paid by a certain date. Some accounts should also have a cut-off date and only the charges prior to that date will be included in the next payment. All charges during the month are posted to the proper account payable.

Some accounts are subject to a payment discount and when the payment day arrives, the discount is automatically posted to revenue and deducted from the amount to be paid. A check is drawn for the net amount and fully prepared for mailing by the use of proper equipment.

Postings. There will be thousands of variations in the array of postings for purchases. First there is a posting to the proper accounts payable, of which there will be several hundred. Then there will be either an inventory or expense account posting. The expense account will be related to a department. Under the department is the type of expense, which frequently is broken down into classifications. There are also postings to various controls.

For simplification, each array of postings would be identified by number and each number would represent a fixed method of posting. The postings related to the number can be kept in machine memory or an instruction card can be cut for each and inserted in a reader each time. The instruction would include the department, the type of expense or balance sheet account, the classification under the type, and the proper controls, etc. This indicates many ramifications but it all can be arranged in chart form for easy use.

The input clerk would enter the purveyor's identification, the posting number (or instruction card) and the necessary amounts. The invoice—or more probably the purchase record—would be given a serial number produced by the computer and recorded against each posting. In the interest of accuracy there would be a print-out of the postings on the purchase record.

Transfers

A transfer of an asset or service from one department to another is handled in the same manner as a purchase, except that the "purveyor" is the department from which the supplies or service have been obtained. No "cash required" postings need to be made. Postings for transfers will also be made at the central input station.

Payroll

This is a general description of the payroll procedures.

Once an employee's contractual data is entered into the computer the whole payroll procedure is automated from the time he places his identification into a reader device until his payroll check and all other checks for payment to the government, etc., are in an envelope ready for mailing.

An employee is given a machine-readable identification, which identifies his department and gives other necessary information. If an employee does more than one job, he will have two such identifications, both of which will identify him but otherwise refer to the respective jobs. His records, payroll check, etc., would be completed for one person while the expense and control data would be properly distributed in terms of two jobs. Similarly if the employee changes jobs within the hotel during one tax period, his records will still be a single identification to him, but they will provide a separate distribution of expense and control.

Here again the expense of an employee will apply to one department, to one type of service in that department, and to one of several sub-classifications within that type. This breakdown of labor expense differs from purchases in that it is relatively established or fixed for each employee. This simplifies the procedure as each employee's time will be charged according to one plan which is in the computer.

Work schedules are established well in advance. These, however, can be changed in accordance with the hotel's needs provided that proper notice is given to the employee. Also there are extra workers who can regularly be requested to work or when desirable. The computer at a proper time will give the department head a list of these employees and the times they are scheduled to be on duty. The department head will relate this work schedule to anticipated business, make desirable changes, and then return it for entry into the computer as an authorized work schedule. A copy is given to the employee as his authority to work at that time. The timing of the advance notice is determined by the contract with the union.

Each department or area will have an input device in the form of a reader. When an employee reports for duty, he will place his identification in the reader which will record his arrival on the job. If the employee has not been authorized to work on that watch the computer will reject his entry. Similarly, when he leaves he will record his departure. Hotel payrolls generally are based upon time, and wage scales are based upon a week's work of five days with a fixed number of hours per day. If the time record shows a few minutes more or less than the standard day, the variation should be ignored by the computer in computing wages. However, if the employee is authorized to work overtime this authorization is recorded in the computer and a copy given to the employee. The extra time is calculated at the premium rate for the purpose of payment. If overtime has not been authorized the computer will not recognize any time over the employee's watch.

Full information pertaining to wage rate, premium wage rate, payroll deductions, taxes, etc., as required for the functions detailed below will be put into the computer. The computer then requires only a daily input of time worked, as described above, in order to complete full payroll records as indicated below. Payroll checks will be machine produced and an attached mailing machine will prepare them for distribution.

Since there are some days for which the employee is to be paid but on which he will not report for duty, the input in such cases would be made by the department head; and print-outs would be produced in sufficient quantities to be distributed to management, accounting and the personnel office. Such a print-out will record that the payroll expense was due to vacation, sick leave or other proper reason. Because good hotel accounting methods provide an accumulation or reserve for such payroll expense which is properly recorded to department, etc., these expenses are charged against such reserve.

The computer will not only calculate and prepare the payroll but will make all other associated postings.

The computer will perform the following as may be applicable:

1. Calculate the total earnings of the employee.
2. Calculate the take home pay of the employee.
3. By a proper printer produce a payroll check which will be placed in an envelope by an attached mailing machine. It is recommended that this be in the computer center.
4. Calculate all deductions that have been made from the employee's pay as indicated by the difference in the amounts of (1) and (2) above and post them to proper accounts.
5. Calculate all contributions required of the hotel in connection with the employee's pay and post them to proper accounts.
6. Add the items in (4) to the take home pay of the employee (as in (1) above) and post the total to proper expense and control accounts. By this means it will be possible to allocate the expense not only of the cash payroll and meals to the proper department but also accurately distribute the cost of the fringe benefits.
7. Post all vacation, sick leave and similar payroll expense to proper departments.
8. Post all accumulated obligations (accrued payroll and accounts payable) to all proper liability accounts.
9. Post all totals of obligations (accrued payroll and accounts payable) to cash requirement records.
10. Retain all necessary data in proper form so that reports can be made at year end for the employee's tax requirements.
11. Post necessary additional data in proper record form for payroll controls with particular reference to performance controls.

Cash Requirement Posting. Simultaneously with the posting of accounts, the cash requirements schedule will be posted. However, this can be as totals at the end of the day.

Payroll Control Posting. There are two kinds of payroll control: (1) percentage control, and (2) performance control.

Hotels are accustomed to the percentage controls, which require no further reference here. Performance controls have previously been used, but over a period of time such controls have always failed. It is not necessary to relate the causes here, but with data processing this control is practical, accurate, and extremely useful.

Performance Control

The unit of work paid for is related to the amount of work done, which when possible will be related to sales statistics such as occupied rooms, meals served, etc. The following is suggested as useful even though in some instances the relationship between the unit of work paid for and the control or amount of work done may be quite indirect, such as telephone employee days to the number of rooms occupied. Probably three-fourths or more of the payroll can be subjected meaningfully to valid relationships. Performance data is posted automatically.

Performance control must be reconciled to the total payroll. For example: maids, floor housekeepers and housemen may be controlled as such, but in addition there must be a control on all other housekeeping employees and the over-all total reconciled with the payroll expense. While the number of occupied rooms per maid day is controlled as are housemen, etc., there must be a further control of number of occupied rooms per employee day, counting every person on the housekeeper's payroll. Unless the entire staff is controlled, department heads have a way of switching employees from the controlled classifications to the uncontrolled.

Where there is premium pay for overtime, the premium is not recognized in the performance control data. If an employee works an extra day and obtains a day and one-half's pay, only one day is included in the statistics for the performance control. The performance control should record only the persons who actually worked. However, in order to reconcile with the total payroll, employees paid for that day who are on vacation, sick leave or otherwise must also be accounted for.

Where possible, a day might well be the effective unit of work paid for. Even when some employees have an hourly rate it may be better to convert this to a day or fraction of a day. Ordinarily, if an employee reports for work he is given a full day's work. The relationship will be the number of occupied rooms per employee day, etc. If 10 maids each work a full day when there are 150 occupied rooms, the report would show 15 rooms per maid day.

Seven-Day Roll Up. This procedure is described under Food Cost Control and will be used in payroll performance control as well as in percentage control.

Overtime or Premium Pay. This is always a problem in hotels and many department heads are the cause of the problem. For various reasons they may want to give some employees an advantage. By data processing a complete and detailed report can be made available to management so that the amount of premium pay to each employee over a certain time is known.

Central Input Station

Reference has been made to a central input station. It will be further noted that there is no input other than that necessary for check-outs by front office cashiers. They are then free to cash checks, make change and check out guests. When a room is changed, or one person is added or subtracted from a room or any other similar change is made, the record in the computer is changed by the room clerk and there is a new print-out which is given to the guest so that he can verify the new arrangement. There is nothing for the cashier to do other than as noted above.

If an item on an account is questioned the guest is referred to another service, probably the credit department or an assistant manager. All vouchers are filed away from the cashier first by source and then by serial number. (It may be that all vouchers will be tab cards and if so they can be sorted automatically for filing.) Since the serial number is on the front office folio, reference to original signed vouchers is speedy and convenient. The long delays at check out will be discontinued. Guests will have complete freedom to go to any window for check out as all cashiers will have access to all accounts. Moreover, all cashiers can accept payment so that there is no need for a guest to go to two windows or to line up at a window where another guest is having problems.

All charges to both the guest ledger and the city ledger are either:

1. Direct from Source. Rooms, restaurant, beverage, telephone and probably valet charges go directly from the department into the computer. Also check outs to be charged to city ledger are automatic—the computer is instructed to transfer the existing account to the proper account in the city ledger. Here there is a great advantage because if the proper account cannot be immediately located in the city ledger, further information can be had before the guest leaves the telephone or the cashier's window.

2. From a Central Input Station. This station is always open and probably should be part of a new department which would include the general cashier. All other postings—including invoices, laundry, petty cash, paid outs, adjustments (other than those for guests checking out), general ledger items, etc.—enter the system at this center.

It is interesting to note certain controls for accuracy are available with all postings. These along with revenue procedures previously described eliminate the need for night audits. We have shown the continuity of responsibility in food and beverage sales. Since the telephone company charges are entered by the telephone company, an audit is not necessary. The valet control is similar.

"Paid Outs" are different, however. Suppose a hotel tenant (such as a store that leases space) has a C.O.D. for a guest. This is taken to the clerk in the central input station, who enters the charge, and the computer produces an order on the general cashier who pays the tenant and gets a receipt. If the amount generated by the charge on the guest's account is too low, the tenant will not accept it. If it is too high and he accepts it, he would be only wasting his time and would be subject to criticism; for when the guest protests, there is a record of what the tenant received and he would have to return the excess. The general cashier has credit in the computer for the disbursement, the tenant is paid and the proper amount is charged on the right guest's account.

The same procedure applies to petty cash and other paid outs. Transactions of any kind are not valid or included in revenue, expense, or another account until entered into the computer, and then the amount in the computer is the correct one. Since by the same entry the obligation or responsibility is recorded and the computer is accurate, the computer automatically will make the input audit.

With laundry charges, the input machine produces a print-out of all charges posted and this is returned to the laundry. The revenue is not the amount of the charges sent to the input station by the laundry—but the charges listed in the print-out returned to the laundry. If any charges are missing, the laundry department arranges for correction. The original list of charges produced by the laundry is merely a memorandum similar in principle to that used by waiters. All guest ledger vouchers not put into the computer by direct access from the department are posted in the central input station and filed in the proper place in case of challenge.

All input stations have a three-way control. The input is made and the computer in turn immediately prints out the data it has accepted.

In most cases this is given to a person who has a direct interest in it and who is different from the person making the input. In other cases it will be checked and corrections made if necessary.

Automatic Postings

Rent Revenue is programmed to be posted automatically daily. If the rental contract is a percentage of sales, the amount is estimated for a month and then adjusted at the end of the month.

Interest Revenue is calculated on a daily basis and entered automatically each day.

Interest Charges are calculated and the amount is automatically posted daily until there is a change, when the new amount is programmed.

Depreciation Allowance is calculated. It can be a single amount or a series of postings (which is probably preferable), with one for each class of asset to be posted automatically each day. If a new depreciable asset is purchased, or an old one sold or discarded, one of the postings to be made is that of adjusting the depreciation allowance.

Allowance for Bad Debts is also automatic. At the end of the day's transactions the computer calculates the amount of outstanding accounts, which are overdue 30 days, 60 days, 90 days, and over, as well as outstanding checks, and applies the programmed percentages to each to produce a new allowance figure. As the amount varies, the difference is posted to profit or loss.

Profit and Loss and Balance Sheets. It is not necessary to describe further automatic postings. All items are handled through the computer so that it can automatically produce an accurate daily and cumulative profit and loss statement. Balance sheets are automatically available when requested. Since revenue as well as payroll, food cost, and all other major expense items are actual, these statements should vary from the actual only as may be caused by minor estimates such as revenue on a store where rental is based upon a percentage of sales.

Reports

All input and print-out stations in the hotel are peculiar to the department in which they are located. One print-out station designed for reports would be in the manager's office, probably located conveniently near to his secretary but so that access to it can be controlled.

Some hotels are careful to see that reports concerning their business are not available to outsiders. Be this as it may, the accounting office probably has fifty or more employees, many of whom are old and trusted, but others will be new and relatively unknown. Hours in the accounting department are irregular and it is a rare situation when the new employee doesn't have access to most information. Through this new computer system the only source of information is at the print-out station where reports are printed. Since this station can be under the direct control of the general manager there is a high degree of security. As the input is fragmentary, over-all results cannot be obtained from it.

The only need for print-outs in the computer center, other than those desired for convenience such as payroll checks, are the ones for monitoring the system. As these do not need to be complete runs, the data exposed is relatively meaningless to center personnel, who incidentally are fewer in number and higher in grade than many clerks in most accounting offices. At the same time there is a print-out for monitoring in the computer center there can be a print-out in the hotel, so that management is aware of all data thus exposed.

Balance Sheet. When the system is installed the data for the balance sheet is organized in the computer memory. The balance sheet does not need to be complete if management wants further security. Fixed amounts known only to management can be added or subtracted from machine totals to get the actual amounts.

Revenue, Expense, Profit or Loss and Control Reports. All data, the current day's transactions and the cumulative figures are in the computer before each department finishes work the previous day. Most revenue and settlement postings are concurrent with the transaction. Since auditing is continuous throughout the day as part of the input, there is no need for a night audit. Processing of postings other than those concurrent with the transaction are made at the input center and should always be current. There are also some automatic postings, such as interest expense. This means that all data for reports is available early in the morning. Therefore, reports can be awaiting management, or the manager can request them on arrival in his office.

It is to be noted that the data for reports is extensive and given in great detail. As management desires, however, reports can be brief or detailed. It is recommended that reports be fairly complete. There is a very effective aid for fast easy report reading, so that the maximum use can be made of them. This is described below.

Hotels today make fairly detailed forecasts of revenue and expenses. These will now be more accurate and complete. Developing them will be facilitated by data processing. When the forecast is complete the data will be put into the computer. As the daily statement is produced it will automatically compare the daily and cumulative results with the corresponding estimates. In addition to this comparison, it will be possible for the computer to flag all important discrepancies either in relation to the forecast or in terms of unsatisfactory conditions as determined by the controls.

Quantity and performance control pars will be established in the computer for food, beverage, supplies and payroll expense. Serious variations from the estimates and all failures to meet the pars will be highlighted in the printed statements by red arrows (flags). The manager scans the statement for arrows. When he finds one he has relatively complete data from the detailed statements which enables him to determine the cause of the deviation. It is not redundant to repeat that the reports covering full operation up to and including the previous day are available early in the morning; they are complete and accurate; and the data has been kept private.

All checks including payroll checks, checks in payment of accounts, all confirmations of reservations, all statements and collection letters should be automatically produced at the computer center and mailed or distributed from there. Since the functions from the print-out to the enclosing in envelopes and application of postage are automatic, there is still a high degree of privacy.

The staff in a computer center is limited in number, higher trained and well screened, which gives additional overall security.

Audit trail. As the data processing system is developed it will be necessary to see that there is a sufficient audit trail for government and other necessary purposes. This should not be difficult.

Staff Reductions

Night audit is eliminated.

The accounting office staff is very substantially reduced. It is suggested that one might like to reread this description of the system and note the almost complete lack of reference to any accounting office activity except at the central input station.

Room clerks do nothing but rent rooms and the supporting staff for reservations, mail, information, etc. is reduced in numbers.

Front office cashiers only cash checks, make changes and handle check outs. Almost all guest charges are sorted down for filing by data processing equipment.

Circuit operators are eliminated.

Food and beverage checkers are eliminated.

Timekeepers and paymasters are eliminated and as the personnel department will be properly located without any increase in staff it will supervise the back door. The personnel department will prepare payroll data to be put into the computer when an employee is hired, etc. The input will be at the center.

19

MANAGEMENT'S NEW ROLE

Peter F. Drucker

The major assumptions on which both the theory and the practice of management have been based these past 50 years are rapidly becoming inappropriate. A few of these assumptions are actually no longer valid and, in fact, are obsolete. Others, while still applicable, are fast becoming inadequate; they deal with what is increasingly the secondary, the subordinate, the exceptional, rather than the primary, the dominant, and the ruling function and reality of management.

To a considerable extent, the obsolescence and inadequacy of these assumed "verities" of management reflect management's own success. For management has been the success story par excellence of these last 50 years—more so even than science. But to an even greater extent, the traditional assumptions are being outmoded by independent—or at least only partially dependent—new developments in our society, in our economy, and in the world view of our age, especially in the industrialized countries. To a large extent, objective reality is changing around the manager's basic role—and fast.

Managers everywhere are very conscious of new concepts and new tools of management, of new concepts of organization, and of the "information revolution." These changes within management are indeed of great importance. But more important yet may be the changes in the basic realities and their impact on the fundamental assumptions underlying management as a theory and as a practice. The changes in managerial concepts and tools will force managers to change their behavior. The changes in concepts and tools mean a change in what a manager *does* and how he *does* it. The changes in

Peter F. Drucker is Professor of Management at the Graduate School of Business Administration of New York University. He specializes in business and economic policy and in top management organization.

"Management's New Role" from *Technology, Management & Society* by Peter F. Drucker. Copyright © 1969 by Peter F. Drucker. Reprinted by permission of Harper & Row, Publishers, Inc.

reality demand, however, a change in the manager's role. And a change in his basic role means a change in what a manager *is*.

In this article, I shall first briefly mention the traditional assumptions that most men of management—practitioners and theoreticians alike—still take for granted. Then I shall attempt to formulate different ones that correspond to the management realities of today.

The Old Assumptions . . .

In my considered judgment, there are five assumptions that may have formed the foundation of the theory and practice of management in the last half century. These assumptions deal with the scope, the task, the position, and the nature of management.

Of course, few practitioners of management have ever been conscious of them. Even the management scholars have, as a rule, rarely stated them explicitly. But both practitioners and theorists alike have accepted these assumptions, have indeed treated them as self-evident axioms, and have based their theories and actions on them.

Number One
Only business has "social responsibility."

This view derives directly from the belief—which is widely held, although not necessarily by business—that business is the one exceptional institution. According to this belief, the university or hospital is not assumed to have any social responsibility, primarily because of not being within the purview of the traditional vision. In other words, neither the university nor the hospital is seen at all as an "organization." Moreover, the traditional view of a social responsibility peculiar and confined to business derives from the premise that economic activity differs drastically from these other human activities.

Number Two
Entrepreneurship and innovation lie outside the management scope.

This assumption takes the view that the primary, and perhaps the only, task of management is to mobilize the energies of the business organization for the accomplishment of known and defined tasks.

To a large extent this assumption was a necessity during the last half century. The concern of the world of 1900 was the large and complex organization for production and distribution with which the traditional managerial systems, whether of the workshop or of the local store, could not cope.

Thus the invention of the steam locomotive was not what triggered concern with management. Rather, it was the emergence some 50 years later of the large railroad company, which could handle steam locomotives without much trouble, but was baffled by the problem of coordination and communication between people and by the problem of separation of their authorities and responsibilities.

But the focus on the *managerial* side of management—to the almost total neglect of entrepreneurship as a function of management—also reflects the reality of the economy in the half century since World War I. It was a period of high technological and entrepreneurial continuity—a period which required adaptation rather than innovation, and ability to do better rather than courage to do differently.

Number Three
It is management's task to make the manual worker productive.

The manual worker—skilled or unskilled—has been management's concern as a resource, as a cost center, and as a social and individual problem.

Thus to have made the manual worker productive is indeed the greatest achievement of management to date. Frederick Winslow Taylor's *Scientific Management* is often attacked these days (though mostly by people who have not read it). But it was his insistence on studying work that underlies the affluence of today's developed countries; it raised the productivity of manual work to the point where yesterday's laborer has become the semiskilled worker of today's mass production industries with a middle-class standard of living and guaranteed job or income security.

As late as World War II, the central concern was still the productivity and management of manual work; the central achievement of both the British and the American war economies was the mobilization, training, and management of production workers in large numbers. Even in the postwar period one major task—in all developed countries other than Great Britain—was the rapid conversion of immigrants from the farm into productive manual workers in industry. On this accomplishment—made possible only because of the scientific management which Taylor pioneered 70 years ago—largely rest the economic growth and performance of Japan, of Western Europe, and even of the United States.

Number Four

   Management is a "science" or at least a "discipline."

This assumption is based on two propositions. The first is that management is as independent of cultural values and individual beliefs as are the elementary operations of arithmetic, the laws of physics, or the stress tables of the engineer. The other is that all management is being practiced within one distinct national environment and embedded in one national culture, circumscribed by one legal code and part of one national economy.

These two propositions were as obvious to Taylor in the United States as they were to Fayol in France. Of all the early management authorities, only Rathenau in Germany seems to have doubted that management was a culture-free discipline—and no one listened to him. The human relations people attacked Taylor as "unscientific"; they did not attack Taylor's premise that there was an objective science of management. On the contrary, they proclaimed their findings to be "true" scientific psychology and grounded in the "nature of man." They refused even to take into account the findings of their own colleagues in the social sciences, the cultural anthropologists. Insofar as cultural factors were considered at all in the traditional assumptions about management, these were regarded as "obstacles."

Number Five

   Management is the result of economic development.

This assumption holds that management is a result rather than a cause, and a response to needs rather than a creator of opportunity.

Of course, this had been the historical experience of the West, but even in the West the traditional explanation of the emergence of management was largely myth. As the textbooks had it (and still largely have it), management came into being when the small business outgrew the owner who had done everything himself.

In reality, management evolved in enterprises that started big and could never have been anything but big—the railways in particular, but also the postal service, the steamship companies, the steel mills, and the department stores. To industries that could start small, management came very late; some of those (e.g., the textile mill or the bank) are still often run on the pattern of the "one boss" who does everything and who, at best, has "helpers."

I fully realize that I have oversimplified, but I do not believe that I have misrepresented our traditional assumptions. Nor do I believe that I am mistaken in thinking that these assumptions, in one form or another, still underlie both the theory and the practice of management, especially in the industrially developed nations.

. . . vs. the New Realities

Today we need quite different assumptions—more in keeping with today's realities than the assumptions on which theory and practice of management have been basing themselves these past 50 years.

Here, in this section of the article, I shall attempt to present corresponding new assumptions. These, too, are oversimplified—grossly so. They are far closer to the realities of our time, however.

Number One

All institutions, including business, are accountable for the "quality of life."

Because our society is rapidly becoming a society of organizations, all institutions will have to make fulfillment of basic social values, beliefs, and purposes a major objective of their continuing activities rather than a social responsibility that restrains or lies outside their primary functions. In the business enterprise, this means that attainment of the quality of life will increasingly have to be (a) considered a business opportunity and (b) converted by management into profitable business.

This will apply particularly to fulfillment of the individual. It will increasingly be the job of management to make the individual's values and aspirations redound to organizational energy and performance. It will simply not be good enough to be satisfied—as industrial relations and even human relations traditionally have been—with the absence of discontent.

Perhaps one way to dramatize this is to say that we will, within another 10 years, become far less concerned with *management* development (that is, adapting the individual to the demands of the organization), and far more with *organization* development (that is, adapting the company to the needs, aspirations, and potentials of individuals).

Number Two

Entrepreneurial innovation will become the very heart and core of management.

There is little doubt in my mind that entrepreneurial innovation will be as important to management in the future as the managerial function itself is currently. Indeed, it may be more important in the

years to come. Unlike the nineteenth century, however, entrepreneurial innovation will increasingly have to be carried out in, and
by, existing institutions, such as on-going businesses. It will, therefore, no longer be possible to consider it as lying outside management or even as being peripheral to management.

There is every reason to believe that the closing decades of the
twentieth century will see changes as rapid as those that charac-
terized the 50-odd years between 1860 and 1914, when a new major
invention, ushering in almost immediately a new major industry with
new big businesses, appeared on the scene every two to three years
on average.* Unlike the last century, however, these innovations of
ours will be as much social as technical—a metropolis, for instance, is
clearly as much of a challenge to the innovator today as the new
science of electricity was to the inventor of 1870. And also, unlike
the last century, innovation in this century will increasingly be based
on knowledge of all kinds rather than on science alone.

At the same time, innovation will increasingly have to be channeled in and through existing business, if only because the tax laws in
every developed country make the existing business the center of
capital accumulation. And innovation is capital-intensive, especially
in the two crucial phases of development and market introduction of
new products, new processes, or new services.

We will, therefore, increasingly have to learn to make existing
organizations capable of rapid and continuing innovation. How far
we are from this is shown by the fact that management still worries
about resistance to change. Existing organizations will have to learn
to reach out for change as an opportunity, will have to learn to resist
continuity.

Number Three
   It is management's task to make knowledge more productive.
The basic capital resource, the fundamental investment, and the
cost center of a developed economy all rest in the application of
knowledge—that is, in concepts, ideas, and theories, rather than in
manual skill or muscle.

Taylor put knowledge to work to make the manual worker productive. But Taylor himself never asked the question: What constitutes "productivity" with respect to the industrial engineer who
applies scientific management? As a result of Taylor's work, we can

---

*For documentation, see my recent book, *The Age of Discontinuity*, (New
York, Harper & Row, 1969).

answer what productivity is with respect to the manual worker. But we still cannot answer what productivity is with respect to the industrial engineer or to any other knowledge worker.

Surely, the measurements which give us productivity for the manual worker, such as the number of pieces turned out per hour or per dollar of wages, are quite irrelevant if applied to the knowledge worker. There are few things as useless and unproductive as the engineering department that with great dispatch, industry, and elegance turns out the drawings for an unsalable product. The productivity of the knowledge worker is primarily a matter not of quantity but of quality. We cannot even define it yet.

One thing is clear: to make knowledge productive will bring about changes in job structure, careers, and organizations as drastic as those which resulted in the factory from the application of scientific management to manual work. The entrance job will, above all, have to be changed drastically to enable the knowledge worker to become productive. For it is abundantly clear that knowledge cannot be productive unless the worker finds out who he himself is, what kind of work he is fitted for, and how he works best.

In other words, there can be no divorce of *planning* from *doing* in knowledge work. On the contrary, the knowledge worker must be able to plan himself. And this the present entrance jobs, by and large, do not make possible. They are based on the assumption—valid for manual work but quite inappropriate to knowledge work—that anyone can objectively determine the "one best way" for any kind of work. For knowledge work, this is simply not true. There may be one best way, but it is heavily conditioned by the individual and is not entirely determined by physical (or even mental) characteristics of the job. It is temperamental as well.

Number Four

Management will have to be considered as both a "science" and a "humanity."

There are management tools and techniques; there are management concepts and principles. There is a common language of management, and there may even be a universal discipline of management. Certainly, there is a worldwide generic function which we call "management," and which serves the same purpose in any and all developed society.

But management is also a culture and a system of values and beliefs. It is also the means through which a given society makes productive its own values and beliefs. Management may well be considered the bridge between a *civilization* which is rapidly becoming worldwide, and a *culture* which expresses divergent traditions, values, beliefs, and heritages. Management must become the instrument through which cultural diversity can be made to serve the common purposes of mankind.

At the same time, management increasingly is being practiced not within the confines of one national culture, law, or sovereignty but "multinationally." Indeed, management increasingly is becoming an institution—so far, the only one—of a genuine world economy.

Management, we now know, has to make productive the values, aspirations, and traditions of the individual, the community, and the society for a common productive purpose. If management does not succeed in putting to work the specific cultural heritage of a country and of a people, social and economic development cannot take place. This is, of course, the great lesson of Japan—and the fact that Japan a century ago put to work her own traditions of community and human values for the new ends of a modern industrial economy explains why Japan succeeded while every other non-Western country has so far failed.

As a science and a humanity, management is both a statement of findings that can be objectively tested and validated and a system of belief and experience.

At the same time, management—and here I mean business management alone, so far—is rapidly emerging as the one and only institution that is common and transcends the boundaries of the national state. The "multinational corporation" does not really exist so far. Rather, what we have, by and large, are businesses that are based on one country with one culture and, for the most part, one nationality, especially in top management. But it is also becoming clear that this is a transition phenomenon and that continuing development of the world economy both requires and leads to genuinely multinational companies, in which not only are production and sales multinational, but ownership and management as well—all the way from the top down.

Within the individual country, especially the developed country, business is rapidly losing its exceptional status as we recognize that it is the prototype of the typical (indeed, the universal) social form, the organized institution requiring management. Beyond the national boundary, however, business is rapidly acquiring the same exceptional status it no longer has within the individual developed country, is rapidly becoming the unique, the exceptional, the one institution that expresses the reality of a world economy and of a worldwide knowledge society.

Number Five

Economic and social development are the result of management.

It can be said without too much oversimplification that there are no underdeveloped countries. There are only *undermanaged* ones. Japan 100 years ago was an underdeveloped country by every material measurement. But it very quickly built up management of great competence, indeed of excellence. Within 25 years, Meiji Japan had become a developed country and indeed in some aspects, such as literacy, the most highly developed of all countries. We realize today that it is Meiji Japan, rather than eighteenth-century England—or even nineteenth-century Germany—which has to be the model of development for the underdeveloped world.

All our experience in economic development proves that management is the prime mover and that development is a consequence. Wherever we have only contributed the economic factors of production, especially capital, we have not achieved development. In the few cases where we have been able to generate management energies (e.g., in the Cauca Valley in Colombia), we have generated rapid development, which is a matter of human energies rather than of economic wealth. And the generation and direction of human energies is the task of management.

Conclusion

I submit that the new assumptions about management that I have discussed in this article are better guides to effective management in the developed countries today, let alone tomorrow, than the assumptions on which we have based our theories, as well as our practices, these last 50 years.

Not that we are going to abandon the old tasks. Obviously, we still have to manage the existing enterprise and create internal order and organization. We still have to manage the manual worker and make him productive. And no one who knows the reality of management is likely to assert that we know everything in these and similar areas that we need to know.

But the big jobs waiting for management today, the big tasks requiring both new theory and new practice, arise out of new realities and demand different assumptions and approaches.

More important even than the new tasks may be management's new role. Management is fast becoming the central resource of the developed countries and the basic need of the developing ones. From being the specific concern of one (i.e., the economic institutions of society), management and managers are becoming the generic, the distinctive, the constitutive organ of developed society. What management is and what managers do will therefore—and properly—increasingly become a matter of public concern rather than a matter for the "experts." Management will increasingly be concerned as much with the expression of basic beliefs and values as with the accomplishment of measurable results. It will increasingly stand for the quality of life of a society as much as for its standard of living.

There are many new tools of management whose use we will have to learn, and many new techniques. There are, as I have pointed out, a great many new and difficult tasks. But the most important change ahead for management is that increasingly the aspirations, the values, and indeed the very survival of society in the developed countries will come to depend on the performance, the competence, and the values of managers. The task of the next generation is to make productive for the individual, the community, and the society the new organized institutions of our new pluralism. And that is, above all, *management's new role.*

20

THE MANAGEMENT PROCESS IN 3-D

R. Alec Mackenzie

The chart of "The Management Process" begins with the three basic elements with which a manager deals: ideas, things, and people. Management of these three elements is directly related to conceptual thinking (of which planning is an essential part), administration, and leadership. Not surprisingly, two scholars have identified the first three types of managers required in organizations as the planner, the administrator, and the leader.[1]

Note the distinction between leader and manager. The terms should not be used interchangeably. While a good manager will often be a good leader, and vice versa, this is not necessarily the case. For example:

In World War II, General George Patton was known for his ability to lead and inspire men on the battlefield, but not for his conceptual abilities. In contrast, General Omar Bradley was known for his conceptual abilities, especially planning and managing a campaign, rather than for his leadership.

Similarly in industry, education, and government it is possible to have an outstanding manager who is not capable of leading people but who, if he recognizes this deficiency, will staff his organization to compensate for it. Alternatively, an entrepreneur may possess charismatic qualities as a leader, yet may lack the administrative capabilities required for overall effective management; and he too must staff to make up for the deficiency.

---

[1] See H. Igor Ansoff and R. G. Brandenburg, "The General Manager of the Future," *California Management Review*, Spring 1969, p. 61.

R. Alec Mackenzie is Vice President of the Presidents Association, Inc., an organization affiliated with the American Management Association. He is co-author with Ted W. Engstrom of *Managing Your Time*, Zondervan Publishing House, 1967.

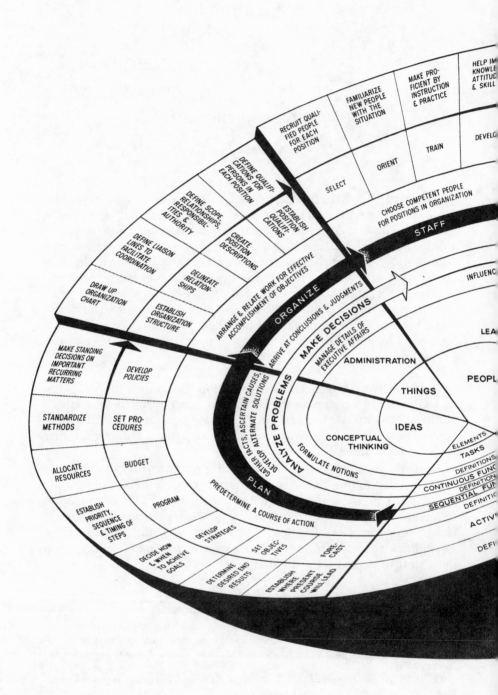

HELP IM...
KNOWLE...
ATTITUD...
& SKILL

DEVEL...

MAKE PRO-
FICIENT BY
INSTRUCTION
& PRACTICE

FAMILIARIZE
NEW PEOPLE
WITH THE
SITUATION

RECRUIT QUALI-
FIED PEOPLE
FOR EACH
POSITION

TRAIN

ORIENT

SELECT

DEFINE QUALI-
FICATIONS FOR
PERSONS IN
EACH POSITION

CHOOSE COMPETENT PEOPLE
FOR POSITIONS IN ORGANIZATION

DEFINE SCOPE,
RELATIONSHIPS,
RESPONSIBIL-
ITIES &
AUTHORITY

ESTABLISH
POSITION
QUALIFI-
CATIONS

STAFF

DEFINE LIAISON
LINES TO
FACILITATE
COORDINATION

CREATE
POSITION
DESCRIPTIONS

INFLUENC...

DRAW UP
ORGANIZATION
CHART

DELINEATE
RELATION-
SHIPS

ARRANGE & RELATE WORK FOR EFFECTIVE
ACCOMPLISHMENT OF OBJECTIVES

LEA...

ESTABLISH
ORGANIZATION
STRUCTURE

ORGANIZE

ARRIVE AT CONCLUSIONS & JUDGMENTS

MAKE STANDING
DECISIONS ON
IMPORTANT
RECURRING
MATTERS

DEVELOP
POLICIES

MAKE DECISIONS

MANAGE DETAILS OF
EXECUTIVE AFFAIRS

PEOPL...

ADMINISTRATION

ANALYZE PROBLEMS

GATHER FACTS, ASCERTAIN CAUSES,
DEVELOP ALTERNATE SOLUTIONS

THINGS

STANDARDIZE
METHODS

SET PRO-
CEDURES

IDEAS

ALLOCATE
RESOURCES

BUDGET

FORMULATE NOTIONS

CONCEPTUAL
THINKING

ELEMENTS

TASKS

ESTABLISH
PRIORITY,
SEQUENCE
& TIMING OF
STEPS

PROGRAM

PLAN

PREDETERMINE A COURSE OF ACTION

DEFINITIONS

CONTINUOUS FUNC...

DEFINITION...

SEQUENTIAL FUN...

DEFINITIO...

DECIDE HOW
& WHEN
TO ACHIEVE
GOALS

DEVELOP
STRATEGIES

SET
OBJEC-
TIVES

FORE-
CAST

ACTIV...

DETERMINE
DESIRED END
RESULTS

ESTABLISH
WHERE
PRESENT
COURSE
WILL LEAD

DEFI...

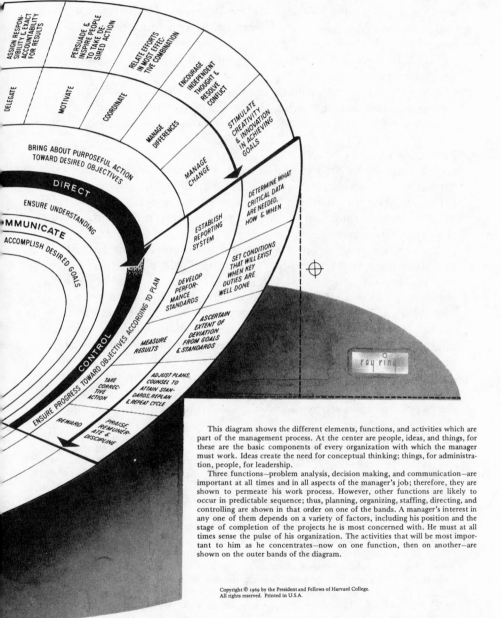

This diagram shows the different elements, functions, and activities which are part of the management process. At the center are people, ideas, and things, for these are the basic components of every organization with which the manager must work. Ideas create the need for conceptual thinking; things, for administration, people, for leadership.

Three functions—problem analysis, decision making, and communication—are important at all times and in all aspects of the manager's job; therefore, they are shown to permeate his work process. However, other functions are likely to occur in predictable sequence; thus, planning, organizing, staffing, directing, and controlling are shown in that order on one of the bands. A manager's interest in any one of them depends on a variety of factors, including his position and the stage of completion of the projects he is most concerned with. He must at all times sense the pulse of his organization. The activities that will be most important to him as he concentrates—now on one function, then on another—are shown on the outer bands of the diagram.

We are not dealing here with leadership in general. We are dealing with leadership as a *function of management*. Nor are we dealing with administration in general but, again, as a function of management.

The following definitions are suggested for clarity and simplicity:

—*Management:* achieving objectives through others.
—*Administration:* managing the details of executive affairs.
—*Leadership:* influencing people to accomplish desired objectives.

Functions Described

The functions noted in the diagram have been selected after careful study of the works of many leading writers and teachers.[2] While the authorities use different terms and widely varying classifications of functions, I find that there is far more agreement among them than the variations suggest.

Arrows are placed on the diagram to indicate that five of the functions generally tend to be "sequential." More specifically, in an undertaking one ought first to ask what the purpose or objective is which gives rise to the functions of *planning;* then comes the function of *organizing*—determining the way in which the work is to be broken down into manageable units; after that is *staffing*, selecting qualified people to do the work; next is *directing*, bringing about purposeful action toward desired objectives; finally, the function of *control* is the measurement of results against the plan, the rewarding of the people according to their performance, and the replanning of the work to make corrections—thus starting the cycle over again as the *process repeats itself.*

---

[2] The following studies were particularly helpful: Harold Koontz, *Toward a Unified Theory of Management* (New York, McGraw-Hill Book Company, 1964); Philip W. Shay, "The Theory and Practice of Management," Association of Consulting Management Engineers, 1967; Louis A. Allen, *The Management Profession* (New York, McGraw-Hill Book Company, 1964), a particularly useful analysis of managerial functions and activities; Ralph C. Davis, *Fundamentals of Top Management* (New York, Harper & Brothers, 1951); Harold F. Smiddy, "GE's Philosophy & Approach for Manager Development," General Management Series No. 174, American Management Association, 1955; George R. Terry, *Principles of Management* (Homewood, Illinois, Richard D. Irwin, Inc., 1956); William H. Newman, *Administrative Action* (Englewood Cliffs, N.J., Prentice-Hall, Inc., 1950); Lawrence A. Appley, *Values in Management* (New York, American Management Association, 1969); Ordway Tead, *Administration: Its Purpose and Performance* (New York, Harper & Brothers, 1959); Peter F. Drucker, *The Practice of Management* (New York, Harper & Row, 1954).

Three functions—analyzing problems, making decisions, and communicating—are called "general" or "continuous" functions because they occur throughout the management process rather than in any particular sequence. For example, many decisions will be made throughout the planning process as well as during the organizing, directing, and controlling processes. Equally, there must be communication for many of the functions and activities to be effective. And the active manager will be employing problem analysis throughout all of the sequential functions of management.

In actual practice, of course, the various functions and activities tend to merge. While selecting a top manager, for example, an executive may well be planning new activities which this manager's capabilities will make possible, and may even be visualizing the organizational impact of these plans and the controls which will be necessary.

Simplified definitions are added for each of the functions and activities to ensure understanding of what is meant by the basic elements described.

Prospective Gains

Hopefully, this diagram of the management process will produce a variety of benefits for practitioners and students. Among these benefits are:

—A unified concept of managerial functions and activities.

—A way to fit together all generally accepted activities of management.

—A move toward standardization of terminology.

—The identifying and relating of such activities as problem analysis, management of change, and management of differences.

—Help to beginning students of management in seeing the "boundaries of the ballpark" and sensing the sequential relationships of certain functions and the interrelationships of others.

—Clearer distinctions between the leadership, administrative, and strategic planning functions of management.

In addition, the diagram should appeal to those who, like myself, would like to see more emphasis on the "behaviorist" functions of management, for it elevates staffing and communicating to the level of a function. Moreover, it establishes functions and activities as the two most important terms for describing the job of the manager.

21

PROJECTED LABOR COSTS IN FUTURE FOOD SYSTEMS

M. B. Burritt

We all plan ahead. Even the eight-year-old boy walking down a country lane, swinging his arms and whistling to everyone within earshot plans ahead. He skips along, stopping now and then to pick up a stone and throw it further down the road. In one hand he carries a long pole with a string attached to it and in his pocket he carries a few bent pins. He is happy and secure, for he made plans for this morning as far back as yesterday—a long time in his life!

An adult, to be successful, must plan his future more carefully and think much further ahead. Running a restaurant, or any other type of food operation, requires so much foresight that we run the risk of being ineffective if we do not plan ahead for several years.

Food Systems of the Near Future

Food service operators are going to continue to have labor expenses in future food operations, despite the sometimes popular concept that one day we'll have kitchens without employees. I don't see this type of a kitchen in the foreseeable future. Without doubt, though, there will be fewer employees in the kitchen of tomorrow to reduce payroll.

The emphasis on better kitchen equipment and layout will make for considerable increase in worker productivity. As a result, we (Horwath and Horwath) foresee considerable reduction in payroll expense, probably somewhere between five and 10 points. We also foresee a reduction of possibly as much as 20 percent in the number of employees required to do a given amount of work. Food cost will be a little higher. Hopefully, profits will be higher, too.

We visualize a shifting in the importance of jobs in certain categories. The old rule of thumb of "thirds"—one-third of the payroll

From the *Cornell H.R.A. Quarterly*, May 1967, pp. 55-64. Reprinted by permission.

for production, one-third for food service, and one-third for ware-washing and cleanup—may change considerably. We're positive that the commotion to be found in the kitchen, causing considerable "travel time" of employees, will and must be reduced.

Elements of Future Food Systems

What will be the important elements of future food-service systems? We visualize them as comprising:

1. Increased mechanization.
2. Increased use of convenience or ready foods.
3. A break with tradition encompassing many changing concepts in food service and menus.
4. A change in the physical layout of the kitchen or production areas, and a vast improvement in the employees' environment.
5. A different type of worker in the kitchens: a worker who will be more skillful, more intelligent, and have a higher social and economic level than did kitchen workers of the past.

Mechanization and Automation

There have been several recent attempts to create complete or at least partial automation of food service. One is AMFare's installation, described in *Drive-In* magazine in late 1966, and in *The Quarterlies* of May 1965 and May 1966. AMFare, as many know, is an almost totally automated drive-in production unit that operates from an electronic control system to provide a limited but adequate menu, either for self-service or waitress service. Two AMFares are presently in operation and these units are available for rental.

Another example of current automation is the Kayway Rotary Cafeteria Food Services installation. The Kayway system is a scramble-type cafeteria—but instead of the customer moving along the cafeteria line, the cafeteria line rotates in front of the customer. As this large rotary counter circulates, it is replenished from the kitchen or service area, enclosed behind the scenes and invisible to the customer. You might term this a large-sized "lazy Susan."

In talking about automation we cannot overlook the Automat operations which have been with us for many, many years. The "automation," of course, is principally the method of serving food and collecting payment rather than the food preparation methods. Nevertheless, the Automat is an example of long-time food service automation.

Still another example of mechanization is the vending machine. Although used for many years, this equipment is undergoing a drastic change. Many units now offer hot as well as cold food and provide considerably more variety with much less mechanical difficulty.

The development of many different types of automatic equipment will be an increasingly important factor in future food systems and will have a direct effect on labor expense. Such new equipment as the silver sorter, the pot washer, the conveyor belt, change-makers, tabulators, micro-wave ovens and the electronic device designed to test the degree of "doneness" should prove to be important labor-savers.

Increased mechanization of food production will not be achieved without problems. Although human hands cause high payroll, it seems the chances are better of getting consistent food quality with knowledgeable hands than by mechanically dispensing pre-cooked, pre-portioned foods. In other words, we face the question of whether or not we can improve present standards of quality through the use of various mechanized food service methods.

Convenience or Ready Foods

The second important element in future food service systems will be the increased use of convenience foods. Referring to a report on the Food Facilities Engineering Society Seminar held last May in Chicago, we note that numerous speakers emphasized that there will always be a kitchen or food production area of some type. In other words, it seems obvious that even when convenience foods are used, a considerable amount of work is involved in getting them ready for customer service.

There are two ways to use convenience foods. In the first method, the food products are purchased from a purveyor, or requisitioned from a commissary, in a state of pre-preparation, requiring only re-constitution for service. In the second method, food is purchased raw, then prepared and frozen on the premises, where it is stored. When needed, this frozen food is requisitioned from storage and held refrigerated for quick reconstitution and service. Later in this article, the type of preparation we visualize for future food systems will be discussed. It is obvious that the size of such production areas and the amount of work required will have obvious effects on payroll expense.

New Concepts in Food Service

The third important element to be found in future food systems will be that of a break with tradition, which would of course include changing concepts of food service. If we look about us today, we will see that there are already many breaks with tradition with regard to food service. For example, we see that paper has replaced china in many instances. Paper also is beginning to take the place of linen in some areas, particularly since the newer paper products feel and to a certain extent look like linen.

A recent issue of *Institutions* magazine, shows good-looking, well-designed disposable containers being used in place of china for service to patients in hospitals on the West Coast. The meals served were gourmet in type and looked extremely attractive. It was our understanding from reading this article that most, if not all, of the containers used in this hospital service were made of a hard material.

It seems certain to us that the emphasis on self-service, which of course is nothing new, is going to increase, rather than decrease. Even in some restaurants today, you are given a bowl of lettuce and the makings for salads, and it is your job to make the salad to your own specifications. For a long time it has been an attractive "special" of some restaurants to allow guests to make their own ice cream sundaes. We look for a continued upturn in the "help yourself" or "self-service" type of operation.

Better Layout and Worker Environment

The fourth important element will be progress in layout and an emphasis on a different type of training. The principal changes in layout of a kitchen or food service area are likely to be intended to make work simpler for the employee to reduce his "traveling time," to cut down the number of motions he must make to complete a given task, and generally, to help him get the job done with less commotion.

Job training by means of the task-unit approach is a method widely advocated by Dr. John Welch of the University of Missouri [*See the February and May 1966˙ Quarterly.*] This approach has valuable and necessary applications in food service.

Another means for achieving better physical layout and new training methods is to determine, through work sampling, the best layout and essential task training. Work-sampling techniques have also been described by Dr. Welch.* Perhaps one of the most interesting examples for ascertaining optimum equipment arrangement is the method used by the U.S. Navy in determining the size and layout of the galley for the new atomic submarines.

---

*The Task Unit Concept for On-the-Job Training in Food Service, Missouri Extension Division Manual No. 66. Address Mailing Room, University of Missouri, Columbia, Missouri and include $1.50.

In general, we favor the "smooth traffic approach" to achieve good layout. This means that a product enters the rear of a food service facility and travels without interruption in a straight path through the storage, using, preparation, and service areas to the point of customer consumption. The "smooth traffic" approach, of course, can only be achieved when equipment is properly placed.

The Future Kitchen Worker

It is important to analyze some of the possible duties and tasks to be performed in future food operation. It is also important to consider the type of person who may be hired to operate these facilities. When we say "type of person," we think of his social standing and his earning capacity based on his education and ability. If a more intelligent and better-trained worker is be be attracted to the food service industry, it is important to provide good environment in the food preparation and service centers.

The following six factors, we think, enter into the tasks to be performed and help to determine the type of person who will perform these tasks in the future.

1. There will be fewer of the highly paid workers generally associated with the chef and his assistant.

2. Employees in future food systems will likely be tending machines rather than using their hands to prepare food or serve it.

3. The worker of tomorrow will have a much pleasanter place in which to work than we find in today's kitchen. In other words, environment will play a much more important part in brightening the work-day of the employee in future food systems.

4. As a whole, we expect future employees to have a better education than today's workers; be psychologically better adjusted, more highly self-motivated. Or, to put it another way, we expect the employee to move from the blue-collar group into the white-collar group.

5. We expect that there will be more specialized training but that present training of a long duration—such as that now required to become a really good cook or chef—will be reduced considerably.

6. The future should also bring a saving in payroll expense beyond that realized by having to pay wages to fewer employees. The smaller number of employees would mean that there would be a sizable saving in employee benefits and related expenses as well as in actual payroll expenditure.

From the foregoing analysis, it is likely that the payroll situation in the future will change radically and there will be fewer employees.

More important, there will be a decline in the over-all expenditure required to get the job done.

How Design Can Reduce Payroll

Five methods of food service are presented below, which we consider a partial answer to the requirements of future food service operations. These concepts are illustrated in several instances. We have also shown some methods, now usable without drastic remodeling of premises, and without waiting for "ready foods of the future" to become available and for the problems to be solved of obtaining consistent quality by means of automated equipment. In brief, there are some changes which will be widely adopted in the future that can be put into operation immediately.

Five types of design are presented in this article:

1. The scramble buffet.
2. The waitress-cook concept.
3. The open kitchen concept.
4. A ready-food kitchen without commissary.
5. A ready-food kitchen with commissary.

*Scramble Buffet (*Figure 1*)*

Figure 1 illustrates a "scramble-type" buffet. This buffet is planned so that customer lines should not develop. Similar to the "scramble" cafeteria, its effectiveness is probably greatest for breakfast and luncheon service.

Note in Figure 1 that sufficient separation has been allowed between the various food groups—appetizer, meat, salad, vegetables, etc.—so that the customer can go direct to a particular food group or pass it by if he chooses. When this system is effective, the customer's longest wait should be for no more than two or three persons ahead of him. People can wander back and forth along the buffet table, selecting whatever they wish, but there should be no queue. When enough service help is behind the buffet table, there is no line-up.

Other details essential to the effectiveness of the "scramble" buffet are concerned with control of customer checks and the need to provide bread and butter and the beverage—and possibly dessert service—at the customer's table.

Anyone desiring to try this food service concept can readily do so if he has a few chafing dishes and some long banquet table. Nothing else in the way of special equipment is needed, but if this type of service proves successful, a permanent buffet installation may prove advisable.

Figure 1. Scramble Buffet

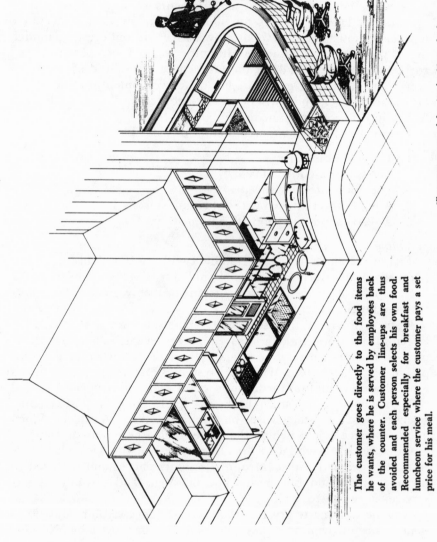

The customer goes directly to the food items he wants, where he is served by employees back of the counter. Customer line-ups are thus avoided and each person selects his own food. Recommended especially for breakfast and luncheon service where the customer pays a set price for his meal.

Illustrations prepared by Aurelio Marin, kitchen engineering draftsman, under the supervision of John E. Markham, head of kitchen design in Horwath & Horwath's Miami offices.

Figure 2. Waitress-Cook

LEGEND

1 COFFEE MAKER & STAND W/ DRAWERS
2 UTILITY STAND W/ SINK SECTION & TOASTER
3 WATER STATION W/ BUTTER PAN & ICE BIN
4 STEAM TABLE
5 SALAD & DESSERT CASE
6 CUP, SAUCER & GLASS DISPENSER
7 ROLL WARMER W/ TOASTER & COFFEE WARMER
8 WATER STATION W/ BUTTER PAN & ICE BIN
9 BOTTLE COOLER

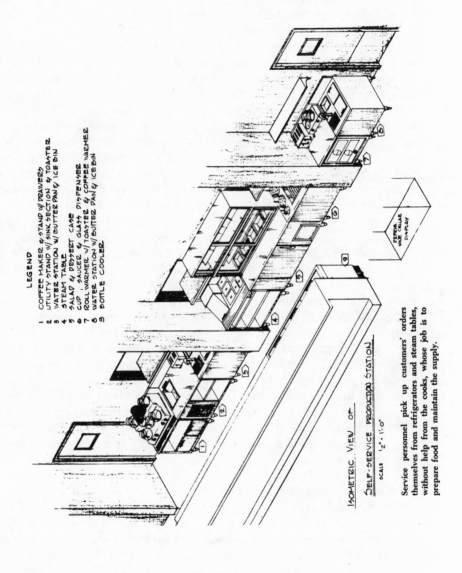

ISOMETRIC VIEW of
SELF-SERVICE PRODUCTION STATION
SCALE ½" = 1'-0"

Service personnel pick up customers' orders themselves from refrigerators and steam tables, without help from the cooks, whose job is to prepare food and maintain the supply.

*Waitress-Cook Concept (*Figure 2*)*

The waiter or waitress-cook concept refers to showing service personnel how to provide food for their customers by picking it up themselves—salads and desserts from glass-enclosed refrigerators, and hot entrees from a steam table.

There is nothing new about this type of service. It has been effectively utilized in such well-managed restaurant operations as Howard Johnson's, Hot Shoppes, and others. Recently we saw installations where a steam table had been added to the service pick-up section.

This service replaces having a high-salaried cook dishing out entree and vegetables with the waitress helping herself—making for efficient utilization of personnel. To be effective, some problems must first be resolved, such as the overall pay of the employees, possible union objections, the volume of business and how items with heavy demand are to be handled. Since local conditons will dictate how these problems will be handled, they are not discussed in this article.

To restate the point being illustrated, Figure 2 is a food-service arrangement wherein the waiter or waitress and a counter-employee do a great deal of work without the assistance of highly paid chefs and cooks. Certainly cooks and chefs will be required in this type of food service—but to prepare the food and see that food is replenished in the equipment where service personnel have ready access.

Observe that the counter is placed to provide ample room for two people to pass behind the counter and also between the counter and the service equipment. Note also that the waiters or waitresses can reach their service equipment from any point in the dining area.

Another waitress-cook concept is used by the John R. Thompson Company in its installations. Thompson uses a Flexo Steamer behind the cafeteria counter. In these installations, a "line" employee cooks vegetables and other items in small quantities to insure their freshness and keeps the customer counter supplied, thus spending a minimum of travel time.

*The Open-Kitchen Concept (*Figure 3*)*

The "open hearth" cooking concept for steaks and service of roast beef has been in vogue for years as an atmosphere-creator. Display areas and a uniformed chef in high hat are typical of the open-hearth display, although much of the actual cooking is done behind the scene. What the guest views is usually for show, although there are exceptions. In many such operations, these open-hearth type arrangements have added people to the payroll instead of saving personnel—which may be justified as merchandising.

Figure 3. The Open Kitchen

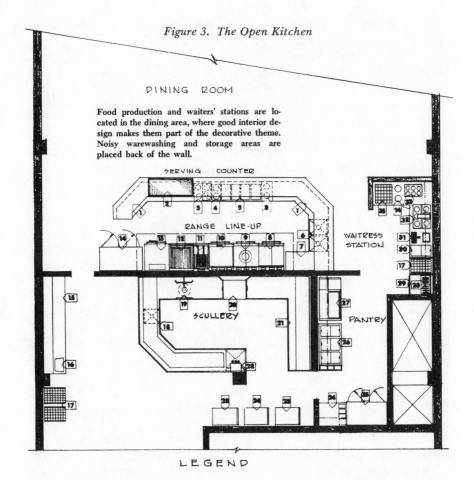

DINING ROOM

Food production and waiters' stations are located in the dining area, where good interior design makes them part of the decorative theme. Noisy warewashing and storage areas are placed back of the wall.

SERVING COUNTER

RANGE LINE-UP

WAITRESS STATION

SCULLERY

PANTRY

LEGEND

1	COUNTER	18	SOILED DISH TABLE
2	COLD PAN	19	PRE-RINSE UNIT
3	DISH DISPENSER	20	DISH-WASHER
4	SOUP WELLS	21	CLEAN DISH TABLE
5	STEAM TABLE	22	GLASS WASHING
6	SINKS	23	DISH CARTS
7	WORKING TABLE	24	WORKING TABLE
8	RANGE	25	REACH-IN
9	RANGE	26	ICE CREAM CABINET
10	GRIDDLE TOP	27	ICE-MACHINE
11	FRYER	28	TOASTER
12	CHARC-BROILER	29	ROLL WARMER
13	UP-RIGHT BROILER	30	ICE-BIN
14	DUAL-TEMP REACH-IN	31	WATER STATION
15	UTILITY CABINET	32	COFFEE MAKER
16	HAND SINK	33	SILVER HOLDER
17	GLASS DOLLIES	34	SAUCERS DISPENSER
		35	CUPS DISPENSER

The open-kitchen concept that is becoming prevalent today, however, actually places the entire kitchen in the dining room. In the future, this will be done in many of the more expensive type of restaurant.

The advantages of the open-kitchen are numerous. One of the more important is that the waiter can always be seen by his customers. So there is less likelihood that the waiter will disappear for a smoke or other reason. The customer should receive better service because the waiter is always available—or the customer can see that the waiter is actually busy.

Another important reason for using an open-kitchen is that waiters do not need to travel nearly so far in the combined preparation dining areas as they do when the kitchen is in the back of the house. A third important point is that a well-designed open-kitchen can actually form the nucleus of the restaurant's decorative theme.

This open-kitchen concept represents a "break with tradition," one of the changes that lie ahead in future food service. Its principle advantage—other than possible aesthetic appeal—is the reduction of worker travel time. This makes for greater efficiency because fewer employees are needed and better service can be given to more customers.

Ready-Food Kitchen Without Commissary (Figure 4)

This kitchen design is based on the availability and use of food ready for reheating or simple assembly when purchased, that is, of high enough quality to please customers. Figure 4 shows a ready-food kitchen of the future which employs the concept of having all food brought into the establishment either in unit or multiple-unit servings in a dried or frozen state. Such food moves from the rear entrance of the restaurant—following the previously mentioned "smooth traffic flow" procedure—to the reconstitution center and customer service. In this way, ready foods can be utilized with the minimum number of employees.

In this type of ready-food kitchen, there can be a reduction of more than 25 percent in employees in relation to the conventional kitchen operation, but the food cost may be slightly higher. It is assumed, in this example, that all food will be purchased ready for reconstitution.

Ready-Food Kitchen With Commissary (Figure 5)

For this concept, it is assumed that production and service employees will have considerable idle time between meal-service

Figure 4. Ready Food Kitchen Without Commissary

Cooked frozen food is brought into the restaurant in portion or multiple-portion sizes. Here it is reconstituted, while salads and other items are prepared fresh for service. The kitchen is an assembly center. (*Scale: 1/4" = 1'*.) *Designed by Horwath and Horwath.*

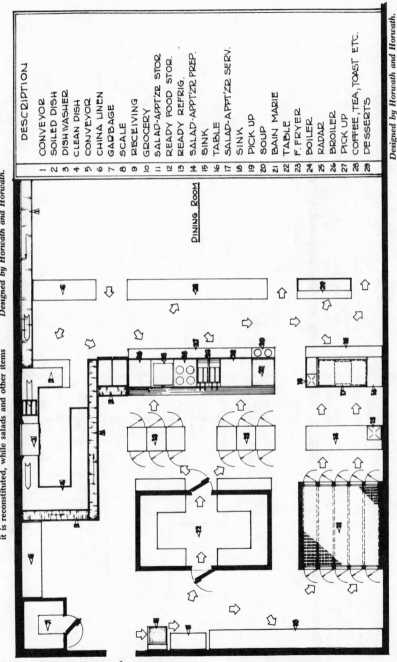

	DESCRIPTION
1	CONVEYOR
2	SOILED DISH
3	DISHWASHER
4	CLEAN DISH
5	CONVEYOR
6	CHINA LINEN
7	GARBAGE
8	SCALE
9	RECEIVING
10	GROCERY
11	SALAD-APPT'ZR STOR.
12	READY FOOD STOR.
13	READY REFRIG.
14	SALAD-APPT'ZR PREP.
15	SINK
16	TABLE
17	SALAD-APPT'ZR SERV.
18	SINK
19	PICK UP
20	SOUP
21	BAIN MARIE
22	TABLE
23	F. FRYER
24	BOILER
25	RADAR
26	BROILER
27	PICK UP
28	COFFEE, TEA, TOAST ETC.
29	DESSERTS

DINING ROOM

Designed by Horwath and Horwath.

Figure 5. Ready Food Kitchen and Commissary

► Food enters the receiving entrance at Point 7 and is processed at Points 8, 9, and 10. Next it is stored in Items 11, 12, 13, and 21. Previously prepared and packaged food is stored for service in Items 22, 23, 24, 25, 26, 33, etc. Service is from Items 30, 31, 32, 41, etc. When employees are not engaged in regular service — presumably at times between breakfast and lunch and between lunch and dinner — they utilize their time to work in areas outlined with heavy black lines that represent the walls of the preparation areas.

► Utilizing Items 15, 16, 17, 18, 19, etc., employees prepare food, package it and then store it in appropriate areas.

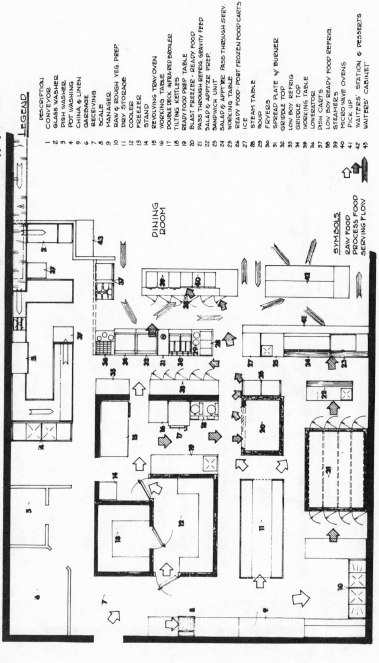

LEGEND

	DESCRIPTION
1	CONVEYOR
2	GLASS WASHER
3	DISH WASHER
4	POT WASHING
5	CHINA & LINEN
6	GARBAGE
7	RECEIVING
8	SCALE
9	MANAGER
10	RAW & ROUGH VEG. PREP.
11	DRY STORAGE
12	COOLER
13	FREEZER
14	STAND
15	REVOLVING TRAY OVEN
16	WORKING TABLE
17	DOUBLE DECK INFRARED BROILER
18	TILTING KETTLES
19	READY FOOD PREP TABLE
20	BLAST FREEZER - READY FOOD
21	PASS THROUGH REFRIG. GRAVITY FEED
22	SALAD & APPETIZER PREP.
23	SANDWICH UNIT
24	SALAD & APPETIZER PASS THROUGH SERV.
25	WORKING TABLE
26	READY FOOD - PORT. FROZEN FOOD CARTS
27	ICE
28	STEAM TABLE
29	SOUP
30	FRYERS
31	SPREAD PLATE W/ BURNER
32	GRIDDLE TOP
33	LOW BOY REFRIG
34	GRIDDLE TOP
35	WORKING TABLE
36	LOWERATOR
37	DISH CARTS
38	LOW BOY READY FOOD REFRIG.
39	STEAMERS
40	MICRO WAVE OVENS
41	PICK UP
42	WAITERS' STATION & DESSERTS
43	WAITERS' CABINET

SYMBOLS

RAW FOOD
PROCESS FOOD
SERVING FLOW

DINING ROOM

periods. These slack periods would be used to prepare, package, freeze, dry or otherwise process food to be stored for later use. This kitchen utilizes the ready-food concepts developed by the Research Section of Cornell's School of Hotel Administration.

This is a hypothetical operation. But we have prepared estimated staffing tables for such a restaurant using conventional food preparation methods and for the same restaurant using the ready food concept. Figure 6 compares the staffing and payroll expense of the two operations. Note that the salaries and employee benefits of six employees are saved in the ready-foods concept. Further note that annual earnings per employee have dropped from about $3,800 to $3,350 for the ready-foods restaurant. (The pay rates are hypothetical and will vary in different parts of the country.) The payroll is lower in the ready-foods concept because fewer highly paid cooks are needed and most cooking can be done during the regularly scheduled work week.

To Sum Up
The menu you are now using should be gradually revised, if changes are needed. The gradual phasing out of items will not raise the doubts that a drastic change will create in your operation—or in

---

Rules for Conversion
to the Use of Ready Foods
Rule 1. Change the menu gradually.

Rule 2. Select menu items which can be pre-cooked, packaged and stored without loss of quality when reconstituted.

Rule 3. Develop proper preparation methods for one ready food at a time. Test several different preparation methods from initial preparation to customer service.

Rule 4. Instruct your service personnel in how to be of assistance in the new ready foods early in the game.

Rule 5. Observe the use of ready foods used by the larger chains and prepared in their own commissaries. (You can tell, because of your own experience, which items are likely to have been pre-processed.) Your opinion of palatability will serve as a guide in your own operation.

Rule 6. Keep informed by every possible means of all new developments concerning ready foods—preparation, packaging, freezing, processing, reconstitution.

the minds of your customers. Although people basically want and expect change, they resist sudden ones.

Next, determine which popular menu items can be prepared in quantity and then frozen, dried, or otherwise held for later use. If one of your popular specialties is standing prime ribs of beef, this item should be prepared and served in the traditional manner. But, in the instance of Seafood Newburg, this item may lend itself to pre-cooking and freezing.

No one is able to state when food systems will be completely changed; perhaps the time will never come when customers are offered only reconstituted, pre-processed food. But one needs only to be caught in the squeeze between spiralling food and labor costs and customer price-resistance to realize that something must be done without the sacrifice of standards of service.

Figure 6. Conventional kitchen vs. ready foods kitchen— Payroll Differences, Horwath & Horwath, December 1966

CONVENTIONAL KITCHEN

	No. of Workers	Daily Rate	Daily Total	Annual Total
Manager	1	$27.00	$ 27.00	$ 9,855
Chef	1	25.00	25.00	9,125
Cooks	1	20.00	60.00	21,900
Breakfast cook	1	18.00	18.00	6,570
Preparation	2	15.00	30.00	10,950
Dishwashers	4	11.00	44.00	16,060
Pantry men	2	16.00	32.00	11,680
Hostess-cashier	2	15.00	30.00	10,950
Waitresses	16	5.00	80.00	29,200
Busboys	4	9.50	38.00	13,870
Total	36		$384.00	$140,160

READY FOODS KITCHEN AND COMMISSARY

	No. of Workers	Daily Rate	Daily Total	Annual Total
Manager	1	$27.00	$ 27.00	$ 9,855
Cook	1	20.00	20.00	7,300
Pantry-breakfast	1	18.00	18.00	6,570
Helpers	2	14.00	28.00	10,220
Dishwashers-cleaners	4	11.00	44.00	16,060
Hostess-cashier	2	15.00	30.00	10,950
Waitresses	16	5.00	80.00	29,200
Busboys	3	9.50	28.50	10,403
Total	30		$275.50	$100,558
Savings	6 employees			$ 39,602

22

EMPLOYEE SHORTAGES IN HOTELS AND MOTELS

A.L. Winsor

This report deals with a survey of the labor shortage in 2,100 hotels and motels in the United States and Canada. It was made by the Research Division of the School of Hotel Administration of Cornell, at the request of the Research Committee of the American Hotel and Motel Association. The problem was to get the best possible estimate of actual industry shortages of technical and managerial applicants available for employment, so far as could be determined by managers or employment officers.

Managers of hotels and motels with 100 rooms or more in Canada and the United States were contacted by mail and requested to indicate on an enclosed card the kinds of employees in short supply in their area. Replies were received from these officials in every state in the U.S. and from every province in Canada.

Over 500 managers estimated the personnel shortages they experienced in their recruitment efforts. These were reported on the card supplied them or by means of a longer descriptive letter telling of their supply problems. Some of their efforts at recruitment had been national in scope, while others were local. These replies constituted the basis of this report. The data collected will ultimately serve to re-enforce current attempts by the industry to improve the personnel problems in the industry.

For the industry as a whole, 63 different jobs were reported as being difficult or impossible to fill with qualified men or women. Some shortages appeared to be local or temporary and thus cause the industry no serious concern. Others, however, were extensive and chronic and definitely limit successful operation. An examination of the columns in Figure 1 will show the departments in hotels with the greatest shortages and those with less severe needs.

From the *Cornell H.R.A. Quarterly*, November 1963, pp. 62-66. Reprinted by permission.

It will be observed that a surprisingly high percentage of all jobs in short supply have to do with the procurement, preparation, and service of food. This finding will not surprise most hotel executives. It has been assumed for years, but the extent and nature of the situation has not been determined before on a national basis. It appears that the earlier supply of chefs from Europe is no longer available, and no local supply has been developed by the industry.

Respondents from every section of this country and Canada wrote in exasperation of their difficulty in finding competent, honest, reliable and sober people for key positions in the food services. Some confessed their only recourse at present was to entice cooks or chefs from other establishments by offering more money or more elaborate fringe benefits, which they disliked doing. Others suggested some reasons for the situation the industry faces and in some cases offered corrective efforts they felt might help. These suggestions will be presented later in the report.

Figure 1. Relative Seriousness of Worker Shortages by Departments

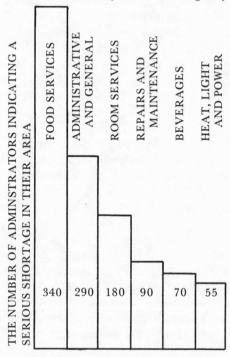

Next to food services, the department showing the greatest short-age was the administrative and general. Even though the actual num-ber of hotels reporting needs in this area are fewer than was reported in foods, the significance of these limitations may be even greater in the success of hotel operation—particularly when the need is for managers, assistant managers, and potential supervisors.

Over 300 officers reported they were having difficulty getting promising young men for beginning administrative assignments. Too few young Americans seemed interested in employment in orienta-tion jobs that might ultimately lead to responsible positions of man-agement. Whereas eager young men formerly sought positions such as a front office clerk in the hopes that an apprenticeship would lead to a more responsible position, today they seem not to be interested. Complaints about the quality of the applicants were as frequent as these about the lack of enough of them.

The increase, in recent years, in the number of college programs in hotel administration has been helpful in supplying qualified candi-dates for these posts. Yet the number of graduates is entirely in-adequate for the rapid growth taking place in the industry. In the 1940's, the Cornell School of Hotel Administration Placement Office received about 100 requests annually for its small class of graduates. In the 1960's, more than 500 requests are received each year—and of course they do not have enough men to meet this demand. Boys fresh from high school show little interest in basic hotel occupations. The hotel as a place to work seems to have lost the glamour of the "bowl-and-pitcher" period.

The adoption of automatic machines seems to be creating greater need for employees, at least in the accounting field. From most of the large hotels throughout the country came reports of a serious need for N.C.R. operators. This need is so new and urgent that it would seem more training programs should be set up to make it possible for hotels to move ahead in this field. One manager in Chi-cago suggested that full instruction about front-office accounting machines be taught in all hotel schools.

In many other divisions of administration—particularly from the larger hotels and motels, and the chains—the need was stressed for well-trained and highly specialized men such as sales promotion men, executive assistant managers, personnel directors, operation analysts, and payroll control men. An executive in one large middle-western hotel reported having made a nationwide search of four months to obtain the services of a competent director of sales. All applicants for the position lacked what was considered the essential qualifications for this key job.

Traditional positions of the administrative department that were reported as hard to fill include auditors, bookkeepers, and accountants familiar with hotel procedures. Even secretaries were listed in some sections of the country as being difficult to employ. In desperation some hotels, particularly in the South, have given up hunting for suitable employees and have established schools to train their own.

In the rooms division the dominant need expressed was for room clerks. In spite of the natural attractiveness and importance of this post—as well as the outlook it offers for advancement—many complaints accompanied the listing of this as a critical area. In the minds of many executives the lack of quality of the applicants, as well as the small number, was serious. They reported lack of interest, lack of stability, lack of skills, and lack of ambition on the part of the young men they interviewed or tried out.

Another major shortage in this department is the job of housekeeper. It appears that an executive housekeeper with good supervisory ability is hard to find in many sections of the country. One or two managers suggested men be selected and trained for this work instead of trying to employ the right kind of woman. In some cities, chambermaids were listed as difficult to get; this, however, was not a widespread need.

In the repairs and maintenance department, the most urgent need was for good all-around maintenance men, who could also take care of air-conditioning and refrigeration systems. It was pointed out that too much specialization of technicians and more favorable work for them outside the hotel-motel made it difficult to get the type of man the smaller establishments needed.

In the beverage department, the major need is for knowledgeable, sober, stable bartenders. There seems to be enough applicants for the posts, but few meet the requirements of honesty and sobriety. The other need is for trained beverage controllers and managers. Here again quality was stressed more than quantity.

Salaries up to $12,500 per year are reported as having been offered in vain for well-qualified chief engineers to operate in the larger hotels of the Middle West. Stationary engineers, particularly for the heating and cooling system, are very scarce in some areas of the country. The demand for young engineers in other industries seems to reduce their availability for such work as the hotel or motel has to offer.

In Figure 2, the distribution of the 15 most frequently listed jobs are shown without regard to the department to which each belongs. It will be noted that cooks, chefs, front office clerks, and N.C.R. operators are the jobs that might be considered critical. From every state in the Union and every Province of Canada came indications of distress in trying to fill these posts. Some managers spoke of abandoning cooking and resorting to frozen foods as a way out of their dilemma.

Distribution of Shortages by Sections of the States

An examination of the managers' replies grouped according to sections of the country, showed some needs common to all, with some differences in the relative needs in different areas. In every section of the States, the shortage of workers is greatest for cooks and chefs, with variation in the extent of the supply in other departments.

Figure 2. Distribution of Worker Shortages by Jobs

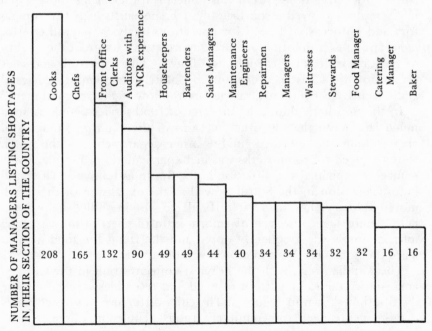

In New England, despite the fact that there has been persistent unemployment for years, the shortage of food service people is serious. A total of 62 hotels or motels reported a disturbing limitation in this department. Room service needs are second in severity in this resort area, while jobs of an administrative nature are not so short as in other sections of the country. In general, other departments follow the national pattern of supply except for engineers. Here there appeared to be a greater shortage, due (according to the report) to the shorter work week and higher pay available to these men in other industries.

On the East Coast as far south as Virginia, the pattern of need resembles the New England pattern as far as administrative and heat-light-and-power people are concerned. In spite of the high concentration of large hotels, room service people are second to food services in the shortage reports. Next in importance are administrative and general workers whose jobs are frequently highly specialized because of the very large establishments or chains of which they are a part in New York City. It was from this concentration of large hotels that many reports showed a shortage of such specialists as N.C.R. operators and an occasional need for operations analysts, payroll control men, and sales promotion people. One executive wrote of the quality of men available for these jobs as follows: "The advertising and sales promotion field has an oversupply of fakirs. Experienced managers' and executive accountants' salaries are too low to attract good men."

In the Southern states, the shortage of food service people seemed much less acute than in other sections of the country, though still greater than the shortages in the other departments of the hotel. Here the need for room clerks was high, particularly in Florida. Some managers explained the situation in the South as follows: "The rapid industrialization in the South as well as the expansion of the hotel-motel industry, has made it difficult to obtain skilled help down here." Here again, the lack of ambition on the part of those seeking jobs in hotels was frequently noted and the trend for good men to leave the hotels for work in motels was observed.

The Middle West, with the heaviest concentration in the Chicago area, shows the same pattern of need and resembles very closely the distribution shown in Figure 1. The chief difference in this section is a more acute need for competent foods people. In this area, 145 hotels reported difficulty in getting satisfactory food workers and many of them urge action by the industry to relieve the situation. New legislation with respect to the sale of beverages in Iowa has created at least a temporary demand for good bartenders there.

In the Southwest, again the need for food service people exceeded all others. Almost every manager expressing an opinion felt that his general operation was definitely handicapped for want of good cooks and chefs. The need for good engineers was greater in the Southwest and assumptions were offered that engineers could do better in other industries. Some hotels in Texas reported having established their own training programs to improve the situation.

The pattern of need on the West Coast (including Hawaii and Alaska) and in the Rocky Mountains resembles more that of New England and the South. While qualified foods people are still the greatest need, room service—particularly good room clerks—is a close second. Administrative people are high in the need column and the rest of the departments follow the national pattern of being urgent but not so important as those of foods, room service, and administration.

One manager wrote: "It is not so much the shortage of help but the shortage of interested and competent help that poses problems out here. Long hours and comparatively lower rates of pay do not attract the higher type of people to the service openings in hotels and motels." Another reply from the San Diego area noted, "There seems to be no one entering this line of work anymore—newcomers are misfits or rejects that came to Southern California for the climate."

The western provinces of Canada report no shortages of any type of hotel employees but the central and eastern provinces report needs similar to those of the States, with a particular need for good advertising and sales promotion people. One manager reported his observation that in general "the staff today has no ambition and no interest in learning to get ahead in the industry."

In replying to the request for judgments on the personnel shortages in the hotel-motel industry, several managers expressed their ideas on the causes of the unhappy state of affairs which the survey reveals. While this report is not primarily concerned with this phase of the problem, it seems wise to include these comments by experienced and thoughtful executives on causes and remedies for these disturbing shortages.

L. E. Schoenbrunn, General Manager, The Chase-Park Plaza Hotel (St. Louis, Missouri) listed these significant causes of the shortages and the best way to resolve them as he saw them:

1. The communications between the hotel and restaurant field with the counselors in the high schools and employment services has been very poor and is in need of prompt remedial action. Very few

of the students in schools are aware of the opportunities in the hotel field.

2. There is a lack of well-qualified teachers for hotel and restaurant personnel.

3. The unions must be made to realize that they have an important obligation in insisting upon a training program for hotel personnel that would be comparable to the apprentice program of other trades.

4. There is a definite complacency on the part of most hotel and restaurant operators in that they will not take any action themselves, and leave it up to one or two members of a local organization to do all of the necessary work in establishing a training program.

5. Current unemployment legislation is much too lenient.

6. Management and supervisory personnel must be alert to promising personnel on their staff and encourage them to further their education, pointing out the possibility of bettering their earning power when the training program has been successfully completed.

Managers in other sections of the country suggested these additional causes:

1. That the food industry is handicapped still by restrictive U.S. immigration policy that cuts off the former supply of chefs from Europe.

2. That recent raising of salaries of chefs and cooks in Europe reduces the advantages Americans formerly had in inducing these men to accept work here.

3. That low pay and longer hours of work in the hotel industry is the cause of the problem.

4. That there are too few of the right types of vocational training facilities in this country.

5. That the whole problem is due to a lack of initiative and persistence on the part of the industry and the unions in creating a more favorable attitude toward hotel work.

In a current survey being made by school districts in New York State, only 11 junior high school boys out of 2,867 contacted expressed an interest in food service occupations, while 251 of them were interested in auto mechanics as a life's work.

In Summary
The general implications of this survey for the hotel-motel industry seems to be that:

1. More young, capable workers should be induced to take up careers in the industry.

2. Opportunities for on-the-job training should be made available to employees.

3. Policies of improvement and advancement should be maintained to keep present employees in the industry.

23

STEPS YOU CAN TAKE TO MEET
THE UNION DRIVE LAWFULLY

Benjamin Werne

Employers in the restaurant business are well aware of union claims that new organizing drives are "sweeping forward" (to quote a recent issue of *CIE*, journal of the Hotel & Restaurant Employees Union). There is no doubt that activity is on the upswing, with an accelerated pace forecast for the future. Increasing competition between the AFL-CIO and the newly formed Teamster-Auto Workers axis, the ALA, will help to guarantee this.

What management does not understand, apparently, is that there *are* specific steps which can be taken to counter a union's campaign —and still stay within the letter and spirit of the Labor Management Relations (Taft-Hartley) Act. Some managers seem to have the impression that they either must "cave in" to union pressure at the first sign of a drive, or that the only alternative is to try to work out some kind of a "deal."

The courts and the National Labor Relations Board (NLRB), which enforce the statute, have repeatedly ruled that an employer has every right to conduct a vigorous and "hard-hitting" counter-drive. In fact, management has an *obligation* to put the facts before employees! Let them decide after hearing *both* sides of the story. They may not be aware of some of the disadvantages of unionization—and they certainly won't learn about them through the union organizer.

During a drive, you must be concerned with two major groups:

Employees—the facts must be put before them, by word of mouth or through letters or leaflets. You can let them know exactly what

---

238

they might experience from unionization, i.e. strikes, picketing, assessments, fines, etc. Remind them also about the benefits they presently enjoy, all granted without union interference or paying dues.

Supervisors—they must realize their responsibilities in a drive. They are closest to the employees, and are in the best position to "feel the pulse" of the group. There should be no letdown in discipline, so long as all are treated fairly and in the customary manner.

You can and should tell the employer's side of the story to the employees. You may campaign freely within certain limits. Remind employees that the law protects those who wish to stay out of the union as well as those who want to join. Your campaign should be concentrated during the period between the designation of a representation election date and the actual date of balloting.

There are certain actions that you must carefully avoid:

—Don't threaten or say anything that *implies* a threat against employees who favor the union. Don't say that you will close down, or that they will lose their jobs or benefits.

—Don't ask any employee how he feels about the union, or if he is a member, or what the union's plans are.

—Don't promise any benefit, if employees will stay out of or vote against the union.

—Don't change hours, wages or working conditions during the period of the drive without checking first. Any such action may be viewed as an attempt to influence employees unlawfully. Maintain the status quo; carry on as you would have prior to the drive.

—Don't discharge or discipline or penalize an employee because of union activity.

Remember, too, that you are held responsible for any unlawful statements or actions by your supervisors, although unauthorized. Be explicit. Tell them how they should act, what they should do.

You must continue to treat all your employees just as you did before the drive began. You may not discriminate against those who favor the union, or those taking part in its activities. This means that you cannot be more strict in enforcing the rules just because a pro-union employee is involved.

Also, you may not treat those who oppose the union more favorably. Any such acts of discrimination or interference with a legitimate union campaign can lead to unfair labor practice charges before the National Labor Relations Board. More than that, such moves often backfire and turn employees against you.

Union agents do *not* have a free hand during a drive. If they are employees, they are to be treated like everyone else. They must abide by the same rules, and they must perform their jobs properly. A union drive is no excuse for a breakdown of discipline, for inefficiency or other conduct that would normally not be tolerated.

If you have to discipline or discharge a known union adherent, be sure that you have substantial proof of the offensive conduct. Also, be sure that you are proceeding just as you would with any other employee. Make certain that no one can accuse you of coercion or discrimination in your handling of the individual case.

Peaceful picketing is generally protected by the federal statute, but some means can usually be found to deal with conduct that interferes with business, threatens damage to your property, or interrupts normal dealings with customers and suppliers. Picketing may have an illegal objective or be conducted in an unlawful manner. Unfair labor practice charges might be filed against the union. A speedier means to relief may be through the state courts which can enjoin certain conduct.

For review, below is a list of 20 steps to help you carry on your business, and put your best foot forward with your employees in the event of an organizational drive:

Step 1. Maintain discipline. Do not be frightened into permitting conduct that would not be tolerated under ordinary circumstances. You must continue to run your restaurant business. Your customers are interested in service—no excuses.

Step 2. Do not discriminate between union and non-union sympathizers.

Step 3. Except for areas open to the public, keep non-employees off your property at all times.

Step 4. Adopt the rule that "working time is for work." Do *not* restrict the activities of employees during their own free time such as rest periods, lunch hours, before and after work—so long as they are in areas not used by the public.

Step 5. If an organizer poses as a customer and bothers employees or interferes with their work performance, ask him to leave. If he refuses, turn the matter over to local authorities.

Step 6. Do not prohibit employees from wearing union buttons or other insignia on their clothing or personal property—neatly and inoffensively. Do keep union slogans, insignia, and literature off company bulletin boards, menus, tables, chairs, counter tops and other equipment.

Step 7. Tell your side of the story to the employees in a positive manner. Detail the benefits they have been given and are presently receiving. Do not engage in debating union charges or making counter-charges since this gives the initiative to the union as to subjects to be discussed.

Step 8. Carry on your business in a normal manner. Do not change your *established* practices with regard to wage increases, work assignments, overtime, shifts, etc., merely because a union drive is on.

Step 9. Do not ignore routine complaints or defer their settlement.

Step 10. Do not make or imply promises to employees for the purpose of influencing them against the union. Likewise, do not threaten pro-union employees with retaliation.

Step 11. Do not question employees about their union sympathies or activities. (But you don't have to close your ears if someone volunteers information.)

Step 12. Do not initiate or assist in the preparation of anti-union petitions or other employee anti-union activities.

Step 13. Keep a record of all apparent union activity. Do not, however, engage in spying nor surveillance merely for the sake of keeping such a record.

Step 14. If the union approaches your suppliers and asks them to stop doing business with you, get advice on filing secondary boycott charges.

Step 15. If the union threatens anyone with violence, alert local police. Your attorney will consider ULP charges and a state court injunction.

Step 16. Do not conduct a campaign of home visitations to dissuade employees from joining the union. Do conduct an information campaign by means of speeches, letters, circulars.

Step 17. During the 24-hour period immediately preceding an NLRB election, do not make election speeches to the employees on your premises. Last-minute letters or circulars are generally permitted.

Step 18. Caution all managers or other supervisors that the law considers them to be the representatives and agents of the company. You will be held responsible if they threaten or coerce employees who are sympathetic to the union.

Step 19. Advise supervisors and executives of their right to express opinions that are non-intimidating and not coercive. They should be encouraged to give their *opinions* to the employees.

Step 20. Always be courteous in dealing with union delegates. You may have to negotiate a contract some day!

24

THE MIAMI BEACH HOTEL STRIKE

Edwin B. Dean

The Miami Beach hotel strike began on April 13, 1955 and ended on January 5, 1957, but its effects on all the hotels in the United States have never been fully assessed. Before the ripples would subside, all but the smallest hotels in the entire hotel industry would be placed under the jurisdiction of the federal government for the handling of labor disputes. Further, the "solid South," which had been so impervious to the organizing tactics of hotel unions would see renewed assaults, this time with the help of the Labor Management & Relations Act, 1947, otherwise known as the Taft-Hartley Law.

It was truly a historic event, when, for the first time in this industry since the San Francisco strike in the thirties, an international union tried to organize an entire city's hotels. The union was the Hotel Restaurant Employees and Bartenders International Union, with headquarters in Cincinnati. A change in leadership, caused by the death of its aged former president, Hugo Ernst, brought to power Ed Miller of Kansas City as the new president. He had long had plans to organize Miami Beach.

This union, the fourth largest in the AFL, historically had represented the majority of hotel employees in organized hotels in cities in the North and West. Like most, it was woefully weak in the South, and Miller saw in Miami Beach an opportunity to gain a foothold under the circumstances which he felt were more favorable than those in any other non-union southern city.

Edwin B. Dean, Executive Director of the Southern Florida Hotel and Motel Association, was Assistant Vice President in charge of personnel and labor relations for the Hilton Hotels in New York and with Hotels Statles Co., Inc. He has also taught in the summer program of the School of Hotel Administration at Cornell University and in the first Cornell in Hawaii program.
From the *Cornell H.R.A. Quarterly*, February 1962, pp. 80-86. Reprinted by permission.

Why Miami Beach?

Among the favorable circumstances in Miami Beach was the intense competition in an area which had almost 350 hotels with 30,000 hotel and motel rooms on a strip of land covering only seven square miles. The post-war boom was in full flood, and many hotels were being sold, re-sold and often operated by men who were without previous experience in the industry.

The union felt that it had allies among the employees—many of whom were so-called "snow-birds"—who were loyal union members in their northern home cities during the off season.

Finally, it was the union belief that the hotel patrons—who were not only vacationers and seekers of rest and relaxation, but convention and business groups too—would not put up with the inconveniences which usually attend labor difficulties. Nor would patrons from the increasing number of groups allied with organized labor wish to become involved with picket lines.

Little did the union realize that before the battle was over it would have spent in excess of $1,500,000 on the Miami Beach effort for legal fees, soup kitchens and other strike costs. Nor did the hotelmen realize that their Miami Beach Hotel Association would founder on the rocks of union recognition, and their membership stay divided for years afterward.

Laying the Groundwork

There had been several previous attempts at organizing the hotels in Miami Beach, for the area was a tempting target. However, each had resulted in a setback and the matter rested until the General Executive Board of the union in January of 1955 made the decision to commit the resources of the international union in the fight.

During 1954, in a preliminary move, the union decided to create a specific local for the purpose, and on March 1, 1954 Local No. 255, Hotel Employees Union, was chartered and given jurisdiction. Since the new local had to be financed by the international union, it was soon placed under trusteeship, with Albert H. Berlin as trustee. (In a trusteed local, there are no officers or by-laws. The trustee had powers limited solely by the parent organization under the laws at that time.)

Thus the structure of the local union was ready, and a Greater Miami Hotels Organizing Committee was named to coordinate the drive. In addition, to Berlin, the roster included the top union officials in Chicago, Los Angeles, Atlantic City, Boston, Detroit, St. Louis, Philadelphia, Cincinnati and New York, all of whom had much experience in organizing workers.

This committee was under the direction of the international president, and one of its first acts was to authorize Berlin to hire key employees to work as organizers in the hotels. To facilitate communications and maintain morale, a four-page union newspaper was established.

By February of 1955, David Herman, at the time president of huge Local 6 in New York City, was drafted for temporary duty to head the effort on a full-time basis. International vice president, Mrs. Myra Wolfgang of Detroit, and the president of the Los Angeles Joint Executive Board, John Cooper, were sent to aid him. Soon after his arrival, Herman began serving demands on Saul S. Cohen, Association president, to meet with him as the representative of the workers. Cohen and the hotelmen refused, and after the third formal refusal the union called a mass meeting of the employees on April 12, 1955.

The Strike Begins

Early the next morning, the workers at the Saxony and Monte Carlo hotels walked out and picketing began. Two days later the Roney Plaza was struck, and in quick succession was followed by the Casablanca, Sherry Frontenac, Sans Souci and Sorrento. A week later the Algiers, Sea Isle and the Lombardy were struck, bringing to nine the number of hotels with picket lines.

The employers rushed into court seeking injunctions against the picketing. When the local courts denied their requests, the Empress was struck, followed two days later by the Di Lido, as the attorneys for the employers prepared appeals to the superior courts.

The hotels rallied quickly to the challenge, and organized flying squads of department heads and key employees who would rush to the scene of new picketing and keep the hotels operating while recruiting efforts were speeded up to replace the strikers. Housing within the hotels was provided for workers who remained loyal to management; others were brought in by teams of recruiters operating in other cities, and the struck houses were able to maintain service. Employment offices were set up in hotels not yet struck or picketed, and at one time hotelmen established their own employment agency.

Union pickets were well instructed, and, while there were instances of violence and intimidation, most of them took place in areas away from the picket lines. The final U.S. Supreme Court decision years later would note that there had been no violence involved in the cases before it. (The union did not appeal those cases where violence had been established). At the high tide of picketing, sixteen hotels were involved, though not at the same time, and seven others were on the unfair list.

Legal Phase

Both parties to the struggle were surprised at the strength of their opponents. The hotels maintained operations in the face of the picket lines with only some initial difficulty and pursued their efforts to stop the picketing through legal action. Thus began one of the longest and costliest legal battles in the history of the industry.

The tactics of both adversaries were brilliant,[1] and the final results could not become known until the United States Supreme Court handed down its decision in the Saxony Enterprises and eleven other cases on January 12, 1959, almost four years later and long after the strike was settled.

The union won the first round when the Dade County Courts refused the applications of seven of the first nine hotels for injunctive relief. Its victory, however, was short lived, for on application by the hotels to the Florida Supreme Court the decision was reversed and picketing was banned. From that point on it was a see-saw battle. As the union established new picket lines, the employers would get injunctions, and the picket lines would be removed, to be re-established elsewhere where the process would be repeated.

Florida Labor Laws

Florida happens to be the very first of the "right-to-work law" states, and its law was embodied in the Declaration of Rights in the Constitution of the State of Florida, which says in part:

> The right of persons to work shall not be denied or abridged on account of membership or non-membership in any labor union, or labor organization; provided that this clause shall not be construed to deny or abridge the right of employees by and through a labor organization or labor union to bargain collectively with their employer.

Yet it wasn't the "right-to-work law" which proved so troublesome to the union. Another statute called the "Union Regulation Law," in the union's opinion, was responsible for bringing them to the brink of disaster. While appearing to require an employer to bargain with a union representing a majority of his employees, it failed to establish any method of proving in law whether a union had a majority. It stated in part:

---

[1] Principally Marion E. Sibley for the Employers and Jacob W. Brown for the union.

It shall be unlawful for any person . . . to participate in any strike, walk-out or cessation of work or continuation thereof without the same being authorized by a majority vote of the employees to be governed thereby provided, that this shall not prohibit any person from terminating his employment of his own volition. (Fla. Stat., Sec. 447.09 (3) 1953).

The union soon found that it was in the position of being unable to establish the fact that it represented a majority of the employees in a specific hotel, for it feared to show authorization cards because of possible employer retaliation against the signers. There was no governmental agency authorized to conduct secret elections or to protect the voters against possible reprisals.

In one of the court cases involving the San Marino Hotel,[2] a local judge ordered such an election to be held, but that part of the decision was stayed on a writ of certiorari by the Florida State Supreme Court. The union's efforts to conduct "elections" under the auspices of a local radio and television commentator had no standing in law, and of course were not recognized by the employers.

By December of 1955 there were 22 injunction cases in the courts, and, while local courts denied the hotels' requests for injunctive relief, in every case they were overruled in the superior state courts, especially in the Florida Supreme Court.

A typical case which was later to make legal history was the one involving the Saxony Hotel, titled "Sax Enterprises vs. Hotel Employees Union Local No. 255,"[3] which went all the way to the United States Supreme Court. Management alleged that it was being coerced to sign a contract designating the union as the exclusive collective bargaining representative so that the contract could then be used to force individual employees to join the union.

Federal Law Invoked

As case after case was being lost in the Florida Supreme Court, the union decided to invoke federal law and reversed its long standing position opposing jurisdiction of the hotel industry by the National Labor Relations Board. Its attorneys filed a petition with the NLRB's Tenth Regional Director in Atlanta, (NLRB Docket 10-RC-3155, August 9, 1955) requesting certification as bargaining

---

[2] Thos. Jefferson, Inc. vs. Hotel Employees Union Local 255, 81 So. 2d (Fla. 1955).

[3] 80 So. 2d 602 (Fla. 1955), 93 So. 2d 591-598; and 358 U.S. 270.

representative for the employees in the hotels. The director denied the petition, on grounds established earlier, including the Hotel Association of St. Louis case (92 NLRB 1388,1951) in which, ironically enough, the union had supported the employers' plea opposing jurisdiction.

The union then requested a hearing before the full board in Washington, which was held on August 9, 1955, with the American Hotel Association intervening on behalf of the employers. On August 26 the board upheld the action of its regional director. An appeal to the board to reconsider was denied on October 11, and at this point the union decided to file a suit in the Federal District Court in the District of Columbia against the NLRB and its chairman, Boyd Leedom.

The District Court affirmed the decision of the NLRB, whereupon the union appealed the case to the U.S. Court of Appeals, which in turn upheld the lower court. However, the dissenting opinion of one of the judges in the appeals court raised points which were successfully used by the union in its last-ditch appeal to the U.S. Supreme Court. On November 24, 1958, the U.S. Supreme Court held that "Dismissal by the NLRB of petitioner's representation petition, on the sole ground of the board's long established policy of not asserting jurisdiction over the hotel industry as a class, was beyond the board's power."[4]

NLRB Assumes Jurisdiction

In May of 1959 the NLRB, after a series of public hearings, formally assumed jurisdiction of the hotel industry. Its first case was destined to involve another Florida hotel, the Floridan in Tampa.

While the battle to force the NLRB to assume jurisdiction was in progress, litigation in the Florida State courts over the picketing continued. By the strikes' end there had been 37 trials of temporary and permanent injunctions in the Dade County Circuit Courts, and 23 cases argued before the Florida Supreme Court. Each case was argued and tried on various motions, cross petitions, requests to hold elections, etc., and some cases were argued three or four times in the Florida Supreme Court.

The final rulings in that court were adverse to the union's position, and because of their serious effect on the union's right to picket, it decided to appeal the case to the United States Supreme

---

[4] 101 U.S. App., D.C. 414, 249 F (2d) 506, reversed and case remanded.

Court. There were 11 cases which were combined for argument with the Saxony Enterprises case, and on January 12, 1959 the U.S. Supreme Court said:

> There being no violence involved, the Florida State Courts were without jurisdiction to enjoin the organizational picketing of the Florida resort hotels here involved, whether it was activity protected by Section 7 of the National Labor Relations Act or prohibited by Section 8 (b) (4) . . . even though the National Labor Relations Board refused to take jurisdiction . . . reversed.

Economic Phase

While the union did its best to dramatize the picketing by selecting pretty girls in halters and shorts to carry picket signs, it soon began to complain of a news blackout in the northern cities regarding the strike. And as the picket lines were removed through court injunctions, the union intensified its campaign to have sympathizers honor its "invisible picket lines."

Newspaper display ads were prepared for insertion in northern newspapers, titled "Official Notice to Members," proclaiming a work stoppage in seven named hotels (later 12). The union was bitter because the daily newspapers in at least five cities (St. Louis, Washington, Detroit, Cleveland, and Philadelphia) refused to accept the advertisements.

Thus began a campaign without parallel in hotel annals to bring employers to capitulate through publicity and economic pressure in the major cities from which patrons came. The AFL through its president, George Meany, wired its full support, as did the CIO and its then president, Walter Reuther. The International Labor Press, through its 285 member newspapers, coined the slogan, "Stay out of Miami until it's over—don't spend your union dollars in a non-union town."

In New York the largest hotel union, Local 6, together with the Hotel Trade Council representing other unions, bought space in the papers, and arranged for radio and TV announcements to tell the story of the strike.

In Los Angeles there was a five-minute work stoppage in the Ambassador Hotel, owned by the Schine interests as were the Roney Plaza and McAllister hotels in Miami Beach and Miami. Later the Seagram Building on Park Avenue in New York was picketed because the Schine Enterprises Corporation had offices there.

Travel agents were visited, owners and minority hotel stockholders were contacted, and every possible labor connection was exploited to put pressure on the employers to sign, and on patrons to pass up Miami Beach vacations.

Convention groups were likewise pressured, the most prominent being the American Legion whose convention was held in Miami in October of 1955 but which was subjected to repeated demands to cancel.

In Congress, union sympathizers, among them Senators Paul Douglas and Herbert Lehman, called for legislation compelling the NLRB to assume jurisdiction.

At the AFL headquarters in Washington, a special committee of seven AFL presidents was formed in June 1955 to broaden support for the by then sagging strike. In July George Meany made a nation-wide radio broadcast from the New York State Federation of Labor Convention in Buffalo titled "Misery in Paradise."

In August, Governor Leroy Collins was asked by the union to help settle the strike but without success.

The 1955 Labor Day parade in Miami was featured by a torchlight parade headed by the Dade County Central Labor Union and 1,500 members of the Hotel Employees Union, as the adversaries jockeyed for position for the forthcoming winter season. A number of conventions were canceled. The Association charged the union with the "rule or ruin" tactics when it was discovered that the union had somehow secured access to lists of tourists who had written the Miami Beach Chamber of Commerce requesting information in response to advertising paid for by municipal funds. The union was accused of writing the tourists to stay away from Miami Beach until the strike was settled.

The Mayor of Miami Beach's sister city to the west, Abe Arono-witz, at a Union rally on September 27 said: "The hotels must learn that they have used all the technical means of trying to stop the workers and realize that there is a great moral issue at stake. Miami cannot afford a continued hotel strike."

This rally was important in another way, for the union announced a change of leadership in the local.

Bert Ross, a former Miamiam and an International Union vice president from the Mid-Atlantic States, replaced David Herman, who returned to his duties as president of Local 6 in New York City. Ross' arrival was heralded as a change in policy by the union, from the militant and aggressive methods of Herman to the quiet, soft-sell and reasonable persuasion of Ross.

The first faint cracks were beginning to appear in the solid wall of employer opposition. The Monte Carlo, one of the two originally struck hotels, signed a contract on October 14, 1955. (The Delano, a non-member of the Association, had signed before the commencement of the strike. Two smaller hotels, the Vanderbilt and the Patrician had also signed). Then the newly built 300-room Seville, scheduled to open on December 20, announced three days earlier that it had signed a contract. Yet Christmas week and the impending winter season saw no apparent let up in the determination of both parties to fight to the finish.

The union published ads in northern cities warning members that they would be subject to fines and expulsion if they took jobs in struck hotels. (Later, some 57 union members at the Fontainbleau were fined $100 each and expelled from the union for crossing the picket line).

On December 21, the Fontainbleau was struck. The union claimed it was in protest of management's action some days earlier in requiring employees to sign so-called "Yellow Dog" contracts under penalty of dismissal.[5] The picketing began at 6 a.m., and by noon had been enjoined by the courts upon the application of the employer. This was destined to be the last picket line on Miami Beach until the strike's end.

Greater New York-Miami Strike Aid Committee

The previously formed Greater New York-Miami Strike Aid Committee in New York City went into high gear in pursing its three principal objectives: (1) cutting off the supply of skilled workers; (2) promoting a boycott among prospective patrons; and (3) cutting off TV and radio talent at the source.

This committee was successful in stopping recruiting efforts on lower Manhattan's employment agency row for New Year's eve. Waiters and bartenders jobs were offered in Miami Beach hotels plus round-trip passage by air for a package price of $25. Pickets were placed in front of the employment agencies doing the recruiting, and a tumultuous picketing episode involved turning back fifteen waiters at Idlewild Airport as they were about to emplane for Miami Beach. These incidents got the first comprehensive publicity of the strike in New York City papers; in fact, more in four days than in the entire preceding period of the strike.

Picket lines were also established at NBC in Radio City to try to dissuade NBC officials from going through with planned television shows in Miami Beach, such as the Steve Allen show. That show was

---

[5] An agreement in which the worker states he does not wish to join a union.

held as planned at the Saxony, although the stagehands' union pick-eted it and were promptly enjoined. Two days later NBC announced it would originate no more shows in Miami Beach as long as the labor dispute in the hotels continued. In a few days, ABC and CBS did likewise.

On the customer front, the committee established an "information center" on the Miami Beach strike just off Times Square, where through signs, pamphlets and word of mouth they sought to discour-age patrons from going to the struck hotels. Governor Leroy Collins of Florida, on a tour to sell northern industrialists on the advantages of Florida for industry, found himself greeted by pickets outside his hotel in Pittsburgh.

The Strike Continues

These activities stirred up a hornet's nest of opposition to union tactics in Miami Beach. The City Council, the Miami Beach Tax-payers Association, and the Presidents Council, consisting of the presidents of most of the city's civic organizations, denounced the union for trying to "ruin the Beach." But after the flurry of charges and counter-charges was over, the strike grimly continued.

On February 9, 1956, President George Meany, of the AFL, speak-ing at a large labor rally in Bayfront Park, in neighboring Miami, announced the signing of the 300-room Di Lido Hotel, an association member, to a union agreement.

On March 12, the newly built 350-room Eden Roc Hotel signed an agreement, as did the 148-room Hotel Shelborne. Union jubilation was tempered by President Miller's warning that "the union has a long way to go before the Miami Beach Hotel Association can be declared decisively defeated."

At this point, the union published an eight-page brochure for dis-tribution to labor, business and convention groups. The booklet con-tained photographs and quotes from the hotelmen who had previ-ously signed union contracts extolling the business advantages ac-cruing to them.

On April 26, 1956 the union launched an advertising campaign in the North to counteract its former efforts to dissuade travelers from coming to Miami Beach at all. The emphasis was on "Now Miami Beach has a union label" and it urged the public to patronize only the nine union hotels. Convention groups which had scheduled head-quarters in the 21 remaining struck hotels were pressured to switch to union hotels, and several did.

On June 15, the 145-room Sea Gull Hotel signed. In July the first motel on the "strip" north of town signed, the 300-room Colonial Inn. Then the small Bel Air Hotel signed and in November the 248-room Empress, followed by the soon to open giant of Bal Harbour, the 475-room Americana.

During the late summer of 1956 there were persistent rumors of an impending peace pact between the warring parties. Before it could come to pass, there was another change in the leadership of Local 255. In August, Bert Ross was summarily dismissed for reasons which have never been made public and shorn of his vice presidency at the next General Executive Board meeting.

Peace Overtures

By October 17, the rumors had reached the stage where the union felt compelled to call a membership meeting to report on the peace efforts. General Counsel Jacob Brown reported to the meeting that Abraham L. Bauman, a New York labor attorney and specialist who had the confidence of both parties, had been attempting to mediate the dispute, and that the first face to face meeting of the disputants was imminent.

October passed, as did November and December. On January 5, 1957, before TV cameras and reporters, in the City Council Chambers in Miami Beach City Hall, the parties signed an association-wide master contract bringing to an official end, after twenty-one months, the longest and costliest strike in hotel history. The contract was for a ten-year period, with yearly reopenings for wages, hours and working conditions, with compulsory arbitration if agreement was not reached. Immediate wage problems were deferred until May 1, 1957 and subsequent arbitration.

The importance of the signing of the master agreement was emphasized by President Miller of the Union in his report to the 34th General Convention in Chicago in March of 1957, when he said: ". . . prior to January 5, we had gained recognition from thirteen hotels and one motel in twenty-one months, a rate of less than one a month; between January 5 and March 15, we have gained recognition from nine hotels and three motels, an average of more than one a week."

For the union, the master contract meant that the costly part of the battle to sign up individual hotels was ended, and the organized opposition of the MBHA had been eliminated. The Hotel Association, while approving the signing of the agreement by an almost unanimous vote at a sparsely attended meeting, had already split wide open with the formation of a dissident group which unsuccessfully tried to force postponement of the signing.

In the end, only the hotels represented by the members of the negotiating committee signed the new master contract at the ceremony. It would be two years later before the organization showed any sign of recovery, at which time under the new name of the "Southern Florida Hotel and Motel Association" it picked up the pieces and again began to function as a trade association.

No One Really Wins a Strike

The entire cost of the strike may never be known. As of February, 1957 the union had spent $1,000,606.41 out of its own treasury, and another $504,536.35 from affiliated locals and sympathizers. There is no record of the sums spent by the employers, nor of the losses of business and wages. In this strike, as in so many others, no one won. The union had been bled white by the costs of establishing its beachhead in the South.

The effectiveness of the union's northern boycott has been a matter of dispute, for the years 1955 and 1956 turned out to be the highest point in the tide of post-war business in Miami Beach. What probably turned the scales was that whatever group business was diverted, especially conventions, had an effect which could be seen and measured. And, the growing number of "this year's hotels" which signed prior to opening in an effort to avoid labor troubles undoubtedly had an effect on their neighbors, who realized that once the dike was breached it would only be a matter of time until their turn would come.

Effect on the Hotel Industry

The repercussions on the entire industry are still going on, for a new bargaining climate has been established. Hotels which conform to the standards defined by the NLRB ($500,000 yearly volume) are now governed by federal law rather than state law unless violence is involved. The fight to organize hotel workers continues in a dozen states.

Now that hotels are subject to federal law in the field of labor relations, renewed pressure has been felt to bring them under other federal laws, particularly the Fair Labor Standards Act, commonly known as the Minimum Wage Law. To date hotelmen have been successful in avoiding what has been called an impending disaster.

25

SOLVING THE RESERVATIONS RIDDLE

from *Hotel & Motel Management*

The Downtowner Corporation maintains its own chainwide reservations system. Downtowner's system is linked to a national network run by International Reservations Corporation, which connects to the ATAR travel agent computer terminal, which will soon link circuits with the American Automobile Association.

Confused? Don't feel silly. Most innkeepers are too. Reservations systems are springing up faster than most hotels and motels can absorb their potential impact.

Despite the confusion, it does mark an advance. Only three years ago many industry skeptics scoffed at the idea that it might be possible to operate a reservations system larger than a single company chain. Today the concept is so well accepted that the question now is not whether it will succeed but whether the next few years will produce a marriage of competing reservations systems into one or maybe two worldwide networks.

If it *is* to be a winner-take-all game, the biggest questions facing innkeepers is which systems to put their money on. "It's true that confusion exists," says the marketing VP of a leading contender. "Each of the salesmen—ours included—tends to talk only about his own system without bothering to help the hotel or motel manager see the big picture.

"As a result, we're finding that decisionmakers for hotels and motels seem to fall into four categories. One type feels that all reservations systems are *more or less the same*. He's apt to base his decision on the eenie-meenie-mo method. Next, we have the man who is confused, and so will probably wind up buying from the salesman he likes best. A third type is also uncertain, but hedges his bets by subscribing to perhaps two or three reservations services, using the

Reprinted with the permission of *Hotel & Motel Management,* Clissold Publishing Co.

lowest down payment possible on each. He wants to see how each does before choosing—which, actually, is rather smart if you can afford it. Then fourth we have the large chain operations which can afford to assign at least one systems analyst to study cost comparisons in depth."

Unfortunately, those with the resources to assign a systems analyst are far too few. The great majority are ticketed to fly by the seat of their pants.

If that includes you, *Hotel & Motel Management* might be of help. The editors have compiled a brief listing of the leading external reservations systems (as opposed to intra-chain) which we hope will serve as a starting point for those trying to solve the reservations riddle. Should you have additional questions about any of the systems mentioned below, we will be happy to forward your inquiry to the proper company.

ATAR

Operated by Atar Computer Systems, Inc., Sherman Oaks, Calif., which, in turn, is owned jointly by Informatics, Inc. (a computer software firm), and Hayden Stone (a large investment brokerage house). Atar was designed under agreement with the Air Traffic Conference to serve as a unified airline flight-scheduling and booking system for all travel agents and other accredited airlines selling agents. Eleven major airlines have been signed as subscribers so far.

When operational, the system will link an anticipated 2,700 desktop terminals at travel agent offices with a central IBM 360 computer. Cost to travel agents will range from $110 to $160 a month, depending on their volume of transactions.

Atar itself will not involve lodgings reservations. However, in July the firm disclosed an agreement with International Reservations Corporation to link Atar travel agents in a common system with IRC's inventory of hotel/motel rooms and rental cars. Hence, Atar-linked travel agents would not only be connected to every hotel or motel on the IRC system, but would be able to book complete package tours by way of Atar. At the same time, both IRC and Atar stated that each system will continue to operate independently.

Atar is obligated by contract to become operational within 11 months of approval by the Civil Aeronautics Board. Its petition for approval, however, has been opposed by the Justice Department and Telemax Corp., as inherently monopolistic because it would require all participating airlines to refrain from dealing with all reservations systems other than Atar. Several hotel groups have also protested on grounds that Atar would have dictatorial rights over which hotels and motels got airline traveler business. Atar, in turn, has pointed out that hotel reservations systems other than International Reservations Corporation are free to join the system. So far they haven't.

A CAB hearing on the matter had been scheduled to begin September 3, but was postponed at presstime pending a review of the written arguments.

EECOTEL—Totel Systems

Totel Systems Corp., Bridgeport, Conn. Internal computerized reservation system that automatically types, stores and verifies room reservation information instantly. Utilizes console containing a CRT display (TV-type screen) and keyboard, a high speed typewriter, a magnetic tape unit and a mini-computer. Stores data up to one year. Gives daily print-out of management reports. Cost is dependent on complexity of system required.

AM-EX Express Reservation Services

"Space Bank" American Express Co., New York, N.Y. World-wide room reservations service with 247,642 rooms under contract: Approximately 3,000 in Europe, 5,000 in the Far East, 5,800 in Hawaii, remainder in continental United States. Major chains include Pick, Ramada Inns, Western International, Rodeway Inns, Master Hosts, Del E. Webb Hotels, Royal Coach Motor Inns, Hyatt House, Stouffer's, Roger Smith Hotels, American Motor Inns. System uses two IBM 360 computers; cost depends on subscriber's choice of sender: $75 per month for receiver only unit; $200 per month for intermediate sender/receiver. Additional charge on each reservation: 5 percent (minimum of 75 cents) of total bill when reservation made through Express Reservation Center; 25 cents for each intra-chain referral; 50 cents for each inter-chain referral. Receiver-only equipment utilizes Bell Telephone receiver and a teletype (desk-size); others use standard key-punch terminal. Subscribers must accept American Express credit cards. Expansive development of international market planned for immediate future.

American Automobile Association National Reservation Service

AAA, Washington, D.C. Contracted to operate with International Reservations Corp. Not yet in service. Target date: January 1970. Will link many of the 12,000 AAA-approved accommodations (800,000 rooms), as well as car rental agencies, airlines, etc., with AAA's 12 million members. Projections suggest 48 million reservations over the five-year contract term. Subscribing firms will have option of using toll-free telephones or desk-size terminal computer equipment. Rates for terminals around $190 a month, which includes 120 free reservations, 90¢ charge for each additional. AAA plans additional service to include international reservations, new domestic portion is functioning.

NARS

NARS (National Accommodations Reservations Service) Computer Systems, Orlando, Fla. Claims 170 units with 10,000 rooms including Dutch Inns of America, Congress Inns, American Motelodge, Emmons Walker Best Eastern. Subscribers may use terminals (key-board punch) or WATS-line telephones for transmittals. Charge is $1.25 per reservation delivered. Rental fee for terminal, $125.00; no installation fee. Will add Management and Scientific Service of Jamaica to subscribers on November 1, 1969; 104 hotel/motel units; 5,000 rental cottages. Future plans include expansion into Canada: date undetermined.

In-Control

UMC Electronics Co., North Haven, Conn. Electronically-installed internal reservations monitor. Keyboard recording console makes permanent record of reservations on three-part, pre-printed forms at the time reservations are made. Automatically records total of rooms available on panels, each of which shows a 30-day forecast. Customers may use as many panels as desired, allowing unlimited forecast on reservations. Complements an external computer reservations system by giving management independent, instant information on room reservations and rooms availability. Equipment can be leased or bought; cost is dependent on complexity of the system necessary.

International Reservations

International Reservations Corp. Wholly-owned subsidiary of Planning Research Corp., Los Angeles. Features desk-top terminals (keyboard punch) linked to master IBM computer facility in McLean, Va. Subscribers pay installment fee of $250 and monthly $80 rental fee plus 90¢ for each reservation delivered. Subscribers also receive 40¢ per reservation placed with another participant in the network.

System is one year old, not yet operational. IRC reports 100,000 rooms (1,000 properties) ready to go, including such chains as Downtowner/Rowntowner Motor Inns, Superior Motels, Howard Johnson's Motor Inns, and Royal Inns of America. Recently linked up with Atar network of airlines and travel agents. Now plans to join with American Automobile Association in 1970, adding many more units. 1970 plans also include master computer facilities in Great Britain (already installed), southern Europe and Japan. Each overseas computer center will carry room inventories of American hotels—and vice versa.

Reservations World

Litton Industries and Diners Club, Los Angeles. Claims more than 500,000 rooms. All major hotel/motel chains and car rental firms included. No special equipment. No subscription fee. Reservations are booked for subscriber until notified of no vacancy. Transmitted by telephone or teletype. Cost is based on a percentage of customer's bill: 10 percent when communications are by telephone; 9 percent when by teletype; 6 percent when customer uses Diners Club card. To initiate requires only a letter of agreement to pay commissions.

(At presstime we learn of the purchase by American Airlines and the Continental Corp. of Reservations World from the Diners Club. American and Continental have formed a partnership to acquire the system, which will be managed by American as part of its broad range of travel services).

SEARCH

SEARCH (System European Automatique de Reservation des Chambres d'Hotel), Lloyd Outremer Co., Paris, France. System will be put into operation by January 1970. SEARCH, with plans to serve all of Europe, will be controlled by British-built Honeywell computer system linked to international teletype network. Subscribing hotels will be listed according to class, price and location in catalog published by Lloyd Outremer, which will be supplied to teletype subscribers who wish to use reservation service. Reservations can be made by direct communication from any subscribing station to computer in Paris. Computer confirms reservations immediately or, if they cannot be filled, gives details about alternate hotels in same area and class. Service will also provide records for participating hotels by giving each a detailed list every night of rooms reserved, with dates and names of persons making reservation. Cost details not available.

Tele-Res

Data Architects, Inc., Waltham, Mass. Computerized system for smaller chains and independents. Not yet operational in the United

States. Used in England to hook up eight motels with a total of 1,000 rooms. Priced at $3,900 per month per chain, regardless of number of units or number of rooms. Line charges connecting equipment additional. Necessary equipment includes a general-purpose computer to be placed in unit most central to the entire chain. Also input/output interface hardware and teletype terminals for each accommodation. Computer belonging to one chain can be hooked up with computer of another chain to provide nationwide service. Manufacturers claim Tele-Res can handle bookings, confirmations, amendments and availability searches. Also reportedly provides accurate records of room inventories for 12 months in advance, and prints out daily summaries of arrivals, projected occupancy and release bookings. Tele-Res is available on a three-month delivery schedule. Data Architects provides operation manuals and a training course for reservations clerks.

Tele-Status

Offered by Tele-Status Corp., Wyoming, Mich. Designed primarily for use by all hotels and motels within a metropolitan or small regional market. Computerized system with desk-top terminal sets allows each participating innkeeper to inform others in the network of his exact occupancy and vacancy status. Among the other benefits claimed: (1) assures that guests won't have to leave the area in search of rooms until all are filled; (2) relieves busy clerks from making phone calls to find rooms for overflow customers; (3) enables participants to replace late cancellations promptly by instantly alerting others in the network to the new vacancy. In addition, the company can install Tele-Status monitors at airports, convention bureaus, etc., so that incoming visitors can quickly check the list of available rooms in the area.

Telemax

Maxson Electronics, Westchester County, N.Y. Computer-backed comprehensive reservations system. Claims more than 200,00 rooms on inventory. Major chains include: Quality Motels, Marriott Motor Hotels, Marriott Inns, Hotel Corporation of America, Best Western, Canadian National, Realty, Gotham. Also all national car rental firms and 12 airlines: American, Frontier, Air France, BOAC, Japan, KLM, Qantas, SAS, Irish International Airlines, Lufthansa, Swissair, Olympic Airways. Necessary equipment includes desk-sized terminal computer equipment hooked into the Telemax UNIVAC computer center. Sender/receiver is simple to operate and can make and confirm reservation in less than five seconds. Rent is $98 per month. In addition, there is a 60¢ charge for each reservation made. Toll-free telephone service is also available through the WATS line to the Omaha-based reservation center.

National Data Corporation Instant Reservations

National Data Corp., Atlanta, Ga., working with Mobil Oil Corp. Only equipment necessary for hotels and motels is a telephone. NDC's room-sized computer keeps an automatic daily room inventory that subscribing hotels and motels can add to as often as necessary without charge. Computer lists properties' basic facilities and rotates room availabilities on a "fair share" basis. NDC operator will answer and check out any telephone request within seconds and give guest and property a special "confirmation number." No initial fees or minimum charge. A charge of $1.35 is made for every guest that shows; no payment required for no-shows.

"Private" Nomenclature Adds to Confusion

Major organizations which have their own computerized reservation system, or which have affiliated with a reservation system, may wish to retain their own identities. Travelers are bombarded with advertisements selling such systems as:

	Group	Affiliation
Holidex	Holiday Inns	———
Instant Host	Howard Johnson's	International Reservations
Phone-A-Towner	Downtowner Corp.	International Reservations
Qualimax	Quality Motels	Telemax
Quick-Pick	Pick Hotels	AM-Ex Reservation Services
Ramada Inn-Stant	Ramada Inns	AM-Ex Reservation Services
Reservatron II	Sheraton	———
Royal Express Reservations	Royal Coach Motor Hotels	AM-Ex Reservation Services

26

THERE IS NO RESERVATIONS RIDDLE

from *Hospitality*

"Reservation systems are not new," said Robert Wigger, vice president of Booz, Allen & Hamilton, recently.

"Most people think they are because they are now emerging in the hotel-motel industry, but basically the hotel-motel industry had reservations systems for hundreds of years. We just added a new gadget which is called a computer."

Mr. Wigger was participating in a panel discussion on reservation systems at the annual convention of the Massachusetts Hotel-Motel Association, in Provincetown. His point was well taken.

Although confusion over reservation systems does exist, most of it stems from the lodging operator's lack of knowledge about computers and data processing equipment. The service performed by a reservation system is the same service that was formerly performed by telephone and, before that, by mail. Reservation systems simply make it easier for your customer to make a reservation. There is no riddle over reservation systems.

Of course there are different reservation companies, and each offers a distinctive program. Some confusion over reservation systems does result from this difference. Basically, however, there is little to be confused about. You don't have to be a computer technician to belong to a reservation network and benefit from it.

What the Systems Do

All of the reservation systems employ computers. Each system's computer is linked to the system's reservation offices throughout the United States (and in some cases, the world). When a traveler telephones one of these reservation offices and inquires about a room in Phoenix, the reservations girl instantly contacts the system's computer. She uses something called a VDT—a television receiver and a

From *Hospitality*, December 1969. Reprinted by permission.

typewriter—to communicate with the computer. She types the guest's requirements, date of arrival, number in the party, etc., and then asks the computer if accommodations meeting these specifications are available. The computer immediately checks its files and reports back. If the caller has requested a particular lodging facility, the computer checks the availability at that motel or hotel and reports back.

Most systems also offer sending and receiving equipment to their member motels and hotels. Each lodging property with this equipment then becomes—in effect—another reservation office. When a reservation is made through another motel or hotel, or through the regular reservation office, the computer checks its files for availability and then automatically sends the reservation information to the lodging property where the guest will stay.

If the lodging property does not have its own terminal (teletype or special device installed by the reservation company), then the computer sends the reservations information to the nearest reservation center, which in turn calls the property and advises it of the reservation. Some reservation companies will provide equipment for receiving only, but most systems prefer to install both sending and receiving equipment.

How to Evaluate a System

Mr. Wigger, whose company has just completed a study of reservation systems for the American Hotel & Motel Association, says there are four important factors to consider in evaluating a reservation system.

"Number one," said Mr. Wigger, "is the ability of the reservation service company to gain and maintain availability in their computers. Their stock in trade is having your availability." The more available rooms the computer has stored in each area of the country, the greater the service provided to the traveler. The greater the service, the more frequently travelers will use the system.

"Number two is the ability of the reservation service company to have the traveler or his representative call its centers for reservations," said Mr. Wigger. "In other words, they must advertise, and they must get what we call penetration. The traveling public must call them."

The third factor is extremely important, said Mr. Wigger. It is, "the performance of the company in total and its computer-to-computer linkage with airlines, auto rental and reservation companies." The term system does not mean a computer, Mr. Wigger said. It means the quality of service from the telephone reservation center, the accuracy of their billing system, the technical services provided, and the training and education of the staff.

The fourth factor is the placement of a terminal at each location, when it is justified by volume of reservations received. "The essential element in the future," Mr. Wigger noted, "will be the number of terminals that company A or B actually has out in the market place."

What About Independents?

Although all of the major reservation systems sought to sign motel and hotel chains initially, nearly all of them are now interested in independent properties. The first thing that independents should do, says Mr. Wigger, "is to sign up with several reservation companies, so as to provide maximum exposure at a minimum cost.

"We are seeing in the hospitality industry the same characteristics in American business that we see in the distribution of products. Historically, if we were back in the early '40s and '30s, we had delineations—a drug store, a market and so forth. If you wanted aspirin, you went to the drugstore. After World War II, we had a revolution in that manufacturers were interested in getting maximum distribution for their products. Thus, today you see aspirin displayed in a wide variety of stores. Traditional characteristics of defining a drugstore or even a gasoline station have been shattered by the distribution of products at multiple points. I think in the lodging industry you are going to see a similar effect."

Lodging operators should want maximum exposure for their properties, Mr. Wigger said. As travelers become more sophisticated, he predicted, they'll want a simple and easy method of making reservations. The lodging property linked to a reservation network that includes other hotels and motels, airlines, travel agencies and rent-a-car outlets will therefore be offering its services and facilities to a much broader market.

When the volume of reservations indicates which reservation company is providing the most business, the lodging operator may then consider the selection of a particular terminal.

What About the Future?

The study prepared for the American Hotel & Motel Association by Mr. Wigger's company predicts that "all small and large lodging industry chains will have their own reservation systems or use the services of reservation companies by 1972."

In addition to anticipating the use of reservation systems by chains, the study concluded that independent motels and hotels will be storing their room availability data in one or more hotel-motel reservation systems by 1972. By 1974, the traveler will be able to make lodging, transportation and car rental reservations with one call to an airline, travel agent, hotel or motel. Further, it is expected that technology will be available in 1974 to produce and deliver transportation tickets and reservation confirmation forms automatically. Copies of the External Reservation Services Analysis are obtainable from the American Hotel & Motel Association, Membership Services Department, 221 West 57th St., New York, N.Y. 10019. Price is $1.50 to members and $2.50 to non-members.

The Big Four

There are many reservation systems, with more being introduced every quarter. For all practical purposes, however, presently only four offer the advantages of a large reservation network. In alphabetical order, they are: AM-EX Express Reservation Services, Inc., 67 Broad Street, New York, N.Y. 10004; International Reservations Corporation, 1100 Glendon Avenue, Los Angeles, Calif. 90024; Reservations World, P.O. Box 1068, Ansonia Station, New York, N.Y. 10023; and Telemax Corporation, 6 Kingsbridge Road, Fairfield, N.Y. 07066.

Nearly all of the major lodging chains and referral organizations, without systems of their own, belong to at least one of these four systems. Each of these systems has a large network of independent members as well. All of these systems are considered highly reputable by Hospitality editors.

Other Systems

Many other systems are in the process of development or are already competing with the big four. Several of these hold promise. The International Telephone and Telegraph Corporation is currently developing "a worldwide computer reservation system linking the airlines and travel agencies." Eventually, there may be two systems. The first will link travel agencies with airlines. The second will connect transportation companies, hotel and motel reservation systems, travel agents and other service organizations.

Another system that is somewhat different from the other systems is the Eecotel International Reservation Computer System. Standard Eecotel systems are tailored to each hotel's requirements. They can book reservations for up to one year, store them away according to date of arrival, name, type of room and stayover period, and print out a written confirmation in one operation. Most reservation systems experts say internal reservations systems will ultimately be linked to external reservation systems. Eecotel Computer Corporation is located at 4695 Main Street, Bridgeport, Conn. 06606.

27

MOTELS

David Shulman

Motel? Hotel? Tourist Court? Name it, the definition of what constitutes a lodging facility is so difficult to pin down that even the dictionary falters. When it conducts its Census of Business, the Department of Commerce simply allows each lodging property to specify its own classification (motel, hotel or motor hotel), without using a definite formula. Whatever the label, motor-oriented lodgings come in all sizes, all shapes and with all types of services.

A far cry from yesterday's stop-overs for stagecoach passengers, the multi-storied Marriots, Holidays, Sheratons, etc., satisfy any physical requirement. All offer fine accommodations. Swimming pools, color TV, direct dial telephones, coffee-in-the-room, relaxor beds, fine furniture, rooms with a view, just name the service and the room price—today's motel/motor-inns have what you need.

Motels emphasize service, and personal attention is apparently still in vogue. Restaurants, from gourmet to snack shops, are finding their way into more and more motel facilties.

You may wish to enter the motel business as a franchise investor or as an investor/operator. To better acquaint you with the growth industry, *Franchise Journal* has collected some statistics of interest. Due to the confusion in terminology and to reporting techniques, the figures may not be precise, however, they do give an adequate picture of general trends in the industry.

First, it is important to know that basically there are four kinds of motel operations besides the independent owner type. They are:

Franchise Chains: Builders and operators are licensed to use the name and must conform to standards set by parent firm. Franchise fee and continuing per room royalty is charged.

One-Operator Chains: Single ownership networks with no ownership by operator. Staff supplied by parent company.

Referral Chains: Independently owned motels agree by membership to use a common name, in addition to their own, share reservation networks and generally agree to maintain certain standards.

Co-Owner Chains: Owned in a partnership arrangment between the parent company where the investor owner-manager usually owns as much as half the stock in the facility.

Tourist Court Journal, a trade publication in the field, supplied us with the following statistics. In 1967, over 1.1 billion people were accommodated in motels and that number is increasing by the thousands daily, due to the interstate highway program, the demise of railroad travel, the changing face of business complexes, as well as more leisure time.

In 1967, there were about 60,400 motels which had 1,234,000 rooms. In 1969, there are reported to be about 60,000 motels, but they maintain over 2,100,000 rooms. If hotels are included, the accommodations increase to an estimated 2,600,000 rooms, according to *Hotel & Motel Management,* another trade paper.

Here are more revealing statistics:

40 percent of all motels are located beyond the city limits but on the highways leading to that city.

20 percent of all motels are located in suburbs.

27 percent are located in fringe downtown areas.

13 percent are located in downtown areas.

37 percent have restaurants but estimates indicate that 75 percent of to-be-built motels will have them. (Yet the increase in occupancy percentage shows restaurants to increase occupancy by only one percent when they have restaurants.)

44 percent presently have swimming pools and 78 percent of the new motels will have them.

92 percent presently have TV sets and this will increase to 95 percent with new motels.

Only 57 percent presently have telephones in the room and 77 percent will have them.

15 percent have a liquor license but 54 percent of the new ones will have one.

75.6 percent are owner-managed and 95 percent are presently independent. *(Motel Newsletter* reports that independents thought to be on the wane receive a new lease on life through present day referral membership plans available). These numbers should be tempered by the fact that many of the present motels included in the statistics, of course, are old, small and out of date. Today, however, the giants, the chains of one type or another, account for over 70 percent of all *new* construction so the figures above will probably change rapidly.

Here are some additional facts:

The hotel/motel industry reported gross receipts of $7.4 billion in 1968. Estimates through 1975 indicate at least $8.5 billion is to be expected.

Allowing an adjustment for the large percentage of smaller motels, the average number of rooms per modern motel is 60, with some facilities having hundreds of rooms in one motel.

The average occupancy rate is 73.6 percent and room rates average about $11.42 per room.

The average *construction cost per room* appears to be about $7,000, and that is drawn from a range of $4,500 to $15,000.

The average gross room income in 1968 according to *Tourist Court Journal* was $3,000 per room. Motels with 10 and under rooms showed an income of $1,655 per room, per year, while income of 101-unit and up showed an annual room income of $3,891 per unit. Income is also produced from services. The range of income from the rental of sales rooms averaged 11.8 percent, sleeping rooms 83.64 percent, and other 4.5 percent. Operating expenses averaged about 52 percent while capital expenses averaged about 31 percent. The average profit was about 16 percent on an advantage investment

Figure 1. There is a direct ratio between profit and the number of rooms per facility, and a similar ratio in the occupancy rate. Here's how they read:

		Occupancy	(before capital expenses) annual profit per room (1968)	(after capital expenses) annual profit-per room (1968)
Motels with	1-10	64%	$1,053	$364
	11-20	67%	1,226	439
	21-40	72%	1,381	488
	41-60	74%	1,682	541
	61-100	73%	1,749	642
	101 up	78%	2,218	769

of $359,200. It is important to remember that these facts are based on averages, which include wide variances between geography and number of units. Therefore a comparison with information received from a specific operation may seem to bear very little resemblance to these averages.

The factors which should be studied in this business are basically the net profit ratio; the net return on investment; the owner's return for labor and management; operating expenses; gross operating profit; capital expenses; average percentage of room occupancy; average room rates and depreciation methods and practices.

It would seem that although the cash investment requirements are high that there are several methods of entering the field. The firms listed here offer many different approaches and concepts and it would appear that most every requirement can be filled.

The science of site location in the motel business is often handled by independent firms. If the investor already owns a piece of property, or is considering one, a feasibility study is usually conducted by companies specializing in this business.

Training will vary from company to company. Some firms suggest or pay for a private motel training school, and others offer involved and sometimes expensive training schools. Holiday Inns is building a complex training school for the purpose.

The single point which most firms seem to agree on is that in the motel business, the operator is the single greatest factor for success. The financial statements notwithstanding, the man who finds people interesting, who can promote, build goodwill and involve himself in his community will make his motel investment profitable. Motels are good investments for either owner operators or for investment and your thorough investigation of the listed firms could be a worthwhile one.

Franchise Journal is indebted to several trade magazines and the American Hotel & Motel Association for the collection of our statistical information. Those interested in investigating the motel industry as a franchise investment should subscribe to any or all of the publications available for a continuing exposure to the activity in the motel business. For more information on the motel business write:

Tourist Court Journal. Temple, Tex. 76502;
Hotel & Motel Management. 105 W. Adams St., Chicago 60603;
The Motel Newsletter. 2315 Broadway, New York City 10024;
Hospitality Magazine. 5 S. Wabash Ave., Chicago 60603;
American Hotel & Motel Association. 221 W. 57th St., New York City 10019.

Alamo Plaza

Alamo Plaza Hotel Courts is one of the oldest motel chains in U.S., having been founded in 1933. Firm now has 41 motels in South, all of which are continually being updated and redecorated.

Alamo Plaza's aim is to provide the most comfortable rooms possible at economical prices. Rooms rent from $7.50 to $9 for a single, with carpeting, air conditioning, color television, and swimming pools. Convention and banquet facilities are available at some locations.

Contact W. H. Farner, Alamo Plaza Hotel Courts, 1830 Sylvan Drive, Dallas 75208.

Downtowner

Downtowner/Rowntowner Motor Inn franchises are available for one-time charge of $10,000 upon application, regardless of number of rooms. Downtowner Corp. also charges royalty fee of two percent of gross room revenue, plus national advertising fee of one percent of room groups; these are paid on monthly basis.

Cost of constructing and equipping 120-room Downtowner/ Rowntowner complex is between $7,500 and $9,500 per room, plus cost of land. Room cost is prorated to include commercial building, lobby, furnishings and fixtures. All motels offer coffee shop and/or restaurant, meeting room, swimming pool and cocktail lounge (where law permits).

Franchisees are required to send their innkeepers to parent firm's training school in Memphis, where they receive minimum of 30 days of classroom and on-the-job training.

At no cost to franchisee, Downtowner Corp. provides a member of its staff for a period of five days when the inn opens; this operational man assists in supervision of all requirements at all times. In addition, the parent firm is responsible for making an on-the-site inspection twice a year and furnishing franchisee with a written report on its findings, along with specific recommendations.

Prospective investor must first find city that doesn't have Downtowner/Rowntowner already open or committed. Prime sites for Downtowners will be located in heart of downtown business and financial area; prime sites for Rowntowners would include interstate highways, metropolitan airport areas, etc.

In addition to having suitable land (from 25,000 sq. ft. up to three acres), franchisee must submit certified financial statement on himself and any other investors who might be in his group. Careful analysis is made of the financial statement to determine that potential franchisee has sufficient capital resources to assure success of the venture.

Downtowner Corp. now has 81 motor inns in operation, 47 of which are franchised; another nine complexes are under construction, eight of which are franchised.

Contact Franchise Director, Downtowner Corp., 202 Union Ave., Memphis, Tenn. 38101.

Econo Lodge

Econo Lodge Inc. offers franchise with national promotion for the motel operator with under 50 rooms, as well as for large operators. Unless they can be assured of above average accommodations, particular travelers will pass by small motels.

Licensing is available to any new motel, provided planned layout, design, construction, furnishings and facilities meet with approval of Econo Lodge staff. Franchisor provides architectural, feasibility, legal, accounting, engineering, construction and management consultant services when requested.

Econo Lodge program requires an area franchise director, who contracts with parent firm to organize and supervise substantial area on exclusive basis. He develops and controls, within this exclusive territory, a sort of network within a network.

Parent firm trains all new owners in various phases of operation through complete training program. Franchisee may operate his own motel, or Econo Lodge will supply management.

Professionally planned and executed public relations combined with national-regional advertising program provides franchisees with continuous promotions to build Econo Lodge image.

Restaurants may be under the same ownership as motel or they may be leased or separately owned. Econo Lodge advises franchisee to have some control over restaurant to assure full cooperation.

Financing and investment projects are always individual considerations, so cash requirements vary; of course, backers of any projects must be strong enough to meet current financing qualifications. This is determined by cost of project, along with financial terms and trends in that particular market area.

An Econo Lodge area director pays $2,500 per area. Area is determined by present population and potential growth including number of existing motels within area.

Econo Lodge Franchise Inc., a privately owned concern, now has 23 locations.

Contact the firm's franchise representative, General Franchise Bureau, 3645 Warrensville Center Rd., Suite 202, Shaker Building, Shaker Heights, Cleveland 44122. Or write Russell C. C. Terry, president, sales and franchises, Econo Lodge Inc., 147 Front St., Vestal, N. Y. 13850.

Econo-Travel

Made expressly for traveler who desires clean, comfortable overnight accommodations at economy rates, new Econo-Travel Motor Hotels feature built-in economies. For instance, two-story building design keeps construction costs at minimum, yet is functional and eye-appealing.

Cost of Econo-Travel Motor Hotel is about $278,000 for building, $12,000 for paving and landscaping, $41,900 for furnishings, and $4,300 for sign (land is not included in total). There is no cash franchise fee.

Rooms run from $7 for single and $9 for double (one family), to $10 for three or four (one family). Econo-Travel doesn't franchise states or complete cities, but rather locations. Firm often desires to locate near one or several of large national chain motels; although this is not prerequisite, competition with their higher room rates seem to help rather than hinder Econo—travel operation.

Some of services parent company offers franchisee are: help with site selection, full working plans, mortgage loan assistance, bookkeeping and reservation systems, uniform equipment and furniture package, trained manager, continued management training.

Generally, only small amount of capital is required to obtain franchise, however, financial statement showing reasonable net worth and/or business experience is needed. Investor groups are encouraged. If potential franchisee does not know any other prospective investors, Econo-Travel can put him in touch with one interested in local partner for each city in which motel is established.

Contact Lloyd T. Tarbutton, president, Econo-Travel Motor Hotel Franchising Corp., #1 Tidewater Executive Center, Norfolk, Va. 23502.

Hilton Inn

Investor who wishes to obtain Hilton franchise for newly planned hotel/motel property must meet following requirements: (1) Site must be located in area which has recognized need for hotel or motor inn—a need supported by feasibility study; (2) plans must include minimum of 100 modern, first-class guest rooms plus restaurant-bar, swimming pool, and supporting banquet and meeting facilities; and (3) investor must have sound business reputation and workable program for financing project.

Formal financial arrangements need not be concluded prior to applying for Hilton Inn franchise. Hilton will provide estimates on amount of financing necessary and will suggest lending institutions where mortgage financing is available at favorable rates.

Once the franchise is granted, investor has access to Hilton Inn prototype plans (plans for both high-rise and garden-type facilities are available). Independent architect may develop original plans for Hilton Inn, however, Hilton reserves the right to review and approve all plans as condition to granting franchise.

Hilton advises franchisee in selection of manager, then trains him in working situation at existing hotel. In addition, firm provides on-the-job Hilton training for any other staff members.

Restaurant and bar service should provide healthy contribution to profitability of franchise, so Hilton franchise manual details Hilton method for its operation. Included is information on purchasing, menu planning, kitchen procedures, pricing, training techniques, bartending, controlling spoilage, etc. If franchisee desires working consultant to assist him with his restaurant and bar during opening months, Hilton will provide—at cost—highly trained specialist.

To protect franchisee's investment and value of his franchise, Hilton has established standards which every franchise operation must meet. Each Hilton Inn is inspected four times annually; these inspections serve as periodic quality control checks and help franchisee appraise efficiency of his staff.

Joining 360 cities and linking them to 160 member hotels all over the world, Hilton Reservation Service generates room sales. Each year, computerized communications system processes more than three million reservation requests.

More than $16,000,000 is invested annually in marketing of Hilton Hotel rooms and services throughout world. In direct sales, more than 500 people devote full time to sale of Hilton rooms and Hilton convention, banquet and meeting facilities.

Initial franchise fee is $100 per room, not to exceed $20,000. Once in operation, Hilton Inn franchisee pays monthly fee of four percent of total room sales. These fees are exclusive of Hilton Reservation Service fees or of separate fees for consulting and special services over and above those specified in franchise agreement.

Contact Lloyd Farwell, vice president-franchise division, Hilton Hotels Corp., 9880 Wilshire Blvd., Beverly Hills, Calif. 90210.

Holiday Inn

Holiday Inns was born in 1952, when home-builder Kemmons Wilson erected his first motel on one of main highways in Memphis. It was so successful that he built three more inns in city within next year—including first inn with convention facilities.

Wilson discussed his Holiday Inn dream with another Memphis home-builder, Wallace E. Johnson (now president of firm). In 1953 they formed partnership that a year later became Holiday Inns of America Inc.

Today the publicly-owned company has 1,100 inns (180 of which are company owned) located across U.S., Canada, Puerto Rico, Bahamas and throughout the world.

Cost of building and equipping typical 120-room Holiday Inn ranges from $9,000 and $11,000 per room (prorated to include commercial building, lobby, furnishings and fixtures). This amount does not include cost of land; firm recommends that land cost does not exceed $1,000 per room.

All Holiday Inns offer full-service restaurant, meeting room, swimming pool and cocktail lounge. Generally, franchisee's investment should be $200,000 to $300,000 over and above first mortgage obtained. Minimum license fee is $10,000 plus $100 additional per room over 100 rooms. For example, license for 60-room inn would be $10,000 as it would be for 100-room inn. Franchisee would pay $12,000 license fee for inn with 120 rooms, and $15,000 for 150-room development.

In addition, franchisee pays royalty fee of three percent of gross room revenue or minimum of 15 cents per room per night on monthly basis. There are also monthly operating fees for following: sign lease; wall script sign lease; Holidex Reservation equipment lease; metropolitan sales office reservation service; Holiday Inn University; fund for national advertising.

Investor may select any location not already committed to other parties. For typical two-story inn of 120 rooms, site should range from 3½ acres to five acres.

Contact Franchise Sales Department, Holiday Inns of America Inc., Box 18127, Holiday City Station, Memphis 38118.

Horne's Int'l

Stand 'n Snack of America Inc., Jacksonville, Fla., based food franchisor, recently acquired Horne's International Inc., from the Greyhound Corp. Horne's is wholly-owned subsidiary and will operate as separate entity out of Topeka, Kan.

There are presently 18 franchised units in operation, with opening of 19th location set for September 15 in Hartford, Conn. The Hartford motor lodge has 120 rooms and is first Horne's motel with "middle rise," featuring four stories; it can be expanded at later date to eight stories and 243 rooms. Horne's constructs contemporary as well as special design facilities.

Restaurant section, which includes dining room, coffee shop and cocktail lounge, may be leased or owned. With approval of parent firm, franchisee may operate restaurant under supervision of regional manager.

Room rates vary from $8 to $12 for single, and $10 to $16 for double (local market conditions are taken into consideration). Each motel complex contains no less than 120 units.

Franchisees are responsible for supplying personnel, but may enlist parent firm's assistance through its personnel placement connections.

To be considered for Horne's franchise, prospective investor must have minimum of $400,000 in liquid assets and show net worth of $750,000.

Contact Phil Sewell, Horne's International Inc., Suite 1100, Merchants National Towers, Box 1711, Topeka, Kan. 66601.

Howard Johnson's

Howard Johnson's Co. opened 20 Howard Johnson's restaurants and 13 motor lodges during the first half of 1969; of these 12 restaurants and three motor lodges are company owned. Firm also acquired eight restaurants and three motor lodges from licensees. As of July 15, there were 836 Howard Johnson's restaurants, 375 motor lodges, and 21 Red Coach Grills. In addition there are 37 motor lodges and three Red Coach Grills under construction.

Franchise agreement for Howard Johnson's Motor Lodge provides franchisee with use of trade name, trademarks, designs, advertising, architectural and other unique features associated with company. Initial fee is $20,000; monthly fee is $8.50 per room or 5 percent of gross receipts, whichever is greater. There is no other royalty or fee paid to firm, but Motor Lodge National Council, composed of elected franchisees, expects each operator to participate in cooperative advertising program. Howard Johnson's doesn't finance any of the investment, but it may assist licensee in preparation of presentations to financing institutions.

Investment includes cost of land, buildings furnishings and equipment, swimming pool, site improvements, utility installation, landscaping, paving of parking area, and fees to architects and contractors. Cost of installation is subject to many variables and varies widely in different geographic areas. Howard Johnson's can usually apply licensee with comparable costs of similar facilities in similar regions. In cases where prospective investor does not have specific location, company may assist in selecting site. Each motor lodge site must have potential for adjoining Howard Johnson's restaurant.

Franchisee may build, equip and operate motor lodge, or he may have landowner who will build motor lodge and lease it to licensee.

Howard Johnson's management training school is located at motor lodge operated by company in Westbury, N.Y. Four times each year two-week course is held to acquaint franchisees and managers with company concepts, standards and operating procedures.

Write the Franchise Director, Howard Johnson's Motor Lodges, P.O. Box 4541, Miami 33101.

Kelly Inn

Kelly Inns of America's franchised facilities consist of two-story brick buildings with shutters and olympic-sized swimming pools. They may include restaurant, depending on size and requirements of individual motel; restaurant is owned by franchisee.

Motels range in size from 40 to 125 rooms and cost approximately $5,000 to $6,000 per room to build. Kelly Inns makes efforts to be flexible to needs of franchisee and does not have any definite requirements for qualification. However, it is possible to become *co-owner* for as little as $20,000.

A co-owner motel is owned in partnership with parent company. Local investor-manager usually owns up to half stock of motel, the balance being held by parent corporation which selects site, designs, finances, builds and furnishes structure and supervises its operation.

Kelly Inns' franchise is offered on nationwide basis. Firm has locations associated with its referral program in Washington, California, Arizona, New Mexico and Texas.

In addition to offering complete training to franchisees, firm provides management contracts to franchise holders.

Contact Howard T. Kelly, president, Kelly Inns of America, 1332 N. First St., Phoenix 85004.

La Quinta Inn

La Quinta Motor Inns are being franchised by La Quinta National, subsidiary of Barshop Motel Enterprises. Design of the building is Spanish with flat white stucco beneath a traditional red tile roof enhanced by archways, wooden shutters, iron grillwork at windows, and authentic period lanterns. There is color television in each room and swimming pool.

Every La Quinta Motor Inn is freestanding building with 80-120 rooms built around central court. Highrise revolving sign with "caballero" symbol is leased to franchisee by parent company.

La Quinta chain, which is about a year old, currently comprises 13 motels in Texas, Louisiana and New Mexico; of these, 11 are company owned. Company projections call for 200 complexes to be completed over next 10 years. Franchise rights for California have been sold, with 40 motels planned.

Complete training of motel managers, assistant managers and housekeepers is conducted by parent firm at its headquarters in San Antonio. Management responsibilities for each franchised unit is assumed by investor, with advice and assistance of franchisor, or La Quinta is prepared to operate motel with complete management service for reasonable fee.

Franchise can be either investor/operators or investors. La Quinta franchisee should have net worth of about $500,000.

Contact Sam Barshop, president, Barshop Motel Enterprises, 1710 N. Main Ave., San Antonio 78212.

Marriott Inn

Marriott Inn Franchises Inc., wholly owned subsidiary of Marriott Corp., assists franchisee with site selection, financing, architecture, engineering, decorating, construction, training of personnel, and operation of Marriott Inn.

Only applicants who are experienced, financially stable and of good character are considered for franchises. Initial fee is $150 per constructed guest room (minimum fee $22,500), plus continuing franchise fee of 4 percent of gross room sales. Franchisee's contribution to national advertising program is 8¢ per constructed room per day. Firm can help franchisee find adequate first mortgage financing after his site has been selected and his mortgage package prepared and approved.

In general, Marriott Inns are two or three-story buildings providing transient guest rooms and public facilities. Site selection must include free-standing restaurant building which incorporates food, beverage and meeting facilities, preferably connected with inn by covered or enclosed walkways. Size and serving capacity of restaurant facilities must be compatible with size of inn and needs of community and it must be in keeping with Marriott standard of quality.

Minimum number of guest rooms in inn must be at least 150, and ultimate development is not to exceed 350. Adequate lighting and parking facilities must be provided, as well as activity court, outdoor lounging area and swimming pool.

Marriott Inns trains key inn personnel on-the-job and in classroom, and trainees are under direct supervision of parent company's staff. In addition, staff of qualified consultants is maintained for every type of property assistance required by franchisee. Consultants are paid by franchisee when and if they are needed.

Marriott now has about 300 units in operation, including 22 in Europe and eight in Latin America (principally airline catering). First franchised Marriott Inn will open in California this month.

Contact Franchise Director, Marriott Inns Inc., 5161 River Rd., Washington 20016.

Quality Motel

Minimum requirements for Quality Courts Motel include at least 75 rooms offering 24-hour desk and telephone service, restaurant, complete public services including meeting room and lounge where appropriate, computerized Qualimax advance reservation service, not less than 1,000-sq.-ft. swimming pool and televisions in every room.

Depending on local conditions, cost of construction will vary from $6,000 to $7,500 per unit. This figure includes pool, restaurant, paving and landscaping, but not land, furnishings and restaurant equipment.

Initial franchise fee is $12,500, which covers package of "conception to opening" services. When unit is opened, franchisee pays monthly royalty fee of 2½ percent of room gross. Advertising charge of 8¢ per available room per day is assessed to cover Quality's national advertising program.

Unless franchisee is planning to personally manage his motel, or already has experienced manager available, Quality will assist in locating and hiring qualified motel manager. Shortly before motel's opening, manager attends firm's management training school where he will be oriented to techniques used by chain throughout U.S. and Canada.

During "count down" period before opening of franchised motel, Quality provides franchisee with experienced personnel to activate all systems and procedures under which he will operate. For grand opening, firm supplies complete kit which sets forth entire program and how to make it meaningful introduction to community.

There are over 425 Quality motel operators in chain, referring travelers from one to another and contributing to national advertising program. Advertising includes national network and local television and radio, annual direct mail campaign, highway signs, consumer and trade publications, etc.

Contact Franchise Sales Manager, Quality Courts Motels Inc., 11161 New Hampshire Ave., Silver Spring, Md. 20904.

Ramada Inn

Ramada Inns Inc. is a publicly held corporation with motels operating in Mexico and Morocco. In U.S. firm has more than 220 company owned and franchised inns open and operating, with about 50 under construction and another 200 in various stages of development. By 1975 firm projects 1,000 Ramada Inns around the world.

Franchise owners are supplied with comprehensive operating manuals and have guidance, counsel, and knowhow of the executive staff and department heads of parent organization available on continuous basis. Included at no additional fee are services such as periodic inspections, with confidential reports to franchisee.

Franchisee fee for Ramada Inn is $12,500: monthly royalty fee is 2½ percent of gross room sales. Other monthly expenses include assessment of 8¢ per room per day for national advertising, and $232.50 for sign.

Minimum requirements for membership in the Ramada Inns chain are 60 rental units, with coffee shop, restaurant and cocktail lounge. If franchise applicant has site in mind, franchise division and its qualified specialists can help him evaluate it. If prospective franchisee does not have site, Ramada's Six Way Realty Co. possesses knowledge of most profitable areas to explore and works with him to acquire good location.

In the event that franchisee does not want to operate his Ramada Inn himself, parent firm can recommend sources for personnel. Ramada's franchise package includes on-the-job training for motel manager.

Contact Franchise Director, 3838 E. Van Buren St., Phoenix 85008.

Rodeway Inn

Preliminary plans and specifications for use in getting construction costs and financing are furnished to Rodeway Inns franchisee without extra cost. After thorough analysis of feasibility survey, firm makes recommendations as to practical number of rooms for motel, and size and type of restaurant most appropriate. Customized preliminary plans and specifications are then drawn up by franchisor's architects to fit site.

Cost of preliminary plans is included in initial franchise payment. Investor may launch career in motel business for investment as little as $12,500, plus his credit qualifications along with necessary equity capital required over and above mortgage financing obtained for a project. Royalty fee is 2½ percent of gross room sales. In addition, there is assessment of 5¢ a day per room for national cooperative advertising and promotion program.

All Rodeway Inns are built with Colonial architecture beckoning traveler to old-fashioned hospitality. Even though each Rodeway is custom designed, all bear family resemblance that it is quickly identified.

Currently Rodeway Inns operates motor hotels at airport locations in El Paso, Dallas and New Orleans. Other airport locations under development with openings anticipated this year and 1970 are Atlanta, Portland, San Francisco, Orange County (Calif.), Phoenix, St. Louis, Kansas City and Chicago. Downtown locations with high-rise motels are now under construction in Denver and St. Louis. In addition, a 16-story hotel will open in November in Honolulu; eight locations are planned for Mexico. Rodeway Inn also looks to expansion in Canada, Puerto Rico, Virgin Islands, South Pacific and the Far East.

Write Gray McCullah, vice president-franchising, Rodeway Inns of America, Box 1392, Phoenix 85001.

Royal Inn

When Earl Gagosian founded Royal Inns of America in 1965, he had a basic concept—provide more luxury in motels at reasonable rates, not the lowest but somewhere in the middle. With attractive rates, he would add sauna baths, therapy pools, heated swim pools, color TV in all rooms, central air conditioning, built-in refrigerator bars in all suites, satin bedspreads and draperies, over-sized beds and private terraces or balconies.

Royal Inns feature high-rise buildings. Erected in conjunction with most inns are two wholly-owned subsidiaries, Jolly King Restaurants and Lost Knight Cocktail Lounges. Both were organized in 1968 to add to Gagosian's "total complex" idea.

Prospective investors in Royal Inns have choice between 50/50 partnership (co-ownership) with parent firm, or as franchise under Royal Inns franchise plan. Managing co-owner plan offers 10 percent of gross income as monthly salary, rent free living in Royal Suite and 50 percent of net profits. Cash requirement is $2,500 to $3,000 per room.

Royal Inns' franchise plan requires initial one-time investment of $12,500. Then monthly royalty fee of 2½ percent of gross room sales is charged. Of course, in return franchisor provides the franchisee with his expertise in form of services.

All corporation services are provided both co-owner and franchisee including referral, centralized purchasing, company credit card and telephone reservation system, training program, insurance, computerized accounting, construction financing, site acquisition, architectural and design plans, and nationwide advertising and publicity. All franchisees and co-owners must contribute 3 percent of gross room sales to general advertising fund.

Plans call for 35 Royal Inns, 21 Jolly King and 10 Lost Knights to be open and operating by end of 1969.

Contact Franchise Division, Royal Inns of America Inc., 4855 N. Harbor Dr., San Diego, Calif. 92106.

Saddleback Inn
Saddleback Inns of the Americas made its debut in franchising about a year ago. Firm now has three inns operating in Norwalk and Santa Ana, Calif., and Phoenix. Three more are scheduled to open early in 1970 in Woodland Hills and San Bernadino, Calif., and Denver: each location will have 150 rooms and entertainment lounge.

Future plans call for acquisition of two operating hotels, one of which is located in Mexico. In addition, firm is constructing Saddleback Inn Bunkhouses (60 rooms each) in four California communities, with opening set for first quarter in 1970. Saddleback Inns hopes to have operations in 12 cities by end of 1970: Of these, at least six will be company-owned.

Each Saddleback Inn has at least 100 rooms surrounding poolfountain patio complex, with dining room, lounge/bar, coffee shop and banquet facilities. Restaurant section is owned by franchisee. Shops for clothing, sundries, hair styling, travel, etc., are generally part of every hotel. Architecture and height of facility is dependent upon location; each inn identifies closely with heritage of community.

Average construction cost per room for Saddleback Inn (100-room hotel), including banquet, restaurant and lobby and on-site improvements, all completely furnished, exclusive of land cost, ranges from

$10,000 to $15,000. Saddleback Inn Bunkhouses (minimum 50 rooms), with swimming pool, lobby and furnishings, except for land cost, runs from $8,000 to $10,000 per room.

Investor in Saddleback Inn must make an original investment of $100 per planned guest room, a minimum of $10,000. He must also have sufficient strength to qualify for financing, because the parent firm does not guaranty leases, as it does in Bunkhouse programs. Cash investment for exclusive Bunkhouse franchise is $5,000, or $100 per room if complex contains more than 50 rooms. Franchises are available all over U.S., Canada and Mexico, with initial emphasis and primary development in west.

Contact Bruce Gelker, president, Saddleback Inns of the Americas, 1655 E. First St., Santa Ana, Calif., 92701.

Scottish Inn

Publicly owned Scottish Inns of America is a new franchise. Although there are no franchised locations open as yet, 11 states have been franchised on territorial basis. Six company owned units are already in operation.

Current approved design for 100-unit motel involves restaurant facing highway with one 50-unit wing extending back from restaurant; second 50-unit wing extends to side, forming L backwards. This leaves room for another unit paralleling first and forming a U. Pool is placed to right at juncture of first two units. Restaurant is owned and operated by the franchisee.

Rooms run $6 single. $9 double and $12 family. This low figure is obtained through prefabricated construction and other economies. Scottish Inns operates as wholly owned subsidiary of Units Inc., manufacturing center for production of building components. Units handle pre-construction of all motel rooms, restaurants and much of motel's furnishings. Company's expansion plans call for the establishment of centrally located Units Inc. branches to serve each franchised territory. Individual motel rooms can be built ready for installation at rate of one per hour, then sped by truck to motel site.

Contact C.E. Scott, president, Scottish Inns of America Inc., 125 N. Kentucky St., Kingston, Tenn., 37763.

Sheraton Inn

Sheraton Inns Inc., wholly owned subsidiary of ITT Sheraton Corp. of America, grants franchises to existing hotels and motels which can meet Sheraton's standards, and to planned properties which agree to meet firm's site, building and other requirements, which are not dictated by any standard architectural design.

Initial fee for inn in planning stages if $12,500, which covers market demand study, preliminary conceptual plans, and architectural and design consultation up to time of opening inn for operation. There is monthly continuing fee of 25¢ per room per night or four percent of room sales, whichever is greatest.

Firm expects combined ownership of Sheraton Motor Inn to have net worth in excess of $1,000,000. Equity investment in individual property should be at least $250,000 over and above first mortgage commitment. Per unit cost in construction of low-rise property will range from $8,000 to $12,000; per unit cost in high-rise construction will range from $10,000 to $15,000. Furnishings for guest rooms cost between $1,200 and $1,500 per unit.

Sheraton Inns now has 148 franchised locations in the U.S. and Canada, of which 97 are in operation and 51 either under construction or in planning stages.

Sheraton maintains fully staffed departments in areas of architectural design, engineering, interior decorating and kitchen engineering, as well as specialties in variety of other fields. These activities are part of Sheraton Design & Development Inc., wholly owned subsidiary which performs this type of work for all Sheraton properties, franchised and company-owned. For all new properties, Sheraton reserves right of approval of all plans, specifications, furnishings, color schemes, interior finishes, etc. Each complex has 70-350 rooms, restaurant, cocktail lounge, meeting or banquet rooms, adequate parking space and swimming pool.

Contact Director of Franchise Sales, Sheraton Inns Inc., 470 Atlantic Ave., Boston 02210.

TraveLodge

TraveLodge Corp. recently announced that it is embarking on an expansion program adding approximately 37,500 rooms to present 23,000-room network during next five years. Expansion is being made possible through the use of a new hotel design known as tri-arc building; some 50 buildings will be constructed over next three years. All will be managed and wholly or partly owned by the corporation.

TraveLodge already has 317 motels either owned or wholly owned. In addition, there are 108 locations which are franchised. An international organization, TraveLodge has motels in U.S., Canada, and Mexico.

Motel complexes have anywhere from 54 to 340 units. Each has restaurant, which can be leased, separately owned or operated by franchisee himself.

Training program is conducted TraveLodge Center for all franchisees. It lasts two weeks and exposes student to various aspects of motel management—bookkeeping, advertising, public relations and operations.

In addition to training, firm has corp of trained operational specialists in field at all times working with motel operators to improve their techniques, buy better and advertise better. TraveLodgers meet periodically to exchange and formulate ideas for their mutual benefit; annually all gather for general conference to review operating policies.

TraveLodge maintains free telephone reservation system whereby anyone near a telephone can make a reservation simply by dialing 800-255-3050 and talking with trained reservationist at Reservation Center.

Each franchisee contributes portion of gross income to advertising fund, which supports ever-expanding program of national advertising in newspapers, magazines, billboards, radio and television.

Contact Franchise Division, TraveLodge Corp., Box 308, El Cajon, Calif. 92022.

Treadway Inns

Treadway Inns Corp., hotel division of Restaurant Associates Industries Inc., currently has 36 locations from California to Maine to Florida. Firm plans to open its first overseas hotel in Manila, Philippines, in spring of 1970. Franchises are available in all states and all overseas free countries with suitable locations.

Treadway has no stereotyped physical appearance or layout. Its goal is to serve community, to harmonize and fit into it—this principle dictates architectural style. As far as possible, firm tries to provide recreational facilities—indoor/outdoor pools, tennis, saunas, golf, etc.

Restaurants are included in complex. Firm does not favor separation of food and rooms under two managements so franchisee usually operates restaurant.

Initial franchise fee is $100 per guest room, with a minimum of $10,000. Minimum number of rooms required for building is 150. Royalty fee of 3 percent of room sales, plus 1 percent for food and beverage sales must be paid on monthly basis. In addition, there is .5 percent fee of gross room sales for national cooperative advertising.

Franchisee supplies personnel. Treadway will assist in selection of innkeeper and department heads and will train them (one week for department heads, six weeks for innkeeper).

Treadway also provides technical assistance during planning and construction phases. Included are utilization of site, inter-relations of hotel/motel functions as they affect building design, engineering requirements, and design of public spaces and service areas. Costs and expenses of outside professional consultants are paid by owner.

Contact Will Raymond, director of development, Treadway Inns Corp., 30 E. 42nd St., New York, N.Y. 10017.

28

THE MOTEL POOL

Sam L. Warrington

Today's discriminating traveling public demands sparkling, clear pool water. In fact, where to spend the night is quite often determined by an inviting pool. Keeping the pool fit for the most discriminating guest can be a nightmare to some managers. Does it have to be a headache? How can this needless headache be avoided?

Obviously, the only easy method is to hire competent pool service people to take care of the pool. Another method is to hire a competent well-trained pool operator. Contrary to the popular belief, the pool operator has a responsible position. The same care should be given to employing him as is given other personnel in responsible positions. No manager worth his salt will make a chef out of "anyone needing a job." Similar care should be given the employing of the pool operator.

Let's assume that the best available person has been employed, but he knows nothing about pool operation. Where can he learn how to operate the pool? Many local and state health departments conduct short courses locally. Pool service people, operators, safety instructors, and health department personnel teach the courses. If a short course is not available, what is another means? If your city has a surface water treatment plant, your water superintendent will be about the most knowledgeable man in town when it comes to water treatment. Perhaps no industry has as many "sidewalk superintendents" posing as experts, than are found in swimming pool operation. Even the 12-year-old swimmer gives erroneous advice with such remarks as "shut off the chlorinator, my eyes burn."

Finally, what other suggestions do you have? Well, a short, short course follows:

The water available when the pool is first filled is usually from a city main. In general, this water is bacteriologically safe, fairly turbidity free, chemically stable so that it will not corrode the distribution system. Although the city water looks perfectly clear in the bathtub, usually it will not be perfectly clear when looking through a depth of 10 feet or more.

After the pool is opened and people begin swimming, everything is added to the pool constantly; it must be kept out, skimmed out or filtered out. A partial list of things being brought into swimming pools is: soda pop bottles, ice cream sticks, glasses, sandwich wrappings, grass clippings, sand and dirt from the sidewalks, lint, hair, make-up, face creams, soap, suntan lotion, perspiration, body waste and bacteria. It can be seen, readily, that many of these larger items can be kept out by a few enforced swimming rules; however, the smaller particles must be filtered out.

Experience has shown that by passing water through sand, suspended and colloidal matter are partially removed; the chemical characteristics of the water are changed, and the number of bacteria is materially reduced. These phenomena are explained on the basis of four actions; mechanical straining, sedimentation or absorption, biological metabolism and electrolytic action.

Mechanical straining removes the particles of suspended matter that are too large to pass through the interstices between the sand grains.

Sedimentation and absorption account for the removal of colloids, small particles of suspended matter and bacteria. The interstices between the sand grains act as minute sedimentation basins in which the suspended particles settle upon the sides of the sand grains. These particles adhere to the grains because of the presence of a gelatinous coating formed on the sand grains by previously deposited bacterial and colloidal matter.

Biological metabolism is the growth and life process of living cells. This, together with electrolytic actions, causes chemical changes that occur in a water filter. Matter is used in the metabolism of all organisms. Chemical combinations of this matter are altered by the growth of the organism. Since there are living organisms on sand filters, it follows that the chemical makeup of the matter put upon the filter will be altered by the growth of the organisms on the bed.

The action of a filter occurs principally at the surface and in the layer of matter deposited thereon. Other actions take place in the gelatinous coating on the sand grains, within the body of the filter. The surface layer consists of zoogloeal jelly in which the biological activities are at their highest. On a rapid sand filter, the surface layer is composed principally of fine particles of floc. The sand of the filter may be deeply penetrated by this floc, the depth depending to some extent on the rate of filtration, the head loss through the filter, the density of suspended matter in the water, and porosity of the filtering material, the temperature and the floc index.

Rapid gravity filters and pressure filters are used in swimming pool repurification systems. More than 80 percent of the recirculation pools in this country are equipped with pressure filters as are indoor pools and small pools where space is limited. This type of filter is preferred unless the water is very hard. For large outdoor pools the gravity-type rapid filter is suitable and is preferred by some. Where the water is very hard and commentation of the filter medium is likely to occur, the open type of filter is preferred.

Batteries of four or more filters, arranged in parallel, are preferable to a single unit in order to obtain a proper wash rate where the same pumps are used. A special wash water pump may be considered desirable, but such a provision is rather infrequently made and no serious operating difficulties have been noted due to the lack of a special pump.

Filtering material should be at least 24 to 30 inches in depth and consist of suitable grades of screened sharp filter sand or crushed quartz and filter gravel. There should be at least 24 to 30 inches of free board above the surface of the filter material to the overflow troughs or pipes of rapid sand filters to permit proper washing without loss of filter sand.

Pressure filters must be equipped with pressure gauges on both the inlet pipe and the outlet pipe for determination of loss of head or back pressure in the filter medium. Pressure filters should have a proper sight glass installed on the waste discharge pipe by which the operator may watch the progress of filter washing. Such glass should be readily removable for cleaning and should be kept clean. Each pressure filter should be provided with an adequate air release, connected to the filter shell at or near the high point. The arrangement and number of valves and interconnecting piping, or "valve nest," for necessary and convenient operation of rapid filters is fairly well standardized, and a discussion thereof will be omitted. The heart of the pool is the filter and recirculating system. Thus, the next section is outlined for easy reference.

Operation of Filtration Equipment

A. Pressure Sand Filters

Operation. These filters are supplied with a filtering mat of coagulant material and operated 24 hours a day at three gallons per square foot per minute until the difference in pressure between the influent pressure gauge and the effluent pressure gauge is in the range of five to seven pounds per square inch. They should then be back-washed at the rate of nine gallons per square foot per minute (eight gallons per square foot per minute for anthrafilt media filters) for about five minutes or until the backwash water appears clear for two minutes.

Operational Problems. 1. Air Binding—Short-circulating of the fil-ter inflow can be caused by air trapped in the top of the filter. An air release valve located in the top of the shell will release this air. Automatic or manual valves are available. Manual valves should be opened several times a day. When painting the filter unit, do not paint the automatic valve shut.

2. Mechanical loss of filtering mat—Shutting down for extended periods of time, such as during the night, will not only preclude good operation based on filter design, but will result in a partial loss of the uniform filter mat.

3. Inability to read pressure differential—High reading gauges should be replaced with those that read in the range of the filter's operation. In general, gauges reading up to only 30 pounds per square inch are desirable. Another operational difficulty may be avoided by mounting gauges on the tops of filter lines to preclude clogging with sediment.

4. Rate of flow change through filters—With the pump running at the same speed, different amounts of water will pass through the filter throughout a filter run. In order to deliver a continuous three gallon per square foot per minute through the filter, a rate of flow controller should be installed. This piece of equipment is only justi-fied on large pools.

5. Filter media difficulties—Filters that are failing to produce a clear effluent should be inspected by removing the manhole cover and inspecting the sand surface after backwashing.

(a) Clean sand surface—This would indicate satisfactory opera-tion.

(b) Dirty sand surface—This would indicate unsatisfactory con-ditions. The filter should be backwashed slowly and the rising water observed.

(1) Water "breaks" evenly during test backwash—More water is needed for backwashing in this case. While the trouble may lie in an inadequate backwash pump capacity, temporary relief may be obtained by removing the top layer of sand and

washing it in a lye (caustic) solution. Another technique is to give the whole sandbed a "caustic bath" by applying one pound of lye per square foot of filter surface after allowing the water to drain down to within two inches of the sandbed surface. After four to six hours of soaking, the filter may be drained and then thoroughly backwashed.

(2) Water "breaks" unevenly during test backwash—This would indicate obstructions in the filter bed or underdrains.

This might be caused by "medballs" or accumulations of dirt and sand held together by organic growths. This sometimes can be corrected by applying two ounces of calcium hypochlorite per square foot of filter surface and practicing a soaking operation as described above. Maintenance of adequate backwash rates and application of pool disinfectant chemicals ahead of the filters will probably prevent this difficulty from reoccurring.

Some success has been reported with the use of an "acid bath" for correction of clogged filters and underdrains. Two pounds of sodium bisulfate per square foot of filter area is added and then filters permitted to soak as described above. Thorough backwashing is critical after this type of treatment to prevent damage to the metal parts of the system.

Commentation of sand grains due to mineral compounds normally in the water or added in water treatment may preclude correction by these treatments, in which case the sand might have to be replaced.

Sodium hexamentaphosphate may be fed into water to prevent the undesirable effects of excessive hardness. Dosing in the range of 5ppm is generally accepted. One suggested method for batch feeding is to add 10 pounds of the compound for each 250,000 gallons of pool capacity at the start and two pounds for each 250,000 gallons every other week. The pH should be closely watched using this method as this chemical is strongly acid and will lower its pH below desirable ranges.

B. Gravity Sand Filters

Operation. These filters are supplied with a filtering mat of coagulant material and operated 24 hours a day at three gallons per square foot per minute until the difference in pressure is eight feet. The filter should then be backwashed at the rate of nine gallons per square foot per minute for five minutes.

Operational Problems. 1. Mud deposits near the surface can frequently be broken up by washing with a stream of water under pressure and with rakes.

2. Algae growth on troughs and walls may be prevented by hosing and applications of copper sulfate.

3. Mudballs may be broken up with rakes or other tools. A higher rate of backwashing can also be adopted.

4. Mounds and craters on top of filter bed usually means that the underdrain system is clogged or damaged. Mud deposits on the surface of the gravel can also cause this. Cleaning of underdrain and filter media will prevent this.

5. Jet action is caused by the lack of uniformity of the upward flow of water during the backwashing. This is due to mud deposits on the gravel or to any condition in the underdrain which may cause uneven distribution of water. Cleaning filter sand and gravel and cleaning underdrain is necessary to remedy this.

C. Dyatomite Filters

Operation. These filters are equipped with various types of filtering surfaces which are covered with diatomaceous earth prior to their being put into service. They are generally operated at two or three gallons per square foot per minute and operated 24 hours a day.

Pressure filters are backwashed when the influent and effluent pressure differential is in the range of 10 to 25 pounds per square inch, depending on the type used. Vacuum filters are backwashed at a vacuum gauge reading of about 15 to 20 inches of mercury.

Operational problems. 1. Short filter runs—While a shorter filter run than is obtained with a sand filter is expected with this type of filter, extended hours of use can be obtained by careful attention to the application of body feed throughout the operation of the filter cycle.

2. Clogged filter elements or septa—Elements made of metallic material or synthetic fiber "cloth" may be freed from encrusted debris by one of the following treatments:

(a) Diatomite and organic matter clogging—This may be removed by soaking the elements in an 8 percent solution of sodium hexametaphosphate (one commercial compound containing this is Calgon) for two hours and then scrubbing them with a brush.

(b) Iron clogging (rust colored deposit)—This may be removed by soaking in Calgon.

(c) Manganese clogging (gun metal deposits)—This may be cleaned by soaking in a solution of hydrochloric acid to which a small amount of sodium sulphite has been added.

(d) Calcium and magnesium deposits—Water hardness chemicals can be removed from the elements by the application of hydrochloric acid as noted in (b) above.

3. Loss of filter cake—Shutting down the filtration operations for even a short period of time will result in "sloughing" of the filter cake of diatomaceous earth. If the filter is shut down for any reason, it should be backwashed and a new precoat added.

4. Failure of filter elements—Early filter elements were subject to excessive operational breakage. Newer elements and different filtering procedures have largely overcome these difficulties.

Other Pool Operation Problems

Algae. These plant forms are brought into the pool by the wind and with fresh make-up water. If uncontrolled, they will grow abundantly in the presence of sunlight. They are found in the free floating and clinging varieties. The clinging type will embed itself into pores and crevices in pool floor and walls and is a more persistent type of threat. Algae is nature's way of oxidizing organic waste material. From the decomposing of this waste material, CO_2 is released, and it is the CO_2 that is necessary for algae to live.

Objectional features of algae: (1) More chlorine is consumed; (2) Water turbidity; (3) Slippery surfaces; (4) May foster bacterial growth; (5) Causes odors.

Algae, being plants, require carbon dioxide in order to manufacture food. In the process of taking carbon dioxide out of water, there is a definite increase in the pH. This may be seen in a radical jump in pH (from 7.5 to 8.0 as an example) in several hours, before there is any noticeable growth in the water.

Methods of Control

Routine Chlorination. The maintenance of free chlorine residual in the pool at all times will prevent the start of algae troubles.

Pool Shading. Since algae need sunlight for growth, the shading of the pool with a carport-like device will tend to slow down the growth, but will not prevent it.

Temperature. When the pool water is at a temperature of less than 80 degrees F., the algae problem is minimized.

Application of Copper Sulfate to Pool Water. (1) Shock treatment—A treatment dose of five pounds per million gallons of pool water can be introduced by putting crystals of copper sulfate into a porous bag and moving it through the pool water or into a skimmer or hair and lint strainer so the crystals will be dissolved before entering the pool. (2) Maintenance dosing—Pools that experience continuous algae difficulties due to some uncontrollable factor may practice preventive application of copper sulfate. This may be done by introducing an initial dose of 0.5 ppm and maintaining a 0.3 to 0.5 ppm level by dosing every five to seven days. (3) Difficulties involved in the use of copper sulfate. *Effect of Hard Water.* The effective portion of the copper compound is precipitated by alkaline carbonate and rendered ineffective. *Effect on Swimmers.* The compound may discolor swimmer's suits and hair. Excessive amounts of copper sulphate are very drying to the mucous membranes. *Production of an Inky Precipitate.* When hydrogen sulphide is present in the water, it will cause a precipitate of copper sulphide.

Application of Quaternary Ammonium Compounds. These compounds are not intended to supplant the use of a disinfecting agent, but will permit the disinfectant to have greater effect in attacking algae, because of the lowered surface tension of the pool water. The usual dose is one gallon per 50,000 gallons of water initially and subsequent dosages of one quart per 50,000 gallons every six days.

Superchlorination. One of the most effective treatments is the development of a 10ppm free chlorine residual in the pool during non-swimming hours.

Excessively high residuals may be reduced to permit swimming by adding sodium thiosulfate to the water at a rate of 1.0-1.5 ppm for each 1.0 ppm of residual chlorine being removed.

Pool Scrubbing. As a last resort the pool may be drained and the bottom and sides scrubbed with a 5% hypochlorite slurry or copper sulfate solution to remove tenacious algae growths. Scrubbing will also remove any dead algae that have turned black and are clinging to the walls.

Pool Paints. A durable, smooth surface created by painting with a rubber-base, waterproof enamel paint will resist the intrusion of clinging algae.

pH of Pool Waters

General. Hydrogen ion concentration, or pH as it is commonly called, is an important measurement in swimming pool sanitation. Optimum coagulation, disinfection and swimmer comfort depend upon maintenance of proper pH level.

pH is a quantitative measure of acidity or alkalinity, expressed in terms of hydrogen ion only; seven being the neutral point and 14 being the complete absence of hydrogen ions and the presence of only hydroxyl ions. The opposite end of the pH scale approaches "0" with strong mineral acids prevailing, giving a pH range of 0 to 14.

Colorimetric determination of pH is based on the ability of certain organic materials called indicators to change color in varying hydrogen ion concentration. Addition of a small quantity of the indicator to the sample and comparison with a color standard permits rapid determinations of pH to be made.

pH Test—Color Comparator Kit
Equipment. The following procedure should be carefully followed when using a pocket comparator:

1. Fill the two test tubes with 10 ml of water to be tested and place them in the comparator. The tube in the left-hand opening of the comparator is the "Compensation Tube."
2. Add 0.5 ml (about 10 drops) of indicator to the test tube in the right-hand opening.
3. Match the colors by turning the disc until the color of the sample and that of the disc most nearly match. The reading is made directly in pH units.

Compensation. The function of the second tube is that of optical or color compensation, insuring the comparison of similar media (liquid against liquid). In most cases difficulties due to color or turbidity in the original sample will thus be eliminated.

Indicator. Phenol red indicator measures a pH range of 6.8 to 8.4 and is probably the most useful one for swimming pool water.

pH Control Feeding Equipment
Operation. These devices feed control chemicals previously described, in order to maintain optimum pH conditions.

Operational Problems. Partial loss of "floc" mat—after *batch* dosing with soda ash, it is possible that a part of the sand filter mat may dissolve and carry turbidity into the pool. This, of course, is not a problem with diatomaceous earth filters. It may be prevented by either continuous maintenance of pH level by slow feeding techniques or by adding batch doses of soda ash or other control substances after backwashing, before beginning the alum feed.

Creation of a Precipitate in the Pool. Soda ash when thrown into the pool in powdered form can cause a precipitation of hardness compounds. This can be prevented by feeding ahead of the filters in the normally prescribed manner.

Feeder Maintenance. In general, the same maintenance and cleaning procedures applied to hypochlorinators will be effective with these devices.

1. Daily cleaning. Flushing all parts with clear water will do much toward maintaining the parts in operating condition. The strainer connection on the suction side of the pH control feeder must be brush cleaned daily to prevent clogging of the intake orifices.

2. Semi-monthly cleaning. Treatment of the valves and other important parts of the pH control feeder with acid solutions will be necessary to remove chemical deposits. This is particularly true with pool waters that are high in carbonates, sulfates and iron. Dilute muriatic (hydrochloric) acid, dilute acetic acid or undiluted vinegar may be used for the cleaning solution. Brushing with a stiff bristle brush will facilitate cleaning.

Importance of Proper pH Level

Coagulation. When using filters equipped for the addition of coagulant chemicals, pH is an important factor in the proper production of a "floc." The optimum point for alum flocculation is about 7.2 to 7.6, depending upon the hardness and total alkalinity of the water.

Disinfection. If the pH becomes too high, the effectiveness of chlorine disinfection is greatly reduced.

Swimmer Comfort. A pH level below 7 or above about 8.4 may result in skin and eye irritation to the swimmer.

Optimum pH Level

In any case the pH of pool water should be above 7.0. A balancing of the advantages and disadvantages involved dictate an optimum level of 7.2.

Factors Affecting pH Level

Disinfectants. Chlorine gas lowers pH. Pure bromine lowers pH slightly. Hypochlorite—These compounds raise the pH.

Coagulants. Alum, the most commonly used coagulant, lowers the pH, but should never be used for this purpose.

Fresh Water. The make-up water added to the pool can cause a considerable change in pool water pH if it is high in alkalinity or acidity.

pH Raising Compounds

Soda Ash (sodium carbonate). This compound will raise a depressed pH and may be fed through a feeding device or be placed in briquet form near a recirculation outlet of the pool. In the latter

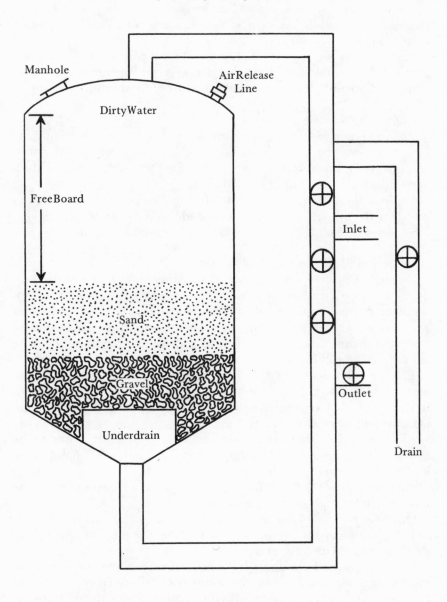

Schematic drawing of sand filtering system for swimming pools shows process of water filtration

Manhole

AirRelease
Line

DirtyWater

FreeBoard

Sand

Gravel

Underdrain

Inlet

Outlet

Drain

technique, the briquet is slowly dissolved by water movement. Also, soda ash may be fed manually through make-up tanks, swimmers or even hair and lint strainers in fairly large doses.

Caustic soda (sodium hydroxide or lye). This compound is more hazardous to use but has more effect in raising pH, pound for pound, than soda ash.

Lime (calcium hydroxide). Lime will raise pH, but is not recommended for use at pools because it may result in turbidity in pool water and possibly lead to cementation of the filter sand.

pH Lowering Compounds

Dilute Hyperchloric (or sulphuric acid). The use of this compound is a hazardous procedure from the standpoint of injury to the operator, the swimmer and the equipment. Furthermore, it may disturb alum coagulation and increase turbidity.

Sodium Bisulfate (sodium acid sulfate). This compound is safer to use than the mineral acids and has the additional benefit of removing lime deposits from chemical feed lines, filter sand and piping.

Disinfection of Swimming Pool Water

General. Chlorine, in common with other oxidizing agents, produces a strongly colored yellow compound by reaction with orthotolidine. A small amount of chlorine will give a yellow, and larger amounts an orange color. Quantitative estimation is carried out by comparing this color with color standards representing definite amounts of free chlorine.

Chlorine Residual "Flash" Test (Range 0.0 to 1.0ppm). Equipment: The following procedure should be carefully followed when using the pocket comparator. Procedure using other types of comparators will be essentially the same.

Procedure. Fill the two test tubes with 10 ml. of water to be tested and place them in the comparator. Tube in the left-hand opening of the comparator is the "compensation tube."

Add with force 1.0 ml. (about 20 drops) of orthotolidine to the test tube in the right-hand opening.

Quickly (within 10 seconds) match the colors by turning the disc until the color of the sample and that of the disc most nearly match. Reading is made directly in parts per million.

Compensation. Function of the second tube is that of optical or color compensation, insuring the comparison of similar media (liquid against liquid). In most cases difficulties due to color turbidity in the original sample will thus be eliminated.

29

THE MOTEL BATTLE FOR SURVIVAL

Douglas C. Keister

Motels in the 15 units or less category are what the hotel industry people call "Ma and Pa" motels. Most are located in small communities where it is not feasible to have large motels. Because they are small, they can be run by "Ma and Pa." The wife can take care of the rooms and rent the facilities, thus giving her husband the potential opportunity to hold down another job in addition to working at the motel.

The type of motel with the most troubles right now is the motel with 15 to 50 units. In this group the battle for survival is really raging. These motels are too big to be handled by "Ma and Pa" and too small to afford the professional management and consultation which are frequently needed. All motels, especially those in the general category of 15 to 50 units, need evaluation in terms of financing, sales, marketing and management. They need good management, good planning, and plenty of know-how if they are to live through the battle for survival.

Valuation of Motels

People invest in motels for various reasons. Some do so to consolidate their investments, to earn a return on their investments, or to build up an estate. Some invest in and operate a motel because they think it will be a form of semi-retirement.

What is your motel worth right now? The changing market conditions of the motel industry in the past few years have probably altered the value of your motel. There are various techniques used to estimate and evaluate the worth of a motel.

Book Value

This is the most common means of stating what a motel is worth. Book value is the value you claim for your motel on your books. It is the original value minus depreciation. Depreciation is nebulous, but it is a real fact of life. Your motel may be worth more or less than the amount at which you carry in on your books. Book value is seldom a true indicator of the value of the property.

Selling Price

Your motel may be worth approximately what a motel similar to yours was recently sold for.

A motel is worth what someone is willing to pay for it. A buyer may pay more that it's worth or he may get a bargain, but the only valid way to learn your motel's selling price would be to sell it. Your own estimate of what your motel's selling price would be is not very dependable unless you really do sell it. Then you'll know.

Appraised Value

There are different approaches to the appraised value method of valuating your motel property.

One method corresponds to a selling price method. It bases the worth of one motel on the sale price of a similar motel.

Another type of appraised value often used by tax appraisers is to figure the cost of duplicating the motel at today's cost of construction. Then depreciate the property for the number of years it's been in existence on the basis of this new value for the motel. The fallacy in this—and what makes this method rather unrealistic—is that many existing motels would have been built differently or not built at all if today's costs had been involved when they were built. Conditions have changed drastically. If a lot of motel owners had a choice, they would not have the type of facility they do have. Considering the circumstances today, they would prefer a larger motel or a smaller one. In many cases, they could not have afforded to build it now at all.

Liquidation Value

Liquidation value is the value of the motel's land, buildings, furniture and fixtures if they are sold off individually. Under liquidation value, the furniture and fixtures are worth practically nothing. The land has usually increased in value. The building is usually worth little or nothing. In reality, liquidation value is usually the value of the land minus the cost of demolishing and disposing of the motel and its contents. When the motel buildings have been razed and the land has been leveled, the property will generally be of value for other more profitable enterprises.

Many 15- to 50-unit motels are located in rural and suburban areas where land values have not appreciated substantially as have many urban land values by comparison. Consequently these motels will not be valued very highly under the liquidation value concept.

Liquidation value does set a rock bottom price on the value of your establishment.

Capitalized Earnings Value

There is only one valid method of valuing a going motel concern. You value it on the basis of its earnings. A motel is worth what it can earn.

You compute capitalized earnings value as follows:

1. Divide 100 percent by the rate of capitalization.
2. Multiply the answer by earnings.

For example, an incorporated motel earns $15,000 per year after taxes. If the rate of capitalization is 10 percent, then you divide 10 into 100 percent. The answer is 10, which you multiply by $15,000. The capitalized value of the motel is $150,000.

If the rate of capitalization is 20 percent, you divide 20 percent into 100 percent. The answer is 5, which you multiply by $15,000. The capitalized value of the motel in this example is $75,000.

From the above it can be seen that the rate of capitalization is the key factor in determining the value of a motel.

Investment is computed as your original investment plus any plowback of earnings. When you establish a rate of capitalization for evaluating your investment, you consider the following: (1) Return on money you invest; (2) return on risk you take; (3) return on services you render.

In today's money market a return on money only should be about 6 percent.

The return on risk is very difficult to calculate. The motel industry involves more risk than many other industries.

In addition, it's hard to estimate and evaluate the money worth of the service (including labor and capital) which the motel operator provides.

I conducted an extensive research study of 90 motels in Michigan in 1965.* I found that most of the motel owners involved felt that 15 percent was a reasonable return on investment.

The examples cited above concerned an *incoporated* motel. Perhaps your motel is a proprietorship or a partnership. If it is not an incorporated motel, the picture changes considerably. ·

An incorporated motel is allowed to deduct salaries paid to an executive even if the executive is the owner. If, however, you own a proprietorship motel, under tax law you are not allowed to deduct your salary from earnings. If your motel earns $15,000 a year and you subtract a salary of say $7,500 per year for the services you perform, then the earnings of your motel are $7,500. If you multiply this by 10 (10 percent capitalization rate), the motel is worth $75,000. The incoporated motel with the same 20 percent capitalization rate was worth $150,000 because the salary deduction was in expenses.

The main things to remember in evaluating your motel are:

1. A motel is worth what it can earn.
2. Rate of capitalization is a factor in the evaluation of earnings.
3. The way your business is organized for tax purposes (whether or not the owners' salary is chargeable to the business as it is in a corporation) will have a bearing on evaluation.

Sound Financing

Obviously, your motel should have sound financing. It will do better if it does. My own study, mentioned above, indicated that motels which have a debt of more than 60 percent of the value of their assets are apt to periodically encounter financial difficulty. The demands for cash for debt retirement and interest may place too heavy a burden on the operation.

At times motels with a debt of more than 60 percent will find themselves lacking the cash to meet their obligations, and the situation can become dangerous. The condition of periodic cash lack where debt is more than 60 percent is especially true of motels which have wide seasonable fluctuation in their volume of business.

Sales and Marketing

One thing you can and must do to have a better chance of succeeding in the motel "battle for survival" is to analyze and under-

---

*A study of the nature of the ownership and management of selected Michigan motels. Thesis for the Degree of Ph.D. Douglas C. Keister, 1965. Unpublished dissertation.

stand your own market—your customers. Motels are profit-oriented businesses. They can exist only if they make a profit. Profits come from sales of services to guests. You must understand what your market is in order to attract and satisfy the guests who constitute your market.

The motel's market is made up of commercial travelers (anyone who travels away from home for business reasons) and tourists. Whether the commercial traveler or the tourist is more important to your own operation will depend on whether you are in a vacation setting or not. Most motels must rely on the commercial traveler as the backbone of their business. The tourist is usually a secondary market, but a very important one which can make the difference between profit and loss for the motel.

The motel operator should ask himself:

1. What facilities and services which I offer (or should offer) do my guests actually want and/or need?
2. To obtain these services and facilities will they be willing to pay rates which will give me a reasonable profit?

Many guests want much more than you can offer but are not willing to pay for it. You must know what services and facilities you can sell, you must know how to sell them, and you must know what type of guests—and how many of them—will be able and willing to buy.

It is a mistake in this business to try to be all things to all people. Your major selling efforts should be concentrated on your own major market.

It all boils down to this:

1. What main type of traveler stays at my motel.
2. How can I attract more of them.

Room Rates

In order to obtain a reasonable profit (a profit which gives you a reasonable return on your investment in your motel) you must charge rates which are fair to the guest and fair to you.

Rates used to be set on the basis of $1 room rate per $1,000 value of the room. For example, a motel that cost $70,000 to build and had 10 units would have a value per room of $7,000. Each room would rent for $7. Today this rate guide has in many instances been raised to $1.50 per $1,000, so the room would rent for $10.50.

The above is only a guide. Your motel may be worth more or less than $10.50 per single occupancy, depending upon the type of services you offer. The rate charged should be in line with your costs, with the services you offer, and in line with services your guests want and will pay for. The motel which offers its guests a swimming pool, wall-to-wall carpeting, a private telephone in each room and 24-hour-a-day telephone service, private television, etc., is in many cases worth more to the guest than the motel that does not offer all or any of these services. The rate charged must, in the final analysis, be reasonable to both the motel operator and to the guest.

Commercial Rates

In the 1965 study of 90 Michigan motels, I asked each operator, "Do you have commercial rates?" Only two of the 90 said yes. I asked one of these two why he did give a commercial rate. He answered, "Because everybody does." The study showed two out of 90 did.

The 88 operators who did not give commercial rates were asked why not? Many felt that commercial rates would be unfair to many of their guests. They said that many guests who frequently visited their motels would not qualify for a commercial rate. They felt that a commercial rate set-up would give a break—solely because they were commercial travelers—to businessmen who might be guests only once and were on an expense account, but would penalize vacationers and other non-business travelers who stayed at the motel on a repetitive basis.

Most motel operators in my study felt it was important to charge a minimum rate for single occupancy by anyone, regardless of the type of room occupied. Most motels located in vacation settings did give a seasonal adjusted rate. They earned most of their income for the year during a very limited seasonal time period.

Some motel operators did have a "one-in-ten-club"—a guest's eleventh stay at the motel was on the house. But this "one-in-ten-club" applied to all guests of the motel, not just commercial travelers.

Most of the 90 motel operators felt it was more important to sell service than to attract guests by rates alone.

Rate Cutting

One of the real dangers of our industry is the motel operator—perhaps there's one in your own area competing with you— who says to himself, "I'll get all of the area's customers coming to my place simply by lowering my rates. If my competition charges $10, I'll charge $8 and I'll get all the guests around here to come and stay at my motel."

Guests do not always respond to price alone. Some will continue, for various reasons, to pay $10 at another motel. The rate-cutting operator may wind up taking care of approximately the same number of guests as he did before but he'll earn $2 less per unit.

If he does succeed, though, in attracting extra guests at his $8 rate, the other motels in his area will probably be quick to respond. They'll lower their rates to $8 and he has lost his price advantage. As a consequence, all motels in the areas will be offering their services and facilities for less money than they did before. In this case, rate-cutting benefits no one but the customer, who is happy to save $2 but would have continued to pay $10 if $10 was a reasonable rate.

It is best for the motel industry and for the individual operator if there is competition through trying to offer better services and facilities than competitors, not through price war and rate cutting. Rate cutting can hurt the rate cutter himself as well as the other motels in his area.

The Need to Manage

The motel business has changed and it's pretty sure to keep on changing. Now, more than ever before, the manager must be alert to what's happening to the industry. And he must really *manage* his motel. He cannot afford to let the motel "run itself."

He should analyze what type of guests he does or should cater to and make every effort to provide what will attract them. He should know his competition and know what they are doing. He should know his own costs of operation. He should put together a total planned program of goals, controlled budgets, and realistic objectives in order to achieve an efficient motel operation.

At the same time he must retain the concepts of providing the traveling public—in a courteous, friendly way—with convenient services they want and need at costs which are fair to the travelers and fair to the motel. These are concepts which originally made motels popular.

An adequate profit, based on an adequate return on investment, does not just happen. It has to be worked at and worked at constantly. The motel manager should be aware of all facets of his operation. He should understand his motel, its present functions and its potential for the future. He should carefully plan operating strategy and react appropriately as change occurs. If he does, his motel will have a better chance of succeeding in the motel battle for survival.

30

THE ADVANTAGES AND DISADVANTAGES OF LEASING

Brooks Walker, Jr.

Typically, when cycles of "tight money" set in, several things occur to credit in the following sequence: (1) interest rates go up, (2) the term length of loan diminishes, (3) the size of the average loan is reduced and (4) companies with weaker credit standings often find themselves cut off from bank credit.

We have recently seen the first step—interest rates are being raised and the pattern has begun. In a word, the availability of credit is now being reduced by cost, by term length, by amount, and by elimination.

This new cycle of "tight money" comes at a time when the liquidity of many hotel operators is at an extremely low point. The pinch will thus be felt even more.

In the past five years, the liquidity ratio (the ratio of cash and marketable securities to current debt) has declined from .44 in 1960 to .36 in 1965. This represents a drop of 18 percent. Yet the industry's new building plus modernization of older units in these five years has increased the need for working capital.

Growing companies need a reservoir of credit to protect themselves against the periodic droughts that afflict the money market.

While the cost of these funds is important, the *availability* of credit is even more important. Larger companies are not greatly affected by the swings of the credit cycle. They pay the going rate, but *availability* is no problem. Larger companies can go to other banks, to insurance companies and pension funds, and to the public through the sale of securities.

But what does a company do that doesn't have access to public security markets, to a whole string of banks or to insurance companies?

Brooks Walker, Jr. is the President of the United States Leasing Corporation. From *Hotel Management Review & Innkeeping*, August 1966, pp. 38-41.

One answer that has helped many hotels during past tight money periods, has been equipment leasing. Aside from its many other aspects, equipment leasing is a form of *intermediate term* financing. This technical banking term refers to the three different types of loans: short-term bank loans that are under one year and are normally self-liquidating; intermediate term loans that run from one to 10 years, usually require instalment payment and are usually available to top companies only, and long-term financing that runs beyond 10 years, usually available through sale of bond issues, etc.

Equipment leasing because it normally runs from one to 10 years falls in the intermediate term area. In its financial aspect, a lease covering equipment worth $50,000 is equivalent to a loan of $50,000 from the leasing company, for a period of up to 10 years. Most leases are much shorter, but that depends on equipment life.

What has made leasing especially attractive during tight money periods is (1) that it is a financial commitment for a period of years, with interest costs stabilized for the whole period, and (2) the money involved represents a *second* line of credit. That is to say, a lease of $50,000 represents a line of credit over and above whatever other credit lines a business may have with a bank or other financial institution. A lease cannot be "called"; a lessee cannot be told to "clean up" his loan. The commitment stands as long as the lease runs.

Before turning to some of the drawbacks of leasing, we should itemize some of its advantages. Leasing permits companies:

1. To obtain long-term financing without taking in partners or selling stock to the public.
2. To increase profits without a corresponding increase in capital investments.
3. To obtain needed equipment without waiting to accumulate retained earnings and depreciation.
4. In inflationary periods, to pay for equipment in cheaper dollars.

Now, let's look at some of the drawbacks of leasing.

For one thing, the *dollar* cost of leasing may be more than the *dollar* cost of buying the same equipment. In an example to be elaborated below, it will be seen that to purchase $56,000 worth of equipment through a bank loan involved spending $61,344; to lease this same equipment cost $70,080. This is total dollar outlay, not net outlay. Yet this company chose to lease for reasons which the example will disclose.

Secondly, at the end of a lease the equipment remains the property of the leasing company. If the lessee still wishes to use this equipment, he must pay the leasing company the equivalent of its salvage value either by renewal or purchase. This adds to the cost of a lease.

These are the two major drawbacks to leasing commonly cited. Companies should consider these drawbacks before rushing into a lease.

How serious are these drawbacks? In 1959 the *Harvard Business Review* reported that 53 percent of all business corporations were leasing equipment. In 1964 the percentage had risen to 78 percent. Lease volume in 1959 was $392 million; in 1965 it was almost $1.35 billion. In the hotel-motel industry, lease volume last year totalled $14 million.

In other words, there must be some substantial benefits to leasing that overcome the two drawbacks cited above.

That is to say, while all methods of intermediate term financing provide funds to industry, they all have drawbacks also. There is no such thing as a perfect method that fits all situations better at all times. It is the job of the wise manager to select the best method for his company at the given time it needs financing.

For example, intermediate term financing from a bank or insurance company often involves restrictions on changes in the borrower's business (can't sell assets, can't merge without permission, can't make major changes in management); no other long-term debt may be assumed without the lender's permission; minimum current ratio requirements are written into the loan agreement; salaries, dividends, and so on, are restricted until the loan is paid off.

Almost all banks today insist on a compensating balance of 20 percent, i.e., the borrower must leave on deposit with the bank 20 percent of his loan. This cuts down usable funds by 20 percent (and also raises the true rate of interest by more than 20 percent).

None of these particular drawbacks apply to leasing (whose own drawbacks I cited above). Leasing companies do not impose restraints on their customers' businesses nor do they limit salaries, dividends, other borrowing, and so on.

Similarly, purchasing equipment on a five-year installment basis has its drawbacks. These include the requirements for a sizable down payment (anywhere from 10 to 33 percent), higher interest charges, etc.

Depreciation is another significant subject. When equipment is purchased, no matter how, it must be depreciated according to government regulations. If the useful life is 10 years, then that is the depreciation period. But no matter which accelerated depreciation schedule is used, this equipment cannot be written off as rapidly as it can under a three or five-year lease. By definition, lease payments are fully tax deductible as operating expenses.

The significance of this advantage is illustrated by the accompanying chart based on the example of a resort hotel which leased $56,000 worth of kitchen and refrigeration equipment. What we will do here is to compare the actual net lease cost over the five-year lease term with what would have been the net cost of a three-year low-cost bank loan to acquire the same equipment.

Lease rentals are $1,168 per month for five years, and to arrive at the *actual cash cost* we deduct from these rentals all those items which actually are deductible in cash, to arrive at the *net actual cash cost* to our client company.

As shown in the chart, the true actual net cash cost of leasing $56,000 worth of equipment over a five-year period is $36,450. Now, let's turn to the conventional purchase plan, financed through a three-year bank loan at 6 percent simple interest. (For purpose of comparison the following chart shows no down payment, which is contrary to bank practice, which normally requires 25 to 33 percent down payments.)

The results, while startling, are clear: the actual cash cost under leasing turns out to be $4,258 less than under the purchase plan. And this occurred despite the fact that under the lease plan payments which total $70,080 compared with total purchase payment of $61,344. There's nothing magical about this: it is a simple demonstration of the powerful effects of more rapid cash recovery of equipment costs afforded by leasing than is available under the most rapid depreciation.

This brings us to the other drawback of leasing: at the end of the lease the equipment does not belong to the lessee, but to the leasing company. This is true. To continue to use that equipment will cost him a small payment per year—two or three percent in renewal payments. Or he can purchase the equipment at a fair price. Or he can have the leasing company take its equipment. Or he can trade in this equipment against a new lease on new equipment. Good options—but they do cost the lessee additional money.

In the hotel industry, the major reason why companies lease is their need for working capital. Obviously, if a company needs $50,000 worth of equipment and wishes to save its credit for other current purposes, it must lay cash on the barrelhead. This is taking $50,000 out of working capital.

Cash flow comparison. Lease vs. 3 year bank loan at 6% simple interest

	1 YEAR	2 YEARS	3 YEARS	4 YEARS	5 YEARS	
LEASE						
RENTAL $1,168/MONTH	$14,016	$14,016	$14,016	$14,016	$14,016	(1)
TAX SAVING 48% OF (1)	6,726	6,726	6,726	6,726	6,726	(2)
NET CASH COST (1) MINUS (2)	7,290	7,290	7,290	7,290	7,290	(3)
CUMULATIVE NET CASH COST	7,290	14,580	21,870	29,160	36,450	(4)
3 YEAR BANK LOAN AT 6% INTEREST						
PAYMENTS $1,704/MONTH	20,448	20,448	20,448	—	—	(5)
DEPRECIATION DBL DECLINING OVER 10 YEARS	11,200	8,960	7,168	5,734	4,587	(6)
INTEREST (OR FINANCE CHARGE)	2,882	1,798	666	—	—	(7)
TAX SAVING 48% OF (6) PLUS (7)	6,759	5,163	3,760	2,752	2,202	(8)
NET CASH COST (5 MINUS 8)	13,689	15,285	16,688	2,752	2,202	(9)
CUMULATIVE NET CASH COST	13,689	28,974	45,662	42,910	40,708	(10)
CASH ADVANTAGE						
AMOUNT OF CASH STILL AVAILABLE (10 MINUS 4)	6,399	14,394	23,792	13,750	4,258	(11)

EQUIPMENT COST: $56,000
TOTAL RENTAL PAYMENTS OVER 5 YEARS: $70,000
TOTAL PAYMENTS ON 3 YEAR BANK LOAN AT 6% SIMPLE INTEREST: $61,344

There are varying ways to calculate the value of these funds, one of the most common being to discover what this amount of money would earn if used in the primary business.

What is working capital worth? According to Dun & Bradstreet, working capital in U.S. industry in 1964 earned almost 15¢ net after taxes. That is to say, for every $1 in working capital in industry, the average company earned 15¢ net profit. To remove $50,000 in working capital from an average company means the sacrifice of $7,500 in net profit per year. Leasing permits a company to retain its working capital in the business, and acquire the use of equipment without straining its working capital position, without loading its balance sheet with more fixed assets, and without distorting the company's balance sheet ratios.

Thus, by and large, companies in three situations usually will find that leasing's drawbacks outweigh its benefits: companies that do not need new equipment (though a sale-leaseback of old equipment may be useful to raise new working capital), companies with idle working capital, and companies whose earnings are too low to take advantage of the benefits that flow from the release of capital (though in some instances the addition of new equipment will recify this and increase profits).

For all other companies, however, the benefits of leasing must be thrown into the scales against the drawbacks and weighed for their effect on company growth, particularly in net profits. And they must be measured against other methods of providing intermediate term funds.

With the onset of the present cycle of "tight money" the availability of intermediate term funds will become a prime consideration for many hotel operators. For many of these companies leasing may prove the vital technique that enables them to maintain and increase their rates of growth.

How Leasing Works

A hotel company wishing to lease specifies the equipment desired, the price to be paid, and the supplier from whom it is to be purchased. The leasing firm then buys the equipment to specification and instructs the supplier to deliver the equipment directly to the company.

The lease payments normally do not commence until the equipment has been delivered and has been accepted by the company.

Term of Lease

Leasing is long-term. Normally it ranges from three to eight years, depending on the company, the equipment involved, and the size of the lease. Payments can be on an equal monthly basis or can be tailored to any particular requirement.

At the end of a lease, it can usually be renewed on a year-to-year basis at reduced annual cost.

Types of Equipment

All types and combinations of non-expendable equipment—both new and used—can be leased.

Termination of Lease

Upon the expiration of a lease, the equipment can be returned; the lease can be renewed; the equipment can be traded in for new equipment; or arrangements can be made to purchase the equipment.

Purchase Option

A purchase option can be written into the lease but is not recommended. The inclusion of a purchase option could result in the transaction, from a tax standpoint, being classified as a conditional sale. In such a case, the company could not treat the lease payments as a deductible, operating expense.

31

BASICS, PITFALLS OF LEASES ARE DETAILED

Stephen W. Brener

Since leases are a vital and negotiable part of many motor hotel operations, I thought it a good idea to review the basics of the lease and point out some of the pitfalls.

Existing leases are examined whenever a motor hotel is to be sold, to be leased, or it seeks to obtain financing.

The major types of lease arrangements are (1) flat rental—this calls for a fixed dollar amount per year, which need not be the same each year, and which may be subject to adjustment via an inflation clause; and (2) percentage rental—such a lease defines rental to be paid as a percentage of sales or profit.

A percentage lease usually contains a base minimum rental to provide the landlord with a guaranteed return.

A percentage lease arrangement may be based on gross income or profit. It may require a minimum rental payable monthly, in advance, plus a percentage on sales or profit.

Some percentage leases are based on total sales; others require an acceleration in the rental percentage based on increases in sales volume.

Another type of percentage lease is based on a division of profits. The main problem here is to determine the meaning of profits—are they to be calculated before or after depreciation of capital expenses?

Some of the possible pitfalls to be checked out are:

1. *Term of lease.* Since many leases are made for a definite period of time with renewal options, it should be clear which party has the option to renew.

Stephen W. Brener is Vice President of and a hospitality consultant for Helmsley-Spear, Inc.

From *Hospitality,* June 1966. Reprinted by permission.

2. *Time rent payment commences.* The lease should specify the exact time that the rent is to begin and when the tenant is to take possession; these may not be identical.

3. *Inspection and acceptance of premises.* There should be a clause in the lease which states that the tenant has seen the premises and accepted them "as is" or as shown in a plan.

4. *Rental and form of payment.* A clause describing payment must be included. It should state the type of rental plan, the manner of payment, and provisions for adjustment.

5. *Security deposit.* Clauses should also be included covering the form and amount of a security deposit.

6. *Subleasing or assignment.* Spell out whether and under what conditions the lessee has the right to sublease.

7. *Taxes and insurance.* Ascertain who is to pay real estate taxes and insurance, and specify any special lessor requirements regarding the type and amount of coverage.

8. *Repairs.* State who is responsible for interior, exterior, and structural repairs, and the manner in which such repairs are to be made.

9. *Personal property.* If the furniture and equipment are part of the leased premises, an inventory is necessary. Define the lessee's liability as to upkeep, replacement.

10. *Right of inspection.* Lessor will want the right to inspect premises, and in the case of a percentage lease, suggest all lessors get some annual operating information as part of a lease. Detail time, method and approved agent.

These are only a few of the areas that should be discussed and covered in a lease agreement. Because it is impossible to anticipate all the circumstances that will befall a tenant or landlord during the term of the lease, all future problems cannot be anticipated. All areas with which the lease deals, or should deal, must be carefully investigated and treated.

32

FINANCING A NEW MOTOR HOTEL

Stephen W. Brener and A. Carmi Gamoran

What's Your Theory of Deal?

The Fourth Annual Census of motor hotel industry in continental United States, prepared by Stephen W. Brener, shows a decreasing rate of increase in new motel properties may be developing.

Even though there has been tremendous expansion in the mass lodging industry throughout the country in the past four years (1965-1968), the yearly rate of increase appears to be slowing down, both relatively and absolutely. The year-to-year net increase in motor hotels, according to Brener's census, has declined from 613 in 1965-66, to 523 in 1966-67, to 442 in 1967-68. This indicates a yearly rate of increase that has declined respectively in each year from 13 percent to 10 percent to 8 percent.

The reasons for the apparent decline are several. Among these are higher construction costs plus increases in both operating and maintenance expenses. Another reason is the present cost of money coupled with a general tightness in the money market.

This high cost of money and lack of lendable capital, especially funds for construction financing, call for new and imaginative ways of creating dollars needed for a new hotel or motel project.

Yesterday's Mortgage Deal

The traditional source of financing real estate has been by employing passive investment funds via the real estate mortgage. From an investment point-of-view a real estate mortgage is an instrument

---

Stephen W. Brener is Vice-President of and a hospitality consultant for Helmsley-Spear, Inc. A. Carmi Gamoran is Director of Systems and Research for the Hospitality Division of Helmsley-Spear. Both men conduct courses in real estate administration at the School of Hotel Administration of Cornell University.

From the *Cornell H.R.A. Quarterly*, November 1969, pp. 5-8. Reprinted by permission.

under which the owner of the property (mortgagor) borrows money from the lender (mortgagee) pledging the property as security for the payment of principal and interest. In the case of a hotel or motel, the mortgagee also may have first claim upon the chattels (personal property) in the buildings. Sources for mortgage money have been savings banks, insurance companies, pension funds, Federal savings and loan associations, and so forth.

In the hotel business, the mortgage always has been a common instrument of financing and institutions have been the prime source of hotel mortgage money.

Lenders usually look to the real estate as security for the mortgage, but it is patent that in a hotel/motel situation the success of the business venture itself is intrinsic to the value of the improved real estate. If the hospitality venture is not going to be successful because of poor location or bad market for transient rooms, then the hotel is not the "highest and best use" of the land—and certainly in the case of a new hotel ought not to be built in the first place.

It is for this reason that lenders retain consultants experienced in the hospitality industry to advise them on their hotel/motel investments, market studies, feasibility reports or other form of economic analysis to document the investment potential of a new hostelry.

Studies alone are rarely enough to satisfy the lender. The reputation of the developer is of prime importance. The credit standing of the developer is also carefully reviewed. If it is weak, it may be enhanced by a sound contractural arrangement with an operator of proven worth and success.

The lender also takes into consideration the preliminary plans, the estimated cost of construction, the forecasts of operating results during the early years and the anticipated results in future typical years. All that has been recited before is typical of financing a hotel via a passive mortgage. Thus the lender, if he is satisfied that the project will be successful, advances the money and looks to the borrower to repay the mortgage over a stated period of time and retain a fixed rate of interest on the unamortized portion of the mortgage. There is no further financial participation by the lender in the success of the hotel.

With the advent of increasingly expensive money, lenders are being forced to obtain higher and fluctuating rates. At times, this results in less amortization in order to earn a greater rate of interest and not permit the constant to increase too drastically. This is causing would-be borrowers serious problems—for reducing of amortization forestalls refinancing benefits quite a bit. Thus, the way in which the financing of today's hotel is put together must be carefully planned.

The manner in which a transaction is financed we term "theory of deal," and it is important that this arrangement always be thoughtfully worked out.

The New "Kickers" in First Mortgage Financing

Let us first examine how some lenders try to create mortgage financing in today's money market. In addition to charging higher interest rates, lenders look to ways of protecting their investments from erosion by inflation.

For short term positions such as a construction loan, an increase in the "points" or charge for the loan is being used. For long term loans, a variable interest rate, based on fluctuations in the prime rate, is often considered. Another method involves a percentage of sales or profits as a method of increasing the loan interest rate.

These "kickers," as they are referred to in the trade, have the effect of increasing the cost of money to the developer. They also tend to dilute his return. The likelihood is that this trend will continue until such time as our money supply grows to a point that demand catches up with supply. Obviously, a reversal in our economy or a stopping of the inflation quickly will change this situation.

Raising Debt Money

Given the "kickers," the tight money situation and so forth, what happens if the amount offered by the lender is inadequate? How can additional money be raised?

The obvious way has been via a second mortgage, i.e. a claim secured by the real estate and chattels which comes subsequent to the first mortgage. Rates for the second mortgages are, of course, higher than those of the first mortgages.

To carve out adequate financing in a new hotel/motel venture, one not experienced in this area should retain professional help.

When counseling clients on financing a new venture, one often attempts to fragment the transaction into its components. A typical motor hotel deal could be divided into (1) land, (2) building, (3) furnishing and equipment, and (4) operations.

1. The land is often the initial equity contributed by a developer-investor. It can be owned outright, mortgaged or leased.

2. The building is generally the item requiring the greatest financing. Conventionally this improvement is financed with a mortgage pledging land and building as security.

3. Furnishings and fixtures are financeable as separate transactions via leasing, chattel mortgages, and conditional bills of sale.

4. Operation refers to, in this case, the working capital that will finance the pre-opening costs and inventories, operations and early years' losses.

Let's examine a hypothetical venture in today's market. A developer-investor owns land, as if free and clear, which is suitable for a motor hotel. He has at least $300,000 in cash which he is willing to invest in the project. He hires a consultant to advise him on the project and prepare a market report and an architect to draw preliminary plans.

This developer goes to his investment banker or mortgage broker to discuss financing. Lo and behold, the project is estimated at over $1,500,000 plus land and the lender will only advance $1,000,000. He therefore needs $200,000 in addition to the $300,000 cash he has and the land he is willing to contribute.

How is this additional financing created?

Using Land. Land is frequently the important variable which dictates whether a hotel feasibility study will be favorable. The many possiblities or ramifications in which a land deal is consumated makes it difficult to explore most of them in this article.

Since the developer owns the land he might sell it to a party who would be willing to lease it back over a long period of time for a motor hotel and subordinate his rights to a first mortgage.

Owning of subordinated land by an investor is not uncommon. The proceeds of the sale of the land adds to the financing package and allows the developer to proceed with the improvement. Quite often, the leasehold rent is subject to escalations. The rent formula may be a minimum against various percentages of gross sales. The new owner of the land will also want to reflect the appreciation of his land in the future years of the lease and may restrict eventual refinancing.

Building. Perhaps a second mortgage can be placed on the project. However, first its high cost, usual short term and other restrictive features have to be carefully reviewed.

Furnishing and Fixtures. These may be financed by chattel mortgages, conditional sales agreements, equipment leases and so forth. When we review statements of new properties, we find that all too often they are overburdened with high rate, short term debt. The cost of this money averages 50% over prime and its amortization requirements are usually from three to six years annually.

Operation. Does the developer intend to operate the motor hotel himself or would he prefer to negotiate a sound agreement between himself as owner and a recognized hotel company as operator? If the developer prefers self operation he may wish to consider affiliating with a national chain by purchasing a franchise. Aside from the benefits of referral, national advertising, identification of the hotel with a national company may loosen the purse strings of the lender. This, of course, depends on many factors, including the standing of the franchisor.

On the other hand, if the developer is interested in having a national chain operate his motor hotel it may open up a variety of financing opportunities:

1. The national operator may propose joint venture and actually contribute a portion of the equity cash.

2. The national operator might be willing to lease the land and build the hotel.

3. Perhaps the national operator is only willing to act as manager, based on some division of profits by means of a formal management agreement. Even in this case, the strength of the agreement may enable the borrower to obtain additional money and, in addition, might reduce the investment if the operator agrees to certain investments such as operating capital, inventories, etc.

4. The joint venture in Item 1 or the management contract in Item 3 may be further modified, for the operator might execute guarantees of certain portions of the mortgage. These may help create additional financing.

5. In almost all instances, the managing company (in Item 3) will contribute a portion of the working capital of the operation, therefore, creating the cash the developer needs.

There are a whole host of possibilities and combinations that might be worked out in negotiating a transaction between developer and operator. These are often negotiated with the purpose, among others, of creating the maximum financing possible for the new venture.

What we have cited in this article is an example of the kind of situation that a hospitality consultant often is faced with. While consultants are responsible to advise on availability of financing, they are not mortgage brokers. Very often mortgage brokers and bankers are introduced by the consultants to obtain loans. However, it is the theory of transaction worked out that creates the loan and the relationship between equity and debt.

Summary

The rate of hotel/motel expansion has been slowing down. One reason for this is the high cost of money and generally tight credit market. Hotels and motels are being financed today despite these problems. This is accomplished by imaginative arrangements between developers and investors. It is obvious that the theory of deal properly set up and negotiated affects the amount of financing. By employing financing theory for land, building, furnishings, and operating a profitable package—fair to developer, operator and lender-investor—it is possible to create most of the capital necessary for a new hostelry.

33

WHEN DOES IT PAY TO REMODEL?

from *Canadian Hotel and Restaurant*

"There is only one reason why more money should be invested in an old hotel and that is to make money. The decision should in no way be influenced by public sentiment. On the other hand, a hotel has a heart and deals with the very personal comforts of its guests. If you treat it like a factory or an assembly line, it will come out looking and feeling like just that."

So speaks Alan Tremain, project manager, who is spending $4 million of Canadian Pacific's money to put Victoria's Empress Hotel on the convention map in big letters without doing violence to thousands of sentimental memories. Results so far, judged both by the cash register and public comment, are excellent as "The Project" or "Operation Teacup" passes its halfway mark.

From his background of successful management of half a dozen top class hotels which have gone from red ink to black, Mr. Tremain says:

Before one spends a penny on any refurnishing or remodelling program, it is necessary to evaluate the hotel and its position in local business. What market is it catering to, or what should be its market? You should take a long look at policy and management: make sure they are not as old as the hotel itself. It is generally true that eagerness and willingness of staff depreciate along with equipment and furnishings; yet no amount of new paint and carpets will automatically up-grade mediocre service, nor cause a mad rush to either restaurant or guest rooms.

Alan Tremain is a Fellow of the Cookery & Food Association and a founder-member of the International Society of Chefs de Cuisine.

From *Canadian Hotel and Restaurant*, March 15, 1968, pp. 40-41. Reprinted by permission of the publisher.

A feasibility study is your first step. Here the point is not to hire too calculating a consultant. It is easy for such a person to come back with a study proving that your occupancy should be 75 percent, and how on paper it can be, etc., etc., etc. I don't think you can put faith in such a report. The crux of the matter lies in the operation of this particular hotel itself. The person doing the study must be someone involved in hotel management—the kitchens, the housekeeping department—someone who has worked in all departments, knows their ins and outs of staff and operation.

Given the preliminary study, the budget must be determined, not by how much you can spend, but how much you should spend and can afford to spend, and how much new business this re-investment will bring in.

An architect or interior designer can sell you a marvelous presentation, with excellent renderings which can lure you into a great deal of expense. In selecting a design firm, the most important consideration is to choose a team with extensive hotel experience—a team which realizes that improvement is for profit, not an exercise in aesthetics.

It is agreed that remodelling pays off in higher room rates and perhaps increased business in the dining room, but the amount of investment in rooms must be carefully controlled so as not to subtract money from public spaces and function areas. These latter are very important and necessary to the bringing in of new convention business. The non-revenue-producing public areas must be looked at very closely, and their remodelling done along very practical lines.

Guest rooms are expensive. For a complete refurnishing program, you should allow about $1,500 per room. Carpets vary enormously in quality and price; you should be able to buy good carpet for about $8 or $9 a square yard, but, in budgeting this, don't forget to take into account freight, tax, underlay, Smoothedge and laying—also to make allowance for waste in cutting.

If you order case goods custom-made in less than the factory's minimum amount you naturally pay considerably more. But any furniture which is not good will very soon depreciate.

Present trend among designers to eliminate the centre ceiling lamp and use desk and floor lamps can add greatly to the cost of lighting. You can spend many thousands of dollars on lamps. To get your money's worth, avoid the plaster type which gets knocked over and chips easily. Choose a substantial type of shade. Also consider base switches; these are more practical than those located inside the shade.

"Bathrooms," says Alan Tremain, "are a nightmare. A bathroom can cost twice as much as your bedroom. In many cases where installations are satisfactory, you might be wise to leave the plumbing alone and revitalize the room with vinyl wall paper. There is a lot of charm in some old style plumbing, and the addition of a shower and attractive shower curtain may be sufficient. Please beware of bathrooms! Once you touch an area of plumbing, expense can spread right through the hotel and cost you a quarter of a million dollars before you know it."

One of the easiest areas to overlook in appropriating money is that of corridors. But these are very vulnerable—subjected as they are to the wear and tear of continual guest traffic. Carpet must be of good enough quality to stand up. Naturally, new carpeting calls for new wall finishes, vinyl is a good choice. Add lighting and you must tie up a lot of money where no direct return of revenue can be gained.

If you plan converting manually operated elevators to automatic operation, have plenty of money available. A couple of passenger elevators and a service elevator can cost you a quarter of a million dollars. It is true that this can be recuperated in time by cutting down elevator staff but this saving is far from immediate. Initially, the money must be found, and perhaps taken from something else.

Your telephone system is a doubtful area. Whether you should go in for automatic dialing, message waiting system, wake-up systems, and so on depends entirely upon what kind and volume of traffic your hotel is dealing with. But beware of imagining that you will cut down a staff of half a dozen operators to one or two by going automatic: you still have to cover 24 hours a day and allow for mealtimes and holidays. In a large city hotel, I don't think you can avoid the step to automatic unless you can justify retaining personal service.

Television is an expected thing with which you must keep up, but beware of allowing the sets to dominate guest rooms. Remember that the TV will probably be used for only an hour or so and that it is in a small room.

A small set is entirely adequate. Also be sure that it is a combined radio-TV. I think the practice of renting these sets is agreed by most hotelmen to be the most economical one. Be sure, however, that rental covers service and maintenance, and that the company providing the sets puts clear, easy operating instructions on them.

Colour TV is debatable. Competition will eventually bring the changeover, but at present bearing in mind that you are *not* buying, colour sets should be limited to luxury suites."

Turning to the hotel's public areas, Alan Tremain stresses versatility is the key to maximum profit: "Function rooms, correctly planned, can serve for both political and social activities, as well as accomodate art displays and other attractions which bring traffic to your hotel. To serve as proper meeting rooms, you need not only correct seating, but air conditioning, public address systems and careful attention to acoustics. These add to cost, but increase profit potential."

Author of two books on food and winner of top international awards as a master chef, Alan Tremain says:

Restaurants and dining rooms, with their kitchens, can become so expensive as to be an absolute nightmare. But as they are large revenue bearing areas, it is your business to turn them into areas of maximum profit.

In thinking out the method of operation and economy of running a restaurant, you must first decide very clearly what type of business you are going into. This decision includes the type of customer you are catering to, what the set-up will be: self-service, coffee shop, dining room. Next you plan the menu, which will dictate the type of equipment you should have in your kitchen and dining room.

Working out your projected revenue is the next step—not an easy job and one which takes a specialist. Working back from revenue to a fair percentage for labor costs enables you to determine the number of staff. From this you double check the floor plan of the restaurant to determine necessary seating. When planning seating, be most careful in allotting stations to waitresses in accordance with maximum efficiency and economy of motion.

Controlling the flow of customers comes next. Easy access to the cashier and clear marking of entrances and exits are the final steps in planning a smooth operation, with no problems for the guests.

In every case, the hotel's restaurant is a highly important part of the business, with no room for guesswork. Design must be as efficient as in any other hotel department. You must be able to project the method of operation and profit, be able to work out the number of staff, the hours you will be open, and the amount of revenue you are going to take. If you cannot do all these things, you should not be in business.

In the beverage department, emphasis is on control—whether the bar in question be an exclusive cocktail lounge, or a large self-service bar turning over 10,000 gallons of beer a week. Very careful thinking must go into every aspect: the number of bars, their type (such as

English pubs, oyster bars and other specialty premises if they are in keeping with the type of customers you can expect). Design of the actual bar, its operation and equipment, must always relate cost to revenue and profit protection. You must also assure the right type of control system so far as accounting is concerned, and that the right type is employed to suit your particular premises and customers.

Alan Tremain concludes: "So far as I am concerned, a project for rejuvenating an obsolete or outmoded hotel is an experience. If you can blend the gracious art of the hotelier of Europe with the American knowledge of modern methods, you can achieve something worthwhile."

34

THE VACATION-CONVENTION HOTEL

E. Truman Wright

The premise is accepted that a hotel of 200 or more rooms, located in a resort area, must have group business to survive. Smaller properties may not need group business to the same extent, although many are now adding meeting rooms and extra dining facilities to bid for this market, a market reckoned at over $2 billion annually when transportation is counted in.

While serving conventions and other groups, the resort hotel must also retain its regular vacation-guest market. None can afford to become strictly a convention hotel as few conventions meet in summer. Both markets are essential for successful year-around operation.

The Greenbrier is in its 187th year of resort operation. Before white settlers moved into the area in the middle 1700's, the Indians had used the waters at White Sulphur Springs for medicinal purposes. A modest inn was built there after the Revolution. The first guests arrived on horseback; later they came in covered wagons, westward bound. The first resort hotel (The White House) was built in early ante-Bellum days when White Sulphur was part of the Virginia Colony and served as a social and mating center as well as a watering spa for well-to-do Southern families. Stage coaches and finally a railroad made The Greenbrier more accessible. (Now many guests come by air.)

In 1910 the Chesapeake & Ohio Railroad purchased the property and built The Greenbrier's present main structure between 1910 and 1913. Two large wings were later added between 1929 and 1931, after "Old White" had been torn down in 1922. It is remarkable, of course, that anyone would make a substantial investment in a resort hotel after October 1929, but the commitment had been made

E. Truman Wright is the Vice President and General Manager of Greenbrier, a resort hotel at White Sulphur Springs, West Virginia.

From the *Cornell H.R.A. Quarterly*, November 1965, pp. 32-39. Reprinted by permission.

earlier in the year and work started, so that the new wings had to be finished. In this, The Greenbrier's construction somewhat paralleled the case of the present Waldorf-Astoria in New York, which was also built after 1929.

Resort hotels in remote areas were sorely hit by the travel and other restrictions of World War II. Thus, in 1942 the railroad sold the property to the United States Government for interning Japanese and German diplomats. And as soon as these nationals had been exchanged for our own diplomatic corps the property was converted into Ashford General Hospital, in which capacity it served until late in 1945.

The Greenbrier obviously earned money for its owners in the 19th Century or it would not have grown famous. But from 1910 until 1942, the hotel served the railroad principally as a fine means of entertaining big shippers and, from time to time, many other guests. The emphasis was on proper operation and on giving these customers a pleasant holiday. There was no emphasis, I am told, on whether the final figure at the bottom of the financial page was red or black. So, in a very real sense, the railroad was relieved of a financial burden when the Government purchased the property during the War.

It is obvious from things done when The Greenbrier was sold that the railroad never again expected to enter the hotel business. Some valuable pieces of furniture, paintings and other works of art were donated to Washington and Lee University and similar institutions in the East.

A post-War series of circumstances led to the railway company's re-acquisition of the property. Later on, changes in the Federal administration, in the railroad, and in our economy created pressure to re-convert the property into a hotel and get it in operation promptly.

Under such circumstances, it was natural that insufficient thought was given to the market the hotel would serve. There was not adequate planning for the future. Mr. Robert Young, then chairman of the board of the Chesapeake & Ohio Railroad, expressed the opinion that the hotel should cater to the nation's elite, with no thought given to conventions or conferences.

The first year of operation, the extent of the loss was such that everyone changed his mind. All realized that a proper planning job had not been done. Emphasis was shifted to booking group business as promptly as possible. Overbooking sometimes led to confusion. During this time The Greenbrier tried to accommodate 300 to 400 convention guests and 200 to 300 individual vacationing guests in the same facilities. The theater was taken away from the vacationing guests in order to serve evening convention meetings and there were several more complicated situations. Yet at this time The Greenbrier had some of the most able management available in our nation.

The problem was that they had neither planned for, nor been equipped to handle, the type of business they were doing. This was the situation the present management encountered when it assumed direction of the property in 1951.

After a thorough study of the entire operation, it was obvious to the new management that we would need to make many changes. These required additional capital investment. Several of my friends have said to me, I hope they're only kidding, "Why sure, any of us could operate beautifully if we had a wealthy railroad as a landlord or as our owner." I think it's true that we have a very successful railroad—I don't think anyone can dispute that the Chesapeake & Ohio Railroad is one of the most successful railroads in the country. But I assure you the officers and directors are very astute and demanding businessmen. They are willing to make an investment only if they can foresee a prompt return.

One advantage we have—and this I am very grateful for—is that we can borrow money from our owners without paying interest. For capital investment, this is a great advantage. During the past 12 or 14 years we have borrowed about $7 million, and to date we've paid back more than $6 million plus dividends.

As I said, the physical property required many additions. One great problem, one that management had been unable to convince ownership to aid in solving, was establishing facilities to accommodate convention guests and vacationing guests at the same time. This problem was resolved quite by accident. In 1952 Harry Cohn, then vice president of General Motors, came to The Greenbrier to inspect the property for General Motors' annual executive conference. He spent three days with us, looking over guest rooms and going through the plant, before coming to my office. "Wright," Mr. Cohn said, "The Greenbrier is perfect for our executive conference but we can't bring it here." "Why not, Mr. Cohn?" I asked. He replied, "You do not have a meeting room in which 800 men can sit comfortably in armchairs and see the stage." I said, "Oh, yes we do. It's here in my file on a blueprint." He said, "Let me look at it." So I brought it out, he went over it, and said, "This is exactly what you need."

Harry Cohn went back to Detroit. I heard later that he had a series of luncheons with some of the top officers of the Chesapeake & Ohio, and we got our building. We had to pay for it, but General Motors is helping us pay for it.

Once our house was put in order, the improvement in staff morale and employee attitude and performance led to guest satisfaction, reflected in an upward income trend. We had better business not only from vacationing guests but also from large groups in terms of convention reservations.

In 1956, to round out our facilities further, we added a large outdoor swimming pool. There had been an indoor pool at The Greenbrier since 1910. Why did we need an outdoor one? Today, people don't like to swim indoors unless it's snowing outside. In 1957 we added an attractive gun-club and also built an informal picnic lodge on a mountainside above the hotel. In the lodge we can throw a steak-and-beer party for 600 to 700 people. This new facility has paid off, as it provided a change of pace from our otherwise formal atmosphere.

In 1961 and 1962, we added a third 18-hole golf-course. We'd had many complaints about the crowded conditions of our golf-courses. Our limousine drivers, after taking people on long trips to airports, would say to us: "Now don't think we were intentionally eavesdropping on these guests, but we heard Mr. So-and-So, president or chairman of the board of So-and-So Company, say that he would come to The Greenbrier again for a meeting if it were held here, but he wouldn't plan to stay over a day or two to play golf. He had to wait much too long to tee off and play a round." To keep such people interested, we had to build a third 18-hole golf course, which was completed and opened in 1962. And, based on October 1964 business, we're going to have to build a fourth golf course during the next five or six years.

At The Greenbrier, we place great stress on prompt reports from the auditor, reports which give us daily our employee count (we have over 1,000 employees), payroll cost, and departmental profit or loss. Also we have a condensed weekly report on operations. The accounting procedures, installed with the help of the railroad's financial men, give us our final operating figures on the third working day of the month. This gives us an opportunity to promptly correct situations which might otherwise miss our attention. Instead of waiting until the 10th or 15th of the month, we can immediately take advantage of the information supplied by the accounting department.

From our experience, the key to successful operation seems to be:

1. Determine your problem.
2. Analyze it.
3. Take corrective steps, which may involve calling in outside consultants.

You are on the way to success when you have analyzed and solved some of your particular problems, and can offer your guests a properly planned, completely equipped, perfectly maintained physical property, staffed with expertly trained and genuinely courteous employees.

Don't pass over lightly the matter of having genuinely courteous employees. We get compliments on some of our service staff, and we have unions. You can appeal to the unions through the pocketbook as well as through the heart. We've told our employees repeatedly that if their performance in serving the guests is genuinely sincere and makes them feel welcome, if their performance matches or even approaches the magnificence of The Greenbrier's physical property, then we have no competition in our class elsewhere in the world. From guest-reactions, we seem to be getting through to our service staff.

The combination of people, buildings and facilities must be guided by a team of management personnel, each expert in his work, thoroughly knowledgeable, and sincerely interested in people. Sincere interest in people must come from the top, and be evidenced in your employees as well as in your guests. I would put it in that order, for if your employees don't take proper care of your guests, you won't have guests very long.

This combination has produced for us a smooth-functioning, co-operative team-operation that leads to a high percentage of repeat sales. People often ask, "What percentage of your business is group business?" On an annual basis, 70 percent of our revenue comes from conference business. Of that 70 percent, 65 percent is repeat business—either annually, bi-annually, or one year out of three.

Forecasting the future in an era of rapid change is obviously hazardous. In my opinion, group business will continue to be of paramount importance to the large resort. Conferences are held even in periods of economic recession or depression. We should continue to cultivate the individual vacationing guest and his family, for they are of vital importance to us. Yet a sudden fluctuation in the stock market, a sudden heavy paper loss, will cause individual guests to cancel their personal vacation plans. We've had it happen to us many times.

If prophecies are correct, Americans will have far more money and leisure time to spend in the future. As hotel men, we must find ways to educate these millions in the art of travel. People who have not travelled, who have never visited a resort, have a natural hesitancy almost bordering on fear of resorts. They are uncertain about how to make reservations. Will they look right to other guests? Will their children behave? How do you read a railroad and airline timetable? They will not be knowledgeable about many other matters, including tipping (which I wish all of us could eliminate). People will have so many questions and problems that we must find some way to provide answers without talking down to them.

In a recent talk, Mr. Sadler, president of the American Airlines, said something which appealed to me very much, and I think it is worth repeating. He said, "We have advertised and promoted airlines, hotels, motels, and restaurants, but these are not what the customer wants. We will always have only limited success so long as we confine our promotional efforts to the product itself. What we are really selling is a fuller life. We're selling pleasure. We're selling broader horizons. We're selling America."

Now this is a novel and new approach. We must tell our prospective guests what a resort visit will do for them in terms of a broader, fuller, and more enjoyable way of life. Possibly some of you saw the issue of *Hotel Industry,** in which the results of a Center for Research-Marketing survey were presented.

It was particularly interesting to me because the caption read, "Wives want luxury travel, husbands prefer lazy vacations." Ed Wallerstein, executive director of the Center, reported on a survey sampling about 400 housewives in the northeast of our country which indicated that 60 percent initially said that they were just planning to travel; 15 percent were planning to go camping; 13 percent indicated that they would go to a resort; and 11 percent were planning to stay at home. So they rephrased the question. "Suppose you had a vacation and were planning to go away from home. What would you most enjoy?" When the question was put that way, the simple mention of travel declined to 48 percent, the resort figure went up to 41 percent, and the number of those who would go camping or rent a cottage dropped to 11 percent.

---

*"Wives want luxury travel—husbands prefer lazy vacations," Ed Wallerstein, *Hotel Industry*, Christmas 1964 issue, p. 8.

The important thing, it seems to me, is the large percentage of those who want to combine their travel with a vacation at a resort hotel. It clearly indicates that housewives want to get away and have a vacation without household cares and responsibilities.

The mother of three young children in northern New Jersey said: "We always go up to a cottage in Vermont. And there I wait on my children even more than I do at home. My husband likes to rough it; I'd like some luxury when I go on vacation."

Another housewife answered: "I love a resort with people waiting on me, but this means nothing to my husband. He goes to fancy restaurants every day. He travels on business and stays at fine hotels. He likes camping because it's a change for him."

Let me quote one more comment: "A first-class hotel is much more luxurious than almost any motel. But an average hotel is not nearly as comfortable as the average motel." I think that is quite significant.

Several years ago the American Hotel Association (now the AH&MA) embarked on a long-range program which would have done much to overcome the natural fear of travel in those who are inexperienced. Though the proposed public education program was but moderately expensive, it was trimmed from the budget before it had an opportunity to prove itself. What a pity that a program which could be doing so much for us today met with such a tragic end.

Every year the January issues of business magazines contain opinion surveys of investment bankers, economists, and other authorities on the business outlook for the year ahead. In one survey of investment bankers as to the 1965 business outlook, 33 indicated that they expect a strong rise in business during the year, 221 anticipate a slow rise, while 196 expect a leveling out. Taking a look ahead at stock prices, the same bankers indicated the following:

10 said stock prices would rise sharply upward;
347 predicted a moderate rise;
119 foresaw not much change;
158 predicted a moderate decline;
14 said stock prices would go sharply downward.

Conclusion

Again, wouldn't it be great if we knew just what the economy was going to do? The resort hotel business is directly affected by general economic conditions and by serious fluctuations in the stock market. The Janss Brothers, wealthy Californians who recently purchased

Sun Valley, must feel that there is a future in the resort business, because they're not accustomed to losing money or making poor investments. They plan a residential real-estate development in that area.

It is quite possible laws will be passed in Washington or in our respective home states which will necessitate a complete revision of our future operating plans. It is a sad and factual commentary on the extent of government intervention in the areas of industry which I'm sure we all agree rightly belong to honest, prudent management. Many of us may cringe at the thought of becoming personally active in politics. But there can be no doubt that we must devote considerable time and attention to our politicians. We must be alert and informed about proposals made in the legislative halls of our respective states and of our nation. Though this seems rather far afield from hotel operating problems it is of such vital importance as to literally make the difference between a profitable survival and a liquidation of a business.

The Washington office of AH&MA does an excellent job of informing our members of proposed legislation that will affect our hotel and resort business. But it cannot accomplish miracles.

We have a serious obligation to inform our legislators at both the state and national level of the impact that their proposed legislation will have in our industry. It is naive to expect legislators to be impressed with our opinions. Your opinion, my opinion, seems to mean little to them. But if we can reach them, we can present facts, accounting and financial facts, about the effects of proposed legislation. In a personal visit with your legislator, for example, you could by taking any past year's figures and by applying new wage costs show him clearly what the results of proposed laws will be.

It is unfair of us to criticize legislation that is passed unless we have first given our legislators this factual information. I think this is particularly true of many of our remote seasonal resorts, which are frequently the economic life-blood of their respective communities.

Another group that we should inform carefully and fully is our employees. We should tell them frankly the full effect of proposed legislation, not only on our business but on them personally. Since it is impossible for legislators to be completely knowledgeable of each industry or of the thousands of individual businesses within each industry, it is impossible for Congress or any state legislature to enact equitable laws for all business in the area of wages.

None of us wishes to see the cases of severe hardship or employee-abuse which formerly existed in many industries, including our own.

But we certainly do feel that it is not equitable to include the resort-hotel industry in the wage legislation which applies to major industries, where the rate of pay, the productivity of the individual, and the margin of profit are far higher than they are in our business.

Once a federal wage is established for our industry, we face a truly grave danger. Look at the recent statement which George Meaney, president of the AFL-CIO, made at the Labor Congress in Washington: "Federal wage of $1.25 an hour is legislated poverty. We demand and must have at least $2.00 per hour."

And, as we all know, wages are not the only threat to our industry. Proposed legislation includes a limitation of the number of working hours. I doubt if any of us have been able to accurately calculate the total increase in costs that would be caused by the adoption of a 40-hour week, possibly a 35-hour week, in a business which operates 24 hours a day, seven days a week. It should be made clear to service employees that the 35 or 40-hour week will reduce their tips by approximately 16 percent.

Just out of curiosity we held a completely voluntary meeting of the service employees about this matter. We could not insist that they attend, and we spoke with the union business agent beforehand so that we could not be accused of unfair labor practice by talking to the employees without his being present. We told our service employees that as we faced a 40-hour week and a minimum wage, either we would have to increase our rates 20 percent to 25 percent, which might price us out of the market in some areas; or we would have to impose a service charge of a light amount and eliminate tipping. And we asked them to tell us whether they wanted a 40 hour week.

The answers they gave were interesting. The bellmen, 100 percent, said they want to continue just as they are, with a 48-hour week and frequent overtime. They're eager to work. The housekeeping department was split about 60/40 in wanting to keep things as they are. The waiters all wanted no change, but 70 percent of the waitresses wanted a 40-hour week. And regardless of the fact that we explained that this was only a poll to enable us to tell our legislators the true opinion of our employees and that this discussion had nothing to do with their present working hours or working arrangements, eight or 10 employees wanted to know how soon we were going to start the 40-hour week.

Perhaps the one bright spot in affairs at Washington is that the Internal Revenue Service has relented a bit in its harsh drive on business expense accounts. (I thought it almost too dangerous to mention this, lest the new commissioner, Mr. Cohn, pick up where the old commissioner, Mr. Caplan, left off and pursue such activities even more enthusiastically than they were pursued a year or two ago.) But let us hope that Washington has learned a little about the importance of honest expense accounting in our industry.

As we face the rising costs of the future, resort-hotel men must become better businessmen. Years ago our business adopted the Uniform System of Accounts, but we've not been uniform in any of our other business practices. If we offer the public a quality product, we should not be apologetic when we price that product high enough to guarantee us a profit. This is of vital importance as we look to the future.

If we base our room rates properly on investment and operating costs, on size, location and attractiveness of the room, and with the expectation of a profit, why should we cut those rates by giving run-of-the-house assignment to conventions? Why should we extend complimentary accommodations to conventions? Is there any valid reason for granting any complimentary accommodations to any organization, other than the fact that it has become a necessary evil? If we are all astute businessmen, we will have to have the collective courage and business ethics to eliminate it.

You might be interested to know that one complimentary accommodation to convention committees who come to make arrangements and to officials attending the conventions totaled a tariff-schedule volume of $65,000 in 1964. And we do not go overboard—as some of our competitors have in the past—in granting enough complimentary accommodations to "buy" a piece of business.

There is a future for American resort hotels, although nobody knows just what that future may be. Without doubt, the rapidly changing pattern of American life will force us to make many changes in our future operations. I'm confident we can find ways to cope with these changes—as long as we have the freedom to run our businesses ourselves. Though its operations ten years from now may bear very little resemblance to its operations of today, the management that can adapt will still be in business. Constant vigilance is the price of profit.

Questions and Answers

Question: You say that you had to learn how to handle both convention guests and vacationing guests, since chaos arose when you tried at first to entertain both at the same time. I was wondering how you now handle dining?

Mr. Wright: That's a sneaky question. You've been there and seen the one thing that we haven't solved yet. When there is not a banquet, our dining room is still chaotic at times, although we're trying to find a solution to this difficulty. People are funny: on board ship they will accept, without fussing, a first and second seating. But in our resorts they don't like you to tell them when they should go to dinner or when they should do anything else. We do plan to enlarge our dining room space. We have the beautiful new Crystal Dining Room, about 50 feet from the corner of the main dining room. It is a lovely room, but even with live music in it people feel like second-class guests because they're not right in where the main show is. Let me remind you—this difficulty arises perhaps only 15 or 20 evenings during the year; but, in order to maintain our gracious dining, we must make arrangements for expansion of our dining room.

Question: If a vacationing guest requests it, do you let him have the same table and the same waiter in the dining room?

Mr. Wright: If a guest requests the same table, we will certainly grant it. And he will have the same captain. Unfortunately, at the time of re-opening in 1948 the director of personnel knew little of basic resort operation. So he let pass the provision in the union contract which states that waiters and waitresses should rotate around the dining room after each meal. They apparently felt that this would lead to more equitable distribution of gratuities. But it just raises heck with fine resort operation. If the captain is alert, he can, however, correct this situation—because such a captain knows just how John Smith likes his two- or three-minute eggs in the morning and whether he takes cream in his coffee.

Question: How do the guests like this arrangement with rotating waitresses and waiters? Wouldn't guests on the American plan forget that they weren't going to have the same waiter at the next meal, and forget to tip?

Mr. Wright: This often happens. And the one hope we have for removing the provision in the union contract is that the rotating arrangement reduces tipping.

Question: Do you encourage guests to bring their children, especially grade-school age and younger, with them?

Mr. Wright: We have encouraged this family trade with almost disastrous results. The little rascals like to pick up everything that's loose around the hotel. We have a supervised children's program, which is the one area in which we use quite a few attractive college students during their summer vacations. We take children as young as two-year olds off their parents' hands, entertain them, give them their meals, put them down for their naps, and put them to bed at night. The rate for this service is figured according to the age of the child; we have no American Plan charge for a child four years of age or younger.

Question: Could you tell us a little more about your new picnic lodge? Can guests go there any day, or only when special parties are planned?

Mr. Wright: We open this lodge only for special, pre-planned catering, for which there is a charge. Let me describe it for you in more detail: the undercover area is about 100 feet by 300 feet. It's an open structure with an overhanging roof, surrounded by a large picnic area, including a barbecue pit. Undercover are four charcoal grills, two fireplaces and two dance floors. Frequently this lodge is booked on an "if-basis." That is, a convention will plan a picnic for Tuesday night with the provision that if it rains, the picnic will be put off until Wednesday night.

Question: Do you have a definite formula for determining the number of complimentary suites you will offer to a convention?

Mr. Wright: Yes, we definitely do have such a formula. I tried for a number of years to have this accepted in our Resort Hotel Committee meetings, but I had no success. I think that people wanted to retain the freedom to work with this as they saw necessary. Another reason I had no success is that the resort properties vary so in size that no general rule could be made. At The Greenbrier, we give one complimentary parlor suite to a convention of 250 guests. We never offer more than three complimentary parlor suites, even if the group is 800 or 900. And we do not offer complimentary meals with the complimentary accommodations.

Question: Would you tell us more about your arrangements to have daily reports from the departments?

Mr. Wright: Principally, the adjustments are to be given to the head-waiter, and to the kitchen and housekeeping staffs, in order to keep them alerted to the house-count anticipated so that they can staff according to the occupancy. We might find, for example, that certain procedures in scheduling our housekeeping have not been properly checked, and that expenses, other than payroll, are out of line. Since these reports come in very promptly, we can correct errors quickly. If we find that the profit in a certain department isn't right according to the house count, we go to that department and ask about it immediately.

Question: What kind of training do you give a new employee?

Mr. Wright: Two years ago we established classes, which are purely voluntary, for anyone who is interested in working in our dining room. These classes are supervised by one of the assistant head-waiters. The trainees practice all the dining room serving-procedures, using those who eat in the officers' room as guinea pigs. And our laundry bills aren't too heavy. These trainees will serve us for one month, accepting gentle criticism and suggestions.

35

FRANCHISING: IS IT FOR YOU?

from *Volume Feeding Management*

Franchising: defined as the right of a retailer to sell a supplier's products under certain conditions. It is becoming a real factor in the food business. A franchise, in most cases, offers a proved product, easy investment, a careful training and operating program, and an almost guaranteed profit. But . . . *is it for you?*

Do you have some experience in preparing and serving food? Do you have a bit of talent or flair (and interest) in planning a menu? Do you enjoy working out new dishes to spark up your menu? Do you like to experiment with garnishing and plate presentation to create new, rich effects?

Do you dislike repetitive work—the same tasks every day? Do you have an idea for—and a yen to try—a different kind of place that isn't in your area now? Can you put your hands on enough capital to build your own place now?

If your answer to all of these seven questions is "No," then, friend, franchising is for you. And, you're made for franchising; you're the kind of "franchisee" that every "franchisor" is looking for.

They are looking for buyers, make no mistake. No segment of the business is growing as fast, nor proliferating as wildly.

Franchising, in the sense that the name is a household word, and the product known without going in, began with Howard Johnson in 1926. In the intervening 38 years the number of franchise companies offering food has grown to something approaching 300. The growth rate is accelerating; the number is estimated to have doubled in the past 10 years, and may well double again in the next decade. Some firms are expanding so fast that they average a new store a week!

From *Volume Feeding Management,* July 1964. Reprinted by permission of the publisher.

What is a franchise? It is commonly defined as "the right, granted to a retailer by a supplier, to handle the supplier's products under certain conditions and stipulations."

In practice, the deal is spelled out rather carefully. While there are general policies that apply (see Franchising–The Groundrules), you can appreciate that there are contractual differences between, say, a Howard Johnson and a Mister Donut of America.

Still, it is possible to draw a reasonably accurate composite picture of the ground rules. In broad strokes, it would look something like this:

Let's start with a man we shall call John Smith. He wants to buy and operate a franchise store selling some sort of food. He has done some checking into the business* and decides he likes the XYZ company. He writes headquarters for an appointment with Frank Brown, a senior officer.

If Smith fits the common pattern, he is somewhere between 30 and 50 years old. He is likely a salesman, though he may be in another white or blue collar job. His income is between $5,000 and $8,000 a year. He is dissatisfied with his present job. He has one overriding ambition: to work for himself. That's why he turned toward franchising. And that appeal–"Be Your Own Boss!"–has made franchising big business.

We can also rough in a profile of Brown. He is an astute business-man. He has been in the franchise business at least a few years. He probably helped conceive and define his particular operation. He suffered through the first, pilot model, where he tried various foods and combinations. By now he has dozens, or even hundreds of units operating successfully. He knows what makes a unit produce. He knows, too, what qualities are important in the people he lets buy in.

The first thing he checks with Smith is money. Does he have enough money to meet initial expenses? He wants him to feel an investment "pinch." That way Smith is guaranteed to work his head off to make sure he won't lose his investment. And that kind of dedication is the first rule for success.

If he's satisfied about the money, Brown moves on. Does Smith have prior business experience, regardless of type? Can he get along well with people? Does he have an outgoing personality, plus the desire to succeed? Fine.

Does he have any background in food service? Brown hopes not.

---

*The Small Business Administration division of the U.S. Department of Com-merce, the local Better Business Bureau, and the Franchise Boom.

He knows that in most cases that spells trouble. He has learned, from bitter experience, that operators try to change the strict operating formula. They add menu items, individualize decor, experiment with food combination and garnishing, and even adjust prices. *Brown knows his formula works!* So, he generally rejects applicants with a food service background. It saves misery on both sides.

By the same token, he does like previous business experience. A food franchise is more a business than a food service operation. It requires business principles only: keeping records and maintaining controls. The food service thinking has been done by the company. The outgoing personality and liking for people are important to attract and keep customers and help.

If the qualifications and chemistry are right, so far, Brown will now get down to the franchising facts of life. What does Brown expect from Smith? What can Smith expect to get in return? Every company has specifics, of course, but for purposes of our broad picture, we can rough in approximations here.

Smith now gets a dollar figure. This is for his investment. It is rarely less than $10,000, and most commonly runs between $20,000 and $40,000. This money has to go on the barrelhead first. It covers, Brown will explain, four areas: license, building, equipment, and initial operating capital.

First comes the license fee. This gives Smith permission to run a company installation for a twenty-year period. The fee is determined by the individual franchisor: some few have no license fee at all, while others charge as much as $10,000. If there is one, it must be paid in advance. It is designed to cover the initial cost of training and supervising the new operator.

The second topic is the building. Brown's company sets all standards and specifications for the building, including its construction. A company rarely owns these buildings. This would require enormous capital and the basic premise of franchising is spread-out, or individual capital investments. This not only spreads the risk, but insures investor-operator interest. Smith may own a suitable lot. If so, he must supply the funds with which to erect the approved building. Or, he can lease the land and building. The general rule here is a year's lease in advance as security. But whoever owns it, the completed building will be a replica of all the other structures in Brown's group.

Equipment, Furnishings and Opening Costs

The third consideration is equipment and furnishings within the building. This, too, is specified *in toto* by Brown. The price can vary from $10,000 to $100,000, depending on the type of operation. Usually, Smith must put up at least 10 percent in cash in advance.

The fourth part of the initial expenditure is to cover operating costs for the opening months of the installation. These vary, of course, but are generally in the $3,000 to $10,000 range.

And that, Brown explains, about covers the initial investment. There are some other things, though, he tells Smith, that the company does require. So far, neither of us has made any money, he notes. A franchisor has two sources of income, he continues.

The first is a percentage of the gross as a royalty. It varies, usually, from 2-4 percent, depending on the size (or absence) of a license fee, and other considerations. The second is a rule that Smith buys from the company. This may include food, supplies and equipment, and often does include them all. There are good reasons other than profit for this rule, Brown adds. The company image has been built on a certain quality standard; whatever the company sells will meet these specifications. Also, he points out, because of its size, the company can often get a better price than Smith could get for himself.

The company makes other demands, Brown explains. But these are a matter of protection for both of us, he says. Take, for instance, location. There is no help for a poor location, except to close down and start elsewhere. So the company carefully plots each unit before it is built. It knows the location that will work best. It knows, from past experience, what type of people it wants to attract—whether they be men or women, factory workers or college students, drivers or pedestrians. It knows their income bracket, the foods they prefer, and even the hours of the day they will likely stop. As a result, a good franchise company rarely suffers a loss from a poor location.

Every Location Is Planned

It is interesting to note that while food franchise operations are found in all kinds of places—suburbs and downtown, on the highway and in shopping centers—every location is the result of careful planning. Each company has staked out a definite segment of the community as its customers and tries to broaden its sales through that segment. (For example, McDonalds has found its greatest appeal with college students and motorists. So a highway beside a campus is the ideal location. Compromises are made from that point.)

The company also requires a fixed fee—usually one percent for advertising, Brown explains. This, too, helps both parties. It sells the company name and image to prospective customers. It generates a steady supply of new customers for Smith. And, of course, it helps Brown by generating a supply of applicants for new locations.

But the most important of the company's demands, Brown says, is control. And no operations manual was ever stricter or tighter than a franchise manual. Every step of the operation is controlled by the company, Brown says. The reason is obvious: if a franchise is successful, the success of any new unit depends upon following the formula. This formula is a series of controls. These controls standardize the unit, and make it a carbon of every other unit in the company.

Controls Begin With the Menu

These controls begin with the menu. All food franchise companies dictate all or most of the menu. Where this has not been done, trouble has frequently followed. (Case in point is Howard Johnson. The menu plan here was to have the basic items supplied by the company, but allow each operator to add other items as he saw fit. When the company had few units, quality controls could be effected. As it has grown, tight controls became more difficult, with the result that quality varied tremendously among the units. So the company decided to buy back the units and install a master menu, supplied from its own commissary. It is well on the way to accomplishing that goal.)

Because a small menu permits greater control, the trend is in that direction. (A prime example here is Mister Donut of America. It controls every step of its doughnuts, from ingredients, to frequency of preparation, to techniques. Once it tried selling hamburgers in one unit. Sales of doughnuts dropped markedly, as did profits. The experiment ended. As a result of its close control, it has never lost money on one of its units.)

Other company controls, Brown continues, include building design and specifications, furnishings, supplies, serving ware and other accessories. Even sales are controlled, he adds. If Smith's gross sales should drop below a pre-determined figure, company men would be on the spot in short order to find the reason. Most commonly, he relates, the problem is in preparing, pricing or selling his many items incorrectly. The company men will quickly correct the mistake.

Trained Management Is a Must

The last basic control the company wants is management, Brown says. The company knows that you, he tells Smith, must be prepared to devote long hours and many years to achieving success. Often the contract requires that the owner be physically present for the greater part of each working day. Others may settle for a "company-trained manager" on the premises at all times.

We take, Brown says at this point, but we also give. Here's what you, as a prospective operator of one of our units, will get from us. You receive the right to operate one of our units. This means you get a proven name and a quality image. Your sales will start strong the day you open, from people who have been customers in our other stores. We supply you with an advertising and promotion program. We furnish you with recipes and foods which are proved popular and set a price that insures they will sell, and yet return both of us a profit.

Additionally, he notes, you can raise capital that would otherwise consider a food service venture too risky. We supply supervision, to answer your questions and keep you on the right track. We insist you take our training course.

These courses, at company-operated schools, run from two to eight weeks. They teach the novice everything he needs to know to be a success. What this boils down to, of course, is how to follow the rules to the letter. (Some courses go further; Mister Donut, for instance, includes aptitude and psychological testing to help uncover potential problems before they occur.)

But, best of all, Smith will get love and attention from Brown. Brown, and every other franchisor, care desperately about every store. It's not only that profits come from sales and success, but, more importantly, it's the "one bad apple can spoil a bushel" problem. Every unit *must* be good.

What can Smith hope to realize if he makes the investment? Though sales usually materialize almost instantly, thanks to the company name, it takes years to pay off the investment. Estimates vary, but one company suggests eight years as a good target.

Gross Varies More Than Profits

Naturally, some types of food franchises gross more than others. A soft-serve ice cream unit might do $50,000 a year, while a hamburger store might do $400,000. Obviously, costs vary accordingly.

Despite this, strangely enough, operator profits have a startling similarity. The reason, of course, is that the nature of each operation dictates its food and labor costs. This means that if Smith goes for a soft ice cream unit his gross is less than for a hamburger unit, but so too are his costs. He ends up with about the same number or dollars. The variables in profit are not so much the type of unit, as they are in location, and the particular abilities required from a franchise operator.

From this point on, Brown tells Smith, he must decide whether to proceed. If he meets the franchise company's pattern—ambition, some capital, a liking for competitive work and following a routine, a desire to be his own boss—his chance for success is good.

The Experience Problem—Again

If he has had food service experience, though, the problem is greater. Because the company has refined and polished its operation to the last degree, it insists upon these techniques and policies, without deviation. To protect this policy, the company reserves the right, in the contract, to revoke its license or withdraw its name any time its sees fit.

On the other hand, a solid, proved franchise is the next thing to guaranteed success these days. In a business where the mortality rate is very high, good franchise companies rarely lose a unit. The reason is good training at the beginning, with counseling, supervision and support continuously thereafter.

Only the individual can judge whether it's right for him.

Franchising—the Groundrules

Initial Investment

Runs from a few hundred dollars well up into the thousands. Generally, it is between $20,000 and $40,000.

License Fee

Most franchisors, especially those with established reputations, charge some fee for a license. It is usually between $5,000 and $10,000. Mostly it is used to cover the costs of training and supervising the franchise during his first months of operation.

Building

Most commonly the building is leased to the franchisee by a third party, subject to the approval of the franchisor. Location, building design, and specifications are also subject to approval. The franchisee, in most cases, pays all construction costs. These vary greatly with the type of building, and in many instances an already existing structure can be remodeled, reducing the cost to the franchisee. If the franchisee leases from a third party he must put down one year's security.

Equipment

Equipment is paid for by the franchisee, but specified and approved by the company, and usually bought through him. Again, cost varies, and may run anywhere from $10,000 to $100,000, depending on the menu.

Franchisor Profit

The franchisor usually makes his profit in one or both of two ways: (1) Collecting royalties on monthly gross (usually 2-4 percent); (2) Requiring the franchisee to buy all merchandise directly from a franchisor-run commissary.

Franchisee Profit

The franchisee usually keeps his gross, except for the royalties and a 1 percent advertising assessment which most franchisors insist on. He must pay all expenses, including labor and food with this.

36

THE FRANCHISE CHALLENGE OF THE '70's

Howard Cooper and Irma R. Lobe

The franchise fast food market of the '70's will be captured by companies that not only recognize the present competition and trends but, more important, can interpret the needs of the '70's, project the competition of the '70's, and create a strong, unique pattern that will appeal to the market of the '70's.

It is our conviction that in addition to management, location and financing, the key ingredient that will make the difference in the success of any chain catering to the market of the '70's is a powerful, patented, graphic image; an image which is not only strong in architectural form but an image which markets the product and the unit. We believe that in the coming era you can no longer just sell chicken or hamburgers or draft beer; you have to sell a concept, an image and a marketing program.

As examples of the kind of franchise chain that we believe will prosper in the '70's, we will outline the program of Farmer Cooper's Barn and Silo, Inc.* and Barrel of Beer, Inc.,* the two chain franchise patterns that we have developed and are about to launch into national chains.

Problems in Capturing the Suburban
Fast Food Market of the '70's

Real Estate. The key to building a fast food chain for the market of the '70's is the acquisition, the zoning, the construction and the financing of real estate; the organization that will be equipped to

---

*Trademark

Howard Cooper is an expert in the research and development of fast food patterns, and is experienced in retailing and real estate. Irma R. Lobe has an extensive background in handling administrative problems, including those concerned with banking, insurance, legal, and food operations.

From *Fast Food Magazine*, December 1968. Reprinted by permission.

tackle this challenge and do an outstanding job will be a leader in the fast food business.

Prime locations in the heart of the suburbs are becoming almost non-existent and costly. Land on the periphery of a regional shopping center in the 100 major markets of America will average $820 a front foot by 1975.

Municipal governments are becoming more difficult to work with. The codes are becoming tougher; construction costs will rise 30 percent to 60 percent; sign variances will become more stringent with height restrictions of 18 feet to 20 feet becoming the rule rather than the exception. Drive-in units that will provide dining in the car will find it difficult to obtain building permits. Churches, schools, and shopping centers as well as existing competition will present a fierce, united front to prevent the building of new units in the heart of suburbia in the '70's.

The Market of the '70's

Sixty five percent of the fast food market of the '70's will be customers in the 35-and-under age group. Thirty four million families will have annual incomes of more than $10,000, with more time for leisurely dining out. The 1970 fast food market is a $20-billion market with an annual growth of 10 percent.

The suburban fast food market is growing at a faster rate than the urban market, representing 25 percent of the total fast food market by 1972.

On-premises consumption of draft beer in suburbia will increase at an annual rate of 15 percent from 1970 on.

People. The second critical problem facing the fast food franchise chains of the '70's is people.

Working, operating people will be difficult to obtain and costly when you can get them. We are competing with industry. The income in suburbia is above the urban market, therefore housewives, youngsters and the bread-winner of the family do not desire a second job.

The New Competition in the Fast Food
Franchise Business of the '70's

Since real estate is the key to building a chain of the '70's, existing retail chains with strong financial statements will be moving into the fast food business of the '70's because of their ability to acquire prime locations. The developer is interested in financing his lessee. The existing retail chains offer the developer a lease which, in most cases, would result in a 70 percent to 80 percent mortgage commitment from institutional lenders based on the guarantee of a major, existing retail chain. The types of chains that will be moving into the fast food business are as follows:

Department Store Chains. Department store chains such as Federated, Allied and May Company will demand food facilities in the regional shopping centers as an added incentive, before becoming the anchor tenant in the shopping center. In order for a developer to build a regional shopping center with 500,000 square feet or more, he requires a department store as the anchor tenant. The foodservice facilities in a regional shopping center have proved to be lucrative because of the captive shopper market. Department store chains are moving fast to capture the food facility locations in the regional shopping centers with enclosed malls.

Discount Chains. Discount chains such as K-Mart will build freestanding, fast food drive-ins in the front of or adjacent to a new K-Mart discount center. The captive shopper and the employees working at the center will give K-Mart an advantage that a fast food franchisor building a free-standing unit does not have.

Food Chains. Food chains pose the greatest threat to the fast food market of the '70's. Supermarket chains are expanding into the convenience foods field at a fast pace to build profits by serving the young family market of the '70's.

Supermarkets have the locations, built-in traffic, money and consumer acceptance to build substantial volume in carry-out chicken and other types of foods.

Supermarket chains have the real estate and the bargaining power with the developer to develop prime locations for free-standing, prototype units.

Major food chain groups including Topco, representing 32 member chains with gross sales in excess of $1 billion a year, are studying plans to offer their chain members free-standing, prototype packages that will be franchised to one food chain in every market.

Real Estate Developers. A number of real estate developers across the country, because of tax and depreciation requirements, will build small chains of free-standing, prototype, fast food units which they will operate or franchise in a local market. The locations that they own are so valuable that they will not turn them over to a franchisor; they will develop them on their own.

Existing Fast Food Franchisor Chains. Existing fast food franchisor chains and their impact on the market of the '70's will be as follows:

Strong-Image Chains: Chains like McDonald's and Kentucky Fried Chicken, who are the leaders for their pattern of marketing, will open several thousand units during the '70's; as leaders in one pattern of marketing, they have such a tremendous head start that no one, regardless of their resources, will ever overtake them.

Furthermore, McDonald's and Kentucky Fried Chicken with their powerful consumer acceptance will expand the graphic image of the golden arches and the trade name of Colonel Sanders onto their types of prototype units including roast beef, delicatessens, pies and other specialty food operations.

Obsolescence of Present Chains

Several chains that were leaders in the market of the '60's will be obsolete in the market of the '70's. They will be obsolete for the following reasons:

Management Control. Several chains are not receiving an adequate royalty from present franchises to provide the management, training and supervision necessary to build a strong, effective group of franchised units. It will cost the franchisor in the market of the '70's a minimum of 3 percent of gross sales to provide a full-time supervisor for a maximum of 12 units with the constant training and controls required to provide effective supervision for every unit. Chains with inadequate franchise agreements will suffer because they do not have the franchisee fees with which to provide this management.

Obsolescence in Image. Several chains that were leaders in the market of the '60's will be obsolete in the market of the '70's because their image does not fit in with the requirements in the market of the '70's. It is old fashioned; it is hum-drum; it is honky-tonk; it is in bad taste. With hundreds of units in operation, you cannot tear down buildings and change the image over night.

Obsolescence in Physical Plants. Several of the leading franchise chains of the '60's have prototype buildings that are obsolete. The building layout and size do not lend themselves to using the new equipment, production and packaging techniques needed for the market of the '70's.

Obsolescence in Location. Some of the existing chains of the '60's have locations which no longer have a relationship to the population and shopping centers of the new and growing suburbia.

Saturation and Over-Storing of the '70's

Wall Street has been good to franchise chains in recent months. Franchisees have been easy to come by. The franchisees have been willing to lend their names and credit to secure real estate financing. Some franchisors have not employed real estate research techniques, nor hired seasoned, experienced real estate men. All of these factors have resulted and will result in some markets having more units, more square footage and more capacity than the market can possibly support. This will mean that some of the units will have to go out of business.

Developing the Franchise Fast Food Pattern
for the Market of the '70's

With the problems outlined above and the new competition coming into the marketplace, the first question that should come to your mind is: "Is there an opportunity for a new chain to come into being and become a leader in the fast food franchise business of the '70's?

We strongly believe that there is. We believe that a corporate committee cannot create and execute a fast food franchise pattern. We believe that it has to be done by one or two individuals who have the knowledge and understanding of every facet of what goes into the creation of a fast food pattern. It has to be done by one or two people who have the vision and the dream to see the results, but who also have the patience, understanding and determination to put all of the components together to create a striking and a powerful image.

The basic requisites for building a strong fast food chain of the '70's are:

1. A total understanding of every facet of a fast food prototype: real estate, construction, the image, the financing, equipment, food preparation and presentation, packaging, operations and controls and everything that goes into creating a success pattern.

2. Creation of a pattern—an image—unique in your market. No one in our lifetime will ever overtake McDonald's or Kentucky Fried Chicken. They created and did a superb job in building their pattern into a national chain.

3. Management interest in company. We are bringing into Farmer Cooper's Barn and Silo, Inc., and Barrel of Beer, Inc., a group of seasoned and experienced foodservice and real estate executives who are joining our two companies because they have a ground-floor opportunity to create a capital gain situation and take part in the building of a new chain. These are incentives that no established chains can offer imaginative and ambitious people.

4. Owner-Operator. It is our belief that the strongest and most effective kind of management of a unit is a man, his wife and family working in a unit because they have their life's savings and their

future tied up in that unit. Our policy is to franchise an owner-operator to operate one unit and, after he has proved his performance, to expand by owning and operating one additional unit at a time, on a conservative expansion timetable.

5. Real estate oriented company. Farmer Cooper's and Barrel of Beer will provide the owner-operator with real estate and equipment financing so that we can control the unit in the most effective manner and, at the same time, limit the cash requirements of the owner-operator. It is for this reason that the chains will be financed separately, with financing running into several million dollars at the outset. A franchise agreement in the '70's will have very little power in the eyes of the courts. The most effective method of controlling the management effectiveness of a franchised unit is to be the guarantor or the lessor of the real estate.

Building Image: The Key to Creating the Franchise Pattern of the '70's

Land and building represent the major investment in a fast food franchised prototype.

Locations in the heart of suburbia in the market of the '70's will be difficult to obtain, so many units will be located one-quarter or one-half mile away from the shopping and population centers. With fierce competition in the marketplace, you have to create excitement and sell an image and a concept in addition to the product. The building, as an architectural form, will have to relate itself to the total marketing program, in order to build a strong, unique identity for the chain.

A good example of the power of the image is McDonald's. In the early '60's, there were a number of chains that copied McDonald's menu and price structure. In at least 18 locations, there was an independent or another chain unit right next to a McDonald's. However, confidential studies showed that the McDonald's unit, before it was a national chain and before it had national advertising, would gross anywhere from 20 percent to 60 percent more than the other, because of one strong factor—the image. The golden arches captured the imagination of the American public and made a stronger impact than the image of competitive 15¢ hamburger chains.

However, in the coming era, we not only need the architectural form as an image, but to sell a total merchandising story. This is demonstrated in the Farmer Cooper's Barn and Silo and Barrel of Beer programs.

Analysis of Constructing a One-Purpose, Unique-Design Fast Food Building

Cost of Building. The structural design features of the patented Farmer Cooper's or Barrel of Beer prototype building costs anywhere from $7,000 to $10,000 more than a conventional building of the same size, mechanical and site requirements. This would result in an additional monthly rental of anywhere from $70 to $120.

The major cost of construction today is the mechanicals: plumbing, heat, ventilating and air conditioning. The second highest cost is site work. Whether you build a conventional building or a Farmer Cooper's or Barrel of Beer prototype, the mechanicals and site requirements cost the same.

Building Codes: Securing a Building Permit for a One-Purpose Unique-Design Fast Food Prototype. There are problems in getting a building permit for a special designed building. However, there are very few communities across the country that have an architectural pattern where all buildings are identical.

The trend in all types of retailing today, whether it be a supermarket, a dry-cleaner or a fast food unit, is to create a building image. The program of Farmer Cooper's and Barrel of Beer is to franchise owner-operators who will operate units in their own communities. The applicant for a building permit is the local owner-operator who in most cases has lived in the community for a number of years.

Financing a One-Design, Prototype Building. Every fast food building is a special building. The mechanical and interior layout requirements are designed specifically for a restaurant. For the building to be converted to another use, a substantial loss would be taken regardless of the building design. The history of fast food prototypes is that either the pattern is a fantastic success like McDonald's, or an early failure. When it is a proven success, financing is readily available because the building enhances the property, creates more sales and more profits, and brings a greater return to the real estate investor because he receives a percentage of gross sales.

37

WASHINGTON: ARE CONTROLS IN THE WORKS?

from *Volume Feeding Management*

As comfortable as it is with bigness, the federal government has never stopped loving—and looking out for—the small businessman. Now the franchisee, his ranks swelling to an army, is winning special attention in Washington. He is the little guy whose livelihood may be threatened by unfair business practices of his franchisor. But at the same time, he is the symbol of a new and very promising approach to small business—one which may help him survive in a world of bigness, and provide minority groups a promising avenue to the American Dream.

Ironically, both these views reflect the essential nature of franchising. The individual who signs such an agreement wins access to market-tested management techniques, financial resources, promotion and advertising backup which he could hardly manage alone. But along with these benefits comes necessary sharing of authority and profits. The big question being asked around Washington agencies and in Congress: how much of his freedom should a franchisee be asked to give up.

The answers will be far from academic, since they will affect how franchising may work under the antitrust statutes of the U.S. Activity in the capital on the subject has grown steadily. A number of bills await action in both the House and Senate. The Federal Trade Commission is looking into antitrust implications, and the Justice Department is also involved. The Securities and Exchange Commission is considering tighter rules on stock issues of franchisor companies to protect private investors from some unrealistic accounting practices. The Post Office Department is said to have scores of fraud cases in the works.

On the non-public side, a new organization called the National Association of Franchised Businessmen has set up offices in Washing-

From *Volume Feeding Management,* January 1970. Reprinted by permission of the publisher.

ton to do battle on behalf of franchisees. With an estimated 1,200 franchisors and more than 670,000 franchised businesses ringing up sales of $100 billion, NAFB has its work (in its words, "helping to build a better franchise industry") cut out for it.

One of the organization's first public acts was to support legislation sponsored by Senator Philip A. Hart (D.-Mich.) intended to lay groundrules for franchising. Decrying the "lack of definite legal standards," NAFB ticked off what it considers the chief problems of franchisees, all of them stemming from the terms of franchise agreements themselves:

—"Constant pressure and control by the company to impose mandatory working hours, and high sales quotas;
—"Limited or no rights to transfer franchises;
—"Fear of loss of investment through cancellation or termination for minor contract infringements;
—"Exhorbitant fees and royalty payments that are vastly out of proportion to sales volume;
—"Directed company purchases of merchandise, supplies, and equipment that could be obtained elsewhere for less;
—"Restrictions on selling price and product offerings—regardless of local competitive situations."

Though these super-charged allegations represent the "injured party's" viewpoint, and by no means reflect universal industry practices, they are being considered by the legislators and regulators closest to the situation.

At bottom, these "problems" are all matters for interpretation. Franchisees must agree to restrictions, or else the bedrock of the concept—uniformity—is undermined. But how to stop franchisees from being unduly restricted in a booming field with all kinds of franchises—good, bad, and those in between—is the trick.

The major legislation in Congress aimed at doing this is Senator Hart's proposed "Fairness in Franchising Act."

A key provision affecting the volume feeding industry is the termination of franchise clause. The bill would prohibit cancellation or failure to renew a franchise except for good cause. This is defined as failure on the part of the franchisee to comply with the provisions of the franchise agreement that are essential to the operation of the business, and for bad faith. If the franchisee-franchisor contract provides for the arbitration of differences in the case of possible cancellation, the franchisor would be exempt from the requirements of the legislation. Presently a franchisor can cancel—for any reason—on thirty days' notice.

"Cancellations are now running rampant in the franchise business," a spokesman for the Senate Antitrust and Monopoly Subcommittee told VFM. "A small businessman's life savings can be wiped out on thirty days' notice. This legislation is a strong safeguard for the franchisee."

Senate action on the Fairness in Franchising Bill is expected by the end of this month. No action had been taken on the House bills, indicating delay in possible final passage well into 1970.

The Federal Trade Commission, the Department of Justice, and the Department of Commerce have all taken positions on the legislation. Speaking in its favor, FTC Commissioner James Nicholson said that "not until the problem of cancellation or termination of franchise is resolved can franchising even be considered as a candidate for introducing minorities into the mainstream of our economic life."

Commerce and Justice, on the other hand, opposed the legislation. They feared it could encourage inefficient franchising because the franchisor would not be able to close down inefficient operations easily. Senate leaders feel that the Commerce and Justice reasoning is faulty.

Rufus W. Wilson, Chief, FTC Division of Federal Trade Restraint, adds some more light to the Commission's thinking on franchise termination. "The assumption of many franchisors seems to be that the franchisee has contributed little to the business and that the only intangible asset of any value is the franchisor's trademark, which automatically reverts back to the franchisor. There is little recognition of the fact that the franchisee's investment of effort, time and money may have enhanced the value of the franchisor's trademark in the particular area and that the franchisee may be entitled to a fair compensation when the franchise is terminated or transferred to another franchisee. An equitable franchise arrangement would take into account contributions made by the franchisee to the business. Some provision—for example, compulsory arbitration—might be made to serve in evaluating the franchisee's contribution.

"Failure by the franchise movement to evolve such a doctrine of fairness may invite a vigorous reaction from the enforcement agencies," Wilson warned.

The way things might turn out is suggested by recent precedent. In the Schwinn Bicycle case, a policy against restricting transfers by dealers and distributors emerged. On the basis of the Schwinn approach, according to Wilson, "it could be argued that when a franchisor refuses to allow a reasonable transfer of the entire license —that is, a transfer of the use of the trademarks, processes, and good will to other franchisees—this may amount to unlawful restraint.

"The failure to allow a franchisee to realize in some equitable manner his contribution to the franchise could result in a questioning of the entire franchise agreement under Section 5 of the Federal Trade Commission Act. It may become the view in enforcement circles that the legality of any restriction in a franchise agreement is colored by whether the entire arrangement is equitable. By equitable, I mean that there exists a fair allocation of financial risks between franchisor and franchisee."

Supreme Court decisions during the past few years have directly affected the franchisor/franchisee business relationships, and the antitrust consequences of franchisor control over purchasing has been the subject of review by both the Supreme Court and the FTC.

In the Carvel Corporation decision, the FTC said that a franchisor who designated sources of supply of ice cream mix for its soft-ice cream franchisees did not commit a per se violation of Section 5 of the Federal Trade Commission Act or Section 3 of the Clayton Act.

The Carvel case, in effect, upheld the inherent economic benefits of franchising an entire business. FTC held that without evidence of substantial restraint of competition, buying restrictions such as Carvel's were reasonably related to the need to control a trademarked product's quality and the franchisor's image.

FTC Commissioner Nicholson had this to say about the Carvel decision: "The well-advised franchise operation would contemplate alternative methods for maintaining legitimate control over quality. One less restrictive alternative would be the designation of several suppliers who would be free to negotiate with franchisees over price. Another alternative may be the establishment of quality specifications, together with a system of sample testing to insure compliance."

Unfair exclusivity in pricing, or any other franchisor excesses for that matter, are vulnerable from a number of legal directions. Says Commissioner Nicholson: "The charging of exhorbitant prices could be challenged as an unfair act or unfair method of competition under Section 5 of the Federal Trade Commission Act. There is support for such a position in recent pronouncements by the Supreme Court, which condemned the practice of exclusivity, which resulted from either overt or inherent coercion. Overt coercion was covered in the Atlantic Refining Co. v. Federal Trade Commission (1965), and inherent coercion in the FTC v. Texaco (1968)."

The Supreme Court's decisions as they affect food franchising are mainly concerned with the factor of exclusivity. The Court has ruled in other areas of interest to the franchise industry generally, but these cases relate mainly to tie-in sales—with obvious emphasis on franchises involving consumer goods items.

These misgivings about some management practices haven't even slightly dampened Washington officialdom's enthusiasm for franchising. Its authentic contribution to American business is recognized by all agencies, as witness the Commerce Department's package of programs to aid business development by minority groups.

In fiscal 1971, for instance, the Department expects to make available up to $301 million in federal grants, loans and guarantees. And one of the most significant of those programs is the one devoted to franchising.

Under this scheme, Commerce's Office of Minority Business Enterprise and the Small Business Administration are working out a broad cooperative relationship with franchisors. For its part, the Commerce Department is arranging the procedure under which franchisors and franchisee come together. The SBA role is to get a bank to lend the franchisee the money required to establish the business with enough operating capital to see the enterprise through to profitable operation.

Called "25x25x2," the joint effort is aimed at bringing 25 franchisors to Washington at a time for conferences with Government officials to work out plans for each of the franchisors to open up a minimum of 25 franchise opportunities to minority businessmen over the next two years. Under SBA plans, 200 franchisors will be brought to Washington in groups of 25 over the next several months. Roland Kadesch, SBA Public Affairs Coordinator, told VFM that as many as 500 franchisors could ultimately become involved. In 1970 alone, the number of minority-owned franchises will triple, according to Small Business Administrator Hilary Sandoval, Jr.

Speaking for the Commerce Department, Secretary Maurice H. Stans forecast that eventually thousands of new franchises will be opened up for minority businessmen. Among the initial participants in the new program are Dunkin' Donuts, Dairy Queen, Arby's, Bresler's 33 Flavors, Pizza Hut, McDonalds, All-Pro Chicken, Convenient Food Mart, Carvel, Lums, House of Pancakes, and Burger King.

Significantly, the SBA's attitude toward franchising has changed during the past year. The agency had been a bit leary of franchise operations, particularly over the relative independence of operators. Although it has always made its guaranteed loans available to businessmen interested in franchise operations, it was far pickier over terms of these agreements. The new emphasis is on getting minority individuals set up in business as fast as possible. It is even establishing appeals machinery for franchisors dissatisfied with treatment by SBA field offices. This attitude, coupled with the ambitious plans of the minority program, is ample evidence of the overall confidence Washington is placing in franchising.

38

WALL STREET: PART BULL, PART BEAR, ALL EYES

Joseph S. Coyte

Investors who listen to the oracles of Wall Street before supporting or rejecting any group of stocks are now hearing two distinctly different stories about food franchising.

Around mid-1969, the investment community paused in mid-euphoria, and began a second and more suspicious examination of this growth phenomenon. For a number of complex reasons, these stocks began to take on a double image. The Street had become choosy almost overnight, alternately believing and distrusting, recommending and rejecting, enriching and impoverishing different issues among the dozens that had been making the market scene since the boom started three years earlier.

In a nutshell, here is the two-fold reasoning:

On the one hand, franchising is a genuine economic advance in eat-out food distribution. It will suffer a shakeout—and may even have started one—as all fast-growing trends in U.S. business do. But it will emerge stronger than ever. Its markets are far wider and deeper than anyone had heretofore realized, with important areas of potential barely touched.

On the other hand, franchising's promise of quick riches has attracted some entrepreneurs with little more than an untested idea (and hope) to go on. Out of the thicket have sprung questionable marketing and accounting practices, which in turn have attracted negative attention from Congress, the Justice Department, the Securities and Exchange Commission and the Federal Trade Commission. These developments, along with some severe setbacks, outright failures, and apparent oversaturation in some areas, have placed every franchisor's proft-and-loss picture under sterner scrutiny on Wall Street.

From *Volume Feeding Management*, February 1970. Reprinted by permission of the publisher.

In the real world of stock prices, this good-but-bad image seems actually to have helped the solid, well-managed leaders in the field. Despite a market slump that cut the heads off many leading industrial stocks and kept them off even in the autumn advance, companies like Kentucky Fried Chicken and McDonald Corp. were selling at their highs for the year. The bellwethers were more than holding their own.

Luckily, the excesses of the food franchising boom generally do not run deep. They are more symptomatic of the quantity of the entrants than the quality of the original idea. It is the solid base of franchising—and the equally solid economic reasons for its expansion—that interest Wall Street in the long run. The prime ingredients, from the investment point of view, could probably be reduced to two key factors: demand growth from without and management growth from within.

First, and perhaps most important to the over-capacity-shy analysts, is the still valid prospect for steadily rising demand. The dread that strikes the casual visitor to one of those overgrown strips of roadside eateries is understandable. Some franchisees have suffered disastrous volume decreases as a result, but others have reported just the opposite—a kind of boomlet as customers in an area become accustomed to thinking of a certain crossroads as the place to eat almost anything. It is the shopping center concept all over again.

But as sales volume kept scaling new, almost unbelievable peaks, analysts began to wonder (based on their own tastes) just how much fried chicken, tacos, burgers, franks, frozen desserts and so on the American stomach could handle. Fortunately, Wall Street's latest diagnosis goes beyond that oversimplified view. As one recently released study by a New York brokerage house pointed out, franchise food service is competing as much with *other* channels of the consumer food dollar as with itself. These include not only traditional restaurants, but perhaps even more important, supermarkets. With customer trends indicating more and more acceptance of convenience foods, the low-to-moderate tabs of most franchise operations represent the ultimate in convenience to housewives preoccupied by everything from community activities to wage-earning.

A second demand source that bodes well for franchising is geographic—a fact Wall Street has also caught up with. The boom so far has centered largely in suburban and traffic-dense highway locations. This leaves many urban and more rural areas virtually untouched. Beyond these, there are the beckoning foreign markets, particularly those in Europe, which have to date been spirited imitators of American merchandising ways.

Still another ingredient of solid expansion, as Wall Street sees it, is greater management expertise in the franchising industry overall. This includes the range of internal operations, such as more uniform franchisor-franchisee relations, better financial and accounting controls. Beyond these there's been an upgrading of promotional techniques, research, equipment, and, of course, franchisees themselves. Since the top ten or so chains account for about half of the volume done by franchising, and may become even greater presences as time goes on, these various forms of managerial upgrading are viewed as sure bets for the industry at large.

But as things stand now, the management situation seems to be more worrisome to Wall Street than the demand picture. The growth in franchise food companies is continuing to outpace the total growth of the commercial food service industry—and will likely continue to do so in the next few years, according to recent financial studies. Whether real profitability will accompany that growth in franchises is what is most in question.

One franchise practice has, rightfully, drawn the sharpest criticism. This is the accounting technique of claiming whole franchise fees as current net when in fact agreements call for payment over a term of several years. In cases where this is done before units are in operation or even built, the danger of never earning what has been already counted is evident. And since such fees can often be run through almost completely to net, two other grim spectres appear immediately.

One is that franchisors may concentrate too heavily on selling franchises to keep growth figures rising, thus widening the gap between fee "income" and unit sales necessary to support real growth.

The other is that profit figures may become unrealistically inflated, producing price-earnings ratios all out of proportion to worth. In effect this sets up a high-flying stock issue for an ignominious crash. This is not hypothetical; it has already happened. And Wall Street, once burned, has learned the lesson well.

Just how well came to light in a *Wall Street Journal* article last November which cited a privately circulated study made by the public accounting firm of Peat, Marwick, Mitchell & Co. The study makes four suggestions: (1) that the uncollected amount of fees due the franchisor not be counted as income immediately; (2) that even initial fees be shown separately on profit-and-loss statements; (3)

that related costs should be disclosed and (4) that the accounting method used be spelled out. Although only proposals, Peat-Marwick's checklist appears to agree substantially with the conclusions reached by security analysts on the Street.

These observers are also concerned about the bad press some franchisors have been getting over their relations with franchisees. This, in fact, is the sum of Washington's antitrust interest in the field.

How far franchisors can—or should—go in controlling everything from purchases to resale prices on franchises is the leading question. But as one analyst pointed out recently, this problem is also symptomatic of a fast-growing industry where poor business practices are bound to surface. The further point being made is that high-caliber franchisees themselves are now at a premium. This fact coupled with pressure from Washington should, the feeling goes, dissolve this problem quickly enough.

On balance, then, the analysts and money managers, many of whom became heroes by riding certain food franchise stocks on their heady ascents, are not about to change their minds now. And to protect their own investments of advice and money, it is in their interest to help maintain a clean image for the industry at large. With expansion unabated, the franchising phenomenon is not going to go away. It may falter, but the correction ought to do it genuine good.

In fact, as some observers see it, several built-in factors may already have begun purifying growth. One is ever-tighter money, which means that banks are far more particular about who gets their help. The other is that the Street is shy about new issues of any kind, and is equally sparing with its favors.

While the quality of franchises is on the rise, this does not yet mean that quantity is on the wane. The annual growth rate of convenience food service establishments, figured by one source as 15 percent, has run more than double that of the commercial food service industry for the past half-dozen years. This segment now represents roughly one-fifth of the total. But more than half of this convenience group is made up of the ten or so top companies. Wall Street figures that these leaders will dominate the scene even more in coming years, producing a further stabilizing effect on growth.

Finally, there are those basic factors, sometimes overlooked amid bad market news, which franchising has going for it. By one count, franchise operations make up one out of every ten U.S. commercial restaurants. They did not get there by gimmickry alone.

Underneath, they represent a real economic advance, going the trend to convenience foods one better. Centralized buying and promotion, reduced labor costs through automated equipment, and owner operation with all the extra control that this brings, have helped franchise operators achieve much higher unit grosses than the industry average. Franchise operators, as a result, have a far better record of business survival. They fail, according to one estimate, in 10 percent to 20 percent of cases, against a frightening 80 percent to 90 percent for independent businesses.

In short, Wall Street has seen the statistics, and they work. The message from this point on is that in the right hands, with the right management, food franchising can be a bigger winner than ever.

39

EVALUATING A FRANCHISE

from *Franchise Journal*

The following checklist was prepared for use by prospective franchise investors by the Small Business Guidance and Development Center in Washington, D.C.:

1. For how many years has firm been in operation?
2. Has it a reputation for honesty and fair dealing?
3. Will firm assist you with:
    (a) Management training program?
    (b) Employee training program?
    (c) Public relations program?
    (d) Capital?
    (e) Credit?
    (f) Merchandising ideas?
4. Will firm assist you in finding good location?
5. Is firm adequately financed so that it can carry out its slated plan of financial assistance and expansion?
6. Has franchisor shown you any certified figures indicating exact net profits of one or more going firms which you have personally checked yourself?
7. Is franchisor a one-man company or corporation with experienced management trained in depth so that there would always be an experienced man at its head?
8. Exactly what can franchisor do for you which you cannot do for yourself?
9. Has franchisor investigated you carefully enough to assure itself that you can successfully operate one of its franchises?
10. Did your lawyer approve franchise contract after he studied it paragraph by paragraph?

11. Does franchise call upon you to take any steps which are, according to your lawyer, unwise or illegal in your state, county or city?

12. Does franchise give you exclusive territory for length of franchise, or can franchisor sell a second or third franchise in your territory?

13. Is franchisor connected in any way with any other franchise company handling similar merchandise or services?

14. If answer to the last question is "Yes," what is your protection against this second franchisor organization?

15. Under what circumstances can you terminate franchise contract and at what cost to you, if you decide for any reason at all that you wish to cancel it?

16. If you sell your franchise, will you be compensated for your goodwill or will the goodwill you have built into the business be lost by you?

17. How much equity capital will you have to have to purchase franchise and operate it until your income equals your expenses? Where are you going to get it?

18. Are you prepared to give up some independence of action to secure advantages offered by the franchise?

19. Do YOU really believe you have the innate ability, training, and experience to work smoothly and profitably with franchisor, your employees, and customers?

20. Are you ready to spend much or all of the remainder of your business life with this franchisor, offering his product or service to your public?

21. Have you made any study to determine whether product or service which you propose to sell under franchise has a market in your territory at the prices you will have to charge?

22. Will population in the territory given you increase, remain static, or decrease over next five years?

23. Will product or service you are considering be in greater demand, about the same, or less in demand five years from now than today?

24. What competition exists in your territory already for the product or service you contemplate selling?

   (a) Non-franchise firms?
   (b) Franchise firms?

40

BURSTING BUBBLE: MANY FRANCHISE FIRMS FALL ON HARD TIMES AFTER A 15-YEAR BOOM

James MacGregor

Franchising, says Ray Kroc, chairman of McDonald's Corp., has become the "updated version of the American Dream."

But that dream, says Richard A. Speer, is a nightmare. Five years ago Mr. Speer purchased an interest in a Shakey's Pizza Parlor here. Since then, he has watched $100,000 slip through his fingers like so many greasy slices of pepperoni.

That's not the way Mr. Speer was told it was going to be. Shakey's advertising assured him, and all other comers, that no experience was needed to earn up to $50,000 a year running one of its pizza parlors. By 1968 Richard Speer had five pizza parlors on his hands, none profitable. That's when he quit Shakey's and closed down three of the five shops. The remaining two parlors have been renamed and are showing a profit these days, but not nearly enough for Mr. Speer to forsake his steel warehousing business.

So Richard Speer is in Federal court, suing Shakey's and its parent corporation, Great Western United, for $2.4 million. He charges the company violated antitrust laws by a "tie-in" arrangement that required him to buy pizza ingredients and equipment from Shakey's at seven times prevailing market prices. Shakey's contends that sales arrangement was legal.

A Barrage of Suits?

Earlier this month a Federal court jury in San Francisco ruled that "tie-in" requirements imposed on dealers by another franchising firm, Chicken Delight, were illegal. That verdict is being appealed, but enfranchisers of everything from pancake shops to pet care centers are gloomily girding for a barrage of similar suits from disgruntled dealers.

James MacGregor is a staff reporter for *The Wall Street Journal*.
From *The Wall Street Journal*, May 29, 1970, p. 1. Reprinted with permission of *The Wall Street Journal*.

Dealer revolt is plenty to worry about, but it's just one of a growing number of problems plaguing hundreds of enfranchisers. Once considered the darling of Wall Street and the savior of the small businessman, franchising today is spurned on Wall Street and cursed on Main Street. Many enfranchising firms are sinking deep into the red. Others are hurriedly resorting to both expansion, and contraction to stay profitable. Some are diversifying because they and their competitors have saturated the market with one or two products. Others have taken to buying back outlets from the inexperienced and undercapitalized dealers they peddled them to in the first place.

In the meantime, they have watched the price of their stocks plunge at a rate that has outpaced by far the recent overall market decline. And they're facing a dozen Federal and state investigations —inquiries that are certain to produce a tangle of new regulations.

All that is quite a comedown for an industry whose revenues ballooned 3,600 percent over the past 15 years. Franchising, of course, has been around for decades; operators of car dealerships and service stations, for example, are all franchise holders. But in recent years the franchise has spread like dandelions to a variety of fields, most notably the fast food service industry. In 1955, the 50,000 franchise dealers in the U.S. grossed $2.5 billion annually. Currently, there are 670,000 franchise holders in the country, selling everything from potato pancakes to pedigreed poodles and piling up volume of $90 billion a year.

On the Rocks

Any industry that grows that fast is likely to attract more than its share of unscrupulous operators, as well as hundreds of honest but naive recruits drawn by what appear to be snowballing profits. So it is inevitable that sooner or later the bubble bursts, or at least shrivels a bit. For franchising, that time is now.

"The shake-out is here," says the chairman of one fast food chain. "There's not much left to generate confidence in franchising's immediate future, when you look at the failures and the earnings reports and the legal problems. I expect to see at least a hundred franchisers, including a couple of the big ones, either on the rocks or over the dam in the next few years."

That executive won't find much disagreement among security analysts, many of whom are warning their clients to shun all franchise stocks. In the past year, investors have administered drubbings to some of the 1960's hottest franchise stocks, including International Industries, whose price plummeted from a 1969 high of $58 to yesterday's close of $12.25. Lum's Inc., whose price dropped from a 1969 high of $26.375 to the current $5.875.

A Glut of Restaurants

Nor will the pessimistic franchising executive find much disagreement along one busy street in a Cleveland suburb. Five years ago there were four franchised restaurants on a two-mile stretch of the road near a large shopping center. Today the same two miles contain 14 such restaurants, or one every 250 yards. Two of the 14 say they are near bankruptcy. The managers of six others say profits have dropped sharply in the past two years. "There's no money here," says one glum owner. "I'd sell tomorrow if there were a buyer."

In that atmosphere, even franchising companies that are clearly successful are scrambling to stay that way. One such company is Kentucky Fried Chicken Corp., which now has almost 3,000 stores in operation and boasts it has never had a franchise failure. Last month the company reported record first quarter sales and earnings. Nonetheless, the company's common stock has fallen sharply in the past couple months, and KFC has taken two major steps in hopes of maintaining its past growth record: It is buying outlets back from its dealers, and it is diversifying beyond fried chicken to fish, hamburgers and roast beef and even into the motel field.

To date, KFC has bought back over 700 chicken stores from franchise holders. Donald G. Greer, a vice president, says the company owned stores contributed more to 1969 earnings than did all the 2,300 or so franchised stores put together.

Enfranchisers say "buy-backs" give them leverage to make chain-wide changes and serve as a testing ground for experiments with prices, products and marketing. Franchise critics say the enthusiasm for "buy-backs" demonstrates two things: Holding a franchise isn't as profitable as running your own independent retail operation. And selling franchises is one way of getting cheap financing (the capital put up by new dealers) for a quickly expanding operation.

When a company announces it is buying a franchise back from a dealer, the latter often learns he has no choice. Many standard franchise agreements lapse after a few years or give the company the option to repurchase at a set price, usually a low multiple of annual earnings. Less ethical enfranchisers invoke clauses allowing them to cancel franchises for minor violations of complex rules. Cleveland antitrust lawyer Alan Arnold says that "the dealer usually gets little or no compensation for the time and money he has put into building up the franchise's name in his local area."

Some franchising firms terminate a franchise not so they can manage it themselves but so they can sell it to a new dealer—a method of operation that can prove lucrative indeed. Selling the franchise to a new dealer, Mr. Arnold says, "allows the franchiser to collect a whole new set of franchise fees, often without having furnished the services for which the first set of fees was paid."

Quitting the Field

Kentucky Fried Chicken and some other major franchising firms have managed to avoid most of the attacks now being leveled at the industry by legislators and regulatory agencies, but those attacks seem certain to change the industry. Indeed, one operator of two franchise chains, Ward Foods Inc., has said it will quit the franchise business as a result of accounting changes strongly suggested by the Securities and Exchange Commission as well as the accounting profession. Ward reported a $1.7 million loss for 1969 after making the changes.

Some enfranchisers have resorted to what some consider questionable accounting because of the nature of their income. It can take from several months to two years for a purchaser of a franchise to start producing a profit for himself and his franchiser. So to avoid an earnings slump that could ruin their growth reputation, many enfranchisers took to signing up dealers at a constantly accelerating pace and reporting initial franchise fees as immediate income—even though in many cases those fees were payable over a period of years, or were refundable or uncollectable in the case of franchises that never got off the ground.

Under the pressure from accountants and the SEC, most enfranchisers now report such fees as income only when the money is in the hand. This change is causing a rash of earnings restatements and magnifying the slump in some companies' earnings.

Enfranchisers have come under regulators' spotlights for other reasons. Congress is investigating some franchising firms' practice of using the names of celebrities to promote their enterprises. Kentucky Fried Chicken chairman John Young Brown Jr. recently told a Senate subcommittee that celebrities who dabble in franchises are guilty of "betrayal of public trust" for permitting "fast-buck operators to exploit their names. They sell programs they know nothing about."

Falling Stars

Many such franchises haven't done well. The household cleaning services chain bearing the name of television host Arthur Treacher has run into serious financial trouble. Shares in the restaurant franchise chains featuring jazz musician Al Hirt and football star Joe Namath are selling for half their initial price.

Even franchising firms that don't boast a celebrity on the board are under attack for alleged deceptive advertising. Without admitting guilt, Meal & Snack Systems Inc., and Franchise Development Corp. recently agreed to a Federal Trade Commission order prohibiting them from using certain claims in selling franchises to new dealers. A Senate subcommittee is probing alleged misleading franchise advertising that has appeared in a number of the nation's business and financial publications, including this newspaper.

Hit Parade Co. and Bermuda Pools Inc. are among the enfranchisers whose officials have been successfully prosecuted by the Post Office, which now puts franchise rackets at the top of its list of mail frauds. Mail authorities have convicted 220 individuals for franchise fraud since 1964, and they put the losses to franchise buyers involved at over $120 million.

It's clear the spectacular early success of franchising and the ease of entry into the field prompted many entrepreneurs with neither experience nor capital to become either enfranchisers or dealers. The franchise holder today is often no businessman at all but perhaps a plumber or electrician who has been told he needs no experience to profit handsomely and that the enfranchiser will teach him all he needs to know. Some business greenhorns have sunk all their savings into franchises only to see everything evaporate.

Bulging Files

Unhappy franchise holders are fighting back. Robert M. Dias, head of a national group for dealers formed last fall says his office received 1,200 complaints from franchise holders in its first three months. Many a dealer has discovered, says Mr. Dias, that "the earning projections he was assured of are simply out of reach" and "that the assistance he has been promised does not materialize."

There are also bulging files of complaints at Congressional offices, regulatory agencies and Better Business Bureaus. These may lead to some tough legislation before the end of the year. Among the proposals under consideration in Washington and various statehouses are ones that would make mutual consent a condition of most franchise cancellations and severely restrict exclusive "tie-in" buying arrangements between franchising firms and dealers.

Shakey's Pizza, for one, has ended such tie-ins. Great Western United, Shakey's parent company, last month settled a $46 million antitrust suit by its dealers (not Mr. Speer's personal suit). Shakey's agreed to quit selling pizza ingredients to dealers and promised dealers a significant voice in company affairs. Dealers claimed they were paying almost 8 percent of their gross to Shakey's—including payments for bags of pizza spices priced by Shakey's at $21.50 and comparable to spices other firms were selling for $3.05. A competing pizza chain says its dealers pay about 5 percent for foods and services.

Shakey's dealers also claimed they were getting precious little in services for their 8 percent payout. Before the suit was settled, one dealer said he was operating so much on his own that "if Shakey's Inc. went out of business tomorrow, I can't see where it would make any difference at all to my stores."

William M. White Jr., chairman of Great Western United, says, "When we bought Shakey's (for $14 million in 1968) we found the company had not done as much for its franchises as we would have hoped." That, says Richard Speer, is a masterful piece of understatement. Mr. Speer says his stores were profitable—until a Shakey's inspector forced him to raise the minimum drinking age for low-alcohol beer from 18 (as permitted by Ohio law) to 21. His business immediately dropped 40 percent and never recovered. Inspection reports given Mr. Speer noted the low volume but made no suggestions for improvement and gave both the stores and the staff high ratings.

Shakey's did overhaul Mr. Speer's advertising program, but without result; one radio station it recommended didn't even reach the area where one store was located. When Shakey's turned down his request to lower the drinking age, lengthen operating hours and try foods other than pizza, Mr. Speer got out.

41

IT'S TIME TO CUT OUT THE NEGATIVES
AND GET POSITIVE!

Leon Gottlieb

Enough already! The franchise industry has taken its beating! It seems that everyone who has cared to say anything about franchising in public—has tried to make a name for himself at the expense of our industry. They have tried to get on the bandwagon of "consumerism" by knocking franchising. Class actions by dissident franchisees and their headline-happy attorneys; individual lawsuits of even the smallest consequence have received wide exploitation by press and other media. A few years ago these actions wouldn't even have rated so much as a mention in your local newspaper.

People have panicked, or at the very least have chosen to forget the basics of business dynamics, its interrelationship of people, the honesty and moralities and yes, even the dishonesty that unfortunately will always exist. Many of us have conveniently forgotten many of our own experiences and have not related to what we have heard or read. I have a favorite saying wherein I believe there are three sides to every story, namely: yours, his and the truth that's somewhere in the middle.

Headlines and stories that scream, "Cheat" or "Liar" are readily believed as fact when in reality the articles supply little or no information as to the cause or purpose that led to the effects as charged. Newspaper columnists, after sensationalism, have virtually tried and convicted franchisors in print. Sane, intelligent businessmen know better than to accept this kind of nonsense, while the public takes the stories at face value.

Leon Gottlieb was Vice President of franchise sales and marketing for International Industries and President of its Copper Penny division. He now heads Leon Gottlieb & Associates in Los Angeles.

For example in a recent *Wall Street Journal* column (May 31, 1970) entitled: "Bursting Bubble—Many Firms Fall on Hard Times After a 15-Year Boom," by James MacGregor.

The article stated that a certain franchisee purchased five pizza parlors. The article continued to develop the idea that the franchisee had a legitimate suit against the franchisor and one of the events leading up to the franchisee's extreme dissatisfaction was the fact that he purchased not one, but five pizza parlors and that all were losers. Furthermore, that he was taken advantage of etc., etc., etc.

I was a franchisee myself for eight years. And, as a representative of a NYSE franchisor I sold hundreds of franchises to good solid hard working individuals. In my entire experience I can't even imagine what set of ridiculous circumstances would prompt any franchisee to buy more than one franchise if his first were not going well. He might buy two if the first were marginal with potential, but only wherein the franchisor showed and gave good solid assistance.

A man who has accumulated from $50,000 to $100,000 (a minimal amount I would estimate that was required) to buy some five restaurants cannot be considered a fool. And, logically it follows, unless he were a fool that he must have had good faith from experience in the company executives and the policies and systems of his franchisor. Would *you* repeat again and again an unpleasant situation if you weren't making money or at the very least happy with your arrangement? I could go on and on to question the veracity of such an individual's actions and the extent, if any, of the research performed by the staff writer.

By way of balancing the scales to show you that there are good ethical franchisors and executives who do care, take this case for example:

I personally sold a restaurant franchise to one gentleman in Oxnard, Calif. He worked extremely hard and we advertised and did what we could to make it go. The area just wasn't ready for our particular family style coffee shop. Eventually it would be, but not then. It was simply not the type of situation anyone could predict. The franchisee is one of the finest gentlemen that I ever had the pleasure of dealing with. Together we faced the problem and I had the opportunity of obtaining another location a year or so later and offered it to this franchisee to help him offset his present losses and to make some substantial profits from a second unit. The unit was in a mid-town Los Angeles main artery and offered little chance of being a loser. The cooperation, faith and goodwill between the franchisee and myself and the entire company enabled us to consummate this multiple sale. Yes, the franchisee paid the normal down payment and signed the regular agreements and he is still doing very well. If anything, his previous experience and knowledge gained in his Oxnard unit paved the way for him and his crew to develop profits virtually from the first week of his new operation. These are the facts and I haven't distorted or omitted any of them. Perhaps though I made my point about what can and usually must exist between franchisees and their parent companies if they are to both grow and prosper. At no time is it ever beneficial to compound a problem by remarrying oneself to unhappy "partners." I ask that you think about it. Think about the possible existence of one or two or more sides to the truth between the example I stated of the pizza parlor multiple operator and his "awful" experience with his company and the multiple operator whom I personally sold and resold.

Unfortunately, the "good guys" never make the headlines. No one ever takes anyone into a court of justice to say how good they are. And, we don't expect it! But, by the same token, don't deny that there exists solid, competent, ethical franchisors.

I pity the poor reading public who for the past couple of years have had a steady diet of reading about how bad the franchise business is and how it's getting worse not only as a personal business opportunity, but as a stock investment. Pardon me if I stand astounded by the ability of some writers, editors, newscasters and analysts to be so darn smart as to know all there is about a franchisee and the franchisors to be able to state so completely that this or that company is good or bad. It's high time that someone stated the positives!

Certainly a company must have a reasonable product or service to render. They should have some pilot models in operation supported by facts and figures, and certainly there should be evidence of company support and know-how. No one disagrees. Take the fast-food business for example. Talk to any knowledgeable person and he'll remark that the location is everything. Some companies are better at selecting sites. Some have more money or financing to afford stronger locations. Many are just better businessmen. Fortunate is the franchisee who buys a franchise with a company who can select and obtain class-A locations. Chances are better that he will succeed. Similarly, purchase a poor location or a franchise from a second-rate franchisor and you take a greater risk but if you do, don't condemn the franchisor—or franchising either.

Few good-location-franchisees ever take their franchisors to court or join in class actions against the very company who made them wealthy. And if they do become unhappy with themselves or others, they usually sell out at a handsome profit. That too is a constructive part of our franchise business. Few people stay forever. They might sign a twenty-year lease, but many franchisees tire of their business just as they tired or became restless in their previous employment or business. Makes sense doesn't it? Think about it. Have you remained in one business or employment all your adult life? If you don't believe me, just look at the business opportunity column in the classified pages of your metropolitan newspaper and realize that a resale doesn't mean that the business was unsuccessful. Many a good businessman moves from one business to another stepping up to greater volume, profits, scope or challenges. And so too, it is with franchisees.

I think many of us tend to be scared by headlines and have a tendency to overlook the good, the practical, the realistic and positives that do exist.

Franchising will remain with us for many years to come, because it's a good, working way of being in business. The long term investment by so many companies and individuals is just too large to be taken lightly. The substance and commitment by so many is so great that you must realize that there are thousands of success stories and positives in the franchise industry.

One trouble is that the "good guys" are busy making money and minding their own stores and tending to their business. Many of the so-called troublesome operators, those that make headlines would do well to expend a similar amount of energy on their business. They might find that there is a positive reaction to a positive effort— specifically more money.

So to those of you who are considering a franchise, don't let your confidence be shaken. To new franchisors I admonish you to learn the lessons learned by those of us who made the mistakes of the past. Realize that franchisees deserve the right to make a profit—and even a loss, and that your every effort must be to the mutual benefit of both.

42

WOMEN IN THE INDUSTRY

from *Institutions Magazine*

A Minority Report

The situation in business today, observes one prominent woman executive, "is certainly better than it was, say, 25 years ago. But women, as a group, still run into more discrimination in business today than any other minority, including Negroes."

True enough for the business community in general. But what about the service industry? Just what is the status of management women in our industry today? Are they accepted more readily and do they function more productively in our industry than they do in others? Most important, is the growth of the industry, with the takeover by the big management complexes, opening up—or diminishing—the opportunities for women at top levels?

To find out what it's like being a woman in our industry, we went directly to the experts: women themselves, some 200 of them, who represent virtually every phase of the industry. We also spoke to a number of male executives to find out how they feel about the smell of perfume in the executive suite.

Not surprisingly, a broad divergence of opinion emerged from our queries, particularly on the subject of woman's effectiveness in certain management positions. But even so, there was general agreement on the following points: first, there's probably more management opportunity for women in the service industry than in most other fields; second, women currently holding down responsible positions function as effectively as their male counterparts; third, women will probably hold the key to the critical middle management shortage.

Needless to say, many problems still confront the career-minded woman who has her eye on those management levels currently held almost exclusively by men, especially in the commercial end of our

From *Institutions Magazine*, March 1969. Reprinted by permission of the publisher.

business. Some of these problems are transitional and should resolve themselves as more women advance in the industry. But other problems, such as the psychological and social forces that determine behavioral patterns in corporate situations, are far more structural and are, therefore, in certain respects almost insoluble. Whatever the case may be, it's clear that women are making their presence felt throughout the service industry—as the following pages should well illustrate.

A Look at Today

Women constitute more than one-third of the working force in the United States, and over one-half of the labor force in our industry. Even so, the number of women earning more than $10,000 per year in the entire country is said to be only one in one hundred. Here, in a statistical nutshell, is the basic dilemma facing the business woman of today: plenty of room at the bottom, very little room up top.

It's a problem; and, as far as women are concerned, a very big problem. What makes it even worse is the fact that the basic pattern of a woman's life in this country has already undergone a revolutionary change.

In 1920, according to a report issued recently by the U.S. Labor Department, the average working woman was 28 years old and single. Today, the average working woman is 40 years old and married.

At the root of this change are, of course, a number of highly significant social phenomena. More women are going to college today than ever before. Labor saving household equipment and prepared foods are easing the burdens of domestic chores. Birth control devices have made family planning a workable reality. And the rising cost of living has put increased economic pressure on the family.

"At one time," one woman psychologist asserts, "there was a practical reason for women to stay home and leave the bread winning up to the husband. But today, in many instances, there simply isn't any reason for it. That's why so many women come to resent their role as homemakers and are so anxious to find meaningful work."

Turning to the service industry, we find a situation in many ways different and more encouraging than in the business community at large. To begin with, there's the fact that well over half of all middle-management and supervisory jobs are held by women. To be sure, many of this group fill what might be thought of by title as typically female jobs: dietitians, housekeepers, nutritionists, etc. (or "female" by market area in such health, education and welfare institutions as hospitals, schools, colleges.) Scattered throughout the

industry are women functioning as owners, and managers and consultants, and, in some instances, in jobs that have been traditionally
masculine, such as cost control, purchasing, and sales. In many companies, in fact, the conventional definitions of what is man's work vs
woman's work are beginning to blur.

"There's no question but that the whole stigma often attached to
women in business is going out of fashion," says Lis Brewer, public
relations director of Hilton International. "And I think the basic
reason, at least in our industry, is sheer practicality. We're needed."

The need in the industry for qualified management personnel is
certainly one situation working to the advantage of women, but it's
hardly the only one. "Women in the service industry today owe a
great deal to history," suggests Kathryn Bruce, former education
director of the NRA. "During the war years, women were kicked,
coddled, pressured and persuaded into management out of sheer
supply vs. demand. That situation gave a lot of women the opportunity to get a firm background—something many of them still
enjoy."

Undoubtedly, too, the very nature of the service industry has had
a great deal to do with the substantial role that women play in it
today. Women have frequently been involved in family-run restaurants and chains where their authority, stemming from proprietorship, transcends gender. And indeed, because the industry tends to
be so disparate and, in its institutional segments, has never been as
tightly managed or as competitive as, say, the automotive industry, it
has had havens—nice, comfortable loopholes where the ladies could
function happily and productively—and frankly, were willing to fill
jobs with neither the paycheck nor status to attract men.

Whatever the reasons, though, it's clear that a substantial and
growing number of women have found a place for themselves in the
service industry, and it can be said, without chauvinism, that the
opportunity for women in management is greater here than it is,
perhaps, in any other field, including retailing. Granted, in terms of
executive positions in the classic corporate sense, women are still
much in the background.

Exploding Some Myths

You couldn't prove it by most males, but the biological truth of
the matter is that women as a species are as equally endowed with
brain power as men. Nonetheless, stereotypes persist: women are
emotional, rely on instinct rather than logic, don't respond well
under pressure, are not serious about their work, and, in general, are

Figure 1. Women At Work (National Figures)

Between 1940 and 1967:
  The number of women in the labor force
    more than doubled in the 35-to-44 age group;
    more than tripled in the 45-to-54 age group;
    more than quadrupled in the 55-to-64 age group.
There are 29,000,000 women currently in the labor force; women represent 37 percent of the labor force. 3 out of 4 work full-time, year-round.

Women at work today are nearly 10 years older than the women at work 25 years ago; the median age is 40. About 3 out of 5 are married; 2 out of 5 have children under 18 years of age.

The higher the education of a woman, the more likely she is to be employed.

Labor force participation rates of women aged 18 to 64, March, 1967:
  Less than 8 years of schooling—35 percent;
  high-school graduates—48 percent;
  4-year college graduates—55 percent;
  5 years or more of college—72 percent.

About 1 out of 7, or 14 percent of all employed women (3.5 million) were in professional and technical occupations in 1967; about 4.4 percent of all working women are "managers, proprietors, or officials."

The *median* wage or salary income of 1967 of year-round full-time workers:
  Professional and technical
    Women $5,826
    Men $8,945
  Managerial, official, and proprietary
    Women $4,919
    Men $9,103

Women still earn only 60 percent of the salaries of male counterparts.

Less than 1 percent of all working women earn $10,000 a year or better.
Less than 2 percent can be classified as real "executives.'

Source: *Background Facts on Women Workers in the United States.* U.S. Department of Labor, Wage and Labor Standards Administration, Sept. 1968.

Our Industry as an Employer of Women

Eating & Drinking Places (April, 1967)
Total, non-supervisory personnel 1,525,261
  Men 627,682
  Women 897,579

Total, tipped employees 516,429
  Men 94,397
  Women 422,032

Total, non-tipped employees 1,008,832
  Men 533,285
  Women 475,547

Hotels, (1966)
Total, non-supervisory personnel 610,000
  Men 309,400
  Women 300,600

Source: U.S. Bureau of Labor Statistics

less effective and productive in business situations than men. Granted these stereotypes, it's no wonder that women—even in our industry— seem to have a wider berth in areas like advertising and public relations (plus, of course, the traditionally "female" roles) than in jobs which require more technical knowhow or entail the making of hard-headed business decisions. Peg Swanson of Armour says, "If you stick to areas like product quality, customer acceptance and service when talking over your ideas to top management, you're on safe ground. But just try to offer your opinions on the economic value or financial implications of an idea, and watch the skeptical look on their faces."

Not surprisingly, many women are ultra-sensitive to this built-in skepticism. "I'm sick and tired of hearing about women's intuition," complains Paulene Roeske, a Wall Street broker who deals in restaurant and hotel stocks. "Women, through their social life, get greater exposure to different kinds of situations and different kinds of men than men do. And this is a big help in business. The more social exposure a person has, the better his ability to make business decisions, all other things being equal."

Still, the presence of this skepticism is often an inducement to work harder. "I've outworked any man I've ever worked with," insists Rosaleen Fitzgibbon, v. p. and general manager of the Irish Pavillion, in New York.

As far as statistics and sociological studies are concerned, science seems to be very much on the side of the woman. Virtually every government and independent study ever conducted indicates that in terms of performance, job stability, absenteeism, and turnover, the differences between men and women in similar management and supervisory capacities are practically non-existent. This even applies to women with growing families. "Highly trained women occupying responsible and skilled positions," one government report concludes, "are seldom absent and rarely quit, even if they have several children to bring up."

But scientific evidence to the contrary, the attitude persists, in our industry as well as in others, that women have their "place," that there are, in fact, positions where women as women function more effectively. "A lot of it has to do with sheer physical stamina," says Georgina Tucker, director of housekeeping, Century Plaza, Los Angeles. "Certain positions in large hotels are extremely demanding in terms of pure stamina and are logically thought of as belonging in a man's domain. These would include managing director, general manager, front office manager, sales manager, food director."

Another problem arises for the woman who needs to raise money to start her own business. "It's hard for a woman to borrow," says Iris E. Ford, president of Friendly Village Inn in Rhinelander, Wisconsin. And Stewart Investments' President Dixie Stewart admits that the most terrifying experience she ever had in business was walking into a strange bank where she didn't know any of the officers.

Finally, there is a feeling among many people that women, as women, simply cannot cope with certain situations which go hand in glove with certain positions. Janet Frisbee, corporate food service director of the Union Carbide Co., New York, says: "Industrial food service is a very difficult area for women to enter. Men can deal better with the labor situation, particularly the foreign element, and unions. At the unit level, men seem to have better control. Women are better in lesser supervisory positions or as overall consultants on design and service."

Conflict of Interests

It would be quixotic—and hardly accurate—to give the impression that women have easy access to the majority of jobs in the service industry. Looking at the restaurant and hotel segment only, ours is not the typical 9-to-5 business, and a woman who has a couple of growing children is understandably more reluctant to work overtime than a man secure in the knowledge that the children are being well taken care of—by the mother. (Paradoxically, one of the attractions in non-commercial institutions has long been the possibility of schedules that meet the needs of family women—even to part-time professional and managerial openings in some areas.)

Figure 2. Jobs Women Think They Can't Do, Don't Want To Do, or Think Men Should Do

Executive Chef
Industrial Food Service Director
School Lunch Food Service Director in Large City
Department Head in a Large or Chain Organization
General Manager or Managing Director of Large Commercial Hotel
Front Office Manager
Sales Manager
Catering Manager
Food and Beverage Director
Superintendent of Services
Hotel Design

The large part of the problem arises from the nature of our society, specifically from the stabilizing role the woman is expected to play in the family situation. Psychologists may produce evidence to the contrary, but the overwhelming majority of women with children won't proceed with their careers unless they are reasonably assured their children are not being shortchanged.

On the other side of the picket fence, problems can also arise. "If a woman gets too cozy at home," suggests Helen Rose, assistant manager of the Drake Hotel, New York, "she won't be able to make that extra little effort to get ahead—which probably explains why more married women aren't top executives." An even harder-nosed view comes from Ruth H. Gaertner, director of residence of Eastern Illinois University. "Let's face it," she says. "A responsible job in the service industry does not blend with marriage, with children, nor with running a home. Your work is your life."

So what it comes down to, apparently, is this. The women who want to advance have to figure out a way somehow to cope with the irregular hours. "You have to live with it," says Evelyn Harrison, General Manager of the Ramada Scottsdale Inn. She also has to work out in her own mind the priorities between work and home. ("Take a lesson from the men," advises Hilda Watson Gifford. "Have competent help at home.") "Married women who have careers have to accept the fact that they have dual responsibilities," says Jean Roeschlaub, vice president of Clifton Cafeterias, Los Angeles. "At the end of the day, a man can clear his mind at home. But a working mother doesn't have that luxury. Maybe it's unfair, but that's the way it is."

Superwomen in the Industry
Evelyn Sullivan: 26 Years, 28 Flavors. In 26 years with Howard Johnson's, she's worked in nearly every facet of the business—from unit operations to top management. "Because I started out with the company in times of change, I've had much broader experience than is possible today. I just worked at whatever needed to be done, and was expected to know how to do everything." A generalist by necessity and opportunity, she currently specializes in development and production of comics, puzzles, games, and menus that become toys or learning tools—souvenir items used in HJ units across the country. Miss Sullivan is also executive coordinator of the HJ cooperative advertising program (local and regional advertising for company-owned and licensed units) and coordinator of marketing programs.

Jean Clinton Roeschlaub: 49er. She and her two brothers have been managing their father's successful Clifton Cafeterias in Los Angeles since 1949. Mrs. Roeschlaub is vice-president and director of foods for the cafeteria chain. She also heads up a new division called "Convoline"—a combination of "convalescent" and "convenience." Though still in the testing stage, its business is daily food service catering to small (25-30 beds) nursing homes. The line: pre-prepared chilled foods, made in the Clifton commissary. Despite her own top position, Mrs. Roeschlaub has her reservations about women in management. "I don't think women can do all jobs as well as men. In counseling and personnel, women are stronger—and women belong with food!"

Lavern Owens: Powerful Pragmatist. Lavern Owens believes that "women are required to produce to a higher level in a man's world," and she is living proof that it can be done. As chief of the Bureau of Nutrition for the California Department of Mental Hygiene, Miss Owens creates and directs the nutrition/food service for 16 state facilities—or 31,000 patients. "But I also think that women should be paid the same as men for the same job," adds Miss Owens. "And let's also face the fact that unqualified men in higher positions are just as big a problem as overqualified women in lower positions."

Dixie Stewart: Lady in Franchising. The company is called Stewart Investments, Inc. Its business: distributor of Bonanza Sirloin Pits in the Southern Louisiana territory. Units: 4. Plans for the future: 17 more in 4-5 years. President: Dixie Stewart. Says President Stewart, "My husband believed in me. He was willing to let me risk a whole chunk of money on my ability as a businesswoman. It has paid off." As area distributor, Mrs. Stewart can own and operate the franchises or sell them. She runs her franchises "the Bonanza way and the Stewart way . . . firmly but respectfully. I watch over every detail. After all, a woman has to fight a little harder." Mrs. Stewart thinks the franchise business is made to order for a woman, provided she has enough capital and a desire to oversee the actual operation. "You get just enough guidance from the home company . . . isn't it a shame there are such a lot of women around with so much unused talent."

Rosaleen Fitzgibbon: A Business Woman Begorrah. "My restaurant is my avocation as well as my vocation. I have to give it almost all my time and energy. I just can't afford to be sick or depressed, and I can't let my staff be, either." Rosaleen Fitzgibbon, vice-president and general manager of The Irish Pavillion Restaurant in

New York, looks the picture of a bonnie hostess, warmly greeting businessmen and lady shoppers at lunch or dinner. But she's just as likely to pitch right into food production and service with her staff of 16. "People must be handled very carefully . . . I never demand. I always suggest."

Doris Forsythe: Airport Pixie. "Very unusual for a woman" is the way a colleague described Doris Forsythe's job as assistant commissary manager, San Francisco Airport—the largest food service operation in Northern California. She supervises 75 hourly employees, has to be able to do everything her boss does. "But once," Miss Forsythe relates, "I worked for a manager who said, 'I have a hard time raising hell with you—sitting there with that pixie haircut!' But a haircut is no shield . . . and neither is being a woman."

Lillian Christie: Service Ahoy! Personnel director for seafaring women, Grace Lines, is her title. Miss Christie hires waitresses, stewardesses, dining room supervisors, linen keepers, and salad makers for all Grace Line ships. She also staffs shipboard parties held in port. Once waitress, hostess, and executive housekeeper for the line herself, she how has 145 women sailing at all times. "This job requires a woman's understanding of other women. Turnover among female ship personnel and competition for prime runs are the big problems . . . The position of women in shipping has gotten better—but certainly not equal."

Althea Laudenslager: Hospital Gourmet. Her menu is, in a word, epicurean. From the wide selection of gourmet items and fine wines, you'd never know it is a menu for hospital patients, created and made a workable reality by Althea Laudenslager, director of food service, Inter-Community Hospital in Covina, Calif. But it was no small feat to develop or defend—especially to cost-conscious male colleagues and superiors. "I had to approach some situations in a round about manner, but be able and ready to unquestionably support a decision or recommendation with facts." Mrs. Laudenslager adds, "I think it's true that women have to work harder at their jobs than men. They have to keep proving they can do not just an acceptable job but an outstanding one."

Lis Brewer: PR and a Pink Typewriter. Until 1964, the director of public relations job at Hilton International had always been held by men. But Lis Brewer (a native of Argentina) just moved her pink typewriter right into the male world of H-I and put her own international and PR background to work. "Frankly," confides Mrs. Brewer, "I find it much easier to deal with men than women. Women bring difficulties upon themselves in business . . . you're either an equal and get treated that way or you aren't and you don't." From her vantage point, Mrs. Brewer adds, "I notice more and more women in management, and I think more men are becoming accustomed to working with women."

Kara Baker: Breaking Ground at HCA. Fresh from Cornell's HRI School, 22-year-old Kara Baker is assistant food and beverage manager at the Charter House Motor Hotel in Braintree, Mass.—and the first woman HCA has put into such a position. Kara's duties include staffing, stocking, receiving, ordering, general cost procedures and cost inventories. "I couldn't stand a 9-to-5 desk job," says Kara. Next step: "Food and beverage manager. But someday I'd like to own and manage my own catering firm."

Nell Woodward: 400 Percent of Her Time. "I wanted a part-time job so I could combine work with a family," explains Nell Woodward. "But I got involved in so many things, it works out to about 400 percent of my time." It figures—two-thirds of her time is given to her job as director of the food service and hotel management department at Orange Coast College in Costa Mesa, Calif., with responsibility for two classes, two full-time and several part-time staff. The remaining third goes to direction of an allied health programs project for the school. To fill in spare time, Mrs. Woodward is also a partner in a business that employs ADA dietitians as dietary consultants to extended care facilities that Medicare now requires. Two more jobs: in-service workshops for dietary consultants, and a guide/workbook for consultants to extended care facilties. "That's what part-time work can get you into," warns busy but enthusiastic Nell Woodward.

Nancy Grudzien: From MSU to Mexico. Only 24, petite, and very pretty, Nancy Grudzien has already compiled an impressive record in the industry. A 1967 honors graduate of Michigan State's HRI School and, before that, a Heinz Scholarship winner, Miss Grudzien is now general manager of the entire food service at the newly constructed Acapulco airport, where she manages the restaurant, lounge, banquet room, and snack bars. Having lived and worked in Mexico at various times, she is fluent in Spanish—and in charm. "Mexico is where I want to be . . . the industry here is just booming. There's so much opportunity and here no one says, 'What's a nice girl like you doing in an industry like this?' "

Sex in the Service Industry

Of all the problems that confront the career woman, whatever the industry, none is as perplexing or as frustrating as the question of her femininity and its place in the business situation. Alas, it seems that a woman manager's femininity is as much a handicap as it is an advantage, and which it is varies with individuals and situations. "I think the fact that I *am* a woman is one of the reasons for my success," says Madame Chiang, owner of San Francisco's The Mandarin. "Patrons always seem to want to help me." And Janette Martin, director of John Hopkins Nutrition Department adds, perhaps, cynically, "I don't think a woman is honest if she doesn't trade on her sex as a way of getting advantages in the business world."

Mostly, though, successful women in the service industry seem to strike the right balance between being all-woman and all-business, which nearly everyone agrees is something that takes a good deal of practice. "Sometimes you have to pretend you don't know exactly what you're doing in order not to alarm the masculine competition," says one anonymous woman executive. But, Carol Balinski, training director of Loew's Hotels, warns that men can usually tell when a woman is acting feminine as a business device. "You simply can't use all those coy little feminine tricks at work that you can use socially," she says. Another bit of valuable advice comes from Jane Dillon, who handles the public relations at the St. Francis Hotel in San Francisco and says, "Feigning helplessness is sometimes very useful."

Significantly, nearly everyone agrees that the one thing a woman can't be is too aggressive. "Men hate aggressive women in business," states a midwestern hotel woman executive. "So a woman has to manipulate them subtly to get what they want." Evelyn Sullivan of Howard Johnson's agrees and goes on to say: "We're dealing here with a basic paradox. A woman has to be aggressive in order to succeed in business. But if she loses her femininity, men resent it. The trick is to be aggressive, but not to let it show." But the dilemma is perhaps best summed by author Marya Mannes, who says, "There is still, let's face it, a deep resistance to the career woman, as such, no matter how feminine she may be. And this resistance is quite understandable in the case of militant females who bulldoze their opinions with strident voices, contorted faces and *guerrilla* tactics. Even worse, perhaps, are those silken-voiced, super-groomed ladies who use the guise of femininity to conceal a vaulting and implacable ambition."

The Woman Executive

Someone once observed that true equality for women would arrive the day two sets of keys were made up for the executive washroom. Most women in business frankly doubt that such a day will ever come, and even in the service industry, most women in supervisory or management positions seem to concede, albeit reluctantly, that top management is strictly a man's world.

Curiously enough, the absence of women in top management positions might well be more the fault of women than of men. Explains one executive: "The feeling that women don't belong in high executive positions might have begun as propaganda but it has now become gospel."

Patricia A. Morey, a supervisor in the sales department of Hilton reservation service, New York, goes so far as to imply that women in business are their own worst enemies. "Too many women," she says, "are willing to accept the male-inspired pigeon hole. The opportunities to rise to top management positions are there, we just haven't pursued them." A somewhat more temperate explanation is offered by Ruth McCloy, public relations manager for Western International's Olympic, in Seattle, who says the reason there are so few top women executives is basically a matter of choice. "Many women,"

Figure 3. Reasons Why Women Don't Make It To The Top

Lack of communication with superiors about:

Problems that bog them down
Higher job goals and qualifications
Failure to pursue opportunities available
Become too functional in lesser jobs

Refusal of men to accept them at policy/decision making level
Acceptance of men pigeonholing women
Belief of men that women are not good administrators oriented to problem-
    solving, and not good supervisors of others, especially of men

Conscious or sub-conscious choice

Not willing to make the extra effort
Don't want the big time headaches and competition

Too "female" (as opposed to "feminine")

Expect too many special favors
Unable to compete forthrightly

Marriage and families

Split loyalties, competing interests
In and out of the job
Job limitations, job immobility
Unavailable to manage

she says, "are simply not interested in giving the necessary hours and energy to achieve top success."

Most psychological studies seem to bear out Miss McCloy's view. High level executives are, in most cases, highly motivated individuals willing to subordinate much of their personal life to the demands of their career. "As much as I like my job," admits one highly placed woman executive, "I would quit tomorrow if I felt it were having a negative effect upon my children."

There are, of course, other factors, but most seem to bear out the contention that women as a whole simply don't want the pressure and responsibility of high level positions. "My feeling," explains Hilda Watson Gifford, Director for Project FEAST, "is that women stop at mid-management because they don't want the extra responsibility and competition. Some stop because they do not wish to appear more capable than the man in their life." Still other women, like Mary de Marco, director of dietetics at the Cleveland Metropolitan General Hospital, hold the view that women simply don't belong in top management.

Whatever the reasons, it is an inescapable fact that the number of women currently holding down high level executive jobs in our industry is negligible, and that it takes a truly exceptional woman to break the sex barrier into the executive suite. As one industrial psychologist explained recently, "Theoretically, of course, there is no reason why women shouldn't strive for and ultimately reach top level executive positions. But so much of the interplay among high level executives is traditional—the men's grill at lunch, golf and that sort of thing—and it's highly unlikely the situation will change."

Money and Status

The Federal Equal Pay Act of 1963 assures women equal pay for equal work. Title VII of the Federal Civil Rights Act of 1964 prohibits discrimination in employment on the basis of sex. At the management levels in any industry, they are unrealistic laws.

It's not the comparative amounts of money that bother women in management, but the fact that they have to work harder to earn the same money as a man. "You need to work harder and be luckier than a man to earn the same salary," says young Sue Riddell, assistant director of cost control for the Century Plaza Hotel in Los Angeles. Life in the non-commercial end of the service industry isn't any fairer, according to Jeanette Martin, director of Johns Hopkins Hospital's nutrition department: "I do feel that women attract lower salaries for the same amount of work and same kind of position than men attract, and in spite of present federal laws, there is still a great demarcation in the salary area."

To some extent, the picture in the food/lodging field is beginning to change as all salaries are upgraded and as men and women move into each other's traditional job areas. "They pay me the same as they pay a man, so I have to perform as a man in doing my job. I made up my mind a long time ago not to let being a woman in a man's job bother me," comments Doris Forsythe, assistant commissary manager of the San Francisco Airport. And Kara Baker, who's the first woman Hotel Corp. of Amer. has ever put into a food and beverage management job, adds: "Actually the pay is fair when you consider I'm a girl going into a man's job."

When you get right down to it, it's not even unequal money that annoys most women in management, but the male prerogative on prestige. "I know more than my department head and have had to teach him," complains an anonymous staffer. "But he gets most of the money and all the prestige."

Whether it's exclusion from the men's executive dining rooms, their "boys only" golf outings, or as simple a thing as no secretary to handle the paper work, women in management in the service industry face what business women at large face: equal in law, but separate in reality.

Witness for the Prosecution

Most men take for granted the superiority of males in the business world. In fact, most are not particularly interested in the plight of women. But oddly enough, male attitudes change as the salary levels go up, with men in upper middle and top management positions somewhat more favorable toward women than men in lower and mid-management level jobs. The one reason for this, no doubt, is that competition between men and women at the lower and mid-management level is much keener than it is higher up on the executive ladder.

Some psychologists will tell you that the negative attitudes of young men toward women managers can be explained as the young male's revolt against female domination in the school and home. Whether true or not, it is still immensely significant that in a study conducted by the Harvard Business Review in 1965, strongly favorable attitudes toward women were voiced more often by men who had been superiors to women, or men on a peer level with them, than by men who had been subordinate to women. (Which tells us quite a bit about the male ego.)

Figure 4. Companies Talk About Women And Earnings

Because of civil rights legislation, companies are understandably reluctant to talk specifically about women and their earnings. But, judging from the management functions reported as being filled by women in a limited survey, the corporate caution is really pro forma, since the majority are "typically female jobs" anyway. And those that are not are said to command a salary or salary range that is without regard to sex. If this is the case, then the following rundown of selected management jobs held by women is probably both typical and accurate:

Chief or head dietitian . . . . $10,000-$15,000
(corporate)

District managers . . . . $10,000-$15,000
(ranging 5-10 reporting managers)

Food technicians or specialists . . . . $6,500-$13,700
(standards, test kitchen)

Regular staff dietitians . . . . $8,000-$12,200

Food service unit managers . . . . $5,200-$12,200
(ranging 10-100 employees)

Sales . . . . $8,000-$10,000
(plus commissions)

Note: These figures are simply broad indications. They do not reflect any one company or type of operation.

AVERAGE SALARIES OF OUR "ELITE," BY INDUSTRY SEGMENT

	Average Salary
Restaurants, Drive-Ins, Cafeterias	$14,833
Hotels/Motels	$ 9,562
Food Management Companies	$13,400
In-Plant Feeding	$12,045
Manufacturers/Suppliers	$19,000
Colleges/Universities	$10,878
Hospitals/Nursing Homes	$12,833
Schools	$13,206
Local, State, Federal Agencies	$11,643
'60-'64 HRI graduates	$10,200
Consultants/Designers/Teachers	$15,416
Miscellaneous	$17,500
Average of all respondents	$13,221

Note: Averages are based on salary information received from 200 "outstanding" women in food service/lodging. They are higher than is typical of the industry as a whole.

Figure 5. Seven Associations Report on Salaries

	Starting Salary or Salary Range	Intermediate or Median Positions	Top Position(s)
Dietitian (member, ADA)	$6,000 (internship)	$10,000-$12,000 (Adm. dietetics or Ass't Dir.)	$15,000 (Head or chief dietitian)
Exec. Housekeeper (NEHA)	$5,000-$6,000 (Exec. in small, Ass't in big est.)	$8,000-$10,000 (Exec. in larger est.)	$15,000-$18,000 (Adm. Dir. or Consultant)
School Food Service (ASFSA)	$6,500-$8,500 (Dir. of small, Ass't in large school/dist.)	$7,500-$10,000 (Dir. of medium school/dist.)	$10,000-$15,000 (Dir. of large school dist.—often man's job)
Home Economist, Foods/Nutrition (AHEA)	$5,300-$6,400 (1967 gov't salaries)		$9,000-$15,000 (Chief Home Economist)
College Union* (ACU-I)	$7,200-$8,750 (Food serv. dir. in small/med. union)	$8,750-$10,000 (larger union or higher adm. rank)	$10,000-$15,000 (Dir. of big union— few women, more in food service at around $10,000)
College/university Housing*			$13,500 (average) (Director of Housing— 95% are men)
College/university Food Service (NACUFS)	$9,000-$10,000** (small school)	$13,000 (med. sized school)	$18,000-$20,000 (Dir. or Principal in food service—most are men)

*Majority of Directors or Principal Officers are men, but women who do hold principal position earn the same as men and have equal status.
**Membership, 1958: 70% women, 30% men; membership, 1968: 40% women, 60% men. Salaries given are men's; women generally earn less, hold supportive positions in bigger schools.

Asked to give his own views on women in the service industry, one prominent personnel executive for a large hotel chain had this to say:

"Let's start by pinpointing a truth. The element necessary to success is a certain amount of aggressiveness, whether in a man or woman. Women in not typically female jobs are doing better all the time in our industry. It's true they've been fighting an uphill battle, but it's just about won. Women have proved their point: They can do a job as well as a man.

"Still and all, I have to deal with the company as a whole, and I have to take into consideration the effect a particular woman is going to have in a situation, particularly when the department head doesn't want a woman.

"Sure, I'd like to see more women in key jobs, but I do think they have a 'place'—that is, places they will function well, such as front offices, sales/marketing, certain management positions, advertising and public relations, and local or regional personnel.

"I have to admit, too, although it would probably get me in trouble with the government, that there are areas which I think are so

Figure 6. 1966-67 Salary Surveys of Graduates (Men and Women) of Selected HRI Schools (4-Year Programs)

	Starting Salary	After 5 Yrs.	After 10 Yrs.
School A	$6,780, B.A. $8,628, M.B.A.	65% in 5-figure bracket	$2,500 a year ahead of engineers 10 years out
School B	$7,500 ($6,000-$10,000)		
School C	$7,000 ($5,700-$8,000)	$10,000	$12,000-$15,000
School D	$7,000-$7,500		
School E	$6,500 min.	$10,000-$12,000 (with dept. head status)	
School F	$7,020-$9,250 (men) $6,500-$7,000 (women)	$12,000-$15,000	$20,000 on up

Source: Directory of Opportunity, Reconnaissance, Inc.

tough for a gal as to almost disqualify her. Food and beverage is a prime example. I simply haven't met that many women tough enough to deal with purveyors and salesmen and even with the executive chef. I almost have to admit another prejudice. I just can't see a woman holding down a job as general manager of a hotel."

A couple of other points from yet another in corporate personnel: "Women in supervisory or management jobs are good up to a certain age bracket, or length of service. Then they become resistant to change. Men, I think, anticipate the fact of change and specific corporate changes better than women. It really isn't a woman's fault, though. It takes so much more for a woman to get *to* a certain job level that, once there, she just isn't geared to change. Their approaches become 'patterned,' probably due to an unconscious job security feeling. It isn't that they become 'tough' so much as 'set.'

"And as far as young women go, I find girls just out of school seem to expect so much more so much sooner. We all know that we're missing out on some of these talented young people, but one of the problems is their refusal to come through the operations ranks. The two-year college graduates are proving to be much better employees. They don't have this 'I've got a big degree' attitude and are willing to start at the bottom and work. Granted, some of the fault is our training programs. But this is a problem that involves the whole industry, and one we're going to have to deal with. We must legitimately erase the conception among young people that training is degrading by giving them better, more useful training programs."

Next witness!

Woman Power

You've heard it all before. Over the next decade the service industry will need a quarter of a million people, with an estimated 75,000 of them in management positions. By straight division, that works out to 7,500 new managers a year—a figure the industry, as it now stands, comes nowhere near attracting.

There are two obvious solutions: one, recruit more young people in the industry; two, make more effective use of the people we already have. Significantly, women can play a key role in both.

First, young women.

Unhappily, the facts concerning young women who are now training or who have been trained for management positions in the industry are not very encouraging. First of all, only a tiny percentage of women are entering HRI schools. Last year, for example, only three of the 82 Michigan State HRI graduates were women—and this was a

Figure 7. Beginning Salary Offers to Women, Bachelor's Degree-Candidates, 1967-68

TYPE OF EMPLOYER

POSITION	Business	Govt.-Fed.	Govt.-Local	Mfg./Ind.	Non-Profit	Other
Accountant/Auditor	$721 $633 $677 127	$590 10	$612 5	$712 $540 $626 20	$580 3	$625 1
Airline Stewardess/Receptionist				$437 $307 $372 92		
Artist/Designer	$469 9			$309 2	$466 2	
Business (General) Trainee	$635 $425 $530 257	$563 $433 $498 32	$542 19	$642 $442 $542 72	$390 1	
Community & Service Orgn. Worker	$537 2	$547 $425 $486 24	$574 $448 $511 136		$517 $391 $454 46	
EDP Programmer/Systems Analyst	$684 $594 $639 217	$692 $438 $565 27	$556 8	$758 $612 $685 228	$624 7	$738 2
Educational Administrator	$412 2	$539 1	$465 3		$410 2	

	1	2	3	4	5	6
Engineer	$812 11	$603 1	$731 2	$878 $668 $773 40		
Home Economist/Dietitian/Home Service Rep.	$486 9	$530 3	$538 10	$510 13	$560 1	
Language Specialist	$573 2	$487 7	$470 1		$370 2	
Library Intern	$775 1	$452 5	$477 6		$411 18	
Mathematician/Statistician	$756 $498 $627 42	$780 $516 $648 34	$562 3	$755 $625 $690 54	$631 3	$542 2
Medical Worker		$463 1	$540 10		$639 $473 $556 68	
Merchandising/Sales Promotion Trainee	$565 $419 $492 125			$543 6		
Research Asst.—Non-Scientific	$620 $420 $520 39	$618 $478 $548 29	$541 8	$565 12	$497 9	
Research and Lab. Assistant—Scientific	$774 $552 $663 24	$529 7	$525 1	$789 $613 $701 43	$542 $422 $482 43	

Secretary/Receptionist	$503 $367 $435 28		$443 5	$425 14	$398 15	$483 2
Writer/Edit./Public Rels. Trainee	$544 $350 $447 57	$506 6	$493 3	$552 10	$472 10	
Other	$621 $391 $506 28	$609 $425 $517 23	$556 8	$622 14	$633 $421 $527 46	$519 7

Arrangement of
Data in Blocks:

High Low
Average
No. of Offers

Highs and lows shown represent the limits within the 80 per cent range of offers as measured by standard deviation; i.e., the average plus and minus 1.28 standard deviations. (Not calculated for less than 20 offers.)

Averages shown are derived from total offers reported (not limited to the middle 80 per cent.)

Blank blocks occur where no offers have been reported.

Source: The College Placement Council, June, 1968

typical year. Even when women do complete four years of HRI school, there's no guarantee they'll stay in the industry. Indeed, three years after graduation 50 percent of women HRI graduates are "not available" to the industry: either they're raising families or are married and living in a place which offers no solid HRI-type opportunities. Worse, a substantial percentage of professionally trained women, many of them single, have already or can be expected to abandon our industry for better paying pastures.

Generally speaking, young women in HRI schools have many doubts about their role in the service industry. Many feel they're over-trained and that the industry isn't really ready for them. "I had an honor's degree from a school of hotel administration," says Cornell graduate Nora Heller Freund, "but what most of the companies who interviewed me wanted to know is whether or not I could type. Maybe I sound bitter, but the whole thing was very discouraging."

It ought to be pointed out, however, that the attitude of young women toward the industry is one shared by young people in general as was seen in "Recruitment at Cornell" (Institutions, June, 1968). As Nancy Grudzien, a recent Michigan State honors graduate explains, "The young HRI girl starts out thinking she's special . . . she's a girl, fighting the male world. She sometimes forgets her male class-

Figure 8. How Female Executives in the Service World Compare

Schooling	Male	Female
Graduate Degree	20.8%	50.0%
College Degree	36.8%	68.7%
High School Graduate	86.0%	88.9%
Compensation		
Salary	$ 12,017	$ 8,580
Fringes	1,986	792
Total	$ 14,003	$ 9,372
Belongs To Trade Groups	73.1%	80.7%
Attends Trade Courses	66.7%	76.0%
BUSINESS RESPONSIBILITY		
Average Yearly Business Purchases	$497,437	$309,372
Employees Reporting Directly	33	30

mates are doing the same thing. Actually, it's their youth, not their sex, that has them disgruntled."

But if there is doubt, restlessness and disgruntlement with the service industry among women HRI graduates, the overall picture is considerably brighter among women *over* 25. "I wish I were about 20 years younger and someone would have told me about the excellent opportunities for women in this field," says Maude G. Galetano, who is assistant dining manager for Illinois Bell Telephone Company. "It's the old story, we get old too soon and smart too late." And 26 year-old Lynn Nutini, from Chicago's Conrad Hilton public relations department says: "I'm one of those who never even knew the industry existed while I was in school. I just stumbled into the hotel field, but I think it's a beautiful spot for a young woman, particularly if there's a competent man to work with. A good guy/gal team is unbeatable in our area because between the two of you, there isn't anything you can't get done—at least this has been true so far."

Of course, many organizations look for their professional women, not on the HRI campuses, but at the many schools of home economics across the country. Even at these female-oriented schools, the numbers are small—in 1966-67, only 733 BA's were granted in foods and nutrition—out of 10,917 total home ec degrees!

Perhaps women should take a more active role in the recruiting process, particularly where the professional schools are concerned. Companies, too, ought to take a close look at their recruiting literature. Most of it seems to have been written as if, in fact, women don't exist. "What we have to do," says one personnel director, "is make it a special point to encourage young women. We have to anticipate their skepticism and distrust and go out of our way to let them know that women are really welcome in the industry. I wonder how many companies are willing to do it."

The Future

In the final analysis, is all the talk about women making it to the top just so much whistling in the dark? Is there really a future for women at the peak of the corporate pyramid? Or are the women who content themselves with comfortable, less demanding (but well paid) staff positions and middle management jobs the realists?

The truth is that women today are working in a business world of paradox—a paradox exemplified by the food service/lodging industry and the direction it is heading.

Our industry is already Big Business. And it's still growing. Power continues to concentrate in the hands of a small number of organizations—the big management complexes. As this trend accelerates, these giant bureaus and corporations tend to add managerial apparatus at the top.

True, women are doing "better" today in terms of salary and authority. Better, that is, if you compare their present opportunities with those available ten years ago. But if you measure status by real distance from the top, women have, in many cases, actually lost ground.

Witness the situation in college and university food service: ten years ago, only 30 percent of campus food service directors were men. Today, it's more like 60 percent. Men are joining the housekeeping team—at the top. Hospitals are recruiting men for jobs that in simpler days were considered feminine territory.

Quite frankly, few women who have served our industry (and its public) faithfully for the past years are equipped by training, experience or temperament to make this new and final jump.

But the paradox is compounded: the distance between management and the public it serves is also lengthening. The very commodity our industry professes to offer—service—is threatened. Service is, after all, a personal thing. It cannot be written into an organization chart or a job description. It does not flow naturally from a headquarters group in one city to hundreds of remote locations.

If women are the equal of men in brainpower (and there seems no reason to doubt this), there remains a basic difference. A woman is far more likely to care about people as people, rather than people as abstracts.

That is the meaning of service. And if this type of caring is the province of the female, then our industry needs her more today than at any time in the past.

Quotes By and About Women

"I have felt at times that it takes a little longer for some men to accept women in management positions. I do not feel, however, that one can change ideas or feelings overnight and since women are relatively new to the management field, I have not expected that they would be accepted as readily in management positions as men are at the present time." Wanda Nickerson, Personnel Officer, State of Michigan, Howell State Hospital, Howell, Mich.

"Have never felt that there were advantages or disadvantages—I was born a female and try to make the best of it!" Constance L. Cockburn, Nutrition Specialist, Los Angeles City Schools, Food Services Branch.

"After much deliberation—the same question arises. Why the concern for greater percentages of women at the top executive level? Let the men battle the world of finance and franchises! I, for one, want to be appreciated for the esthetic talents only a female can bring to our industry." Mary R. DeMarco, Director of Dietetics, Metropolitan General Hospital, Cleveland.

"One good woman in the business raises the chances for all other women in the business." Lee Keenan, Assistant to the President, Inter-Continental Hotels, New York City.

"You need to work harder and be luckier than a man to earn the same salary. If you are capable and flexible you can develop an entirely new job—one which had not been set up in the organization." Susan B. Riddell, Assistant Director, Cost Control, Century Plaza Hotel, Los Angeles.

"When I entered the food and lodging profession, most institutional services were under the management of women, and most commercial ones under the management of men. Now men are managing institutional food services and lodging in increasingly larger numbers, while women have branched over into commercial operations. Personally, I welcomed men into institutional food management because I felt such a balance was desirable." Jane E. Griswold, Director Dining Services, University of New Hampshire, Durham.

"The hours are most disadvantageous ... personally, I feel you have to live with it." Evelyn Harrison, General Manager, Ramada Scottsdale Inn.

"Men helped me so much along the way ... I think if they feel you are really sincere about succeeding, they are most cooperative." Helen Rose, Assistant Manager, Drake Hotel, New York City.

"I suspect that the differences between men and women have been over-emphasized in the past, and that we are getting away from this and looking more at the individual than at the man or woman. I wonder, if sometimes we, as women, may have been guilty of placing the blame for situations or supposed injustices on the fact that we are women when, in reality, this was not true." Shirley S. Bates, Director of Food Services, Texas Technological College, Lubbock, Texas.

"Being a woman is not the question ... but being at the right place at the right time and being ready are sure parts of the answer." Louise Froelich, American School Food Service Association, Denver.

"Women will get out of the technician role when they demand decision making authority, and when they demand and support other women in positions of authority." Ruth Dickie, Director, Department of Dietetics, University of Wisconsin, Madison, Wisc.

"The times that I have been admitted by men, primarily because they were curious to see what a woman has to say, have been offset by the times I have been refused admittance, primarily because I found some reluctance from businessmen to accept me as a representative of my company at a decision/policy making level." Patricia A. Morey, Supervisor, Sales Department, Hilton Reservation Service, New York City.

"Women are sometimes too willing to accept situations which should be changed." Eloise Ross Dooling, Dietitian, Virginia Community Unit No. 64, Virginia, Ill.

"Men are creeping into the profession." Betty Yapp, Chief Dietitian, Lincoln General Hospital, Lincoln, Neb.

"Women do not know exactly what they want and need when it comes to purchasing, and have a tendency to flounder when it comes to budgets and unexpected balances. I know exactly what I want and need and have my specific reasons for justifying the needs." Cynthia Bishop, Chief of Nutrition and Food Service, Texas Dept. of Mental Health & Mental Retardation, Austin, Texas.

*"Once, when I was manager at XYZ Hotel, an irate guest came yelling into the lobby, 'There's no heat in my room! Where's that **!XX Manager?' When he got into my office and saw that I was a woman, he just folded and meekly asked me to turn on the heat."* Helen Rose, Assistant Manager, Drake Hotel, New York.

"Women are often better administrators than men because when they see a problem they solve it before it becomes a big problem." Barbara Turner, Unit Food Manager, Grant Towers, Northern Illinois University, DeKalb, Ill.

"Where details are stressed, food service or lodging is 'special.' In fact, I shall go further to say it is often evident when a woman is connected with management, quality is the woman's place—quantity is the man's place." Patricia Espeland, Administrative Dietitian, Kansas State University, Manhattan, Kan.

"Women are particularly adept at training employees and menu planning. Research and technology are coming fields." Virginia T. Hendrickson, Food Specialist, Douglas Hall, Northern Illinois University, DeKalb, Ill.

"We all belong at home, cooking meals and caring for children, with our outside activities related to our families. Since this just isn't possible, I'm all for taking second place in the world of business." Lucille Skerston, Director of Women's Services, Hilton Hotels Corp., Chicago.

"I think our greatest role is support and stimulation of improvements along any line. Flatter the male boss by letting him think it

was his idea all along, but keep suggestions coming." Myrtle H. Webb, Director of Dormitories, Lawrence University, Appleton, Wis.

"The institutional field is a good one for women; it requires day-to-day coping, a reasonable grasp of many technologies, and a basically warm, interested kind of personality. But, as I've pointed out in the past, this is also true of many men. And not true of many women." Roslyn Willett, President, Roslyn Willett Associates, New York City.

"I do think more women have reached the top in food service than in lodging. Somehow I can't see many women being appointed general managers of large commercial hotels, but maybe this too will change." Mary M. Hesse, Sales Manager, The Netherland Hilton, Cincinnati.

"It's easier for a woman to get ahead in this business than most others, but it's still an up-hill battle." Grace E. Carpenter, Director, Residence Halls Food Service, University of Washington, Seattle.

"Once I worked for a manager who said, 'I have a hard time raising hell with you . . . sitting there with that pixie haircut!' " Doris Forsythe, Assistant Commissary Manager, San Francisco Airport.

"Women don't get included in the preliminary planning stage. I could write a book on this subject." Lydia Stetz, Assistant Director of Purchasing, Milwaukee County, Milwaukee.

"I believe the greatest handicap to women reaching the top is the security her employer feels because of her desire to remain in the area. The majority are married and not free to compete for promotion by accepting positions in other locations." Lois Beckman, Director of Food Service, Sacramento School District.

"Women often become so functional in a position they are overlooked when promotions occur." Georgina P. Tucker, Director of Housekeeping, Century Plaza Hotel, Los Angeles.

"In order to get out of the 'dead-end' competitive business of the corporation, I organized my own business." Dorothy W. Tousignant, Dorothy W. Tousignant & Associates, Food Service Management, Washington, D.C.

"No doubt we are 'shooting higher' these days, though I still don't feel that a woman's place is at the top—president or general manager—assistant to either, OK, but not the top." Lynn Marianna McCarthy, Banquet Manager, Airport-Marina Hotel, Los Angeles.

"There are women who are qualified and capable but have been by-passed and not even considered for promotions, merely because they haven't communicated with their superiors to advertise the fact that they are qualified and are interested in the challenge of a better

job." Virginia Haack, Manager, Indian Village Restaurant, Torrence, Calif.

"We have a number of operations owned by women alone. They are doing a fine job; they are making a fine living for themselves; they have complete independence, and are happy. As always in food service, that woman's touch is helpful and we find that in most of our husband-wife type operations, she is most important." Mary Howell, Dairy Sweet Drive-In Systems, Ankeny, Iowa.

"We can't put women in as managers where we have men cooks— they couldn't stand the language, and the men would feel inhibited." Vice President of a steak house chain.

"Women shouldn't be afraid to achieve and then let men take the glory—they need it more than we do." Lis Brewer, PR Director, Hilton International, New York City.

"If a woman makes a few mistakes, it is blamed on her being a 'woman.' A man is allowed free reign: his mistakes are considered reckless advancement and speculation." Patricia Espeland, Administrative Dietitian, Kansas State University, Manhattan, Kan.

"A woman is prone to talk too much and bother male superiors with too many details. These are her problems and she should solve them. When she does deal with male equals or superiors, she must be logical, concise and not expect to have her own way." Elsie Miller, Director of Residence Halls and University Food Service, DePauw University, Greencastle, Ind.

"Guys today don't have any particular feeling about working with women. The masculinity of men today depends on other things. Keeping women in the home was their fathers' hang-up." Sherman Chickering, former Editor, Moderator Magazine, Philadelphia.

"We hire women as salesmen, particularly experienced dietitians, to sell to the hospitals—they're naturals." A West Coast food processor.

"One aspect I like is the opportunity to move from one part of the country to another . . . This business is a great way to see part of the country before settling down." Carol Pavey, Manager, Progressive Cafeterias at Sunbeam Research Center, Chicago.

"I left the food service industry over three years ago mainly because I felt I could never make enough money to support myself and my child. I was also not devoted enough to a food service career to be willing to devote the many hours of overtime usually required by that career. During my three years of computer programming, I felt I have more than doubled any salary I could have attained in the food service and lodging industry and my working hours are strictly 9 to 5." Bonnie L. Coble, Programmer-Analyst, Northrop Corporation, Hawthorne, Calif.

43

CREDIT CARD VENDING

Fred Amann

Announced two years ago, Canteen Corporation's credit card vending system went into regular operation July 8 for employees of the First Federal Savings and Loan Association in Chicago's Loop.

The credit card plan, which is based on a postpaid payroll deduction system for some 350 First Federal employees, is operable in conjunction with normal coin operation of the seven beverage, ice cream, pastry, milk, hot can food and multi-selection food venders. The machines are in the employees' lounge area and accessible only to employed personnel.

Specially coded plastic cards are issued to employees, and their purchases will be handled through a payroll deduction system. A second credit card installation by Canteen, now installed at Montgomery Ward & Company's general offices in Chicago, will operate on a different "collection" system—employees will be billed by Canteen for their purchases.

Both systems function similarly. To purchase an item, an employee inserts his credit card in a special oblong (card-size) slot on the machine. The card, if validated, is accepted and returned and the employee selects his item. A computerized, punched-tape system at the vending installation records each purchase by date, item, amount and card number. In the event an employee loses his card, he reports the loss and after checking records for his card number, simple removal of a pin in the central credit unit makes future use of that particular card impossible.

In the First Federal "postpay" plan, all purchase data are retransferred from the punched tape system at the vending battery to the location's computerized payroll deduction system.

The First Federal credit card system was put into operation by Canteen after testing internally (at Canteen's own headquarters in

From *Vend*, August 1, 1967, pp. 25-27. Reprinted by permission of the publisher.

the Merchandise Mart, Chicago) for the past two years. The system was originated by Tateisi Electronics Company of Kyoto, Japan, and Canteen has the right to sign an exclusive agreement for sales and distribution of the system in the United States.

Patrick L. O'Malley, president of Canteen Corporation, said further on-location testing under regular operating conditions at industrial, institutional and other "resident consumer" locations, will be conducted for the next year. Then, he said, the credit card system will be offered to the vending industry for use with other manufacturers' vending equipment. (To date, the system has only been installed for use with Canteen's Rowe vending machines.)

O'Malley also noted that the incorporation of the credit card units will cost about $250 per 10-machine battery. This could be reduced as much as 35 percent when the system is put into volume production, he said. The system is designed primarily for new equipment, not adaptation to machines in the field.

First operation of the Canteen-Tateisi credit card system took place at a special demonstration in July, 1965, at the Waldorf-Astoria Hotel in New York City (Industry News, August 15, 1965 *Vend*). At that time two credit card systems were shown. One was the present postpaid system used at First Federal and Montgomery Ward; the other was based on prepaid cards (customer could purchase cards for a specific price). The prepaid cards were retained by the vender. The prepaid "deposit" cards—or strips—were coded for specific coin increment values, and could only be used to purchase items for those specific prices. This prepaid system is not a part of the present programs at First Federal or Ward.

Comparing the two systems—postpaid versus prepaid—O'Malley indicated the credit card (postpay) system the "most practical and promising." The reasons, he told *Vend*: The worker need handle only one card for a number of purchases each day, and payroll deductions—or the system at Ward where Canteen has a post-purchase billing program—is the most efficient way to handle credit card purchases.

"A great and growing number of industrial plants already use payroll deductions for employee purchases in their food cafeterias," O'Malley said.

Improvements in the central punched-tape control unit enable it to accept and record purchases by as many as 10,000 cards. However, single control systems will handle only up to 10 credit card-accepting vending machines. The central system, of course, would not be needed for prepaid deposit card operation.

The originator and patent owner of the credit card systems, Tateisi Electronics, manufactures a varied line of industrial equipment and components. It has also developed a railway commuter ticket vending machine accepting both coins and currency.

How the System Works

Following are the operating details for the credit card system for vending machines unveiled by Canteen Corporation. The postpaid version uses specially coded credit cards which are inserted in the vender and then returned.

Operation

Employs a specially coded plastic credit card, a card-checking device installed in vending machines, and a code control. Customer inserts card; card is "examined" by checking device; a "ready" sign lights to indicate card has been accepted (if check shows unacceptable card, "not accepted" sign lights up and card is returned); customer then makes selection. Venders with more than one price carry a "price-select" button corresponding to the price of merchandise wanted. Customer makes selection after receiving a "ready signal."

Credit Card

Plastic-laminated card (thickness less than 3/64 inch), measuring 3 3/8 by 2 1/8 inches; contains following—period of validity; card alignment information; identity card number; space for user's signature; expiration date. Both optical and electronic means are used to determine validity of card and to prevent counterfeiting.

Description of Checker

Checking unit installed on front panel of vender inspects card to insure that it has been inserted properly, has not expired, has not been forged or tampered with.

Code Control System

Device checks card number signal received from card checker; controls tape puncher; contains memory board circuit used to invalidate lost or mutilated credit cards.

44

HOW TO PLAN A HOUSEKEEPING DEPARTMENT

Gina Tucker

Because space is precious and every square foot that is not revenue-producing is carefully scrutinized, it's very important that you think out in advance your physical space requirements and submit a thoughtfully prepared plan of the department.

Often building-planning teams do not understand the function of a housekeeping department well enough to allocate adequate space, so your needs must be clearly presented.

Before new facility planning or its relocation can be intelligently initiated, it is necessary to discuss with top management just how extensive housekeeping's responsibilities are to be. For example, will maintenance and repair work be performed in the hotel, or contracted outside? Such activities as reupholstery and furniture repair; making uniforms, draperies, conference linens, table pads, etc., require considerable additional space.

Determine at the top level also, before plans are laid out, just which extra guest room conveniences will be provided so that you can plan enough storage and budget for them.

Be realistic. Don't ask for more space than you really need because you'll not be believed again. (This same principle of not crying "Wolf" applies to your budget too. Know what you need and be able to substitute.) To arrive at the best locations for the various segments of a housekeeping department, thoroughly *think through the functions* of that group of employees and *be sure the traffic flow makes sense.* (Consider: Where will the people who perform specific functions come from? Where will they be going? What equipment will they use?)

Gina Tucker is Executive Housekeeper at the Century Plaza Hotel in Los Angeles.

From *Institutions Magazine*, September 1969, pp. 190-192. Reprinted by permission of the publisher.

Whether you are planning a new facility or revising an existing property, these same considerations are valid. In many older institutions, it may be well worthwhile actually to move the department to make it function better and to release potentially valuable space for other purposes. For example, two housekeeping departments in the Western International Hotel chain recently were moved—in one case, closer to the laundry—in another, closer to the receiving dock where laundry is delivered. Significant labor savings have resulted wherever a step in handling has been eliminated.

Naturally, the size and type of your property, and the idiosyncrasies of the existing physical plant will all affect your decision on where to locate the different "branches" of housekeeping. However, here are important points to bear in mind when planning. Let's start with the housekeeping "headquarters."

Employee Check-in Area

This is a gathering place so there should be room for a few chairs to take care of the early-arriving employees. They need a place to wait before signing in for their shift.

There should be space for a time clock or the sign-in boards. (Because we have up to 100 employees checking in on the morning shift, we use a 30-foot long counter for them to sign in and be checked off by the assistant housekeeper.)

Adjacent to this area, display the schedule telling maids and housemen where they will be working that day or week (depending upon the predictability of your operation).

The schedule may be on a blackboard or on a large sheet of plastic marked with grease pencil, or it may be written out on large charts.

Key cabinets should be nearby so supervisors can pass out keys to maids. It's often advisable to have keys on sturdy leather thongs or other obvious holders so maids and housemen can wear them around their waists thus preventing them from being lost.

Communications Center

This is often the heart of the department. It is the point where incoming calls are answered, where the room status system is set up, and where desks of supervisory personnel are located.

The communications officer (traditionally known as the "linen room attendant") has his or her desk here and records all incoming calls in the log. He or she issues orders to employees to carry out special requests from guests and other departments.

This is the usual location of the executive housekeeper's office (although some may prefer to be removed from this hub of activity, depending upon the way in which the duties have been split up with the assistant). This office for the head of the department, should have adequate space, some provision for privacy, good lighting, heating, and ventilation or air conditioning. It should be attractive and well furnished since the executive housekeeper will be receiving visitors here.

In this area the assistant housekeeper may also have her phone and desk. Also, it may be well to plan on having an extra desk, or space for one in the future, in case of expansion or new functions being added to the department.

Consider what forms are needed in the operation of the department and provide places for them. This is particularly important in the case of employee payroll cards. Locked file cabinets should be situated in this central headquarters area.

When setting up the plan for this space, try to use scale models or graph paper and small-scaled furniture (such as interior designers and furniture companies can provide) to simulate the proposed area. This will help you to *think through the functions and review the traffic flow.*

Linen Storage

Ideally, linen storage areas should be located both centrally, for banquet linens, and on the upper floors, for guest room linens. Often this isn't possible, for older hotels may have only small closets on the guest floors. What is most important is that linen storage have proximity to the laundry or the area where laundry is delivered so as to keep handling to a minimum. If linen can be loaded directly onto mobile adjustable-shelf units which will go directly to floors, considerable time can be saved.

Adapting a current hospital technique for distributing linen one might use pre-packed linens for bedrooms and baths. Slipped into plastic bags, these linen "kits" are made up on the basis of the size of the sheets and are picked up by maids as they go to their work areas.

Banquet linens, if you have an ample supply and a range of colors, are perhaps best kept in a central linen storage area, and housemen or waiters can come to the linen storage room as the napery is needed.

This eliminates transfer to banquet storage areas where they may be soiled, for only the frequently laundered items on top of the stacks will be used, and the balance of the linens will become soiled simply through disuse.

Sewing Room

The size and location of the sewing area will depend on what functions it performs—does it do the laundry repairs and mending? Does it make draperies and uniforms? Does it mend uniforms?

The placement and number of the sewing machines will be determined by whether you make draperies. If so, machines will have to be set out from walls far enough to accommodate bins to hold the masses of fabrics. Very large cutting tables are also a necessity for drapery making and cork tops are advisable.

All fabric storage should be in the sewing room since it is usually cleaner there.

Supply Storage

Consider what goods need to be stored near the headquarters areas, which on the guest room floors, and which could be located throughout the institution.

For bulk goods such as cases of toilet and facial tissue, use pallet storage—stacking cases on top of each other. Do not plan on shelving for this area because there is no reason to unpack these cartons and waste labor putting contents on shelves in a remote storage area, only to be moved again.

Cleaning equipment and supplies (brooms, vacuums, etc.) can best be stored on guest room floors or adjacent to public areas where they will be used. To have to transport these items from floor to floor only ties up elevators and wastes time.

Large rag bins, which serve as the source for cleaning cloths for the entire institution, should be located in an area near either laundry or housekeeping headquarters. Since food service employees use most of these, perhaps locating rag storage near kitchens would be advisable.

Give-away items for guest rooms—soap, shower caps, notepads, etc.—are kept in our central headquarters area and from that point the floor supervisors' daily supply orders are filled by high school students late each afternoon. The orders are taken upstairs, to guest room floor storage areas, on mobile, metal adjustable-shelf units. Next morning, maids fill their carts with supplies for their 14 rooms.

What really require large storage areas are roll-ins, cribs and extra furnishings.

If possible, roll-ins should be kept on the floors, so they are handy to guest rooms. The type which can be stored upright takes up much less space than the kind that folds in the middle.

Uniform Storage

The area where the uniforms are stored, issued and turned in should be located so that it is easily reached from a) employee locker rooms, b) laundry or laundry delivery entrance.

The uniform room should be large enough to accommodate all the necessary racks or shelves for different types of uniforms, with proper labels for each employee or sizes marked for the extra banquet help.

There should be sufficient floor space for the large bins which hold the soiled uniforms, and ample ventilation is a must.

A counter on which to place clean uniforms, with shelves below for records and for storage of items to be mended is necessary. The records to be kept (probably in a large ledger) tell how many uniforms are issued daily and to whom.

In some cases uniforms will require a deposit, so a cash box may be needed.

45

BASIC FACTORS AFFECTING TOURISM

Lothar Kreck

... [A]n attempt will be made to enumerate and describe all the factors which are needed in order to bring a traveler into a country or into an area and to keep him there for a period of time. To do so means that we have to provide not only for some type of lodging and feeding but also for things to see and to do. There is hardly a piece of soil on this world which cannot keep a group of travelers occupied for a period of time, whether it be desert or the areas around the poles—or as a matter of fact, the moon.

Accommodation

The first of these factors is accommodation. Accommodation can come in a variety of forms: hotels; motels; inns; boarding houses; hired apartments (as are presently popular along the Costa del Sol in Spain); rooms; villas; bungalows which are rapidly built in northern European countries; mountain refuges; ships anchored in a port and used as accommodation; as well as ships in form of overseas steamers or smaller ships like the ones operating on the Rhine River, going from Holland to Switzerland; boats traveling through the Sunderbans, the jungles of East Pakistan, or cruising the Volga and Danube rivers. Other forms of accommodation include trains and a rather recent newcomer, the "Rotel," a rolling hotel bus with a triple layer sleeping trailer pulled by a regular bus,[1] or the unusual but necessary arrangement of putting accommodations into the trees, like the tree-top motel in the wildlife sanctuary of Nepal. Under accommodations

---

[1] Edward Preston, "Rotel Rambling," *Travel* (1968).

This will be a chapter of a planned text in international tourism. Kreck is presently with the University of Denver, School of Hotel and Restaurant Management, and a member of the International Association of Scientific Experts in Tourism (Switzerland).

must also be mentioned camping and trailer parks, like the ones found in Europe and the North American continent in large numbers.

In order to stimulate the economics of South America, the U.S. government under Roosevelt tried to promote tourism in this area. Soon it was realized that without some form of accommodation no tourism could develop. It was then that the Roosevelt administration asked Pan American Airlines to conduct a survey in regard to the availability of accommodations in South America. As a result of the survey Pan American Airlines formed the Inter-Continental Hotels Corporation in 1946 and opened the first hotel in Brazil in 1949. Today there are more than 40 such hotels throughout the world. Other hotel chains, such as Hilton International and Sheraton, followed suit. It would be a waste of promotional efforts if a country were to try to lure foreign visitors into the country and then fail to provide proper accommodation or hope to build hotel rooms with funds created through tourism. There is no doubt that investment in accommodations has to come first, despite a number of disadvantages in hotel investment. In 1966 there were 18.1 million accommodations available in the world with more than 16 million alone in Europe and North America.[2] Hotel-motel rooms constitute only 29 percent while the remainder is made up by other types of accommodation. The next obvious question is to ask whether or not demand has been met or, in other words, has the lack of availability slowed down the development of tourism? In Europe it was felt by some countries that demand outran supply and some said that this was not the case. However, the majority of the countries felt that in the near future demand can be met. The same holds true for the Middle East, while in Asia and Australia the situation is such that the planned accommodations will not satisfy demand in the majority of countries and will inhibit the development of tourism. The real problem lies in the fact of seasonality. During seasons, let this be in Sweden during August or in India during October, prices of accommodations are increased in order to hold down demand or to guide demand into the next lower price category, while the reverse is partially true for off seasons. (Lower prices will not induce, for example, a Pakistani merchant who used to stay in a normally less expensive Oriental type hotel to move into a more expensive Western type hotel.) A second problem is concerned with having the right number of accommodations at the right place. While the demand is numerically met for the country as a whole, it might be insufficiently

---

[2] IUOTO, *Economic Review of World Tourism* (1968).

met at a particular area, due to construction of a new international airport or the development of a tourist area.

Important to remember is that whatever "hardship" a tourist willingly undergoes during a tourist day—heat, cold, dust, odor, dirt, fatigue, anger, fear, hunger, thirst, monsoon rain, shaking and rumbling—when he arrives at his accommodation for the night he wants to relax completely. He usually expects to find some of the comforts which he left at home. If, on the other hand, he is not able to relax, the whole trip becomes a nightmare and not a pleasing adventure. It is therefore of utmost importance for the governments involved to see that such businesses are helped, for example with legislation which keep the types of accommodations attractive to the majority of foreign visitors. One way of meeting these expectations is after setting up standards of hotel construction and maintenance to favor such hotels and motels which are planned with these standards in mind and maintained after construction. Whatever step is taken, the result in all cases should be a tourist satisfied with his accommodations.

Economic Infrastructure

What other factor affects tourism? Until only recently the word "infrastructure" was used as military jargon, but now it is adopted in the field of tourism and summarizes a condition which is not readily visible. "Infra" comes from the Latin language, meaning "below": the infrastructure of a country in regard to tourism can be divided into two parts, the economic infrastructure and the social infrastructure. Economic infrastructure deals firstly with *transportation*, to and from a country as well as within a country or a city. Transportation is the primary ingredient of tourism. The development of tourism can only progress with the development of transportation, as history has shown, lately following the development of railways, steamships, longrange planes and finally jet, jumbo jet and SST airplanes. Since roads, trains, ships, and airplanes in many cases cross national boundaries, cooperation in the operation of these means is vital. International organizations have been set up to overcome difficulties and to help in regional planning, for example the International Union of Railways, the International Chamber of Shipping (ICS), the International Air Transport Association (IATA), and many others. In addition to these means of transportation, there is one other of prime importance, the car, used either as mass or as individual transportation. Here also a number of international agencies coordinate car travel, such as the International Touring Alliance

(AIT) and the Federacion Inter-Americana de Touring y Automovil Clubes. These organizations, while lacking governmental power are nonetheless instrumental in helping government agencies to carry out special projects, like the Asian Highway which will run from Europe via the Middle East to Southern Asia over a distance of more than 35,000 miles.

A change in means of transportation has been seen in the last decade: a shift from ship travel to airplane travel. Ships of the Trans-Atlantic Steamship Conference reported a decline from 743 crossings in 1957 to 535 crossings in 1968, a total drop of almost 55 percent in only 10 years. (However, there seems to be a revival of cruise voyages.) On the other hand, airlines crossing the Atlantic had a gain of 6.3 percent in passengers in 1968 over 1967.[3] (Air travel between Europe and North America grew from 75 percent to 85 percent of total number of tourists.) In looking at world transport there seems to be two general trends: for short-haul, intra-regional travel, road travel is increasing and rail travel decreasing; while in long distance travel, air travel is increasing and sea travel decreasing. In Europe 88 percent of all travel is short-haul and road travel is dominant.

In North America private cars are used for domestic travel in an almost nine to one ratio over bus, rail and air transport. In the Middle East the automobile is the major type of transport; 55 percent of the arrivals came by car and 35 percent arrived by air in 1965. In Africa air arrivals comprise 38 percent, rail 16 percent, road 23 percent and sea 22 percent of total number of tourists. The contrast between the different means of transportation is less pronounced because of the relatively equal spreading of long-haul and short-haul travel. Asia and Australia show a dominance of air travel over any other form of travel.[4]

In Latin America and the Caribbean the picture is somewhat distorted by Mexico. While air transport is far more important than road travel for the rest of the area, almost 800,000 tourists arrived by road in Mexico as against 600,000 by air.[5]

Efforts are made by carriers, especially the railways, to regain a share of the business, for example, adding faster trains like the one in Japan or a Canadian one between Montreal and Toronto. France is presently experimenting with a train which developed a top speed of 264 miles per hour, and the USSR is engaged in fitting a passenger

[3] William D. Patterson, "The Big Picture", *Asta Travel News* (1969).
[4] IUOTO, *Economic Review of World Tourism* (1968).
[5] IUOTO, *International Travel Statistics* (1967).

coach with two turbo-jet engines, to develop a high speed vehicle.[6] Efforts are also underway to make trains more comfortable as well as a more economical way of traveling.

Governments are directly and indirectly involved in transportation. They may own outright transportation systems, for instance, railways, airlines, or shares of transportation companies. This can be found especially in developing countries. Governments are also spending huge sums on road improvements. For example, Hong Kong is planning a $350 million road improvement, a high amount for a city.[7] Asia and the Middle East spent $2.7 billion and Europe $7.7 billion in 1965. For example, taking into account all expenditures for transportation, Thailand spent 49 percent of its national budget for transport in 1966.[8] On roads alone, $13 billion was spent worldwide excluding the U.S. and almost $27 billion including the U.S.[9] Although other considerations, like national defense and supply of markets, enter the picture in building an effective transport system, it is now generally recognized that without it there can be no development of tourism. A typical example is found outside of Karachi, Pakistan, where are found two important tourist attractions. One is an excavation site, Banbhore, forty miles from Karachi, which dates back to 700 A.D., and the other, Thatta, about 65 miles, the remains of the capital of the former Sind Province dating back to the fifteenth century, the beginning of the Moghul period. Although a road leads to both sites, it was not until 1967 when the Pakistan government bought a modern, air conditioned bus that these sites started to attract foreign visitors and as such contributed to the overall tourism development efforts.

The second factor under the economic infrastructure deals with *communication*. In this is included telephone and telegraph systems, radio and television, newspapers and postal services. No tourist will venture into a country without being able to communicate with his friends at home for at least two reasons: first, to signify that no abnormal situation, as sickness, has occurred, and second, to experience the ego satisfaction of letting people know where he is presently.

In addition, a traveler wants to know what is happening outside the country he is visiting; it might influence his future travel deci-

---

[6] International Union of Railways, *International Railways News* (1968).

[7] "Hong Kong," *Time* (1969).

[8] Dr. C. Kaspar, "The Interdependence of Tourism and Transport and its Repercussions," *Revue de Tourisme* (1967).

[9] IUOTO, *Economic Review of World Tourism* (1968).

418 SELECTED READINGS, HOTEL & RESTAURANT MANAGEMENT

sions. Newspapers will tell him, if he understands the host country's language not only world news but also what events are taking place locally, like shows or exhibits. In a number of countries postal facilities should still be improved. It does not happen too infrequently that letters mailed in the tourist's home country never reach him abroad because the cancelled stamps are pulled off and sold to collectors.

The next factor deals with *utilities,* like gas, electricity, water and sewage systems. It can be said that this factor is still a major problem in many areas of the world. To run a first class international hotel air conditioning and refrigeration are essential, and of course will only work if there is electricity available. Insufficient load factors and actual breakdown of transmission equipment is probably the major reason for frequent blackouts or high variation in voltage which will in turn result in either non-functioning of the equipment or in breakdown of electrical motors. There are a number of efforts made to produce electricity on a big scale only to realize that the present line system cannot take the load. These frequent interruptions in electricity present a daily problem to the management of hotels and restaurants, and are really rather annoying to the tourist. As vital to a tourist as electricity is the water supply. This can also present a major problem. A tourist, especially an American, expects to have water served with his meals. In not all parts of the world is the water supply free of contamination, safe to consume in its natural state.

In these locations, tourists are offered boiled or bottled water or water made safe by the hotel's own purification plant, as in the case of a number of the IHC hotels in Asia. To have a sick stomach does not make traveling enjoyable. The last of the utilities is the sewage system. Its proper development is as vital as a good water supply. Even in cities open sewage ditches can sometimes be found, and major efforts are underway to improve both the water and the sewage systems.

The last of the economic infrastructure centers around the banking system. The ideal situation is that a tourist can exchange his money at an unlimited number of banks, hotels and stores, and that he has the opportunity to send or receive money from abroad without red tape. Unfortunately this is not yet the case. In many countries the number of places to exchange maney is extremely limited, and there are additional restrictions, forms to fill out or other complications. Very often the existing exchange rate is unrealistic, resulting in full swing black market operations. This situation can become a safety hazard to tourists.

Social Infrastructure

In the last few paragraphs the economic infrastructure was discussed. In the following the social infrastructure of a country will be discussed, the first being the *school system*. In what way, then, does the school system contribute to tourism development? All of the factors described as economic infrastructure need people with skills as well as administrative abilities. As an economy advances, the need for these two classes will increase and new skills have to be added. The school system is the one which prepares people to pursue a skill or to work in administration. If the school system is insufficient, the results will prove insufficient. There are still countries on this world with 80 and 90 percent of the population unable to read or write. To develop tourism requires increased development of the school system. Of special interest in this connection are efforts being made by some countries in two particular directions of training: the development of persons interested in the tourist, hotel and restaurant trades. Sometimes the responsibility falls under the Ministry of Education, as in Afghanistan; sometimes under the Tourist Board, as in Ceylon; or sometimes it is a private institution, as in Switzerland, the U.S.A. and others. While traditionally the directions of study, that is tourism and hotel and restaurant management, were separate, the present trend is to open one school for both fields or at least to offer some tourism subjects in hotel and restaurant schools and vice versa. Spain, for example, operates an impressive number of centers teaching skills in both fields throughout the country and maintains an institute of advanced training in both hotel management and tourism in Madrid, the Escuela Sindical Superior de Hosteleria y Turismo. An equal effort is made in India where twenty polytechnics, offering short courses in catering and four Institutes of Catering Technology are available for advanced training. The latter institute, with three or four year programs, graduated more than 2,000 students by 1968, as reported by the Food and Agriculture Organization of the United Nations.[10] Many other developing and developed countries plan or operate similar training centers to help in the development of tourism.

What are some of the subjects taught in tourism training? They include travel economics, travel statistics, planning, accounting, functions of travel agencies, advertising and publicity, travel psychology,

---

[10]For a listing of hotel and restaurant schools see the "Directory of Hotel and Restaurant Schools," Council on Hotel, Restaurant and Institutional Education, Statler Hall, Ithaca, N.Y., U.S.A.

travel geography and sites, travel legislation and foreign languages. Some of the subjects taught in hotel and restaurant training, disregarding university level study, include cooking, restaurant service and organization, menu planning, use and maintenance of equipment, nutrition, cost and accounting, hygiene, housekeeping, management techniques and foreign languages. In many cases the countries themselves provide the necessary teaching personnel; in other cases foreign instructors are hired from other countries or secured through aid programs. Some of the large international hotel companies provide for a director of training for their own employees' training.[11] A second factor of the social infrastructure deals with *health service facilities*. No tourist wants to get sick while on a vacation or business trip away from his country. It is the responsibility of the tourism department to see that a list of names of doctors, surgeons, dentists and hospitals is compiled and publicized for the convenience of the tourist. In many cases the hotels will have addresses available. While becoming sick in a city does not offer too much of a problem, it becomes a real problem when away from the city, and this is not helped by the lack of transportation.

Finally the problem of *safety* should be touched on. The feeling of "being safe," if not properly fostered, can ruin any tourism effort. "Feeling unsafe" can result from at least two causes: first, the entire region might be judged "unsafe" by potential visitors. H. G. Clement reported the result of a study where more than 45 percent of the persons interviewed felt that one or more of the countries in the Pacific and Far East were unsafe.[12] In this case, the effort of the entire region is needed to change the image.

Secondly, the "unsafe" feeling might involve only one country and stem from sources like the form of government or the physiology of the natives. It might also stem from the fact that the police is not a helper but your hindrance in that they arrest tourists for minor violations or "produce" charges in order to squeeze out an extra "income."

This last factor of the social structure, safety, involves really the particular part of the government apparatus which comes into contact with tourists: custom officials, health officials, police, and immigration officials, at home and abroad. If these employees do not act

---

[11]Lothar A. Dreck, "Personnel Planning for Foreign Hotels," *Cornell Quarterly* (1969).

[12]H. G. Clement, *The Future of Tourism in the Pacific and Far East* (U.S. Dept. of Commerce 1961).

as "goodwill ambassadors" for their country, the feeling of safety will never develop. Any tourism rating form should include a "personal safety" rubric.

To summarize, the factors affecting tourism, namely the economic and social infrastructure of a country, have been discussed. While accommodation and infrastructure by themselves will not attract tourists, they are essential. The next group of factors to be discussed, recreation, sightseeing, natural beauty, folklore and special events, are the actual magnets to entice people to visit a particular country or region. However, it should be kept in mind that without accommodation and infrastructure there can be no tourism development.

The factors follow in no particular sequence because it is difficult to attach different values to any one of them. Also it is sometimes difficult if not impossible to clearly put an attraction into one category and not into another or number of others.

With these shortcomings in mind the third factor shall be discussed.

Recreation

Recreation comes in a variety of forms. First of all the sports offered include golf; skiing (Switzerland and Austria have been joined by newcomers like Czechoslovakia with its Carpathian mountains); hunting (Africa, India); mountain climbing (Caucasus, Himalayas, Alps); fishing (almost anywhere, either in rivers or in salt water); yachting (Greece includes the rental of a yacht into round-trip airfare); diving (very often included in a vacation package, available around warm waters like the Mediterranean Sea and Pacific Ocean); canoeing (Colorado River and Austria); swimming and sunbathing (along the coasts of most of the oceans, also along rivers and lakes); photographing (in wild life sanctuaries and everywhere else); and dunebuggy and motorbike riding, two of the sports which are presently popular in the U.S.A.

Another form of recreation is gambling. Some of the better known casinos are in Monaco; Cannes and Nice, France; Baden-Baden, Germany; Puerto Rico; Las Vegas, U.S.A.; and Lisbon, Portugal. Horse racing, a form of recreation and gambling as well is common in Europe and the U.S.A. but can be found on the other continents as well.

Visiting night clubs is often a favorite after-sundown recreation. It is difficult and arbitrary to single out any particular location but Paris and Las Vegas are two prime examples. Clubs can be found in most countries but are not common in countries like Nepal and

Afghanistan and in secondary cities of most of the developing countries in Asia and Africa. One reason is religion, another the fact that former colonial powers had set up clubs for the European population, leaving no demand for commercial type clubs.

Another group of recreational activities includes cultural events and attractions. It should be emphasized here that included here are only such events and attractions which are performed by professional artists, in contrast to folklorist artists which will be discussed later. First, there are the many international music festivals, like the Bayreuth Festival; the Baalbeck International Festival, Lebanon; and the Newport Jazz Festival, U.S.A.. Then there are the mixed festivals with music and drama, like the Edinburgh and Stockholm Festivals, the drama festivals, as in Stratford-on-Avon; and the ballet performances of the Bolshoi Ballet. In addition, many opera houses attract tourists, including La Scala, Italy; Vienna Opera, Austria; and the Metropolitan, U.S.A.. Next follow the many museums, the Louvre, France; Tate Gallery, Great Britain; Palazzo Uffizi, Italy; and El Prado, Spain. It can be noticed that developing countries from Asia or Africa are almost completely missing from the above list. One of the reasons is the strong tradition of Western art. This, however, could be turned into an advantage for the Asian and African countries, in that Asiatic and African art now becomes something to look for when traveling to those regions, for example, finding or collecting the water-colors of East Pakistan.

Sightseeing

A number of tourists prefer sightseeing. It can be divided into cultural, historic, scenic and technical sightseeing. As the cultural sightseeing can be mentioned especially the ruins of Rome and Greece, the pyramids of Egypt, the Taj Mahal in India, and famous churches like the Duomo in Milan, the Stephen's Dome in Vienna, the dome of Toledo in Spain, and the Star Mosque in Dacca.

Historic sightseeing includes famous castles, like the ones in Bavaria, in Edinburgh, in Moscow and Leningrad, and palaces such as Buckingham Palace in London and Schloss Schoenbrunn in Vienna. Portugal, Spain, and Germany have converted a number of castles and palaces into hotel type operations. Also included are places associated with famous people, like the houses of the many composers who lived in Vienna, poets, painters, politicians, inventors. Historic sites are of great interest: battlefields, Okinawa, El Alamain, Normandy beaches, Stalingrad; the site where the first atomic bomb was exploded, Trinity Site near Alamogordo, New Mexico, U.S.A.;

the Bridge over the River Kwai, Thailand; the city of Jerusalem; the Kremlin; the Great Wall of China; and excavation sites like Pompei.

Next there is scenic sightseeing. This should be defined as visiting places of scenic beauty which are man-developed and to a certain degree commercialized, for example, Grand Canyon National Park, Niagara Falls (as opposed to the Angel Falls in Venezuela which according to the below definition belong to "natural beauty"), Sugar Loaf Mountain (Rio de Janeiro), Avenue of the Giants (California, U.S.A.), Rhine river valley, the many mountains which are made accessible to the tourist-hikers, lakes, rivers, passes, oasis.

Finally should be mentioned some examples of interest in technical development, like dams (Aswan Dam in Egypt, Mangla Dam in Pakistan); structures (Eiffel Tower, Golden Gate Bridge, Statue of Liberty, Empire State Building); factories, including car manufacturing concerns; slaughter houses; hydro-electric plants; vineyards; oilfields; mines; technical exhibitions and observatories.[13]

Natural Beauty

Natural beauty, as intended here, includes undeveloped nature, not commercialized. Some of the examples are mountain ranges (the Andes, Himalayas, Caucasus); glaciers (New Zealand, Austria, Greenland); caves, volcanoes (Sumatra, Hawaii, Italy); jungles (India, East Pakistan, Burma, Indonesia); and deserts (Africa, USA). All of the examples of natural beauty are in some form or another utilized today for tourism development. There are conducted trips up the mountain ranges, along glaciers, through jungles and deserts, into caves and over volcanoes. It is not seldom that the more daring a trip is the more attractive it is. Here, as in any business situation, it is a matter of marketing if one wants to sell a product.

Folklore

In contrast with cultural attractions, folklore is concerned with such attractions as are produced or have their origin with nonprofessional artists. The word "artist" is still used because of the high skill involved in many cases. First of all there are the many festivals, like the carnivals of Nice, Rio de Janeiro, Cologne; flower festivals; religious festivals (Buddhist lent, birthdays of saints); seasonal festivals, skill festivals (rodeos, fisherman's festivals). Secondly, there are dramatic performances with either religious themes, as the

---

[13] The United States Travel Service has published a list of factories which conduct plant tours for visitors.

Passion play of Oberammergau or historic themes, depicting people, events or both. There is no place, city or village, which does not have a history which has not been exploited fully. There are also always people willing to participate in a play. Dramatic performances include also ceremonial dances, as performed by the American Indians, the Thai Temple dancers or just performances of folklore groups showing national dances in their particular costumes.

Museums are another category. These can show the history of a people, but also individual events or places like the housing of natives, a wagon train, the first railway, ghost cities, ships, built up villages, etc. Also interesting are the arts as produced by folk artists and into this would fall handicrafts as well. Sometimes in order to start a handicraft industry, the government will call for a competition and will reward successful designs.

There should also be a chance for a tourist to visit local families in order to see how their families live. Some countries, as the U.S.A. and Bermuda have started such a program. Emphasis should also be placed to let the tourist know about the local cuisine. To see sights and to take part in local events is one side of the coin; the other side is definitely to get to know the natives and their way of living.

Special Events

Finally there is the last factor, special events which are not continuing but occur at certain times only, like the festivals mentioned previously (they clearly fall into both categories) but also world exhibitions, as in Paris, Brussels, New York, Montreal, Tokyo; beauty contests; the Olympic Games; and any other type of sport events either by professionals or non-professionals, like fishing and golf tournaments, and finally conventions.

Accommodations, transport and the many tourist attractions (if there are not any they have to be "made") will still not bring tourists into a country until one other ingredient is added: promotion. People have to know what they can expect.
deal with this aspect.

46

U.S. CHAIN'S GLOBAL STRATEGY

from *Service World International*

As American hotel/restaurant chains reach domestic saturation, continued foreign expansion offers new challenges and competition to world operators, and vice-versa.... The market varies: a hotel that can break even on a $20 room rate and 20 percent occupancy in Hong Kong needs $40 and 60 percent in London. Land and labor costs are determining factors. Airline-owned hotel chains are currently the largest outside the U.S. But as franchising is adapted to a world market, fast food operations may catch up.

Organization	Present Units		Future Units		Countries Now Operating	Comments
	Food Service	Lodging	Food Service	Lodging		
ARA	7	..	5	..	Puerto Rico, Mexico, Jamaica, Virgin Islands, Western Europe	Plan expansion of operations in the same countries. Very little of foreign holdings are affected by tourism except for in-flight food services. It is affiliated with National Hotelara S.A. and Versa-food Services.

From *Service World International*, November 1970, pp. 21-24. Reprinted by permission of *Institutions Magazine*.

Arby's International	1	..	6	......	Will go into United Kingdom, Germany, Australia, Japan in '70.
Bonanza International	..	..	..	......	Postponed plans to go into Canada, Australia, Puerto Rico while company concentrates on internal reorganization.
Braniff Airways	15	..	..	Chile, Paraguay, Brazil, Columbia, Mexico, Argentina, Bolivia, Ecuador, Peru, Panama, Uruguay and various military airlift command bases in Pacific	Hotels in South and Central America to house tourists that fly Braniff.
A & W International	268	..	5	Germany, England, Italy, Malaysia, Tahiti, Philippines, Mexico	Further foreign expansion limited at present.
Allen & O'Hara	1	1	..	San Juan	Increases in tourism will determine future expansion.
American Motor Inns	..	..	..	......	Plans expansion into Virgin Islands.

Company					Notes
The Brody Corp.	3	2	1	Norway	Norwegian operations through Restaurant Industri, A.S., 51% Norwegian ownership, 49% Brody.
Burger Chef Systems	..	..	..	......	Plans to expand into Australia & Canada did not materialize last year.
Carrol's Development Corp.	3	..	..	Sweden	No prediction made for this year. Trying to locate sites in England and Sweden, but nothing firmed up enough to be sure of outcome.
Collins Foods International	4	5	..	Australia	New expansion area: Germany.
Continental Airlines	..	5	2	Micronesia, Guam, Okinawa	Banking on expanded tourism in Pacific for operations in Micronesia and Guam. Affiliated with Interisland Resort organization.
Delta Airlines	..	..	..	......	Wants direct route from Atlanta to Montego Bay to expand Caribbean coverage. Applying for direct route to Europe—now Pan Am crews fly Delta planes from Washington D.C. to London and from Boston to Paris.

					Countries	Notes
Denny's Restaurants	11	..	6	..	Mexico	Building hotels in Acapulco
Downtowner	8	3	..	..	Mexico, St. Thomas (Virgin Islands)	Tourism plays a great role in foreign planning. Affiliated with Braniff.
Frostop	3	..	5	..	......	Plans to begin operating in Ecuador, South America.
Greyhound Food Management	11	..	..	..	Belgium	Belgian employee feeding operation going great; will probably expand to other European countries.
Hilton International	165	54	30	7	England, Spain, Malta, Philippines, Martinique, Kenya, Cyprus, Iran, France, Morocco, Italy, Virgin Islands, Malaysia, Israel, Japan, Trinidad, Tunisia, Mexico, Ethiopia, U.A.R., Greece, Thailand, Barbados, Germany, Belgium, Venezuela, Curacao, Puerto Rico, Hong Kong, Hawaii, Nepal, Turkey, Jamaica, Kuwait, Netherlands	Expanded tourism affects foreign plans to a high degree. In 1970 operations start in Martinique, Germany, Malaysia, Switzerland, Columbia, Brazil, and in Iron Curtain Hungary. By end of 1971 they will expand to: Malaysia, Portugal, Brazil, Australia, Libya, Nationalist China, Okinawa, Tanzania, Hungary, India, and Abu Dhabi. Affiliated with AmEx, Diners, and Hilton reservation service.
Holiday Inns	48	48	20	20	Bahamas, Caribbean, Mexico, Morocco, Netherland Antilles, South Africa, Netherlands	Plans to begin operations in Germany, England and Belgium. Tourism plays a major role in foreign planning. Affiliated with AmEx, Bank Americard and Holidex.

Company				Foreign Locations	Notes
Sonesta International (formerly HCA)	6	6	..	6	UK, Bermuda, Nassau, Italy, Canada	Tourism plays significant role in foreign plans, but it does not plan any foreign expansion in 1970. Affiliated with AmEx, Diners, Master Charge, Telemax, I.R.C., Bank Americard.
Inter-Continental Hotels	..	40	..	3	Throughout the world, 7 in Africa, 17 in Asia and the Pacific, 15 in Europe and the Middle East, and 12 in Latin American and Caribbean countries	Plans to open in Guyana and England in 1970; hotels going up in Bombay, Bucharest, Budapest, Ceylon, Hamburg, Helsinki, Kinshasa, Prague, Tehran and Zagreb. Tourism plays a major role in expansion plans. Subsidiary of Pan Am.
International Dairy Queen	434	..	40	..	Guam, Mexico, Panama, Puerto Rico, Spain, Philippines, Iceland, Australia	Opens in Germany in '70. Tourism a plus factor in plans.
Jerrico	..	..	..	......	......	Plans to open in Bahamas, Jamaica and Virgin Islands with Long John Silver's operations.
Howard Johnson	..	..	..	......	......	First foreign property opens this summer in Amsterdam. Choosing sites for 30 to 40 restaurants and lodges in Mexico. Recently broke ground for first Canada lodge. Orange Roof Canada, Ltd., new subsidiary, will open several restaurants by end of summer.

Company			Locations	Plans
Loew's Hotels	..	..	San Juan, Bahamas, London	Exploring possibility of new hotels in Europe. Opening one in London in 2 or 3 years.
McDonald's	38	..	Puerto Rico	Begins in Virgin Islands in 1970. Plans big expansion overseas in '71.
The Macke Co.	..	..	......	First overseas operation would provide the vehicle for developing industrial services throughout the Caribbean area.
Kentucky Fried Chicken	40	135	Puerto Rico, Japan, Nassau, Jamaica, Mexico, Vienna, Austria	Plans a total of 25 operations in Vienna, plus possibly 25 more elsewhere in Austria. '70 plans call for the opening of a minimum of 40 company-owned and 75 franchised outlets, bringing foreign total to 175.
Knott Hotels	..	4	England, Belgium	No foreign expansion mentioned for 1970.
Landshire Co.	..	..	Virgin Islands	Has franchised wholesale sandwich units in U.S. and Virgin Islands. Will not divulge future plans.
Marriott	38	1	Italy, Portugal, Spain, Mexico, Peru, Chile, Argentina, Brazil, Venezuela, United Kingdom	Expanded tourism is important, but no foreign additions are planned for '70.

					Remarks
National Airlines	..	..	..	..	......	New London route later in '70.
Northwest Airlines	1	..	..	..	Japan	Expo '70 will increase business.
Original Pancake House	3	..	3	..	Japan	May open new units in Israel and Hawaii.
Pan American	71	..	3	..	Flies to 40 countries including England, France, Germany, Turkey, Norway, Denmark, Lebanon, Italy, Thailand, Iran, Japan, Hong Kong, Hawaii and Romania	Plans to add Antigua to list of foreign countries served in 1970.
Perkins Pancake Houses	..	..	..	..	......	Expanding in Hawaii, Mexico and the Caribbean.
Pizza Hut	10	..	20	..	Australia, Mexico, Germany	Plans unknown, but tourism does not play a significant role in planning.
Playboy Clubs International	3	2	..	..	England, Jamaica	Planning no foreign expansion for 1970. The tourist trade plays a sizable role in plans.
Price Candy	2	..	1	..	Mexico	Opens cafeteria service at U. of the Americas in Mexico this year.

					Locations	Notes
Quality Courts Motels	3	6	..	..	......	Recently opened branch office in Brussels. Plans to expand in Europe, Canada and Central America.
Ramada Inns	7	7	5	5	Morocco, Mexico, Caribbean	Will expand into Europe in 1970. Affiliated with Diners Club, Am Ex, Carte Blanche, major European banks and travel agencies.
Sambo's Restaurants	..	..	..	..	......	Expanding to Mexico this year.
Sandys Systems	1	..	3	..	Canada	Beginning in Belgium in 1970. Expanded tourist trade only affects planning about 25%.
Servomation	..	..	..	..	Australia	No information available on foreign expansion.
Shakey's	6	..	7	..	Mexico	Plans to begin operations in Australia, Japan, Europe and South America.
Sheraton	70	14	33	21	Aruba, Bahamas, Corsica, Chile, Israel, Jamaica, Kuwait, Malta, Mexico, Puerto Rico, United Arab Republic, Venezuela, Australia	1970 opens Thailand, Sweden and Tunisia. Affiliated with Am Ex, Diners Club, Carte Blanche, Barclay Card; Shell Canada Ltd. 16 overseas hotels now under construction. Open by end of 1970: Bangkok, Santiago and Stockholm; by end of 1971: Bombay, Buenos Aires, Lisbon and Singapore; by end of 1972: Istanbul, Paris, Rio, Toronto and Munich.

Company				Locations	Notes
Sky Chefs	..	..		Acapulco, Seoul	Opens hotels in Mexico City and Honolulu soon. More Flagship hotels planned.
Spencecliff Corp.	2	2		Tahiti	Operates distribution-warehouse facilities to supply all units in Hawaii. Affiliated with Warner & Fawcett Distinguished Hotels, Carte Blanche, Diners, Am Ex.
Spudnut Industries	..	..		Japan	......
Tastee Freez International	546	75		Nicaragua, Honduras, U.K., Nassau, Panama, Venezuela, El Salvador, Mexico, Guatemala, Puerto Rico	Starts in Australia and Jamaica in 1970. Affiliated with Lyons Maid, Ltd.
TWA	2	..		Around-the-world carrier	Owning Hilton International Hotels has helped its "around the world" business. Affiliated with credit cards, car rental systems and hotel reservation systems.
Universal Services	20	..		England, Germany, Angola, Australia	No further foreign expansion planned.
Western International	..	45	9	Australia, Ecuador, Guatemala, Hong Kong, Japan, Mexico, Thailand, Venezuela, South Africa	Building new hotels in Houston, Winnipeg and Singapore.

47

THE PARABLE OF THE SPINDLE

Elias H. Porter

More and more we hear the word "systems" used in discussions of business problems. Research people are studying systems, experts are looking at organizations as systems, and a growing number of departments and companies have the word "systems" in their names.

Just what *is* a system in the business sense? What does it do? What good is it to management? To answer these questions I shall first use a parable from the restaurant industry. What, you may ask, can executives in manufacturing, retailing, or service systems learn from restaurant systems? I readily admit that if you envisage only menus, customers, waitresses, and cooks in a restaurant, you will find no transferable knowledge. But if you see (as I hope you will) inputs, rate variations, displays, feedback loops, memory devices, queuing, omissions, errors, chunking, approximating, channeling, and filtering in a restaurant system—then you should indeed find some practical value in my parable.

The implications of the parable will be discussed specifically in the second part of the article after we have reduced it to a paradigm.

The Parable

Once upon a time the president of a large chain of short-order restaurants attended a lecture on "Human Relations in Business and Industry." He attended the lecture in the hope he would learn something useful. His years of experience had led him to believe that if human relations problems ever plagued any business, then they certainly plagued the restaurant business.

The speaker discussed the many pressures which create human relations problems. He spoke of psychological pressures, sociological pressures, conflicts in values, conflicts in power structure, and so on. The president did not understand all that was said, but he did go

---

home with one idea. If there were so many different sources of pressure, maybe it was expecting too much of his managers to think they would see them all, let alone cope with them all. The thought occurred to him that maybe he should bring in a team of consultants from several academic disciplines and have each contribute his part to the solution of the human relations problems.

And so it came to pass that the president of the restaurant chain and his top management staff met one morning with a sociologist, a psychologist, and an anthropologist. The president outlined the problem to the men of science and spoke of his hope that they might come up with an interdisciplinary answer to the human relations problem. The personnel manager presented exit-interview findings which he interpreted as indicating that most people quit their restaurant jobs because of too much sense of pressure caused by the inefficiencies and ill tempers of co-workers.

This was the mission which the scientists were assigned: find out why the waitresses break down in tears; find out why the cooks walk off the job; find out why the managers get so upset that they summarily fire employees on the spot. Find out the cause of the problems, and find out what to do about them.

Later, in one of the plush conference rooms, the scientists sat down to plan their attack. It soon became clear that they might just as well be three blind men, and the problem might just as well be the proverbial elephant. Their training and experience had taught them to look at events in different ways. And so they decided that inasmuch as they couldn't speak each others' languages, they might as well pursue their tasks separately. Each went to a different city and began his observations in his own way.

The Sociologist

First to return was the sociologist. In his report to top management he said:

> I think I have discovered something that is pretty fundamental. In one sense it is so obvious that it has probably been completely overlooked before. It is during the *rush hours* that your human relations problems arise. That is when the waitresses break out in tears. That is when the cooks grow temperamental and walk off the job. That is when your managers lose their tempers and dismiss employees summarily.

After elaborating on this theme and showing several charts with sloping lines and bar graphs to back up his assertions, he came to his diagnosis of the situation. "In brief, gentlemen," he stated, "you have a sociological problem on your hands." He walked to the blackboard and began to write. As he wrote, he spoke:

You have a stress pattern during the rush hours. There is stress between the customer and the waitress. . . .
There is stress between the waitress and the cook. . . .
And up here is the manager. There is stress between the waitress and the manager. . . .
And between the manager and the cook. . . .
And the manager is buffeted by complaints from the customer.
We can see one thing which, sociologically speaking, doesn't seem right. The manager has the highest status in the restaurant. The cook has the next highest status. The waitresses, however, are always 'local hire' and have the lowest status. Of course, they have higher status than busboys and dishwashers but certainly lower status than the cook, and yet they give orders to the cook.
It doesn't seem right for a lower status person to give orders to a higher status person. We've got to find a way to break up the face-to-face relationship between the waitresses and the cook. We've got to fix it so that they don't have to talk with one another. Now my idea is to put a 'spindle' on the order counter. The 'spindle,' as I choose to call it, is a wheel on a shaft. The wheel has clips on it so the girls can simply put their orders on the wheel rather than calling out orders to the cook.

When the sociologist left the meeting, the president and his staff talked of what had been said. It made some sense. However, they decided to wait to hear from the other scientists before taking any action.

The Psychologist
Next to return from his studies was the psychologist. He reported to top management:

I think I have discovered something that is pretty fundamental. In one sense it is so obvious that it has probably been completely overlooked before. It is during the *rush hours* that your human relations problems arise. That is when the waitresses break down in tears. That is when the cooks grow temperamental and walk off the job. That is when your managers lose their tempers and dismiss employees summarily.

Then the psychologist sketched on the blackboard the identical pattern of stress between customer, waitress, cook, and management. But his interpretation was somewhat different:

Psychologically speaking, he said, we can see that the manager is the father figure, the cook is the son, and the waitress is the daughter. Now we know that in our culture you can't have daughters giving orders to the sons. It louses up their ego structure.

What we've got to do is to find a way to break up the face-to-face relationship between them. Now one idea I've thought up is to put what I call a 'spindle' on the order counter. It's kind of a wheel on a shaft with little clips on it so that the waitresses can put their orders on it rather than calling out orders to the cook.

What the psychologist said made sense, too, in a way. Some of the staff favored the status-conflict interpretation while others thought the sex-conflict interpretation to be the right one; the president kept his own counsel.

The Anthropologist
The next scientist to report was the anthropologist. He reported to top management:

I think I have discovered something that is pretty fundamental. In one sense it is so obvious that it has probably been completely overlooked before. It is during the *rush hours* that your human relations problems arise. That is when the waitresses break out in tears. That is when the cooks grow temperamental and walk off the job. That is when your managers lose their tempers and dismiss employees summarily.

After elaborating for a few moments he came to his diagnosis of the situation. "In brief, gentlemen," he stated, "you have an anthropological problem on your hands." He walked to the blackboard and began to sketch. Once again there appeared the stress pattern between customer, waitress, cook, and management:

We anthropologists know that man behaves according to his value systems. Now, the manager holds as a central value the continued growth and development of the restaurant organization. The cooks tend to share this central value-system, for as the organization prospers, so do they. But the waitresses are a different story. The only reason most of them are working is to help supplement the family income. They couldn't care less whether the organization thrives or not as long as it's a decent place to work. Now, you can't have a non-central value system giving orders to a central value-system.

What we've got to do is to find some way of breaking up the face-to-face contact between the waitresses and the cook. One way that has occurred to me is to place on the order counter an adaptation of the old-fashioned spindle. By having a wheel at the top of the shaft and putting clips every few inches apart, the waitresses can put their orders on the wheel and not have to call out orders to the cook. Here is a model of what I mean.

Triumph of the Spindle
When the anthropologist had left, there was much discussion of which scientist was right. The president finally spoke. "Gentlemen, it's clear that these men don't agree on the reason for conflict, but all

have come up with the same basic idea about the spindle. Let's take a chance and try it out."

And it came to pass that the spindle was introduced throughout the chain of restaurants. It did more to reduce the human relations problems in the restaurant industry than any other innovation of which the restaurant people knew. Soon it was copied. Like wild fire the spindle spread from coast to coast and from border to border.

So much for the parable. Let us now proceed to the paradigm.

The Paradigm

Each of the three scientists had seen a different problem: status conflict, sex rivalry, and value conflict. Maybe it was none of these but simply a problem in the division of work between men and machines and how they are related one to the other: a problem of system design. Let us explore this possibility by observing the functions which the spindle fulfills.

Functions Served

First of all, the spindle acts as a memory device for the cook. He no longer needs to remember all the orders given him by the waitresses. This makes his job easier and less "stressful"—especially during the rush hours.

Secondly, the spindle acts as a buffering device. It buffers the cook against a sudden, overwhelming load of orders. Ten waitresses can place their orders on the spindle almost simultaneously. The cook takes them off the spindle according to his work rate—not the input rate. This makes his job easier, more within reach of human capacity—especially during the rush hours.

Thirdly, the spindle acts as a queuing device—in two ways. It holds the orders in a proper waiting line until the cook can get to them. When dependent on his memory only, the cook can get orders mixed up. It also does all the "standing in line" for the waitresses. They need never again stand in line to pass an order to the cook. This makes their jobs easier—especially during the rush hours.

Fourthly, the spindle permits a visual display of all the orders waiting to be filled. The cook can often see that several of the orders call for the same item. He can prepare four hamburgers in about the same time as he can prepare one. By reason of having "random access" to all the orders in the system at that point he is able to organize his work around several orders simultaneously with greater efficiency. This makes his job easier—especially during the rush hours.

To appreciate the fifth function which the spindle serves, we must go back to the procedures used before the advent of the spindle. In looking at these procedures we are going to examine them in "general system behavior theory" terms:

On the menu certain "information" exists in the physical form of printed words. The customer "transforms" this information into the physical form of spoken words. The information is once again transformed by the waitress. Now it exists in the physical form of written notes made by the waitress. Once again the information is transformed as the waitress converts her notes into spoken words directed to the cook. The cook transforms the information from the physical form of spoken words to the physical form of prepared food. We have an "information flow" which looks like this:

$$\text{Menu} \xrightarrow{\dfrac{\text{Printed}}{\text{Words}}} \text{Customer} \xrightarrow{\dfrac{\text{Spoken}}{\text{Words}}}$$

$$\text{Waitress} \xrightarrow{\dfrac{\text{Written}}{\text{Notes}}} \xrightarrow{\dfrac{\text{Spoken}}{\text{Words}}} \text{Cook} \xrightarrow{\dfrac{\text{Prepared}}{\text{Food}}} .$$

Now every so often it happened that an error was made, and the customer didn't get what he ordered. Of course you and I would have been the first to admit that we had made an error, but not all cooks and waitresses have this admirable character trait. This is rather understandable since the waitress was trying to do things correctly and rapidly (she wanted all the tips she could get!), and when she was suddenly confronted with the fact that an error had been made, her first reaction was that the cook had goofed. The cook, on the other hand, was trying to do his best. He knew in his own heart that he had prepared just what she had told him to prepare. "It's the waitress' fault," was his thought.

So what did the cook and waitress learn? Did they learn to prevent a recurrence of the error? Indeed not! The waitress learned that the cook was a stupid so-and-so, and the cook learned that the waitress was a scatterbrained so-and-so. This kind of emotionalized learning situation and strainer-of-interpersonal-relations any organization can do without—especially during the rush hours.

Changes Effected

Consider now how the spindle changes all this. The waitress prepares the order slip and the cook works directly from it. If the waitress records the order incorrectly, it is obvious to her upon examining the order slip. Similarly, if the cook misreads the slip, an examination of the order slip makes it obvious to him. The fifth function of the spindle, then, is to provide "feed-back" to both waitress and cook regarding errors. The spindle markedly alters the emotional relationship and redirects the learning process.

As errors are examined under conditions of feedback, new responses are engendered. The cook and waitress may find the present order slip to be hard to read, and they may request the manager to try out a different style of order slip. Now they are working together to solve the system's problems rather than working against each other and disregarding the system's problems. Maybe they find that abbreviations cause some random errors. For example, it might be that HB (Hamburger) and BB (Beefburger) get mixed up just a little too often, so the cook and waitress get together with the manager and change the name of Beefburger to Caravan Special on the menu because the new symbol (CS) will transmit itself through the system with much less ambiguity—especially during the rush hours.

Handling Overload

Had I been asked a few years ago to advise on human relations problems in the restaurant industry as a professional psychologist, my approach would have been limited to what I now call a "component" approach. My thinking would have been directed at the components in the system—in this case, the people involved. I would have explored such answers as incentive schemes, human relations training, selection procedures, and possibly some time-and-motion studies. My efforts would have been limited to attempts to *change the components to fit in with the system as designed no matter how poor the design might be.*

But now I would first concern myself with the "information" which must be "processed" by the system. My concern would be centered on the functions which would have to be performed by the system and how they might best be performed. I would concern myself especially with how the system is designed to handle conditions of information overload.

It is significant that in our parable the three scientists each discovered that the human relations problems arose mostly during the rush hours, in the period of "information overload." How a system responds to conditions of overload depends on how the system is designed. Let us look at how various design features permit the handling of conditions of overload in a number of different kinds of systems.

Increase in Channels

One of the most common adjustments that a system makes to an excess input load is to increase the number of "channels" for handling the information. Restaurants put more waitresses and cooks on the job to handle rush-hour loads. The Post Office hires extra help before Christmas. The telephone system has recently introduced automatic-switching equipment to handle heavy communication loads; when the load gets to a certain point, additional lines are automatically "cut in" to handle the additional calls. Even our fire departments increase "channels." If there is not enough equipment at the scene, more is called in. Department stores put on additional clerks to handle holiday crowds. Military commanders augment crews in anticipation of overload conditions. Extra communication lines may be called up. More troops are deployed.

Almost everywhere we look we see that systems are very commonly designed to increase or decrease the number of channels according to the load.

Waiting Lines

But there comes a time when just increasing the number of channels is not enough. Then we see another common adjustment process: that of "queuing" or forming a waiting line. There are few readers who have not had the experience of waiting in a restaurant to be seated. Other examples are common. Raw materials are stored awaiting production processes. Orders wait in queue until filled. Manufactured goods are stored on docks awaiting shipment. The stock market ticker tape falls behind.

We have already seen how the spindle makes it unnecessary for the waitresses to queue to give orders. And we are all familiar with the modern custom in most restaurants of having a hostess take our names and the size of our party. What happens when the hostess takes our names down on paper? For one, we do not have to go through the exasperating business of jostling to hold our position in line. Also, the "holding of proper position" is done by machine; that is, it is done by the list rather than by our elbows.

Use of Filtering

The hostess' list also illustrates the way in which a system can make still a third type of adjustment, that of "filtering." Because she jots down the size of the group, she can now selectively pull groups out of the queue according to the size of the table last vacated. Some readers will recall that many restaurants used to have all tables or booths of the same size and that everyone was seated in turn according to how long he had waited. It used to be infuriating for a party of four to see a single person being seated at a table for four while they continued to wait. The modern notion of accommodations of varying sizes, combined with the means for filtering, makes the use of floor space much more efficient and the waiting less lengthy. We can use filtering in other systems as well:

1. The Post Office handles registered mail before it handles other mail, delivers special delivery letters before other letters.

2. In the case of our other most important communication system, the telephone system, there is no way for dial equipment to recognize an important call from an unimportant call; it cannot tell whether a doctor is dialing or the baby is playing. However, where long-distance calls must go through operators, there is a chance for filtering. For instance, in trying to place a call to a disaster area the operator may accept only those calls which are of an emergency nature.

3. Military systems assign priorities to messages so as to assure differential handling.

4. Orders may be sent to production facilities in bunches that make up a full workday rather than in a first-in-first-out pattern. Special orders may be marked for priority attention.

Variations of Omission

A system can be so designed as to permit "omissions," a simple rejection or non-acceptance of an input. The long-distance operator may refuse to accept a call as a means of preventing the lines from becoming overloaded. The dial system gives a busy signal and rejects the call. A manufacturing organization may reject an order it cannot fill within a certain time. A company may discontinue manufacture of one line temporarily in order to catch up on a more profitable line that is back-ordered.

As another example of how the design determines what adjustments the system can make, consider the way the short-order restaurant system design utilizes the omission process. If waiting lines get too long, customers will turn away. That is not good for business, so restaurants often practice another kind of omission. On the menu you may find the words, "No substitutions." Instead of rejecting customers, the restaurants restrict the range of inputs they will accept in the way of orders. Thus time is saved in preparing the food, which in turn cuts down the waiting time in the queue.

The goal of most restaurants is to process as many customers per unit of time as is possible. With a fixed profit margin per meal served, the more meals served, the more profit. But when people are in the queue, they are not spending money. *One solution to this is the installation of a bar.* This permits the customers to spend while waiting. It is a solution enjoyed by many customers as well as by management.

Chunking & Approximating

Another big timesaver in the restaurant system is the use of a fifth adjustment process, that of "chunking." Big chunks of information can be passed by predetermined arrangements. You may find a menu so printed that it asks you to order by number. The order may be presented to the cook as "4D" (No. 4 Dinner), for example. The cook already knows what makes up the dinner and does not need to be told each item with each order. Preplanning permits chunking and chunking frees communication channels.

Somewhat akin to the chunking process is a sixth adjustment process, "approximating." To illustrate:

A business forecaster may not be able to make an exact count of future sales, but he may predict confidently that the sales will be small, moderate, or large.

An overburdened Post Office crew may do an initial sorting of mail as "local" or "out of town."

An airborne radar crew may report a "large formation" headed toward the coast.

An intelligence agency may get a report of "heightened" air activity in a given area.

An investment house may predict "increased" activity in a certain line of stocks.

Stock market reports state that industrials are "up" and utilities are "down."

Approximating thus means making a gross discrimination of the input rather than making a fine discrimination.

Trading Errors

A rather unusual adjustment process that a system can adopt to cope with overload is to accept an increase in the number of errors made. It is almost as if systems said to themselves, "It's better to make mistakes than not to deal with the input." For example, the sorting of mail is not checked during rush periods. Mail which is missent must be returned, but in a rush that risk is worth the cost; more mail gets sent where it is supposed to go even though there are more errors. Thus, quality control is given up for the sake of speed. On the other hand, some systems are so designed as to be insensitive to errors. The telephone system will permit you to dial as many wrong numbers as you are capable of dialing.

It is interesting to see in the restaurant system design a deliberate making of errors of one sort in order to prevent the making of errors of another sort, during rush hours:

Picture yourself and a couple of friends dropping into a restaurant during the middle of an afternoon. You are the only customers there. The waitress takes your order. You ask for a hamburger with "everything on it." The next person asks for a hamburger but wants only butter and a slice of tomato on it. The third person asks for a hamburger but specifies relish and mayonnaise. The work load is low. There is time to individualize orders.

But during rush hours it would be too easy to make errors. Then the cook prepares only the meat and bun. The waitress goes to a table where there are bowls with lettuce leaves and tomato slices and little paper cups of relish and mayonnaise. On each plate she places a lettuce-leaf, a tomato slice, a cup of relish and a cup of mayonnaise. In most instances she will have brought something that the customer did not order, and in this sense she would have made an "error"; but she would have avoided the error of not bringing the customer something he *did* want.

Other examples of the same type are common. For instance, a sales department sends out brochures to everyone who inquires about a product so as not to miss someone who is really interested. Again, the Strategic Air Command, as a central policy, uses this deliberate making of one type of "error" to avoid a possible error of more severe consequences. The commander may order the force launched under "positive control." It is better to have launched in error than to be caught on the ground and destroyed.

Conclusion

And so we see that there is a new frame of reference, a new point of view coming into use in approaching the problems of organizations. This new frame of reference looks at organizations as systems which (1) process information, transforming the information from one form into another, and (2) are or are not designed to cope with the conditions of overload that may be imposed on them. This new frame of reference is expressed as an interest in how the structure or design of an organization dynamically influences the operating characteristics and the capacities of the system to handle various conditions of information overload.

At the University of Michigan there are some 50 scientists whose primary interests lie in looking for similarities and differences in system behavior of all levels. They examine single cells, whole organs, individuals, groups and societies for the manners in which these systems cope with their environments in common and in unique ways. They search the work of other societies for clues to system behavior at one level that is followed at higher or lower orders or organization. As for the application of this "system frame of reference," one finds such organizations as System Development Corporation, the RAND Corporation, and the MITRE Corporation using it in approaching the complex problems of advanced military systems. Here is just a sampling of specific developments that bear close watching:

Because it is possible to view organizations as systems which process data in a continuous sequence of "information transformations" and which may make numerous types of adjustments at the points of transformation, a wholly new concept of training has arisen. In the past, training in business and industry as well as in the military was largely limited to training a man or men to do a given task in a certain way. Now training can be provided that teaches a man or men to adopt adjustment processes suited to the design of the system and the condition of overload. In other words, training for flexibility rather than rigidity is now possible. It should not be long before internal competition is replaced by internal cooperation as the main means of enhancing production.

Because it is possible to view business or industry as an information processing system, it is possible to simulate the information flow on digital computers and, by controlling the adjustment processes at each point where the data are transformed, to learn what effects and costs would be involved in change. The manager will then be able to test his policies realistically on the computer before committing himself in action. A computer program called SIMPAC (Simulation Package) has already been developed at System Development Corporation for this purpose.

A digital computer program capable of "learning" has been developed. By analyzing how data can be sensed, compared with other data, and stored in the computer's "memory," scientists have been able to "teach" a prototype computer program to recognize letters of the alphabet, cartoon characters and spoken words. One can look forward to the day when, opening a bank account, he will be asked to sign his name in a variety of situations—e.g., standing, sitting, bending over, and maybe even after a couple of martinis. The computer will learn to recognize his signature from these samples, and at the clearinghouse, after that, his account will be automatically debited and the payee's account automatically credited.

Ludwig von Bertalanffy, the father of general system theory, predicted that general system theory would unify the sciences, thus making it possible for a scientist trained in one area to talk in common terms with another scientist in another area.* It also seems certain that business and industry will soon profit from the application of the theory of how systems behave.

---

*"General System Theory," *General Systems* (Ann Arbor, Society for General Systems Research, 1956), Volume 1, pp. 1-10.